THE VOICE OF THE EARTH

OTHER BOOKS BY THEODORE ROSZAK

NONFICTION

The Dissenting Academy, editor and contributor

The Making of a Counterculture

Masculine/Feminine, editor and contributor, with Betty Roszak

Where the Wasteland Ends

Unfinished Animal

Person/Planet

The Cult of Information

Ecopsychology, editor and contributor

America the Wise

The Gendered Atom

*Longevity Revolution:
As Boomers Become Elders*

FICTION

Pontifex

Bugs

Dreamwatcher

Flicker

The Memoirs of Elizabeth Frankenstein

THE VOICE OF THE EARTH

An Exploration of Ecopsychology

With an new afterword by

THEODORE ROSZAK

PHANES PRESS

An Alexandria Book

An Alexandria Book

Alexandria Books explore intersections—
the meeting points between cosmology,
philosophy, myth, culture, and the creative spirit.

PHANES PRESS, INC.
PO Box 6114
Grand Rapids, MI 49516
www.phanes.com

Second edition
© 1992 and 2001 by Theodore Roszak

9 8 7 6 5 4 3 2 1
Printed in the United States of America
∞ This edition is printed on acid-free paper
that meets the American National Standards Institute Z39.48 Standard.

Library of Congress Cataloging in Publication Data
Roszak, Theodore
The voice of the Earth : an exploration of ecopsychology
With a new afterword by / Theodore Roszak
p. cm.
"An Alexandria Book"
Originally published: New York: Simon & Schuster, 1992.
Includes bibliographical references and index.
ISBN 1-890482-81-1 (alk. paper) — ISBN 1-890482-80-3 (pbk. : alk. paper)
1. Philosophy of nature—History. 2. Nature—Psychological
aspects—History. 3. Cosmology—History. 4. Environmental
psychology—History. 5. Psychology and philosophy. I. Title
BD581.R69   2001
113—dc20

For Betty
whose words . . .

*. . . green voices are singing
the dark ecstatic metabolism of hidden Earth.
We may read the shaman's gestures,
we bear the heat of eggs in our bodies,
the clustering amorous atoms, molecules,
miracles of future flesh, magnificence of bone,
arteries, sinews, spangled galaxies
craving form.* *

. . . helped me hear the voice

*From *Rescue and Restore* by Betty Roszak

ACKNOWLEDGMENTS

Acknowledgment is extended to the following for permission to reprint copyrighted material:

Oxford University Press for material from David Layzer, *Cosmogenesis: The Growth of Order in the Universe,* copyright © 1990 by Oxford University Press, Inc.

Bantam Books for material from John Gribbin and Martin Rees, *Cosmic Coincidences,* copyright © 1989 by John Gribbin and Martin Rees. Used by permission of Bantam Books, a division of Bantam Doubleday, Dell Publishing Group, Inc.

Cambridge University Press for material from Paul Davies, *The Accidental Universe,* copyright © 1982 by Cambridge University Press.

George Braziller for material from Erich Jantsch, *Design for Evolution,* copyright © 1975 by George Braziller Co.

Random House for lines from "De Rerum Virtute" from Robinson Jeffers, *Selected Poems of Robinson Jeffers,* copyright © 1954 by Robinson Jeffers, reprinted by permission of Random House Inc.

The American Physiological Society for material by Mario Bunge from *News in Physiological Sciences,* copyright by The American Physiological Society, 1989.

Pomegranate Publications for graphic diagram from poster reprint of "Evolution Mandala" by Dion Wright, used with permission of Pomegranate Publications, Petaluma CA 94975. All rights reserved.

Paul Fayter for his annotated bibliography "God and Modern Cosmology," prepared with the support of The Pascal Centre for Advanced Studies in Faith and Science. All rights reserved.

The Ira Hiti Foundation for Deep Ecology and the Elmwood Institute for support in completing the manuscript.

CONTENTS

◆

Part Two:
COSMOLOGY

And God designed the Earth to be our nurse; also, as she winds round the axis that stretches through her, to be the guardian and maker of night and day, first and most venerable of all the gods that are within the heavens.

PLATO, *The Timaeus*

And what is Earth's eye, tongue or heart else, where
Else, but in dear and dogged man?

GERARD MANLEY HOPKINS

PREFACE
Ecopsychology—A Reconnaissance

In 1901 Sigmund Freud delivered a famous series of lectures titled "The Psychopathology of Everyday Life." His purpose was to acquaint the public with the new and still mysterious science of psychoanalysis. He went about this in a clever way. He used jokes, double-entendres, and slips of the tongue to show how these familiar experiences reveal the repressed sexual and aggressive drives of the unconscious mind.

Today, a similar series of lectures might draw its material from reports of ozone depletion, toxic waste, and the greenhouse effect. These commonplace environmental problems have become the psychopathology of *our* everyday life. They reveal a condition of the soul for which Freud would have had no name.

In the century since psychology was first staked out as a province of medical science, we have learned a troubling lesson. The sanity that binds us one to another in society is not necessarily the sanity that bonds us companionably to the creatures with whom we share the Earth. If we could assume the viewpoint of nonhuman nature, what passes for sane behavior in our social affairs might seem madness. But as the prevailing reality principle would have it, nothing could be greater madness than to believe that beast and plant, mountain and river have a "point of view." We think that sanity—like honor, decency, compassion—is exclusively a social category. It is an attribute of the mind that can only be judged by other minds. And minds exist, so we believe, nowhere but in human heads.

While sex and violence continue to smolder in the depths of minds that do reside in human heads, the anguish of what I will call the "ecological unconscious" has emerged in our time as a deeper imbalance. At this level, we discover a repression that weighs upon our

13

inherited sense of loyalty to the planet that mothered the human mind into existence. If psychosis is the attempt to live a lie, the epidemic psychosis of our time is the lie of believing we have no ethical obligation to our planetary home.

These days we see the prefix "eco" affixed to many words. *Ecopolitics, ecophilosophy, ecofeminism, ecoconsumerism,* even *ecoterrorism.* . . . The result is not always graceful, but the gesture is nonetheless significant as a sign of the times. This tiny neologistic flag flies above our language like a storm-warning meant to signal our belated concern for the fate of the planet. Its often awkward connection with words from many sources—politics, economics, the arts—reveals our growing realization of how many aspects of our life that concern will have to embrace.

This is an essay in ecopsychology. Its goal is to bridge our culture's long-standing, historical gulf between the psychological and the ecological, to see the needs of the planet and the person as a continuum. In search of a greater sanity, it begins where many might say sanity leaves off: at the threshold of the nonhuman world. In a sense that weaves science and psychiatry, poetry and politics together, the ecological priorities of the planet are coming to be expressed through our most private spiritual travail. The Earth's cry for rescue from the punishing weight of the industrial system we have created is our own cry for a scale and quality of life that will free each of us to become the complete person we were born to be.

Once upon a time, all psychologies were "ecopsychologies." Those who sought to heal the soul took it for granted that human nature is densely embedded in the world we share with animal, vegetable, mineral, and all the unseen powers of the cosmos. Just as all medicine was in times past understood to be "holistic"—a healing of body, mind, and soul—and did not need to be identified as such, so all psychotherapy was once spontaneously understood to be cosmically connected. It is peculiarly the psychiatry of modern Western society that has split the "inner" life from the "outer" world—as if what was inside of us was not also inside the universe, something real, consequential, and inseparable from our study of the natural world.

Turn, for example, to the modern psychiatrist's constant companion, *The Diagnostic and Statistical Manual.* The *DSM* is our society's canonical listing of all officially designated neuroses, universally employed for every medical, legal, and insurance purpose. The *DSM* might be said to bear about the same relationship to psychiatric theory that a municipal building code bears to true architecture. Like the building code, the *DSM* is a dry and colorless compendium of guidelines. Yet it can serve as a convenient inventory of modern psychiatric thought, what it includes and what it excludes. In the *DSM,* one finds such exotic categories as "Schizoaffective Disorder in a Narcissistic Personality," or "Childhood Onset Pervasive Developmental Disorder." The categories for drug dependency are especially refined: "Hallucinogen Affective Disorder," "Hallucinogen Delusional Disorder," "Hallucinogen Hallucinosis." But with the possible exception of "Zoophilia" (bestiality, as it might once have been called), there is not a single recognized disease of the psyche that connects madness to the nonhuman world in which our environmental responsibility is grounded.

The alchemists of the ancient world had a teaching: "As above, so below." Four words that contain an entire cosmology. In the alchemical tradition, the heavens above, the Earth below, including its living cargo, were seen as a grand cosmic unity, a harmony resounding in the mind of God. Centuries later, modern science has to a degree substantiated that teaching. We too perceive a unity to the world. We know that the stuff and logic of the universe are everywhere uniform. The same atomic rudiments, the same chemical constituents, the same laws and principles extend from the cellular substance of our blood and bone to the farthest galaxies. We have learned that our planet and all the life upon it are made from elements that were forged in the fiery heart of primordial stars. As the alchemists believed, the baser stuff of the world can be transmuted into precious elements; commonplace hydrogen can be changed into gold—if it is cooked in a stellar core to temperatures far beyond anything their primitive furnaces could achieve and for eons longer than they could imagine.

If the alchemists were right about that much, we assume it was simply a hunch. By our standards, their studies penetrated matter too shallowly to yield exact physical knowledge. But then they may have had something else in mind: a knowledge not of fact, but of the meaning behind the facts. For them, "above" was the *macrocosm,* the world of the heavenly spheres, the angelic hosts, and Dame Nature vast as all the planet Earth. "Below" was the *microcosm,* the human soul. Between these two—celestial intelligence and the inner being of humanity—there was said to be a vital link. Macrocosm spoke to microcosm; microcosm reflected macrocosm. The two were in living dialogue. Understanding the universe was a matter of listening, having ears to hear the music of the spheres, the voice of the Earth. Wisdom meant connecting.

For the better part of two hundred years, keeping these two realms divorced and not even on speaking terms has been the signal endeavor of rational thought and sound science. Matter to one side, mind to the other. *Out there,* the objective; *in here,* the subjective. The one a secure realm of mathematical certitude, the other a murky terrain of shifting emotion, dream, hallucination. Thoughts are not things, things are not thoughts. For us the "macrocosm" has become the province of the exact sciences, the greatest collective intellectual enterprise of modern times, no longer one pursuit, but many fields of study: physics, astronomy, chemistry, biology, each now subdivided into numerous specialized disciplines. And "microcosm," the sphere of mind, soul, emotion, means psychology, the study of human experience as it can be gleaned from confessions made on a psychiatrist's couch or possibly from the introspective revelations of novelists and poets.

Thanks to that separation, the scientists have given us a wealth of knowledge about the structure and function of nature; similarly, the artists and psychologists have discovered startling insights into the human heart. But the divorce of inner from outer, above from below could never be more than a temporary expedient, a way of getting on with fact-gathering. Ultimately science is a creator of continuities, sometimes in spite of itself. Specialization narrows, but theory, which is the great adventure, reaches out; it aspires to wholeness, though cautiously. More and more the discoveries of the sciences unite the myriad diverse areas of inquiry. Today, scientists have high hopes of achieving a Grand Unified Theory, a "theory of everything." Some even labor to include the cultural, the psychological, the religious within that project. Their effort is sincere, if tediously piecemeal. What often came to the mystics in a flash of inspiration may have to return to us slowly and painstakingly by way of disciplinary convergence.

In these pages, we will undertake to reconnect the two realms of being, big and little, high and low, outer and inner. I realize there are scientific purists who object to seeing their intellectual property set upon for such purposes by amateurs, even respectful ones. But great scientific ideas have rarely been allowed to preserve their virginal status for long. Galileo's astronomy, Newton's laws of motion, Darwin's theory of evolution, all were rapidly appropriated by the greater culture; even more so Freud's would-be science of the mind. While pure science is not pursued with an eye to social or ethical significance, my purpose here is quite frankly to span the gap between the personal and the planetary in a way that suggests political alternatives.

That project is overdue. Historians of the future may look back in some astonishment at the last half of the twentieth century, wondering why so few thinkers of this period registered the full importance of the revolution in cosmology that took place in their lifetime. It would be no exaggeration to say that in the course of the last generation, we have passed into a postmodern cosmos as significantly different from the universe of Copernicus, Kepler, and Newton (or even Einstein, Hubble, and Shapley) as theirs was from the cosmos of Ptolemy. Many of the details of that transition may be familiar enough. The discovery of bizarre new astronomical objects like the quasar, the pulsar, the black hole, the measurement of microwave background radiation, the theory of the Big Bang have received the attention of the popular press and the occasional television documentary. But it is one thing to explain the technicalities, another to spell out the living importance of great scientific discoveries.

What the new cosmology lacks is the moral consensus that philosophers and artists once bestowed upon the Newtonian worldview. That consensus held for as long as science grounded itself in divine authority and vouched for the importance of human reason. Nothing has been more futile than our effort over the past few centuries to establish values and define sanity within a cultural context that finds no place for the sacred and views life as a marginal anomaly in the universe. The cosmology that gave us that picture of the human condition has now faded from the scene. The time is ripe for a new dialogue between scientific intellect and human need.

That dialogue is being conducted along two lines, one cosmological, the other ecological. I give fair warning: some of the scientific concepts we will investigate here as contributions to the synthesis of inner and outer, above and below—concepts like the Anthropic Principle and the Gaia hypothesis—are newly hatched and remain the subjects of lively debate. They border on "wild science," ideas still in the formative stage and susceptible to bizarre formulations. Some may feel the use I make of them here is premature, given their fledgling status. But ideas like these, as divergent as they may seem on the surface, emerge as the culmination of a long-term, indisputably secure trend in modern science that cries out for philosophical elaboration. That trend is our deepening appreciation of hierarchical systems in the universe. Gaia and the Anthropic Principle simply raise our rock-solid insight into the intricately structured unity of nature to the most ambitious level of generalization. In so doing, they carry science forward to the boundary of metaphysics. This is ground where many scientists understandably fear to tread. But sooner or later the greater implications of the ordered and evolving complexity of the universe will have to be faced. It may be that the deep systems of nature, from which our psyche, our culture, and science itself ultimately derive, are the new language through which the Earth once again finds its voice.

Part One

◆

PSYCHOLOGY

In our hearts we know there is something maniacal about the way we are abusing the planetary environment. The extinction of species, the depletion of the ozone, the annihilation of the rainforests . . . how often do we read reports of the devastation and say "That's crazy!"

We use the word, but in this context "crazy" has no professional status, no theoretical depth. Our instinctive sense of environmental anxiety is little more than an "ouch!" that does not tell us why we hurt or how to heal the wound. We look to the psychiatrists to teach us the meaning of madness, but our dominant schools of psychotherapy are themselves creations of the same scientific and industrial culture that now weighs so brutally on the planet. Even those who dissent from Freudian orthodoxy remain narrowly focused on what Jung called "urban neurosis." They ignore the greater ecological realities that surround the psyche—as if the soul might be saved while the biosphere crumbles. The context of psychiatry stops at the city limits; the nonhuman world that lies beyond is as great a mystery as the depths of the soul.

Where do we turn to find a standard of sanity that comprehends our environmental condition?

One

---◆---

"PLEASE, SIR, MAY I HAVE SOME MORE?"

The Interplay of Psychology, Cosmology, and Ecology

ANNA IN THE AISLES OF PLENTY

In the early 1980s I met a young woman from Poland, a member of the Solidarity movement who was touring California as a sort of self-appointed, unofficial ambassador. Given conditions in Eastern Europe at the time, she traveled somewhat furtively, her pride mixed with a certain air of desperation.

I could tell that Anna had no clear idea what she expected to find on her journey to the West. Her visit was something of a pilgrimage, more inspirational than political. I was among a number of writers she sought out requesting books and talk. So we talked, and I gave her books. But all the while we discussed great issues, Anna was saying more with her eyes than her lips. Maybe all she wanted was for the outside world to know that Solidarity existed, that she existed, and would we please remember that in the troubled days ahead.

After she departed, the people she had stayed with told me this story. They had picked Anna up at San Francisco Airport. On the way home, needing groceries, they had stopped at the Safeway. Anna asked to come with them. She had heard of supermarkets but had never seen one. When the automatic door opened and ushered her in, she stood a long while staring in all directions. Then she wept. She walked the aisles of the store and the tears kept coming.

Now, some ten years later, we know there was a political significance to Anna's tears of amazement. Their meaning has become front-page news. One way to explain the upheavals that are rocking the communist world might be to say that too many people have been kept waiting too long to get to the supermarket. Does that trivialize the revolutionary ferment we see all about us, and not only in the Marxist societies? Not if one puts the matter in the proper perspective. As Marx himself knew, sheer physical discomfort is not the worst form of suffering. Greater by far is the hardship that results when privation is due to injustice, incompetence, corruption. Then the pain is compounded by the indignity of victimization. There is a kind of material hunger—not for the bare necessities—that transcends the needs of the body. In this sense, access to material goods, even of the most frivolous kind—junk food, blue jeans, transistor radios, T-shirts—can sometimes be an assertion of self-respect and independence. It is not just raw, self-indulgent consumption. Anna reported that she spent a major part of her life each day in Warsaw waiting in line for meager goods. What a crushing social discipline that can be: made to wait, made to waste one's life trudging forward inch by inch to buy a cake of soap, a few pounds of potatoes. And what if when one reaches the head of the line, there is no soap, no potatoes to be had? Worse, what if one must turn away empty-handed knowing—from film and television and magazines—that elsewhere people no more deserving than oneself are headed home loaded with merchandise?

The market economies of the world are so riddled with greed and vicious competition that it is easy for critics to overlook the possibility that, after a contorted fashion, they meet significant human needs. We are so used to seeing our economic system exploited by profiteers that we may be tempted to treat the needs that people bring to the marketplace with the same contempt that we heap upon the hucksters who manipulate those needs. But it is the first rule of a humane sociology to distinguish the aspirations of people from the distorted way in which those aspirations may be expressed. An activity as simple, and seemingly as purely acquisitive as shopping may provide the opportunity for making choices, asserting taste. Admittedly it is a low-grade exercise of social power; but clearly it has come to exert a powerful attraction upon millions in the modern world.

Charles Dickens gave us one of the classic images of privation under early capitalism: Oliver Twist in the workhouse stepping forward to ask for a second helping of gruel. "Please, sir, may I have some more?" But there was no more. The impudent lad received only a drubbing. Marx built his ideology on horror stories like these, pictures of a society where there was not enough gruel to go around. For generations the goal of reform and revolution in the industrial societies has been doling out the necessities fairly, building a floor beneath the ever-precarious economy, and, of course, punishing those who took more than their share. What Marx understandably overlooked was the possibility that one day there might arise, even among the most wretched of the Earth, a new high level of expectation, an appetite for richness that demands more than mere guaranteed subsistence, no matter how equitably shared. George Orwell anticipated this in his anti-Utopia *1984*. There, besides the pervasive physical brutality of Big Brother's police state, the human spirit was forced to endure a more constant and pernicious discipline: the incessant daily drabness and uniformity of life. Equal everything for everybody, but without personal choice or even minimal privacy. At last, this becomes the basis for whatever small sad gestures of rebellion still occur: the secret assertion of sexual diversion, an insistent demand for fineness, for color, even for gaudiness. How many who have visited the socialist societies have come back to report they missed the billboards, the garish advertisements, the little touches of luxury? In many Third World societies that level of expectation is making itself felt even before the gruel has been served out. Wishful images of Western opulence gleaned from film and television are convincing millions in the Marxist world that capitalism delivers the goods and communism does not. They wonder: will there ever be anything but gruel in our larder?

Lest this begin to sound like a smug neo-conservative diatribe, let me hasten to say that this is not intended as an encomium on the delights of limitless consumption in the new world order. The spendthrift excess of the Western economies is the problem to which this book addresses itself, *not* the solution.

For here is another story about supermarkets.

From time to time I give my students an assignment. I ask them to visit their supermarket, not to buy, only to observe. Walk the floor, study the shelves. I ask them to consider: how much of what they see there is real food, real goods needed for survival and health. How much is waste, nothing better than expensively packaged garbage in the making? How much floor space could be eliminated if the store limited itself to selling what people really need? How much of what once might have been food has been extravagantly processed into nutritionally vacuous novelties—crisps and chips and flakes, the stuff of dyspepsia and tooth decay?

Then watch, I tell them, what people buy—even those who must pay in food stamps. Stand by the checkout counter and observe the merchandise going by. The cosmetics and tobacco and liquor, the convenience foods, the bottles of colored sugar-water, the paper goods and plastics. What does all this tell you about our standard of living, about the distinction between wants and needs?

This is intended as an object lesson in applied ecology.

But now each time I make the assignment, I think of Anna weeping in the aisles of plenty.

CAN THE EARTH AFFORD US?

Currently, our best hope for saving the peace of the world would seem to entail bringing that plenty to more and more people, relieving the discontents, translating the animosities of nations into economic competition or even cooperation. In the former communist societies, the demand for access to goods has become a force that is shaking long-entrenched regimes to their foundations. In our own society, an underclass locked away in inner-city housing projects or sleeping on the streets makes the same demand, though in practice it may take the form of sporadic crime, the violence of the drug trade, outbursts of racial and ethnic violence.

If things continue on this track, within the next decade or two, there may be some thirty nations around the world clamoring to enter the era of high industrial affluence. Governments, whether liberal or dictatorial, are discovering that they cannot long hold power if they do not make good on their promise to achieve that goal. Meanwhile, the mature industrial economies of the European Common Market are readying themselves for a renewed burst of coordinated growth that may surpass the affluence of America and Japan. The best business brains in the world are hastening to get in on the great European boom.

By the time the East Europeans, the Chinese, the Indians and Pakistanis, the Koreans, the Taiwanese, the Brazilians, and a score of other nations reach the standard of living that the American middle-class now enjoys, a higher standard will have been set, and a new round in the economic race will have to be run. Upward and onward toward ever higher levels of production and consumption.

Now here is a hard truth:

Nothing like this may be possible, because nothing like this may be even remotely affordable.

Such an endless frontier of abundance may exist only in the delusionary thinking of people who know nothing of the biological foundations of life on our planet. In the United States alone, one study based on figures drawn from the Environmental Protection Agency places the cost of existing environmental programs over the course of the 1990s at $1.6 trillion. This does not include the expense of any new programs dealing with such problems as global warming or ozone depletion, whose costs we cannot even begin to assess.[1]

How much is $1.6 trillion? It is not easy to say. Compared with the Gross National Product of the United States ($5.5 trillion per year) this may still seem to lie within the range of affordability. But numbers like the GNP are really more a part of the problem than the solution. The GNP indiscriminately lumps together all the productivity that has blighted the environment as well as all the costs of cleaning up the mess. Environmental sanity is therefore certain to require eliminating that sort of "productivity," hence to a much reduced GNP. We are just coming to realize, as all the environmental chickens come home to roost, that even the affluent are not as rich as they thought they were.

But how rich or poor are we? We have no universally accepted form of economic analysis (certainly none capable of persuading political leaders and their bewildered publics) that can tell us how close we may be to the limit at which what we must do to protect the biosphere will cost more than the wealth our industrial economies can generate. The study mentioned above, for example, was commissioned by the Center for the Study of American Business; it reflects the views of a significant participant in the environmental debate, a corporate community that has come to be deeply skeptical about the seemingly extravagant prescriptions presented by many ecology groups. It fears that existing environmental policies will become "an increasing drain on the American economy," "an open checkbook with no standards of measurement." Its warning is clear: "Policies that shrink the economic pie have widespread consequences for citizens' well-being"; they are "not in line with the wishes of most Americans."

And this may be true. We may be close to the point at which both business elites and the general public that looks to them for the necessities and amenities of life, as well as for the jobs that will let us buy both, will pay no more to repair the biospheric damage we inherit from the past two centuries of industrial expansion. The private sector of our economy is doing all it can to help them reach that decision. Inspired by their sudden and unexpected triumph in the cold war, the corporations of the Western world and Japan are licensed to feel more aggressively confident than ever about their values, their competence, and their claim upon the public trust. *But the pessimistic scenarios of the environmentalists may nonetheless be true.* The *vox terrae,* not the *vox populi,* may have the last word in this debate. If so, then the current American–Japanese–West European standard of living may be a temporary and tenuous indulgence. The entire industrial experiment may be pressing against an intractable limit from which it will soon be forced to fall back.

Something like this happened before. In the later Middle Ages, after a prolonged period of economic expansion, a young and vigorous Europe all but collapsed into ruins. It was struck down by a sudden shift in the ecological balance it did not understand, could not even see: a virus carried by a flea that rode on the back of a rat. We remember this catastrophe as the Black Death, an ecospasm that nearly destroyed a civilization. For the next century or more, all the once-promising economic indicators of an expansive Europe sank to rock bottom, including population growth—not simply because of an increase in the numbers dying, but also due to a sharp decrease in the numbers being born to those who survived. So hopeless did life seem that men and women packed off to monasteries in record numbers, giving up on the world. In time, over the next two centuries, Europe recovered. When the threat is no worse than a rampant virus, eventually the immune response can repair the damage. Or at least that was the case in preindustrial times. Now, thanks to advanced means of transportation and an increasingly footloose population, a disease like AIDS can circle the globe in a few years' time.

The ecological crisis of our time is either another detour along the open highway of economic progress, or it is the warning of a dead end just around the corner, a disaster far worse than the Black Death, from which it may take millennia to recover. The imponderables are so great in making assessments of the global conditions of life that either of these views could be right. In some cases—for example, the planetary warming of the greenhouse effect, the danger of ozone depletion, the long-range effect of acid rain, all of these potentially more irreparable than the medieval plague—even the best minds cannot arrive at a consensus. We count and measure, measure and count again. But do we have the right numbers? Do we have enough numbers? Do the numbers describe a transient fluctuation or the long-term trend? Our fears have been raised; theories and possibilities have been laid out before us. We are left to choose, but many cannot make the choice. There is not enough evidence one way or the other. The risks may run as high as the threat of human extinction, but *we do not know where we stand in the matter*.

This position of radical uncertainty is even worse than the worst-case scenarios of the gloomiest environmentalists, because it leaves us without the conviction to make the hard decisions that may be demanded of us. Where the argument for apocalyptic pessimism cannot be conclusively proven, it is only reasonable to wonder if there might not after all be a technological fix for every ecological dysfunction. Perhaps then we ought to keep our energy focused exactly where it is: on the limitless expansion of our industrial power. Inertia is the strongest of all social forces; people do not change familiar, long-established ways—especially those that have paid so many benefits in the past—unless they are convinced that they are faced by indisputable necessity.

Even less likely is it that the underdeveloped societies will waive their rights to the industrial plenty of our age. For them—the envious, hungry billions who want their fair share of the wealth—the environmental warnings so familiar to us might as well be written in a secret code. Or, worse still, they increasingly read like a deeply laid conspiracy against the wretched of the Earth. Third World leaders have every good reason to display suspicion of the First World's intentions. What are they to make of a memorandum that was privately circulated through the upper echelons of the World Bank's headquarters in Washington and leaked to the press in 1991? It cynically encourages the accelerated deployment of polluting industries to poor countries, arguing that "the economic logic behind dumping a load of toxic waste in the lowest wage country is impeccable and we should face up to that." The author of the memo, a chief economist at the Bank, observes that the most precious resource many "underpolluted" nations have to offer is their "pretty air," water, and topsoil—just waiting to be used as an international garbage can.[2]

Sad to say, Third World distrust of the industrial superpowers has begun to spread beyond governments and corporations to become broadcast hostility toward Western ecologists generally. In 1991, the World Resources Institute along with other environmental groups spoke out against plans by the Chinese government to increase the nation's use of coal. The director of science at Greenpeace joined in on the condemnation, describing China's decision as possibly "the final deadly puff of greenhouse gases" that would irreversibly alter the world's climate. He may have been right, but two Indian economists were quick to respond to the criticism as "environmental colonialism." Metaphorically referring to the planet's CO_2 "sinks" (the oceans and the forests) as a sort of global recycling bank, they correctly observed that the rich Western nations (especially the "filthy five" that include the United States) are vastly "overdrawn." Not so the Third World nations; they have "credits" to their carbon dioxide accounts. "These nations should be lauded for keeping the world in balance because of their parsimonious consumption despite the Western rape and pillage of the world's resources."[3]

Similarly, Ramachandra Guha, an Indian critic of the Western Deep Ecology movement, believes the goals of "the conservation elite"—biodiversity, steady state economic policy, wilderness preservation—amount to little more than a new imperialism. Trace out the full economic implications of measures like game preserves for endangered species, and they entail "a direct transfer of resources from the poor to the rich." In the underdeveloped nations, sheer survival is the paramount order of the day; equity and social justice head the economic agenda. In these conditions of privation, it makes little moral sense to speak of nature having "an intrinsic right to exist." "Deep Ecology," Guha charges, "runs parallel to the consumer society without seriously questioning its ecological and socio-political basis." The best contribution the industrial nations can make to world-environmental policy is to attend to their own overconsumption and curtail their military spending. Beyond that, let the Third World set its own economic priorities.[4]

As the socialist economies crumble before an irresistible popular demand for affluence and justice, their collapse takes with it into extinction what once stood as the modern world's only serious historic alternative to unrestrained entrepreneurialism. The nations and cultures that would survive must commit themselves to urban-industrialism in its most maniacally energetic variation. All the forces of enlightened reform in the formerly socialist countries, all the forces of progress in the Third World, are gambling their hopes and substance on economic growth. But can the planet afford to pay off on that gamble? Even those who are most sanguine about providing a technological fix for the environmental problems of our society must cringe at the prospect of so many more people joining us in the pursuit of unlimited affluence.

Consider only one contingency. If the Brazilians and the Indonesians continue to burn and cut our (*our* not their) rainforests at the present reckless rate, the effects upon the world's weather patterns are bound to prove massively disruptive. The Amazonian basin as a whole retains some two-thirds of the world's nonpolar fresh water supply. The biomass of these vast forests contains more than a third of the Earth's living terrestrial carbon pool; some experts believe the rampant burning of the jungle accounts for as much as a quarter of the carbon dioxide injected into the atmosphere each year. The jungle canopy of the Amazon—an area larger than the lower United States—plays a major role in governing the albedo, a basic factor in the planet's heat reflectivity. All these are among the Earth's chief means of balancing the climate. Some "catastrophic" climatologists believe that the slightest shifts in these geophysical variables can precipitate sudden, calamitous results. Even in the best case, brutally revising so critical a parameter as the rainforests cannot help but produce erratic, global fluctuations in the world's agriculture and demographics. That is as close to a biospheric certainty as we can expect to come.

The rape of the rainforest, especially in Brazil and Central America, serves as a convenient compendium of social and environmental blindness on the widest scale. In return for such short-term benefits as cheap beef and tropical hardwoods, most of which go to absentee corporate owners, the indigenous poor are exploited as part of ill-conceived schemes for development that put the land to disastrously bad uses. Native cultures are annihilated, species are wiped out by the hundreds, reducing the precious biodiversity of the planet, the climate of the world is deranged. The risks we are running have been well publicized, but the attention has produced no serious, long-term reform in the management of the rainforests. The World Bank, the one institution that might persuade the political leaders of these hard-pressed nations to change their ways, has been laggard in the extreme when it comes to mounting the pressure necessary to halt the devastation. Perhaps this is because corporations that are headquartered in some of its richest member nations—Volkswagen, Mitsubishi, Nestlé, Swift, Armour—are among the chief beneficiaries of runaway deforestation. This makes it all the easier for Third World leaders to argue that they cannot *afford* to do more.

They might go further, demanding the right to do as we have done: ransack the land, pillage the forests, raise up great cities and fill them with factories and traffic, sweep the garbage into the nearest river or ocean. The Brazilians and Indonesians could easily point out that, in the United States, less than ten percent of the virgin forest that spanned the continent when the first white settlers arrived still remains standing. Now our ancient forests survive only as tiny enclaves in the Pacific Northwest. And what is the likely fate of the rainforest we have in our own backyard? The forests of Oregon, Washington, and British Columbia stand an excellent chance of vanishing long before the Amazon basin has been stripped. If the damage is less publicized, it may be in part because the techniques of devastation are more cunning and better rationalized. Under pressure from environmentalists, industrial loggers in North America resort to such deceptions as "visual management corridors": shallow strips of forest left standing along major highways to conceal the clear-cutting that takes place just out of sight. For that matter, some loggers make no apologies for their destructive practices. In a network television documentary made in 1990, a leading Northwest timber executive describes the trees he cuts as "stacks of money standing on stumps." Ancient trees are merely stacks of money standing on *"old* stumps."[5]

THE CLASH OF IDEOLOGIES

When Third World countries look to the developed nations for guidance in the formulation of environmental policy, what they see are governments and business elites working ever more busily to unleash market forces they hope will achieve still greater productivity, still higher profits. The godword of official economic thought and policy remains "growth." We have had a generation of ecological research and reportage detailing the many ways in which unrestricted growth can be cancerous to the body politic. At some levels of our society, the lesson has taken hold; an increasing number of localities—usually well-to-do suburbs and more affluent neighborhoods—have passed ordinances intended to restrict growth in favor of a better quality of life. Nevertheless, growth is still invoked, without refinement or specification, as the panacea that will cure unemployment, stimulate initiative, inspire invention, raise public morale, and dissolve all social dilemmas.

And if the environment must suffer in the process . . . ? The American marketplace has well-developed methods for dealing with the unwelcome and antisocial results of corporate policy. Not a change of policy, but of imagery. Aided by the best public relations talent money can buy, the private sector is finding ever-more cunning ways to disguise its bad ecological habits. The tactic is called "greenwashing," the skillful use of the media to put a good face on corporate policies that may be quite the opposite of what they claim to be. These days every product on the market claims to be environmentally safe, recyclable, and one-hundred-percent natural. The change is often no more than large green lettering on the carton. Plastic garbage bags that will survive in landfills for a thousand years claim to be "totally biodegradable" because they are sure to fall apart someday. A frivolous spray-on cosmetic boasts that it is "Good For The Ozone" because it works with "a spurt not a spritz"—but it wastes more labor, capital, and resources than we can afford.

Even more serious than advertising hype are the richly funded lobbying efforts and front groups that work surreptitiously to circumvent government regulations by wrapping themselves in the rhetoric of sincere environmental concern. What is "The Alliance for a Responsible CFC Policy"? A creation of the DuPont, Dow, and Amoco chemical companies intended to oppose the phase-out of ozone-depleting chlorofluorocarbons. What is "Citizens for Sensible Control of Acid Rain"? A trade association of coal-mining companies and electric utilities organized to undermine the Clean Air Act. And RISE, Responsible Industry for a Safe Environment, is a front formed by the National Agricultural Chemicals Association to shield its pesticides from government regulation. As for the recent, highly publicized "Wise Use Agenda," it is a program formulated by loggers, miners, and ranchers to gain maximum commercial access to national parks, wildlife refuges, and public lands.

Efforts like these usually seek to project a spontaneous grass-roots character. They are on the side of little guys who simply want to enjoy the simple, God-given pleasures of life. Major corporate sponsors bankroll ersatz citizens' groups that purport to be the champions of the hikers, hunters, fishermen, and dirt-bike riders who are the supposed victims of environmental groups seeking to preserve wilderness and protect endangered species. Wherever possible, ecologists are portrayed as bullying spoilsports. One lobbyist from The Alliance for America, a corporate-funded association of outdoors enthusiasts, describes environmentalists as "the perfect bogeyman" and freely admits that his goal is to "destroy" them.[6] Opposition this intemperate readily goes beyond subtle manipulation; it spills over into open hostility. And at that point, environmental politics changes its tone and its nature. It becomes a nasty clash of ideologies potentially more wounding to the planet than any cold war confrontation short of thermonuclear war may ever have been.

Since the advent of organized environmentalism in the early seventies, the prevailing public perception of most environmental activists was heroic. They were seen as nature lovers and responsible citizens struggling to keep the water clean, save the forests, and defend soulful baby seals. Even those in the political and business community who believed the movement to be misguided were forced to concede that their environmental critics were men and women of high principle whose motivations were essentially idealistic. That concession is now in the process of being withdrawn. In the United States, as the cold war fades into the past, conservative elements are more and more boldly targeting environmentalists as their chief adversary, casting them in the nefarious role once filled by a now-defunct Marxist opposition.

At the extreme, the rhetoric can be venomous. A disciple of Ayn Rand, the ultra-capitalist ideologue, virulently condemns environmentalism as a "pure, unadulterated poison" based upon "hatred of man," and every bit as menacing to capitalism as bolshevism or Nazism. Its contention that nonhuman nature possesses intrinsic value is a thin cover for its true goal, which is "nothing less than *the undoing of the Industrial Revolution,* and the return to the poverty, filth, and misery of earlier centuries."[7] A bit closer to the corporate mainstream, the Competitive Enterprise Institute, a conservative study center that promotes "free market eco-management," announces, "There is an intellectual war taking place between pro-market and anti-market forces, to which business should be contributing a vigorous defense of its social role." The CEI's attack upon "the grieving greenies" of "ideological environmentalism" demands that we take still bolder steps "to remove the restraints from those who can and will, if allowed to do so, make the world safe." How is this to be done? By "reducing the barriers to wealth creation" and by establishing maximum private ownership of the environment. Let every corporation become its own Environmental Defense Fund with rules of its own making. With enough ingenuity, we can find ways to bring even the oceans of the world under the protection of the private sector. The sea floor might be divided into plots "much like terrestrial farms" and ways might be found for fish, whales, and seals to be electronically branded by their owners.[8]

Through the 1980s the Mobil Oil Company ran a notable series of "hit back" advertisements directed at the environmental movement. One ad titled "Lies They Tell Our Children" dismissed the cautionary warnings of groups like Friends of the Earth as a pack of pernicious "horrors" and "myths." It went on to cast environmentalists in the role formerly played by the communist menace of the fifties as a diabolically subversive influence out to brainwash the nation's youth into believing that famine, overpopulation, and the greenhouse effect might seriously darken "the bright future already on the horizon." Apparently unbridled optimism is the new orthodoxy of the marketplace.

There is a sad irony to the antienvironmental counterattack. Though it is being mounted by free market zealots, it threatens to vitiate the single most valuable contribution the capitalist system has made, largely in spite of itself, to the environmental cause. Namely, it has bred an opposition lively enough to take its case into the streets, the media, the halls of government and find a hearing. When it comes to the fate of the biosphere, this is what accounts for the difference between the environmental records of East and West.

As destructive as the market economies have been in their treatment of the environment, we now know that the socialist economies have an even worse history. *Glasnost* has revealed a blasted landscape stretching from the Danube to the Bering Sea. As far as we know, no one spoke out against the devastation; few knew it was taking place. It is not that socialism is inherently more antienvironmental than capitalism; rather its political organization has been far more effective in beating down all forms of resistance to centralized power. Left-wing politics, born to a hard, exclusive, and angry focus on issues of social justice, never encouraged the creation of an environmental agenda; worse still, the dictatorial methods of its leaders never allowed others freedom to take up the cause. A society like Stalin's Russia, willing to exterminate its own people by the million, was hardly apt to fret for the well-being of the nation's lakes and forests.

In contrast, the capitalist West has provided sufficient pluralistic space to allow an environmental movement to muster effective resistance. In a world of harsh political realities and imperfect choices, this is no small virtue. Making use of that pluralism to open a searching, worldwide reappraisal of urban-industrial values is one of the great environmental benefits we stand to gain from the end of the cold war. If the Earth can be said to have an interest in our ideological contretemps, this is it.

But just as the communist economies wither away, that vital difference between the market and Marxist systems may be about to wither with them. Western corporate leaders and the many think tanks they have established over the last decade are staging a no-holds-barred offensive against "environmental radicals" whom they now see as a more serious obstacle than any of the traditional left-wing ideologies. Those who must have an ultimate enemy on which to vent their political spleen may yet subject the environmental movement to the sort of McCarthyite witch-hunting that once chilled all political debate in our society. Some have seen in the recent police and FBI harassment of more militant environmentalists like Greenpeace and Earth First the beginning of a "green scare" that too much resembles the red scares of earlier days.

The incentives for pursuing such brass-knuckle tactics are rising rapidly as the former communist countries join the Third World in opening themselves to ever-deeper penetration by outside capital and know-how. There are some worrisome straws in the wind. The great forests of Siberia are among the major carbon dioxide sinks that govern the planet's climate and moderate the greenhouse effect. But already the new Russian government is striking deals with European, Japanese, and Korean companies to exploit these fragile ecosystems. The result could be devastation as globally consequential as that being visited on the tropical jungles. Traveling from town to town within the shell of the disintegrating Soviet Union, foreign loggers and miners can easily drive hard bargains with needy and desperate citizens who are in no position to enforce environmental safeguards.[9] Ironically, in the years ahead, the worst victim of entrepreneurial greed in Eastern Europe may be the lands, woods, and waters of the one-time "evil empire."

SCARE TACTICS AND GUILT TRIPS

As shortsighted, deceptive, and plain vicious as the new antienvironmental counterattack may be, to some degree the ecologists have only themselves to blame for their vulnerability. Their habitual reliance on gloom, apocalyptic panic, and the psychology of blame takes a heavy toll in public confidence.

In part, the problem arises from the way the environmental movement has come to be organized. The pattern resembles the telethon "disease of the month" approach. There are few groups like the Worldwatch Institute, Friends of the Earth, or Earth Island that seek to deal with the planetary habitat as a whole with its myriad problems given some order of priorities. Rather, the biosphere has been balkanized into a landscape of disaster areas. Scores of groups compete for the public's attention and funds, each targeted upon a single horror. Hunger, acid rain, toxic waste, the ozone, the topsoil, the rain forests, the whales, the wolves, the spotted owls. . . .

If one composites all the warnings and alarms of all the ecological groups, there would seem to be little people in the advanced industrial societies can do that is not either lethal or wicked. From the dioxin-laced coffee filters we use in the morning to the electric blankets we cover ourselves with at night, we are besieged by deadly hazards.

Worse still, many of them make us accessories to crimes against the biosphere. It is not that the warnings are necessarily wrong; I take most of them to be correct. It is simply that there are so relentlessly many and they come at us piecemeal often from the most unpredictable quarters. How could I ever have guessed that the material from which my eyeglass frames are made comes from an endangered species, the hawksbill turtle, now nearly extinct as hunters slaughter the poor beast to turn its shell into mere trinkets? Once again, I learn the central ecological truth: that all things big and small are members one of another in the biospheric web. Now that I know, I feel implicated in a great wrong. Bad enough to be ambushed by such distressing news, but too often the reports are grounded in a new environmental puritanism that almost delights in castigating our sins of self-indulgence.

At a lecture in early 1992, the Australian environmentalist Dr. Helen Caldicott, someone whose service to the cause I deeply admire, informed her audience that every time they turned on an electric light bulb, they were responsible for producing another anencephalic baby. She dilated upon the subject, describing in detail the suffering of these infants that come into the world without a brain. An inordinately large number of such babies have been born in the new, largely American-owned industrial centers along the Mexican border where environmental controls are practically nonexistent. Dr. Caldicott's strict advice was for us never to light more than a single bulb in our homes. Her audience cheered; I wondered why. If I thought there was any truth in what she said, I would not want to light any bulbs at all.

Other voices are more precise in their analysis, but no less censorious. The population experts Anne and Paul Ehrlich are two of the most dedicated environmental champions. Once again, I admire their work and accept their demographic analysis of our planetary ills. But I am flattened with guilt when they identify the United States as "the planet's primary environmental destroyer," and trace the accusation into every last detail of the American way of life:

> Few Laotians drive air-conditioned cars, read newspapers that transform large tracts of forest into overflowing landfills, fly in jet aircraft, eat fast-food hamburgers, or own refrigerators, several TVs, a VCR, or piles of plastic junk. But millions upon millions of Americans do. . . . We are the archetype of a gigantic, overpopulated, overconsuming nation, one

that many ill-informed decision-makers in poor nations would like to emulate. Unless we demonstrate by example that we understand the horrible mistakes made on our way to overdevelopment, and that we are intent on reversing them, we see little hope for the persistence of civilization.[10]

Drawing the obvious conclusion from such an indictment, *Earth Island Journal* tells us it is not enough to find "fifty simple things you can do to save the Earth," as a best-selling environmental manual of the 1980s puts it. We need fifty *difficult* things. The list begins

1. Dismantle your car.
2. Become a total vegetarian.
3. Grow your own vegetables.
4. Have your power lines disconnected.
5. Don't have children.[11]

The intention is not entirely humorous.

Nor did another activist have the least humor in mind when, in writing about the Columbian quincentennial, he lamented how "this awful thing called Western culture has now, inevitably, brought the world to the brink of 'ecocide.' . . . How sad, how terribly tragic that it should be *this* culture that needed to go and 'discover,' and thereby conquer and destroy the world."[12]

In the face of jeremiads like these, the English science writer Jeremy Burgess, a stout ecological supporter, is understandably moved to ask, "Is it just me, or does everyone else feel guilty for being alive too? . . . Eventually, and probably soon, we shall all be reduced to creeping about in disgrace, nervous of our simplest pleasures."[13]

From a very different ideological perspective, the Competitive Enterprise Institute also rankles at the constant "poormouthing" of the environmentalists. The environmentalists, it charges, are "anti-human"; their underlying premise is that "every consumer product and every consumer action is inherently anti-environmental." Designating this as "the Green equivalent of original sin," it calls for a return to the proud "Promethean paradigm" that launched the Western world upon its industrial course.

Such words, even when they are the preface to zany and reckless policy recommendations, nonetheless echo the great "gospel of hope" Francis Bacon so proudly announced to the world at the outset of the modern period. That inspiring belief in the future still has its residual appeal. Given the risks we are running in the game of ecological roulette our society has been playing for the past two centuries, prudence may be the proper order of the day—just in case the doomsayers happen to be right. But prudence is such a lackluster virtue. It does not match the exhilaration of the heroic exploits to which the myth of limitless progress summons us. If ecological wisdom cannot be made as engaging as the reshaping of continents, the harvesting of the seas, the exploration of space, if it cannot compete with the material gratifications of industrial growth, it will run a poor second to those who appeal to stronger emotions.

What I say here, I say as one who believes the warnings of the most worried ecologists and endorses the indictment of the angriest among them. I share their outrage and their urgency; I understand why they resort to hyperbole. But we may have reached the point at which the environmental movement must take the time to draw up a psychological-impact statement. Are dread and desperation the only motivations we have to play upon? What are we connecting with in people that is generous, joyous, freely given, and perhaps heroic?

There is a Faustian *élan* to our industrial adventure that summons up many of the best qualities of our species. Others find simpler but no less valuable gratifications in the sense of personal worth that accompanies a bit of discretionary income. If sound ecology comes to us asking that we stop being the animal we are, even if it is for our own good, it will not win many converts. Like all political activists busy with their mission, environmentalists often work from poor and short-sighted ideas about human motivation; they overlook the unreason, the perversity, the sick desire that lie at the core of the psyche. Their strategy is to shock and shame. But it is one thing to have the Good clearly in view; it is another to find ways to make people *want* the Good. That must begin with having some idea why people want what they *think* they want. The zealous tinkerers and technicians who gave us the light bulb, the automobile, the computer were not simply searching for ways to waste the wealth of the Earth; the scientists who invented the first atomic bomb were not deliberately doing evil; the highway engineers who tear up rainforests are not sheerly perverse. Even the leaders of the global corporations who seem to operate from simple avarice probably cling to a mystique of progress or an obsession with competitive self-testing that reaches into deep and secret aspirations. All these have seen something defensibly worthy in what they did, in the things they wanted: matters of dignity, excitement, ultimate well-being.

And Anna who wept so pathetically in the supermarket was not shedding tears of greed. She and all the Third World poor who want their fair share of the material plenty we enjoy seek to play a role in building the world they believe will bring them that dignity, excitement, and well-being.

For my part, I would take it to be little short of a counsel of despair if I thought the fate of the living planet depended wholly on the moral fervor of some small number of our species, overworked groups of ecological activists, each focused on a separate environmental horror with nothing more to draw upon in addressing the world around them except ethical denunciation, panic, or even enlightened self-interest. Is there an alternative to scare tactics and guilt trips that will lend ecological necessity both intelligence and passion? There is. It is the concern that arises from shared identity: two lives that become one. Where that identity is experienced deeply, we call it love. More coolly and distantly felt, it is called compassion. This is the link we must find between ourselves and the planet that gives us life.

At some point, environmentalists must decide if they believe that link truly exists. They must ask where it can be found inside themselves as well as in the public whose habits and desires we wish to change as only love can change us.

IN-HERE/OUT-THERE

Environmental politics needs a new psychological sensitivity, a capacity to listen with the third ear for the passion and the longing that underlie many of our culture's seemingly thoughtless ecological habits. Those habits may be surrounded on all sides by mighty, often creditable, certainly exhilarating human motivations. Psychology is the study of those motivations: the deep needs, the hidden yearnings, the driving ideals. In its therapeutic mode as psychiatry, it is meant to trace the twisted connections between what people say they want and what they really want. There must be some reason why people around the world have decided to undertake the mad devastation of their planet. More important, there must be some way to convince them that nothing they truly want can be gained from that devastation. There are greater endeavors than conquering nature, more reliable forms of well-being than physical dominance; there is a greater richness than the limitless acquisition of things. Changing these perceptions at the deepest level of the personality plays as great a part in dealing with our environmental crisis as any economic reform.

To see the matter in this perspective vastly alters what might otherwise seem like rarefied intellectual questions of epistemology and cosmology. What people expect, want, value in life connects intimately with what they understand their place in the universe to be. The modern industrial societies have been reared on a vision of nature that teaches people they are a mere accident in a galactic wilderness: "strangers and afraid" in a world they never made. What stance in life can they then take but one of fear, anxiety, even hostility toward the natural world? Like children who see their parents as remote, powerful, and punishing authorities, they will feel they have no choice but to stand defensively on guard, looking for every opportunity to strike out. Their encounter with nature will not be grounded in trust and security, let alone love. This is the point where epistemology, cosmology, and psychology intersect. The picture of the cosmos we carry in our minds can dictate a range of existential conditions. We may live sunk in bleak, defensive despair or we may find ourselves gracefully at home in the world. In addition to *what* we know, there is *how* we know, the spirit in which we address the world.

Abraham Maslow, the founder of Humanistic Psychology, was among the few to investigate the emotional tone that underlies knowledge, especially in the so-called objective sciences. He concluded that there are "cognitive pathologies" that can work their way into the foundations of philosophy and theory, and that can then warp everything that is built atop them. Science, he believed, "can be primarily a safety philosophy, a security system, a complicated way of avoiding anxiety and upsetting problems. In the extreme instance it can be a way of avoiding life, a kind of self-cloistering."[14] Acting from such motives, scientists, purporting to be dispassionate observers, may actually be in the grip of an "inflexible, neurotic need to be tough, powerful, fearless, even severe." They may then want a worldview that promises dominance rather than truth.

What we raise for discussion here is one of the oldest and most enigmatic issues in the history of philosophy: the relationship between the inner and the outer, the subject and the object. How does the mind In-here connect with the world Out-there? Can we In-here know the world Out-there as it really is? Can the world Out-there "know" or account for, in any adequate sense, what we are In-here? This is one of those deceptively simple problems whose solution seems to hover in the peripheral vision of the mind; but when we turn to study it, it loses focus and grows fuzzy. At one extreme, there have been those (the radical Idealists) who contend that there is no demonstrable rapport between the thoughts and longings within us and the reality that surrounds us. The mind, working upon the shapeless impressions of the senses, molds the world to the inherent contours of our understanding, but may achieve no accurate reflection of whatever exists beyond our eyes and ears. At the other extreme, we have primitive empiricism, which would have us believe that the nature of things, complete with its laws and first principles, simply imprints itself upon the blank and passive mind—provided the mind is emptied of superstition and pre-conception.

Few would any longer subscribe to either of these extremes. Ideal-ism, pressed to its limit, becomes solipsism, the belief that I alone exist in a mental void where everything else is my illusion. This may be the most unassailable of all philosophical positions; it is also the least inter-esting. Even Immanuel Kant, the founder of Idealism, granted that some faculty other than reason, such as intuition or insight, does manage to bridge the gap between "the starry skies above, the moral law within." On the other hand, modern science, which is the child of simple empiricism, has come to recognize that we see the world through the lens of theory, which is a gift of the imagination rather than a given of nature. The inner and the outer, the objective and subjective exist in some delicate balance, though defining exactly what that balance is may be stunningly difficult. Phrased as a formal episte-mological problem, the relationship of the knower to the known can seem an insoluble conundrum. My argument, like Abraham Maslow's, holds that there is a psychological dimension to the problem that must be addressed if one is to find a graceful way to connect the mind and the world. How clearly we understand the world depends on the emotional tone with which we confront the world. Care, trust, and love determine that tone, as they do our relationship to another person.

Our sense of being split off from an "outer" world where we find no companionable response has everything to do with our obsessive need to conquer and subjugate.

Evolutionary theory may offer us a solution to this dilemma. The very fact that human nature, both in body and mind, emerges from the physical universe must necessarily connect it knowledgeably with the nature of things. Adaptation is life's long, strenuous way of getting to know the cosmos. The point of contact it creates between knower and known may not, however, be "reason," but some other dimension of the personality. The bridge we need to find our way back to a significant sense of connectedness with nature may lie in that shadowed quarter of the mind we have for so long regarded as "irrational," even "crazy." If it has been such a "problem" for modern philosophy to formulate a coherent and persuasive epistemology, this may not be a purely academic matter. It may have more to do with the fact that we have for so long been trying to create a theory of knowledge that consigns too much of mind's capacity to the catch-all category of "madness." We should not then be surprised to discover that, having closed the true "doors of perception," there is so very much we can no longer "see."

It is no coincidence that the advent of industrialism in the late eighteenth century was paralleled by a fascination with madness on the part of artists and philosophers. At every step along the way through the next two centuries, the outward expansion of human power into nature was accompanied by an ever riskier exploration of the unconscious mind and its many strange passions. With each generation, the investigation of dream, nightmare, hallucination, trance, ecstasy has delved deeper into the secret recesses of the psyche. The Romantics, who initiated this descent into the irrational, soon to be followed by the Decadents, the Surrealists, the Expressionists, were a compensatory response to the excesses of Newtonian science: "single vision," as William Blake called it. Blake was among the first to link scientific sensibility to the killing pressure of the new industrial technology upon the landscape. His attack upon "Satan's Mathematick Holiness" only served to qualify him as one of the first mad artists of the modern world.

A generation later, when Percy Shelley produced his famous *Defense of Poetry,* in 1820, the battle lines had been clearly and painfully drawn. The dichotomies on which modern psychiatry would be built had been mapped out. Emotion against reason, the primitive against the civilized, the child against the adult, raw nature against the city, the organic against the mechanical, poetry against science. Shelley, himself a great admirer of the sciences, may have intended his words to heal this lethal cultural rift; but his essay came out, as the underdog's desperate appeal always must, sounding like a polemical counterthrust. In a classic definition of repression, he argued that

> the cultivation of those sciences which have enlarged the limits of the empire of man over the external world has, for want of the poetical faculty, proportionally circumscribed those of the internal world; and man, having enslaved the elements, remains himself a slave. To what but a cultivation of the mechanical arts in a degree disproportioned to the presence of the creative faculty, which is the basis of all knowledge, is to be attributed the abuse of all invention for abridging and combining labor, to the exasperation of the inequality of mankind? From what other cause has it arisen that these inventions which should have lightened, have added a weight to the curse imposed on Adam?

Shelley hastened to nominate poetic imagination as the antithesis of "the owl-winged faculty of calculation." Poetry, he insisted, "is not like reasoning, a power to be exerted according to the determination of the will. It is not subject to the control of the active powers of the mind, . . . its birth and recurrence has no necessary connection with consciousness or will." He meant this to be the imagination's redeeming power; but what he described was *madness,* as people were coming to understand the word, namely the rational mind swept by impulse, fallen to the influence of forces outside its power.

By the end of the century, Freud, seeking to bring that madness into the province of medical science, freely admitted that he had discovered nothing the poets had not known before him. He might have gone farther in paying the artists homage—at least the Romantic artists whom he had in mind. They had not only reached into the depths of the embattled psyche but out into the world around them. Lovers and defenders of the natural beauties, they allied poetic imagination to the wilderness, intuitively recognizing that both were endangered by industrial power. Whatever else he may have borrowed from the poets, Freud, ever the urban intellectual, omitted their devotion to nature.

The result was a psychotherapy that separated person from planet. As much as any Positivist philosopher of his day, Freud toiled under the influence of one of the most powerful yet commonplace images in our language: the spatial metaphor that locates the psyche "within" and the *real* world "outside." The struggle to define and to shift the hazy boundary between these two supposedly segregated realms of experience is the great project of our time, an issue that is at once philosophical, psychological, and political.

THE BOUNDARIES OF THE EGO

There is a catchphrase every freshman student learns to associate with that species of religion we call mysticism: "All is one." Almost by definition, mystics assert the unity of all things, deliberately blurring the critical distinction between inner and outer, subjective and objective. Freud traced this sense of an "oceanic" unity between the person and the world at large to a lingering infantile memory.

> Pathology has made us acquainted with a great number of states in which the boundary lines between the ego and the external world become uncertain or in which they are actually drawn incorrectly. . . . An infant at the breast does not as yet distinguish his ego from the external world as a source of the sensations flowing in upon him. He gradually learns to do so, in response to various promptings.[15]

Recognizing how this primitive ego-feeling is recalled and indulged in yoga and other forms of mysticism, Freud concluded

> I can imagine that the oceanic feeling became connected with religion later on. The "oneness with the universe" which constitutes its ideational content sounds like a first attempt at a religious consolation, as though it were another way of disclaiming the danger which the ego recognizes as threatening it from the external world.

While Freud, in the typically tough-minded manner that was the reigning scientific style of his time, labeled the cultivation of such atavistic practices "neurotic," he was frank enough to admit that "the boundaries of the ego are not constant"; thus, while sanity requires the ego to "maintain clear and sharp lines of demarcation . . . toward the outside," there may be something of a loss involved in the adult's "normal" adaptation to the reality principle.

> Originally the ego includes everything, later it separates off an external world from itself. Our present ego-feeling is, therefore, a shrunken residue of a much more inclusive—indeed all-embracing—feeling which corresponded to a once intimate bond between the ego and the world about it.

This is a startling admission. Freud is saying that the well-formed and defended ego, which his science treats as "normal" and "healthy," is the "shrunken residue" of something greater that once connected harmoniously with the world. "Sanity" would then seem to be a matter of writing off the loss.

The Romantics and their rebellious successors also took it for granted that any larger, more liberated sense of the personality required turning from science toward exotic forms of experience: narcotic hallucination, drunkenness, rhapsodic ecstasies. But they welcomed the adventure, even though indulging these altered states of consciousness could often be hazardous, perhaps permanently damaging. Hence our curious association of aesthetic inspiration with madness. The "mad" artist is our cultural parallel to the "mad" scientist, each a distorted mind clinging to an oblique vision of reality.

This rough dichotomy between inner and outer is a recent and parochial invention of human culture. At the philosophical level, it derives from decisions made, quite deliberately, by a handful of European scientific thinkers in the seventeenth century. Impatiently seeking a practical clarity in their approach to the baffling complexity of nature, they elected to cut away the portion of the world that proved more elusive to observation and more difficult to quantify: the realm of personal experience and emotion. Galileo was prepared to be even more ruthless in reshaping the foundations of consciousness. He believed that the undeniably empirical, but as yet nonquantifiable experiences of seeing, hearing, smelling, tasting, touching were mere "secondary qualities" supplied by the mind to the *real* world of size, shape, motion, weight.

I think that tastes, odors, colors, and so on are no more than mere names so far as the object in which we place them is concerned, and that they reside only in consciousness. Hence, if the living creature were removed, all these qualities would be wiped away and annihilated.[16]

"... if the living creature were removed." What a remarkable proposal this is! The "creature" is the scientist himself, addressing the world with all his senses alert, alive, in contact. Let us ask the question seriously, even though we ask it of the great Galileo. *Is this not a crazy way to view the world?* It asks that this very knower delete himself from existence. The observing senses vanish, and with them, the colors and sounds of nature. But, oddly enough, *not* the quantities. They survive in some impalpably colorless, soundless, inhospitable void that is taken to be the "real" world.

But, of course, that void, at some point in its history, gave rise to eyes and ears, to the sentient beings who use them to explore and enjoy their world, finally to the human mind, which is as much "there" as any star or comet or quark. Galileo's sad, but revealing exercise in epistemological suicide is a greater fiction than any work of art. Ultimately science itself, in its persistent search for the truth of things, would have to admit as much.

Perhaps the brutal bifurcation of the world we see taking place in Galileo's words makes a kind of rough methodological sense for "hard" sciences like physics, chemistry, astronomy, geology in their early, bootstrap phase. In all these fields, the focus of the observer is on discrete objects in the world (or more likely in the laboratory) that one isolates for closer scrutiny. But in other fields of science, that isolation is not so easy to achieve. Biology can hardly subtract the "living creature" and survive. Cosmology, which inherits the responsibility once shouldered by theology to draw a complete picture of the world, cannot sensibly set aside the stuff of consciousness. What is inside the mind—whether it is scientific theory or pure hallucination—is also inside the universe, as much contained by it as any molecule or star. Most obviously, the discipline of psychology must grant consciousness a decent scientific status. And finally there is the field of ecology, which must embrace the human mind as an integral part of any ecosystem it would study fully, if only because the values that reside in that mind determine the relations between people and their environment. Where a judgment must be reached and a change made in our relations with that environment, there must be the power of great conviction, the emotional force that art or religion can provide. As science matures through these higher and subtler levels of understanding, it integrates culture into its view of the universe. And culture—*our* culture—is both the cause and the prospective cure of the environmental crisis.

The great changes our runaway industrial civilization must make if we are to keep the planet healthy will not come about by the force of reason alone or the influence of fact. Rather, they will come by way of psychological transformation. What the Earth requires will have to make itself felt within us as if it were our own most private desire. Facts and figures, reason and logic can show us the errors of our present ways; they can delineate the risks we run. But they cannot motivate, they cannot teach us a better way to live, a better way to *want* to live. That must be born from inside our own convictions. And that birth may have to be a painful one.

Neurosis is that pain functioning in industrial society as the impetus to change, filling the lives of the richest among us with annihilating discontent. A modern science of the soul that is adequate to its task must minister to that discontent as something that is more and other than sexually based, family based, or socially based. In our time, the private psyche in its search for sanity needs a context that embraces all that science has to tell us about the evolution of life on Earth, about the stars and the galaxies that are the distant origin of our existence.

Two

◆

MODERN PSYCHOLOGY IN SEARCH OF ITS SOUL

BART SIMPSON AND THE TIGER

I am sitting in a crowded airport waiting to board a plane that will fly me home from a distant city where I have been attending a conference on Artificial Intelligence. The city is Rio de Janeiro, an ailing Third-World metropolis whose government and financial masters have been maniacally plundering one of the planet's last rainforests. More than it needs computers and expert systems, Brazil needs its jungles. And beyond that, its cities, teeming with violence and cluttered with garbage, need social justice and decent sewers. But almost as if high tech might be the magic wand that will dispel these brutal ills, the Brazilians I have met on this visit have been preoccupied with modems and E-mail and multimedia.

Beside me in the waiting room, a little boy about six years old is casually flipping through an American magazine. He pauses on one page to study the picture of a tiger. The illustration is part of an advertisement for Exxon oil. The boy spends several seconds gazing at the photographed face of the great beast whose image, even in this tawdry commercial version, preserves a certain lordly dignity. Then he turns the page to confront another advertisement. At once the boy brightens. He recognizes the picture. It is an animated television cartoon named Bart Simpson, the current media rage. Excitedly, the boy turns to his mother to show her the picture, which also happens to be emblazoned across his T-shirt.

I think: by the time this boy is my age, Bart Simpson will have come and gone, replaced many times over by similarly ephemeral fictions. And by then the tigers will also be gone, never to be replaced. They may not even survive in zoos; not all the wild things agree to reproduce in captivity for our convenience and amusement. When they have no real place of their own, they quietly surrender to extinction. Someday children coming upon the picture of a tiger will view it the way we view the dinosaurs, wondering if such creatures ever really existed. But the extinction of the tigers—and the gorillas and the wolves and the whales—will be different. *We* will have exterminated these species, unthinkingly, without purpose, without remorse.

I have never seen a tiger in the wild. Nor a gorilla or a wolf. But as citified as I may be, something in me nevertheless insists that it is important these beasts should be there sharing some corner of the world with me. If they perish, it closes an episode in planetary history that represents millions of years of evolution. Granted, extinction is a constant theme of life on Earth, one of nature's ways of pruning, improving, and clearing space. But if it is to happen, best that it happen as part of some grand global transformation that has a certain geological, even cosmic grandeur to it. Some think the dinosaurs met their end sixty million years ago in the wake of a meteoric collision that cast the planet into a worldwide winter. Other species were rendered extinct by the drifting of the continents or the advance of glaciers, only to have their place taken by new types. There is an almost ceremonial magnificence to such processes that matches the magnitude of the calamity. We might consider extinction on such a scale as an "act of God," meaning not only that it happened before our time and beyond our control, but that it happened on whatever we take to be the highest authority.

But the tiger in the Exxon advertisement is not doomed to so dignified an end. The demise of its species will be fortuitously bound up with oil spills like that which Exxon in its money-mad recklessness inflicted upon the Alaskan coast a few years back. Bound up too with this airport where I am sitting, whose planes are fueled by Exxon's oil. Bound up with the devastation of the Brazilian rainforest, which is going on night and day somewhere west of where I sit. And with the high tech that was the subject of the less than necessary conference I have seen fit to travel eight thousand miles to attend. It is even connected along less visible lines with funny little Bart Simpson, whose fictitious existence is dependent on the technology I have just finished discussing with other experts flown in from all over the world.

All these are expressions of heedless power on the part of a human culture that is running amok, wildly expending its technical cunning and industrial energy in all directions. And for what purpose that is worth the death of a species? Too little of what we do with our affluence is done to feed the hungry, heal the sick, comfort the desperate. Between the fate of the Earth and the luxuries, frivolities, and greedy profiteering to which we devote our technological might there is no sane proportion. Yet we live in this imbalance, degrading the planet without the capacity to hear its cries of anguish and anger.

The little boy turns a page. A species dies. A television cartoon takes its place in his life. He does not know, he does not feel. At his age, I was just as uncaring, a child raised on the entrancing illusions of urban culture.

The words of the semilegendary American Indian leader Chief Seattle echo in my mind, a voice that has attained nearly prophetical stature among environmentalists. I know the pronouncement to be apocryphal, but it is nonetheless moving.

> What is man without the beasts? If all the beasts were gone, man would die from great loneliness of spirit, for whatever happens to the beasts also happens to man. All things are connected. Whatever befalls the Earth befalls the sons of Earth.[1]

As greatly as they may differ in theory and practice, all schools of modern psychiatry agree that the question of truth lies at the core of madness. We go crazy when we lie to ourselves, refusing to face painful realities, hiding from our shameful fantasies. Lust for the mother, hatred for the father . . . these guilty secrets have long since been laid bare. But what of the guilt that comes of annihilating whole species of our fellow creatures, not because we must do so to survive, but in ignorance and for the sake of nothing better than ephemeral amusements, petty pleasures, quick riches? We are, after all, in ways that may even be part of our innermost genetic inheritance tied to the beasts from whom we evolve. At what risk of madness do we break faith with them?

THE THIRD OUTRAGE

At its deepest level, psychology is the search for sanity. And sanity at its deepest level is the health of the soul. In these respects, psychology, whatever techniques it may use, is necessarily a philosophical pursuit, a critical examination of ethical conduct, moral purpose, and the meaning of life. Every major philosophical and religious system of the past has grounded itself in a psychology, seeking to heal the soul of its wounds and guide it to salvation.

Modern psychology, on the other hand, has been most distinctively an attempt to disconnect from the supposed subjectivity of philosophy and religion. It has followed the example of other fields—economics, political science, sociology—in choosing a scientific model of inquiry, hoping to escape the hazards of judgment. The Behaviorists of the early twentieth century were the most extreme in their assertion of this ideal. Though their principal study was the human mind, whose passions and yearnings they might be expected to share, they affected the cool detachment of the astronomer viewing a distant heavenly body or the biologist dissecting a specimen beneath the microscope. Clark Hull, one of the founders of the school, once described his methodology as a "prophylaxis against anthropomorphic subjectivism." His goal, he claimed, was to treat the "behaving organism" he was studying as if it were "a completely self-manipulating robot constructed of materials as unlike ourselves as may be"—a capacity that might serve as well in a torture chamber as in a laboratory.

Though he is usually regarded as Behaviorism's chief opposition, Freud struggled with no less determination throughout his lifetime to remain as rigorously scientific as possible—a goal that, for the most part, he fortunately failed to achieve. As a result, his studies were destined to have a far greater influence upon the arts, literature, and philosophy than those who were patterning their study of human nature on rodents and pigeons. Still, while Freud was willing to grant that human nature had a shadowed interior whose secrets might be more elusive than the logic of the reflex arc, he nonetheless hoped to make the psyche's dark forces and hidden fantasies the stuff of objective scrutiny.

A great deal has changed in the theory and practice of psychiatry since Freud's time. Here we will be using him as a baseline because he, far more vividly than the Behaviorists, realized the philosophical implications that were posed by the pursuit of a scientific psychology and pitched the issues at the most ambitious level. In his eyes, psychoanalysis was nothing short of epoch-making. It was the final stage in mankind's long, difficult march from superstition to civilization. Yet as much as the life of reason deserved to be cherished, Freud was frank to admit that it brought no happiness with it. Quite the contrary. The progress of science was a punishing ordeal. "Humanity has in the course of time had to endure from the hands of science two great outrages upon its naive self-love," he declared. The first of these came in the age of Copernicus when the human race "realized that our Earth was not the center of the universe. It was only a tiny speck in a world system of a magnitude hardly conceivable."

Three centuries later came the Darwinian revolution in biology, which "robbed man of his peculiar privilege of having been specially created, and relegated him to a descent from the animal world, implying an ineradicable animal nature in him." Bad enough, but worse was yet to come: "Mankind's craving for grandiosity is now suffering the third and most bitter blow from present-day psychological research which is endeavoring to prove to the 'ego' of each one of us that he is not even master in his own house."[2]

Did psychoanalysis *have* to be another outrage to the human ego? It did insofar as Freud insisted upon creating a psychology that shared common ground with the science of Newton and Darwin. Never one to flinch at public disapproval, he predicted there would inevitably be a "universal revolt against our science . . . and the liberation of opposition from all the constraints of impartial logic." He was prepared to meet this response by forcing the bitter pill down the public throat. It never occurred to him that there might be more to that revolt than infantile petulance; it might betoken a legitimate need for transcendent meaning that his science was too readily dismissing.

At the outset of his career Freud made the key decision to adopt the medical model of psychiatric disease, picturing the injured psyche as something like a broken bone: obvious damage in need of some equally obvious repair. It was a safe, minimal assumption, one that came easily to him as a neurologist and which might be expected to appeal to his colleagues. At times he outdid the mechanistic Behaviorists, speaking of the mind as a repository of pressures, drives, and discharges, as if it were a sort of dynamo inside the head fueled by the instinctual energies. To be sure, a good deal of this clanking, technical jargon was imported into his writing by his translators; Freud did, after all, refer to his subject of study as *die Seele*, "soul" rather than "mind," choosing the German word a poet or philosopher might have used.[3] Still, he did have a weakness for engineering metaphors and for the reductionistic methods that dominated the science of his day. It was Freud's hope that the medical model would guarantee the scientific rigor of psychoanalysis. But in order to live up to that criterion he required an objective measure of mental health. Like the Behaviorists, he felt this could be found in the preexisting social standard of normality. What father and mother, church and state, friends and neighbors, defined as sanity *was* sanity. Seeking to sound as scientific as possible, Freud called the child's assimilation to the adult world the "reality principle." Once the reality principle takes over, the infantile "pleasure principle," with its impractical demand for immediate consolation, is subordinated to a more sensible system of hedonistic budgeting. The child learns to settle for deferred gratifications. If this transition to adulthood ushered children into a humane and fulfilling quality of life, it might represent a decent enough ideal of "normality." But of course it does not. The world of the reality principle is the world of wars, witch-hunts, crusades, pogroms, prisons, criminal violence, class exploitation. Nevertheless, Freud's original position was straightforward and stoical. One must submit oneself to the powers. The psychiatrist's role was to guide the wayward patient back into socially normative paths.

COLLUSIVE MADNESS

Simplistic assumptions like these characterize Freud's early period, when he still hoped to ingratiate himself to the medical establishment of his day. But in his later years, he opened up two extremely rich veins of speculation that are hardly simple and potentially the very opposite of reductionistic.

The first of these derives from Freud's growing doubts about the social context of sanity, a skepticism that eventually led him to question, though not entirely reject, the medical model of neurosis that he had pioneered. The shock of the First World War put an end to Freud's complacent acceptance of consensual normality. What he saw before him in the carnage of the battlefield was a world gone murderously berserk in behalf of ideals, policies, and interests that had long been respected as "rational." How could such a society presume to prescribe criteria of sanity? Can those who fail to adopt its norms fairly be regarded as mad? Was it the psychologist's role to label them as such and whip them back into step with these "communal neuroses"?

Freud was the first to raise the ominous possibility that society itself might be psychopathological and so cannot serve as a standard of health. He asked: "May we not be justified in reaching the diagnosis that, under the influence of cultural urges, some civilizations or some epochs of civilization—possibly the whole of mankind—have become 'neurotic'?"[4] With these words, Freud was on the brink of departing psychiatry to assume the task of a chastising Jeremiah. It was a role he was unwilling to take on. "I have not the courage to rise up before my fellow-men as a prophet," he apologized. Accordingly, he never pursued the political implications of his great insight, nor did he seek to integrate it into his clinical practice. By all reports, Freud the father, husband, teacher was too much the authoritarian to challenge the ruling powers; his political stance was that of the intellectual elitist staving off the revolt of the masses. Ultimately he was willing to defer to official authority even if it was diseased. The alternative, he felt certain, would be anarchy. Caught between crazy governments and the threat of total social upheaval, he resigned himself to the conclusion that civilization was hopelessly tormented by discontents that might turn out to be genocidal: more frustration, leading to more explosive fits of rebellion, leading to more repression, leading to bigger wars.

With the exception of Freud's eccentric disciple Wilhelm Reich— to whom we will return later—it was not until a second World War had come and gone that a school of psychology appeared that was willing to take Freud's hypothesis of collective insanity seriously and to launch out along a different route. R. D. Laing, whose background was as much Existentialist–Marxist as it was Freudian, was among the first to assume an adversarial position on the issue of insanity. Convinced that the mad (or at least some portion of those designated "schizophrenic") may be a rare and endangered species desperately in need of protection, Laing argued that psychological breakdown could be the first step toward enlightened breakthrough. It might be an incipient assertion of true sanity by those who were still at least resilient enough to feel the pain of society's oppression. It is therefore the psychiatrist's responsibility to take the side of the mad against wrong-headed social authority. We live, said Laing, in the midst of "socially shared halluci-nations . . . our collusive madness is what we call sanity."[5] This is the fact from which both theory and therapy must take their bearings. If families are the source of neurosis, then the family must be resisted; if the state makes demands that drive sensitive people mad, then the state must be resisted. Psychiatry is called to a revolutionary task.

From Laing's work and that of Thomas Szasz *(The Myth of Mental Illness),* a small, insurgent school of Radical Therapy (sometimes called "Antipsychiatry") has developed, which sees itself as a sort of Mad Liberation Front, the ally and advocate of suffering souls against all the forces that would "adjust" them to their place in an insane world. One group of Laingian disciples, Activists For Alternatives, which calls itself "an organization of former psychiatric inmates, commonly known as 'mental patients,' " describes its mission in this way:

> Our position is uncompromising. We believe the "mental health" Es-tablishment has conned the American people. The idea of "mental illness" is a misleading and degrading metaphor. "Psychiatric treat-ments" in mental hospitals are for the most part forms of physical and emotional abuse. Psychiatric "diagnoses" are demeaning labels without any scientific validity. . . . There has been no revolution in the treatment of individuals who are psychiatrically labeled: it is an unbroken history of barbaric practices, justified by professionals as medical procedures designed to control patients' ostensible mental diseases.[6]

The project of the Radical Therapists is a brave and compassionate one; but, like many forms of political radicalism, it fares better at denunciation than reconstruction. It speaks out for the rights of rebel-lion but with no clear image of that higher sanity it would place above the authority of family and society. My impression has been that those who commit to Radical Therapy may never get beyond heroic opposi-tion to the psychiatric establishment. The result is often a political cause rather than personal health—though always with the hope that the two can be allied as "a people's psychology" that will provide "the integrating factor of self-awareness within the revolutionary process."[7]

With the Radical Therapists, I accept the premise that neurosis is defined within a political context; it is therefore intimately related to the social health and harmony that surround the individual. I also believe Radical Therapy is correct in challenging any form of psychiatry that sees its role as that of simply imposing its definition of mental illness upon the socially deviant as if this act might not be a subject of controversy. But in these pages my purpose is to connect that controversy with a second great insight in the later works of Freud, one that raises an even greater intellectual challenge than the concept of collusive madness.

THANATOS

When, following the First World War, Freud set about revamping psychoanalysis, the task took him beyond both the pleasure and reality principles. In these uncharted regions of the mind he erected a daring new theoretical framework that would do no less than give psychology a cosmic dimension. Exploring the deepest foundations of consciousness, he concluded that there are instincts deeper than sexuality. Below the level of the libido, we find the elemental biological thrust of life itself, which, Freud was convinced, cuts across the grain of physical nature. Life is an "unnatural" event in an uncaring universe, opposed by the most conservative of all the instincts. Thanatos, the death instinct. Thanatos wants nothing less than to extinguish life and return the universe to its inorganic state. Vitality, Freud believed, is at war with the very physicality it must draw upon to make living bodies and thinking minds.

The attributes of life [he reasoned] were at some time evoked in inanimate matter by the action of a force of whose nature we can form no conception. . . . The tension which then arose in what had hitherto been an inanimate substance endeavored to cancel itself out. In this way the first instinct came into being: the instinct to return to the inanimate state.[8]

Though the idea seems metaphysically rarefied, Freud sought to give it clinical application. For a time he believed the "repetition compulsion" might be connected with the primal biological need to return to some previous pleasure, repeating it over and over. This might issue from the hidden drive in all living things to return to the primordial inorganic state. "The goal of all life is death," Freud believed—a marvelously ambiguous pronouncement that may represent the height of wisdom or the depth of despair.

Because the death instinct longs to soothe away the anguish of existence, Freud also referred to it as the "nirvana principle," the desire for that absolute tranquillity that he felt could only be found in total annihilation. This is a quite illiterate interpretation of what Buddhism means when it speaks of nirvana as the cessation of desire; Freud's reading smacks much more of early German Romanticism. It is closer to the *weltschmerz* of the poet Novalis, who longed to expire before the anguish of unfulfilled existence. It is nonetheless a provocatively ambitious idea. By way of its neurophysiological constitution in the brain, Freud connects the mind with the material universe at large. In this encounter of the quick and the dead, life is the underdog. Nature, Freud was convinced, "is eternally remote. . . . She destroys us—coldly, cruelly, relentlessly."[9] This tragic and inexorable truth is too fearful for most people to face. In its terrible presence, the vast majority of our fainthearted species can do nothing but turn to the illusions of religion or go crazy with terror and grief.

Such desolate views were common among agnostic intellectuals at the turn of the century; the physical science of that period gave life an inconsequential place in the universe. It was seen as the improbable result of random fluctuations among inert chemicals. Only a few theoretical physicists had begun to feel their way into that newly discovered realm of subatomic paradox where all the old Newtonian certainties disintegrate. Even so, the New Physics provided life and mind with no more "natural" place in the quantum universe. For the public at large, matter was still a simple thing: little balls and clusters of dead, insentient stuff, so very different from life that there seemed no way to account for the existence of living things at all except as a freakish accident that has temporarily violated the sovereignty of the second law of thermodynamics. Life was a transient condition doomed to annihilation by the inevitable drift toward maximum entropy; ultimately, every chemical process in the universe would succumb to the great and final "heat death." After that, for all eternity, there would be nothing, nothing, nothing at all except empty space sparsely littered with the wandering cinders of long-expired stars.

At the turn of the century, this vision of inescapable doom permeated philosophy and the arts as well as the sciences. It accounts for the aura of invincible pessimism that surrounds the poetry of Housman and Dowson, the historical studies of Henry Adams and Oswald Spengler, the plays of Eugene O'Neill, and the novels of Thomas Hardy. The poet Swinburne lamented

> Then star nor sun shall waken,
>   Nor any change of light:
> Nor sound of waters shaken,
>   Nor any sound or sight:
> Nor wintry leaves nor vernal,
>   Nor days nor things diurnal
> Only the sleep eternal
>   In an eternal night.

This was the brooding intellectual atmosphere in which Freud set about connecting consciousness with the cosmos. A doctrinaire materialist, he envisaged psychoanalysis as essentially an inquiry into "the demands made upon the mind in consequence of its connection with the body." The body was the reservoir of the instincts; and when Freud spoke of "instinct," he meant the word in its evolutionary sense: that which connects human with animal in biological history. Ultimately, however, Freud's search for the physical foundation of the psyche reached a literal dead end. His vision of a lifeless, uncaring universe was so grim that it proved to have no future in psychiatry. It yielded an image of the human psyche trapped in the desolation of an infinity where it finds no consolation, no remorse, no response to its need for warmth, love, and acceptance. A cosmology like this has nothing to warm the human spirit.

There may be a hearty few who find a certain fatalistic bravado in facing that alien void. The Existentialist philosophers have, for example, characterized human life as a cosmic absurdity that has no meaning except that which is heroically but arbitrarily assigned to it by each isolated individual consciousness. At the extreme, Ernest Becker displays a sadistic delight in brandishing Freudian pessimism like an intellectual whip.

> What are we to make of a creation in which the routine activity is for organisms to be tearing others apart with teeth of all types—biting, grinding flesh, plant stalks, bones between molars, pushing the pulp greedily down the gullet with delight, incorporating its essence into one's own organization, and then excreting with foul stench and gasses the residue. . . .
>
> *Creation is a nightmare spectacular* taking place on a planet that has been soaked for hundreds of millions of years in the blood of all its creatures.
>
> Freud knew better, as he gradually came to see that the evil in the world is not only in the insides of people but on the outside, in nature—which is why he became more *realistic* and pessimistic in his later work. . . . whatever man does on this planet has to be done in the lived truth of the terror of creation, of the grotesque, of the rumble of panic underneath everything.[10]

What does the practicing psychotherapist do with a vision like this? Distressed clients arrive bearing the wounds of unresolved infantile fears and longings, grinding insecurity, debilitating anxieties. Does their physician then heap the "terror of creation" upon them?

Despite their rich metaphysical resonance (or perhaps because of it) the death instinct and the nirvana principle have remained intellectual curiosities in the history of Western psychology. Even before Freud's death, the psychiatrist Edward Bibring had designated these primal instincts as "theoretical," never to be adduced "in discussions of a clinical or empirical nature."[11] Accordingly, psychiatry after Freud has gone off in other, more practical directions. By and large the development can be described as the search for a larger social framework in which to treat the neuroses. The usual criticism of Freud is that his theories are claustrophobically restricted to the intrapsychic mechanisms, the familiar battleground of the ego, superego, and id. His disciples felt the need of escaping from this tiny psychic box into the outer world of the family, the group, the culture at large, in order to find the sources of neurotic suffering. Most of the schools that have grown up this century have been of this character, variations on interpersonal themes that take as their goal a functioning accommodation to social demands.

Freud's followers made an understandable adjustment meant to give their professional work more applicability. But there was also a significant loss that has gone unnoticed. Because these psychiatric alternatives simply ignored Freud's explorations beyond the pleasure principle, they have appeared to be larger, more comprehensive therapeutic systems. In one sense, this is true; they are socially more integrative. But in another sense, they have severely lowered the horizons of psychiatric theory, leaving out the universal dimension that Freud sought to give his science in his later, more prophetical essays. Neo-Freudianism has become, as one might only expect, the psychotherapy of urban industrial culture, sharing that culture's blithe ignorance of the greater natural environment on which we depend in body, soul, and mind.

NORMATIVE ALIENATION

Freud's attempt to qualify psychoanalysis as a branch of medical science led some, beginning with his most gifted pupil, Carl Jung, to criticize his approach to the study of the mind as narrowly reductionistic. The response is by now a familiar one. It holds that Freud sought to trace all human conduct to physical, mainly sexual origins, assuming that once these mainly childhood traumas had been brought back into consciousness, the patient would be cured. Yet, as critical as Jung was eventually to become of Freud's militantly scientific stance, he was among the few analysts to speculate, at least in passing, upon the connection between the psyche and physical nature. In his studies of alchemy, Jung was struck by the prominence of the number four in the religious symbolism of the world. He noted that quaternities (the four points of the compass, the four elements, the four temperaments, the four sides of the square, etc.) frequently appear as images of wholeness. What to make of this "statistical probability" in myth and lore? "I can hardly refrain from remarking—a curious 'sport of nature,'" he observed, "that the chief chemical constituent of the physical organism is carbon, which is characterized by four valencies. . . ." Jung quickly backed off the idea, fearing that "such an analogy" might be "a lamentable piece of intellectual bad taste." One wonders what Jung had in mind. Some deep archetypal recollection of the chemical basis of life, perhaps?[12]

At other points in his writing, Jung dabbled with the possibility that there may be an overlap between depth psychology and the new field of quantum mechanics. The hypothesis relates to Jung's concept of the *unus mundus,* the ineffable unity that lies at the core of mystical illumination. He wondered if quantum mechanics, especially the principle of complementarity, might offer some insight into this otherwise impenetrable theoretical realm.

> If these reflections are justified, they must have weighty consequences with regard to the nature of the psyche, since as an objective fact it would then be intimately connected with physiological and biological phenomena, but with physical events too—and so it would appear, most intimately of all with those that pertain to the realm of atomic physics.[13]

Though Jung undertook an exchange of letters on this subject with the physicist Wolfgang Pauli (who was one of his patients), he pressed the idea little further. Some Jungian theorists, among them Victor Mansfield and J. Marvin Spiegelman, have since sought to resume the inquiry. They suggest that the radically ambiguous relationship of particle to wave in quantum physics might, at least symbolically, express the complementary relationship between the conscious and unconscious mind.

In contrast to Freud, the consummate urban intellectual, Jung always remained sentimentally attached to the rural surroundings in which he was raised. A sympathy for natural beauty and wildlife plays in and out of his writing. In his memoirs *Memories, Dreams and Reflections,* he tells how filled with wonders nature was for him in his childhood. "Every stone, every plant, every single thing seemed alive and indescribably marvelous. I immersed myself in nature and away from the whole human world." In 1923, at one of his earliest professional seminars, he identified the four integral parts of the psyche that he believed had experienced the most serious repression in civilized people: "nature, animals, primitive man, and creative fantasy."[14] Still, in the years that followed, a deepening reaction to the dominant scientific paradigm of his day comes to color Jung's thought. Ambitious theoretical attempts to connect the psyche and physical nature fade from his more mature thought to be replaced by an adamantly nonphysical conception of the psyche. Underlying, or cradling the mind, he envisioned a nonmaterial collective unconscious that contains the compounded wisdom of the human race. The contents of this root mind are written in the language of archetypes, symbols that transcend parochial cultural boundaries, summoning the mind to enlightenment. How exactly this reservoir of salvational teachings came to exist, Jung could not say. But judging by the grandeur and universality he attributed to it, and by the reverence with which he always addressed it, for Jung the collective unconscious was either God or of God. At least that is how he believed people have traditionally understood this "world-system of the spirit." They explained it as a person "and they called this being God, the quintessence of all reality."

As Jung fully realized, the idea of the collective unconscious and its archetypal contents represented a decisive break with Freud's biomedical reductionism. He had at last rejected "the omnipotence of matter" in favor of "an independent psyche that is not determined by the body." His would be "a psychology that does not explain everything upon physical grounds, but appeals to a world of the spirit whose active principle is neither matter and its qualities nor any state of energy, but God."[15] In later years, Freud would mock his once-favored student for his defection, making it clear that he respected only those ideas Jung had developed when he was "a mere psychoanalyst and did not yet aspire to be a prophet."[16]

For many religiously estranged Westerners, Jungian psychiatry has opened doors that were long locked shut by conventionally rational thought. Jung once called his work an effort to heal "the urban neurosis of atheism." Some commentators have seen in Jung's work a modernized form of ancient gnosticism, the quest for illumination through knowledge of the mysteries.[17] The system certainly offers a grandiose perspective for the discussion of sanity. All the highest teachings of the great religious traditions can now be brought back into our culture through the collective unconscious and discussed in a more negotiable, psychologized idiom. Unfortunately, that idiom is not always the best vehicle for spiritual purposes. Too often a Jungian analysis of the archetypes takes on a dry, eclectic flavor. Things get labeled and listed: an example of the Divine Child here, there an example of the Suffering Savior. One pigeonholes the items and moves on. Such an approach may succeed in breathing a small, academic breath of life into the old myths; the recent popularity of the work of Joseph Campbell, the Jungian mythologist, is testimony to the attraction people find in combing through the world's forgotten lore when the project seeks to salvage things of living value. But the approach can become oppressively pedantic.

More seriously, it can have the effect of deepening the very dichotomy between psyche and nature that needs to be healed. This is ironic, since it was Jung's conviction that he was contributing to a "practical psychology . . . one which helps us to explain things in a way that is justified by the outcome for the patient." As he saw it, "in practical psychotherapy we strive to fit people for life. If I recognize only naturalistic values and explain everything in physical terms, I shall depreciate, hinder, or even destroy the spiritual development of my patients." While he professed the desire to do justice to "the physical being" of his patients, Jung's decision was finally to ally himself all but totally with the "psychic reality" that scientific materialism placed under such killing pressure. Like the efforts of so many other humanistic champions, his "practical" strategy finished by surrendering the natural world to a desacralized science and so deepening the rift between the physical and the spiritual. It also transformed certain strains of Jungianism into a quasi-religious sect that other therapists, still concerned to guard their scientific credentials, have been reluctant to follow.

Beyond his undeveloped hypotheses about complementarity and the archetype of quaternity, it seems fair to say that Jung, for all the size and spiritual resonance of his system, is resolutely lacking in the one significant quality that emerges in the later Freud. Though Jung was, throughout his life, most at home in a pastoral retreat surrounded by woods and waters, his formal theoretical work tends to have little sense of *nature* to it, except insofar as it gives scholarly attention to abstractions like the Mother Earth or the Father Sky. Otherwise Jung seems to overleap all the universe to land in the high and rarefied intellectual empyrean. The result is a kind of unfleshed, phantasmal collection of ideas about the mind that seems wholly divorced from the world in which that mind evolved. Like all the post-Freudians, he too accepts our estrangement from forest and sea, rivers and mountains, and from all our brother and sister creatures as given and irreversible. Therapy does the best it can within this condition of normative alienation to replace the "urban neurosis of atheism" with a religiosity that is no less urban.

In later chapters, we will return to certain ecologically promising extensions of Jungianism. Here, let us leave off with noting that although Freud could find nothing kindred or consoling in insensate nature, nature is still there in his work, if only as a tragic backdrop. Human beings are bonded to it. Their psyche is an outgrowth, if an anomalous one, of the material stuff of the universe at large; the forces of nature pulse through us, filling our lives with animal lust and hunger. The mind is the brain, the brain is flesh, flesh is chemicals, atoms, electrical energy, and all these belong to the province of science. Where Jung seems to abandon science, Freud clings to it as the only reliable study of natural objects. And for Freud, though the fact is a cheerless one, the psyche is a natural object.

THE DENATURED ENVIRONMENT

Though it is rarely discussed in the professional literature, Freud's despairing vision of life continues to haunt the major schools of mainstream psychiatric thought. It is a sort of negative presence, unmentioned but always there in the background: the image of a cosmos too alien to take into consciousness. The decision modern psychiatry has made to cut itself off from nature at large and minister to the psyche within a purely personal or social frame of reference follows from Freud's courageous but failed effort to find a humanly acceptable connection between the inner and the outer worlds.

That failure shows up with special pathos in the school of Existentialist therapy that has made one of the most determined efforts to revise Freudian orthodoxy. *Daseinanalyse,* which draws heavily upon German existentialism and phenomenology, sets out to discover the patient's *real* world, "the world in which he lives and moves and has his being." Most emphatically this means that the therapist must—in Rollo May's words—"portray the human being not as a collection of static substances or mechanisms or patterns but as emerging and becoming, that is to say existing." In undertaking this effort to find the patient's living, immediate reality, the Existentialists are careful to include the environment *(die Umwelt)* in their theoretical apparatus. But their understanding of "environment" is sadly revealing. *Umwelt* is only one of three "worlds" in which the psyche resides; it is quickly passed over in favor of the social world *(Mitwelt)* and especially the personal world *(Eigenwelt)*. *Umwelt* is understood to be little more than the sum total of thwarting physical necessities. In May's words, it consists of

> biological needs, drives, instincts—the world one would still be in if . . . one had no self-awareness. It is the world of natural law and natural cycles, of sleep and awakeness, of being born and dying, desire and relief, the world of finiteness and biological determinism, the 'thrown world' to which each of us must in some way adjust.[18]

All this, we learn, was adequately handled by Freud. For the Existentialists, getting beyond Freud does not mean revising his vision of nature but rather building new layers of analysis on top of it. *Umwelt* therefore need only be noted in passing as one moves rapidly into the "unexplored frontier of psychotherapeutic theory." And what is that? The *Eigenwelt,* "the self in relation to itself." This is the distinctly human realm, where we disengage from objective nature and stand above it. It is a true "world" in contrast to a mere "environment." "The animal," as Ludwig Binswanger puts it, "not being able to be an *I-you-we*-self . . . does not have any world. . . . The animal has an environment by the grace of nature, not by the grace of freedom to transcend the situation."[19]

What we have here is the denatured environment precisely as we might expect urban therapists and their clientele to know it: a blank, characterless, somewhat bothersome background to "real life," which is social and personal. As Rollo May would have it, "the aim of therapy is that the patient *experience his existence as real.*" A laudable goal. But the Existentialists understand this to mean turning inward and away from the environment. "The neurotic is overconcerned about the *Umwelt* and underconcerned about *Eigenwelt.*" *Umwelt,* being the world common to all organisms, is of little interest. On the other hand, *Eigenwelt* is a repository of fascinating human anxieties, exactly those traumas that people go to psychiatrists to discuss. In mapping the contours of *Eigenwelt,* the Existentialists, like Freud before them, are prepared to borrow insights from literature and philosophy. But the authorities they favor—Nietzsche, Marcel, Tillich, Sartre, Camus—are one and all specialists in the peculiar *angst* of modern Western man. For all their insight, they are the articulate symptoms of a neurotic culture rather than its medicine. Even the religious among them—like Kierkegaard—begin by endorsing the dead and alien universe of modern science and then working away from it as an agonizing premise. One does not work *through* nature, but seeks to transcend it by a "leap of faith." Nature is the prison we must escape in search of a God who is taken to be wholly other.

Granted there is much to be learned from the study of such gifted and articulate victims of our alienated status. But the main lesson therapy might draw from them is the one question these sensitive, but intensely urbanized minds never raise. What is the source of the "epistemological loneliness" that characterizes modern life? *Can it be our ecological ignorance?* While clients may have to begin their therapeutic quest as pathologically isolated egos, can the impoverished, essentially negative conception of environment we find embodied in *Umwelt* do anything to heal that condition?

Mary Midgley, seeking to delineate the subtle and complex connections between "beast and man" in our cultural heritage, finds the doctrinaire dismissal of the physical and biological worlds to be "the really monstrous thing about Existentialism." The philosophy reasons

> as if the world contained only dead matter (things) on the one hand and fully rational, educated, adult human beings on the other—as if there were no other life-forms. The impression of desertion or abandonment which Existentialists have is due, I am sure, not to the removal of God, but to this contemptuous dismissal of the biosphere—plants, animals, and children. Life shrinks to a few urban rooms; no wonder it becomes absurd.[20]

Similarly, in the Object Relations school, one of the major post-Freudian revisions, the concept of "environment" appears frequently. But upon inspection, it turns out to be the *social* environment, which supposedly takes over immediately upon birth. "The external world to which the human organism must adapt," Jay Greenberg tells us, "is unquestionably a social world."[21] Specifically, that social world is the mother, who, if she were the ideal candidate for her role, would be the "facilitating environment" for harmonious child development. No mother is really expected to be perfect, only "good enough." But whether perfect or merely adequate, the mother's role is a socializing one. She must bring about a smooth separation and individuation of the baby. In the process, gender formation and role training take place, and another certified urban-industrial personality is initiated into the culture, ready to make a career, raise a family, take advantage of what the marketplace offers, and in general carry on in the same state of ecological ignorance as the parents that came before.

To take one last example: even when we turn to the more daringly innovative Humanistic Psychology of the late twentieth century, we find the same cultural limitations at work reducing the physical environment to the status of nonentity. The pioneering work of Abraham Maslow, for example, is "humanistic" in a meek and defensive way; it wears the same air of resignation that surrounds the Humanities in our universities. There the study of literature, philosophy, history, sometimes the arts survives as a ghettoized body of knowledge strictly segregated from the natural sciences. The Humanities attend to those things that happen exclusively inside the human mind on purely subjective ground. All the world outside and beyond is left to the scientists. Similarly, the "growth" and "self-actualization" in which Humanistic Psychology distinctively deals have no connection with the real world outside the mind. They are the private affairs of the solitary psyche.

Psychology, Maslow insisted, has its own "unique jurisdiction." It deals with "that portion of the psyche which is *not* a reflection of the outer world or a molding to it." But of course the only "outer world" Maslow had in mind was the world of social relations. Thus, in reacting against what he took to be the other-directed emphasis of interpersonal psychiatrists such as Harry Stack Sullivan, Maslow moved further and further in championing an "autonomous self or pure psyche." He thus becomes a sad but instructive example of what befalls ambitious psychiatric theory when it lacks an environmental dimension.

Maslow's ideal was "transcendence of environment," understood in purely social terms. Even so, at a certain point, he relented, believing he had pressed his pursuit of the "self-governing character" too far in the direction of detachment. Admitting that it might seem "paradoxical," he suggested that the search for the "real Self" might actually mature into a form of re-connectedness. But since, as a man of the academy and the clinic, Maslow could not imagine anything beyond the social world, his major concession was to admit the possibility of a "biological brotherhood *to all other human beings.*" Thus far and no further Humanistic Psychology.[22]

Such schools of psychiatry are born of a healthy revolt against the dispiriting reductionism and physicality of the Behaviorists and Freudians; but the rebellion finishes by locking itself away in an existential vacuum. One looks in vain in the work of Maslow or the Existential therapists for any sense of the nonhuman environment. It is not there; it has been surrendered to the "hard sciences." Purpose, meaning, and value are left to be improvised within the human heart.

THE PSYCHE AND THE BIOSPHERE

The post-Freudians who sought a larger social context for psychiatry were justified in feeling that the mind had to be freed from the restrictions of classic psychoanalysis. In their desire to create a relevant and helpful therapy, they were also justified in turning away from the route Freud had mapped beyond the pleasure principle. He seemed to find nothing in the outer darkness of the universe that was of practical therapeutic use.

What his successors could not appreciate was the dynamism of an urban culture that would at some point impinge upon the planetary environment. When it did, questions would arise about the relationship between the human and natural worlds that could no longer be avoided. It would then be essential to provide the family and society with an ecological context. Sick souls may indeed be the fruit of sick families and sick societies; but what, in turn, is the measure of sickness for society as a whole? While many criteria might be nominated, there is surely one that ranks above all others: the species that destroys its own habitat in pursuit of false values, in willful ignorance of what it does, is "mad" if the word means anything.

Within such an environmental frame of reference, we may find the beginning of that higher sanity that the Radical Therapists would use as a refuge from oppressive social authority. The scientized psychiatric establishment with which they are at odds is, after all, grounded in the same vision of nature that permeates the official politics of the industrial societies. From this realization may follow a psychology of permanence that transcends the conventional wisdom and transient values of the day. *The two bold departures of Freud's later years—his search for a transcultural standard of sanity and his desire to integrate the mental and the physical—meet within an ecological framework.*

There is a historical dimension to this matter that makes the environmental criterion of sanity peculiarly relevant in our time. In the past, societies have, in their ignorance, blighted portions of their habitat sufficiently to endanger their own survival, but the urgency of the matter was much less than we feel today. River valleys have been devastated, forests denuded, the topsoil worn away; but the damage was limited and temporary. Other societies in distant parts of the world may never have known of the tragic loss. The species with whom we share the planet carried on in blissful disregard of the blunders perpetrated by their human cousins who were so often too smart for their own good. Populations relocated and multiplied. Soon after the calamity—a few decades, a few centuries—the land was healed, the ruin mercifully covered over. The rivers rolled on, the great natural systems of the planet closed upon the damage and continued functioning unaffected.

Now all this has changed. Our power over the global environment has become enormous and practically instantaneous. A single human invention may be marketed and put into use around the world before we realize what harm it can do to the environment. We are being warned that within a few decades industrial culture may, out of simple inadvertence, be able to warp the biosphere in ways that will derange age-old ecological harmonies for millennia to come. The chlorofluorocarbons used as propellants and refrigerating agents are an instructive example of such lethal—and yet utterly casual—dynamism. Following their first commercial use in the 1930s, CFCs were rapidly distributed worldwide before, out of mere curiosity, two inquiring scientists (Frank Sherwood Rowland and Mario Molina of the University of California) began to wonder in the mid-seventies where this odd new chemical might be going once it had been released into the atmosphere. The answer was jolting. The CFCs are eating away the ozone that protects life from potentially lethal ultraviolet radiation. Since the discovery of the first ozone hole over the Antarctic, we at last understand the lethal power of this substance. Yet even now, with evidence of the risk clearly before our eyes, it remains uncertain that people—or rather governments—will act quickly enough, on a large enough scale to heal the damage. For that matter, there are still some experts who question the reliability of the data, as if it might be wisest to run the risk of waiting to act until we are absolutely certain that our survival is at stake.

Yet what we are dealing with here is but a minor product, many of whose uses are little better than novelties. One might almost conclude that as a species we lack some necessary instinctive reflex to respond to problems of such magnitude. Instead we find bad excuses to continue our destructive ways. We say there are jobs at risk . . . investments to be considered . . . conveniences we dare not sacrifice. Can it be that our survival instincts are solely tuned to emergencies of a far more obvious, immediate, and local character? What would we say of a man who could not make up his mind to flee a burning building because he could not locate his credit cards? Confronted with global crisis, we lose our way among similarly petty distractions.

Psychological theory that cannot address itself to irrationality on such a scale is surely deeply flawed. A culture that can do so much to damage the planetary fabric that sustains it, and yet continues along its course unimpeded, is mad with the madness of a deadly compulsion that reaches beyond our own kind to all the brute innocence about us. We are, in ways that have been expertly rationalized, pressing forward to create a monocultural world-society in which whatever survives must do so as the adjunct of urban industrial civilization. Unquestionably such a depletion of the planetary variety is ecologically hazardous, perhaps genocidal. But even short of that dire prospect, our devastation of the biosphere deprives us of the beauty and magnificence of things. And the loss that comes of that crime falls upon us as much as upon any species of plant or animal we annihilate; for the planet will, of course, endure, perhaps to generate new adventures in life in the eons to come. But we are being diminished by our destructive insensitivity in ways that cripple our ability to enjoy, grow, create. By becoming so aggressively and masterfully "human," we lose our essential humanity.

The issue we raise here is at once both ethical and psychological, a debate that pits many increasingly distressed environmental scientists against a far greater number of invincibly optimistic entrepreneurs.

Underlying the controversy lie deep questions about what we perceive to be "real" and what we understand to be "good."

Toward the end of the 1980s, the Science Advisory Board of the Environmental Protection Agency issued a report in which it took to task the priorities that have been set by the EPA during the current politically conservative era. Specifically, it called into question the EPA's willingness to reduce its role to a minimal emphasis upon problems that immediately endanger public health. While recognizing that "healthy ecosystems are a prerequisite to healthy humans and prosperous economies," the SAB argued for greater ethical range.

> The value of natural ecosystems is not limited to their immediate utility to humans. They have an intrinsic, moral value that must be measured in its own terms and protected for its own sake. . . . EPA has paid too little attention to natural ecosystems. . . . [Its] response to human health risks as compared to ecological risks is inappropriate, because in the real world, there is little distinction between the two.[23]

The words may be stilted and academic, but if one listens closely, one hears behind them the impassioned plea of Chief Seattle quoted earlier in this chapter. His lamentation for the slaughter of the beasts who share the world with us sounds through the SAB's demand for an environmental ethic that embraces the rights of the nonhuman.

But across a significant segment of the business community, the SAB's noble appeal fell on deaf ears. It proved no more persuasive than Chief Seattle was in his entreaty to America's political leaders a century ago. A rebuttal authored by one of the country's leading business schools argued:

> If the Science Advisory Board's notion of finding better methods to value natural resources is to attach "intrinsic, moral value . . . measured in its own terms" to natural ecosystems, then the process will degenerate into an ideological dispute to be decided quite apart from sound scientific and economic principles. Protecting an ecosystem "for its own sake" implies a blank-check approach that entails bearing many opportunity costs, including losses in public health and welfare. . . . often what is good for ecological systems is good for human health and welfare. Taken literally, however, Americans are being asked to attach as much significance to the Northern Spotted Owl or the delta smelt as they do

to human beings. Most people are not ready to embrace that they are no more significant in the universe than owls and fish.[24]

Clearly, the "real world" as the SAB perceives it is not that of practical business leaders. Yet approached as the business leaders propose by way of a species-by-species, cost-effective analysis, every environmental issue we face will seem to point to an obvious choice. Is the owl, the smelt, the dolphin, the redwood tree worth the loss of profits, jobs, conveniences to the planet's dominant species? Starting from "sound scientific and economic principles" like these, where will the line ever be drawn short of the wholesale extinction of the planetary variety—if it were within our power to achieve such a nightmarish result?

The narrow-gauged logicality of such thinking reminds one of the paranoid who proves his case point by point with legalistic precision. Each incident makes perfect sense within his tiny universe of unquestioned assumptions; but the pattern as a whole is insane. This is what Lewis Mumford once called "mad rationality"; it reveals itself nowhere more fully than in our relations with the nonhuman world from which our human world rose into being.

Among the commanding figures in Existential psychiatry is Viktor Frankl, who was able to bring the most extreme of "boundary conditions" into his life's work as a matter of personal experience. A survivor of the Holocaust, Frankl had traversed the depths and heights of human nature as a prisoner in the death camps of Nazi Germany. He returned to the world determined to integrate the hellishness of what he had suffered into contemporary psychiatric theory. Though he respected the work of his predecessors, he reflected almost mockingly on the comfortable bourgeois origins of his profession.

> Thank heaven Sigmund Freud was spared knowing the concentration camps from the inside. His subjects lay on a couch designed in the plush style of Victorian culture, not in the filth of Auschwitz. *There* . . . people unmasked themselves, both the swine and the saints.

Thanks largely to Frankl, the horror of the camps and of the war as a whole has forced serious psychiatry to revamp its understanding of the human condition. The task has been a wrenching one; but to avoid it in favor of therapeutic business as usual would be cowardly. Frankl insisted that there were parameters of terror and despair that have to be confronted. "So, let us be alert—alert in a twofold sense: Since Auschwitz we know what man is capable of. And since Hiroshima we know what is at stake."[25]

Now we encounter another landmark in our exploration of the psyche, the most imposing thus far. We come upon it as our technological power attains global closure. What Auschwitz was to its human inmates—an expertly rationalized, efficiently organized killing ground—our urban-industrial system is fast becoming for the biosphere at large, and for ourselves as an inseparable part of that environment. The dimensions of psychiatric theory, and with them our understanding of our connection with all things human, nonhuman, and transhuman, must grow to include the planetary habitat as a whole. Once again, to shrink from the challenge would be cowardice.

In one of his late prophetical essays, Freud pondered the dilemma of collective madness, recognizing that it raises "a special difficulty."

> In an individual neurosis, we take as our starting point the contrast that distinguishes the patient from his environment, which is assumed to be "normal." For a group all of whose members are affected by one and the same disorder, no such background could exist; it would have to be found elsewhere.[26]

What follows is a reconnaissance of "elsewhere." It begins with the oldest psychiatry we know.

Three

$\blacklozenge$

STONE-AGE PSYCHIATRY
A Speculative Reconstruction

EYE OF NEWT, TOE OF FROG

Playfully, we call them "shrinks," acknowledging each time we do so that the psychiatrist's precursor was the head-shrinking witchdoctor, the original healer of souls. Often we use the name sardonically, implying that a certain residue of mumbo-jumbo still clings to our supposedly enlightened science of the mind. But by the same token might there not be something of at least marginal value to be found in the supposedly superstitious practice of witchdoctoring? Have traditional cultures anything to teach our industrial society about the meaning of sanity? The anthropologist Marshall Sahlins, assembling a composite picture of life among the hunters and gatherers, once undertook to reconstruct a "stone-age economics" from which he believed we might learn something about the meaning of wealth and poverty. Is there a "stone-age psychiatry" that can be mined for similarly heuristic insights?

Until well into this century, even trained anthropological observers tended to regard tribal healers as charlatans whose practices were mere quackery. Some scholars classified all shamans as psychotics whose practices were "witchcraft" in the most pejorative meaning of the word. The terms used ranged from the politely technical ("neurotic-epileptoid type") to the bluntly dismissive ("veritable idiots"), but all came down to regarding tribal therapy as the mad treating the mad. Thanks largely to the work of Claude Levi-Strauss and subsequent studies in transcultural psychiatry, we have since come to see that tribal societies possess spiritual and psychotherapeutic traditions that may be more effective in the treatment of their own people than Western medicine, especially when it comes to mental and emotional disorders. The anthropologist I. M. Lewis, standing the question on its head, has gone so far as to suggest that our psychotherapy might be viewed as a scaled down subspecies of traditional healing. "The more meaningful equivalence," he observes, "is that psychiatry, and especially psycho-analysis, as Jung would perhaps have admitted much more freely than most Freudians would care to, represent limited and imperfect forms of shamanism."[1] The remark is not entirely fair to Freud, who readily acknowledged that tribal healers can be as adept as many psychiatrists at creating a "condition of expectant faith" that can have great thera-peutic effect.[2]

Perhaps the most marked difference between psychotherapy old and new is the complexity and breadth of traditional healing. In tribal societies, the distinction between the physical and psychic is far less rigid than we understand it to be. One might almost say that traditional medicine regards all disease as psychosomatic, in the sense that the psyche is implicated in its etiology. Even a frozen foot may be treated by Eskimo shamans as a psychic disturbance. Therefore, thoughts, dreams, memories, emotions must be mobilized in its cure.[3] The prov-ince of stone-age psychiatry is a broad one.

E. Fuller Torrey, taking issue with the "psychiatric imperialism" of Western society, points out that healing has everything to do with the cultural bond that unites therapist and client. A common worldview, a shared diagnostic vocabulary, mutually respected ideas and principles make for the trust and conviction without which healing may be impossible.[4] But if we have learned that tribal techniques can be more effective than modern psychiatry in treating native people, this knowl-edge may have little direct value for us—unless we can find some common ground with tribal peoples that allows us to borrow a portion of their culture. That common ground may be the ground of despera-tion. If our relations with nature are as deeply failed as the environmen-tal crisis suggests, we may have to look for help wherever we can find it, including insights long absent from our own society. Where else are these to be found but in the experience of our fellow humans living different lives in a different world?

But here a serious problem arises for anyone interested in more than an academic survey of tribal psychiatry. The therapies of tribal people come at us in a hodge-podge of exotic, "irrational" practices. The lore that stands behind them is unfamiliar to us; it invokes forces and spirits of a bewildering variety. Every group has its own rituals, its own words of power. As outside observers, we may feel convinced that common themes underlie the many tribal variations; if so, it is up to us to draw them out. Yet this selective and abstracting process is a liberty we take with the living lore of another people. The habit of generalization is a distinctly modern and Western approach to the study of culture. Native healers have little interest in universalizing their methods or principles. We might see this as the natural result of cultural isolation; but on the other hand, no Jungian archetype, for all its sophistication, can do justice to what the buffalo means to the Sioux or the seal to the Eskimo. From the tribal viewpoint, it may seem that plucking indigenous symbols and rites from their cultural soil vitiates their power. There are tribal healers who have denied the validity of any attempt to do so. Sudhi Kakar, studying the methods of Tantric practitioners in rural India, found himself rebuffed when he suggested that the mantras used to excite various psychic states merely symbolized some underlying emotional mechanism. His informants insisted there were unique occult correspondences between the physiological vibrations of certain sounds and the emotions they evoke in the patient. But of course these verbal formulas would mean nothing beyond the village culture of India.

Traditional therapy can be stubbornly parochial; it is embedded in a place and a history, in the rhythms of climate, in the contours of a landscape where the birds and beasts have been close companions for centuries. In local lore, a river, a mountain, a grove may take on the personality of a tribal elder, a presence named and known over the generations. Artifacts assume a peculiarly evocative power. The *manangs* of Borneo come to their patients bearing a bundle filled with strange implements: the horns of the giant beetle, a quartz amulet that is "the stone of light," a wild boar's tusk that can retrieve lost souls. What can these things mean to us? They seem like the proverbial "eye of newt and toe of frog" that make witchcraft appear so ludicrous. Yet the effectiveness of the shaman's method largely lies in its emotional specificity. What we as modern observers achieve by our efforts to universalize is, at last, something of our own, a new creation that may lack the color and force of the original.

What follows is based upon some sweeping, but I think defensible generalizations about the meaning of sanity and madness in tribal societies, together with some admittedly less defensible extrapolations to prehistory. As anthropologists warn us, it is always risky to infer from contemporary to prehistoric tribal groups. Existing tribal societies have experienced as much history as the rest of the human race; in our time, they have all been deeply influenced by a ubiquitously intrusive Western culture. Still, at the very least, those tribal groups that preserve a degree of autonomy suggest something of what culture may have been like among earlier hunters and gatherers before the advent of the city.

Another point worth mentioning at the outset. Seeking to salvage value, I take the liberty of passing over practices one finds scattered through tribal culture (such as hexes, curses, the evil eye, or, at the extreme, human sacrifice) that I would be inclined to agree are authentically "superstitious"—which may only mean these are customs that I cannot stretch my imagination sufficiently to understand or countenance. This is a limitation on my part that would, incidentally, extend to the faith healing, Christian Science, and many forms of New Age medicine widely practiced in my own society today. Each of us works within limits of tolerance and understanding. Here, I do not ask that we ignore the existence of seemingly senseless and benighted practices in tribal culture. While acknowledging the problem they raise, I propose to look beyond them—just as, when we turn back to the "golden age" of Athens for inspiration, we charitably disregard the vices of slavery, infanticide, and mob rule. As Paul Goodman once observed, the political use of anthropology is "to show what of human nature has been 'lost' and, practically, to devise experiments for its recovery." Provided, that is, we regard what is "lost" as worth finding.

THE SACRAMENTAL REALM

As its lingering association with witchdoctors might suggest, psychiatry is an ancient and universal practice, as structured and ritualized among traditional people as among ourselves. The healing of souls always happens in special places, at special times (by appointment only), at the hands of a trained practitioner—and with a fee (possibly a bartered item) for services rendered. In some tribal societies, psychotherapy is even more specialized than in the modern Western world. The

Senegalese have six specialized spiritual healers. Among the Navajos, diagnosis is entrusted to a special "hand-trembler" who intuitively reads the patient's condition by passing his hands over the body. There are fixed, highly refined categories in which the Navajo healer locates diseases; the cure is then delegated to "singers," who are skilled in dealing with one or another of these categories. Some singers specialize in chants related to "moth sickness," others in chanting for "ghost sickness."

If we fail to recognize the highly sophisticated character of tribal psychotherapy, it is probably because elements of what we might call "psychiatry" are inextricably blended with the political, economic, and spiritual life of the tribe. Its categories draw upon folklore and myth, its greatest powers may be tapped in states of trance or ecstasy. The shaman often interprets psychosis as demonic possession for which the prescribed treatment is ritual exorcism, not clinical analysis. Madness mingles with impiety. The contrast this creates with psychotherapy as we know it shows up in many ways.

All psychology, whether traditional or modern, stems from the assumption that there is *more* to the mind than we are normally aware of. Conscious life is the outer shell of a larger, shadowed identity. Even doctrinaire Behaviorists, for whom words like "mind" and "unconscious" are anathema, acknowledge that the action of the well-formed reflex arc drops below the level of awareness into some subliminal gulf of the cerebral cortex. The great issues arise among schools of psychology when we ask how this submerged portion of the mind relates to the body. What is the psychosomatic (the body–mind) continuum? Here we must proceed with care. There is a misleading similarity between what "psychosomatic" means in traditional societies and in our own. In both cases, the term connects the psyche with the body. But what in turn is the status of this body?

In the Western world the biomedical model of the psyche was patterned upon a preexisting biomedical model of the body. The body to which the mind was assimilated was already a disenchanted object. Stripped down to its physiological components, it was understood to be "nothing but" a machine. Anatomical sketches of the seventeenth and eighteenth centuries reveal a fascination with the idea that the limbs and organs of the body can be analyzed into springs, levers, pumps, pistons. This is the distant origin of our conviction that the body can be improved upon by spare-parts surgery. The psyche came to be seen as nothing sacred because the body to which it was attached was nothing sacred. The connection between the two was the nervous system, seen as an electrochemical apparatus. Along these reductive physical lines, one treats the psyche by way of drugs, electroshock, or surgical intervention.

Freud never rejected this model; his background in neurology biased him in favor of a purely physiological approach. Still, almost in spite of himself, he developed a method for investigating the psyche that relied on such intangibles as dreams, memories, and biographical narrative. Psychoanalysis takes *experience* seriously; to that degree it preserves a quasi-spiritual conception of the unconscious. Nevertheless, the therapeutic orientation is wholly secular. Metaphorically speaking, it moves down and then horizontally: *through* the psyche *into* the brain and then *out* into the social world that is the source of conditioning, scripting, or trauma. Among the major theorists, only Jung, postulating a mysteriously disembodied collective unconscious, held out for a transcendent extension of the personality. Even so, Jung's psychology, struggling against Freud's persistent materialism, maintains a fastidiously Cartesian split between the physical and the mental. We do not find this dichotomy in traditional cultures, where the body has not been desacralized. There, quite often, bodily functions and natural objects enter into the healing of the soul. Nature at large as well as the body is viewed as alive, possibly divine. The *super*natural resides in the natural, a constant, intentional presence. Stone-age psychiatry draws on a prescientific psychology; body as well as mind participates in an animistic worldview.

Precisely because the natural realm possesses a sacramental quality, traditional psychotherapy would insist that people must remain vitally connected with it as if there were between them an ongoing dialogue. What Martin Buber called a You-and-I relationship is not restricted to people, or to a transcendent deity. The human must establish a *transactional bond* with the natural; there must be give and take, courtesy and respect. One bargains with nature, apologizes for intruding upon it, begs pardon of the animals one hunts and kills, tries to make good the losses one has brought about, offers sacrifice and compensation. Sanity is just such a matter of balance and reciprocity between the human and not-human. The very idea that the two can be segregated, that the human world should or even *can* be treated as autonomously self-contained, would be the very height of madness for a traditional psychiatry. The connection between the two is not simply a matter of survival but of moral and spiritual well-being. Relations with the environment are understood to be ethical, as much so as one's relations with a fellow human. Or even more so, because the natural realm is infused with divinity; to break faith with it is not only crazy but sacrilegious.

The assumption that the natural world is populated by sentient beings accounts for the "mystical" practices so prevalent in traditional societies. If one is to honor the spirits of nature, one must hold discourse with them. One must speak and hear their language. For this purpose, special states of awareness are necessary involving meditation, drunkenness, the use of narcotics, the dizziness induced by the dance, fasting, or the various forms of self-inflicted suffering that have given tribal people their reputation for "savagery." Within the Christian tradition, mysticism has always been an exceptional, often suspect element in religion. It was offensive not only to religion. During the Enlightenment, mystical ("enthusiastic") experience was targeted for ridicule as the worst transgression against reason and science. But in tribal groups, visionary practices, though they may require rigorous preparation, are not at all unusual and can even be quite casual: a standard part of religious ceremonies. It is understood that different realities demand different modes of consciousness that may be no farther away than each night's dreams. Ecstasy is the medium of trans-human communications.

In modern society, dreams had to qualify as a scientific subject matter before they were taken seriously by anybody besides Romantic or Decadent artists. Many would regard the reclamation of dreams—as "the royal road to the unconscious"—to be Freud's greatest, most enduring contribution to psychiatry. But in tribal society, the dream-life is understood—again quite casually—to be a normal and valuable extension of consciousness. It was the importance tribal people attributed to dreams that convinced many early anthropologists that they were dealing with "primitives"; these people seemed to have no sure grip on the reality principle. Yet, in traditional society it would be considered mad to suppress or ignore the dream-life. Rather, one seeks to stay in constant consultation with the dreaming mind. By civilized standards, many tribal people "waste" an inordinate amount of time attending to dreams, combing through them for guidance and insight. For us, each working day begins with the dream-shattering blast of the alarm clock and a heavy dose of caffeine, the better to clear our heads for the busy demands of the "real" world. One sometimes suspects that in modern society dreams have been split off and delegated to movies and television, the official, electronic fantasy-life of our culture. Among tribal folk, on the other hand, rituals that last for days may be designed to probe the visions of great dreamers; far-reaching decisions about war and peace, about important economic and political matters may be based on the interpretation of such visions. The Oglala Sioux medicine-man Black Elk tells how his uncle, the great chief Crazy Horse, was selected for leadership on the basis of a single powerful dream in which he saw a strangely dancing horse; later, the entire surviving Sioux nation gathered to celebrate one of Black Elk's own great dreams, pinning their very hope of survival upon its promise.[5]

Here we touch upon a crucial point for those like the Laingian Radical Therapists, who demand greater tolerance for supposedly psychotic personalities. When, in obedience to a narrow reality principle, we make the nonhuman world less than it is, we also make ourselves less than we are. More of the mind is split off and driven into that zone of impermissible experience called "insane."

By our standards, tribal societies are in many ways quite restrictive. Their world is so much more limited than ours, perhaps comprising no more than an island, a few valleys, or a small corner of the forest. Yet in some ways their range is greater than ours. Because they regard visionary forms of experience as the basis for communion with the sacred, traditional peoples often handle eccentricity with great tolerance, making distinctions that elude our secularized psychology. There are, after all, forms of "madness" that may betoken a spiritual vocation. We recognize this, if grudgingly, when we make reference to the "madness" of genius. Still, we have no institutionalized way of honoring, let alone encouraging such madness. In contrast, if a child in a tribal society behaves abnormally, the youngster may be left in the care of a shaman who then spends days or months carefully observing the child's conduct. He is watching for some indication that this madness may be divinely inspired. The culture provides criteria for such a judgment. The shaman may decide that the child is indeed inspired, a young shaman in the making, or he may conclude that the child is simply deranged and send it home for care.

Our psychiatry has been a long while coming around to a similarly mature distinction between diseased and gifted madness; one suspects many people would still find it hard to accept. Our cities now teem with mendicant psychotics. The only reason they are not locked away is because the taxpaying public has elected to save the cost of keeping the asylums open. So they roam the streets mumbling and raving, begging and menacing. What criteria would we confidently apply to decide if their delusions are visions? Not many people any longer believe there is a spiritual dimension to the natural world which merits our attention; few can even *see* the natural world for all the concrete and traffic that surrounds us. We frequently refer to mad people as "hearing things" "seeing things" that the conventional reality principle insists are not there. In tribal societies, there is very much more to see and hear. The mountain speaks, the bear speaks, the river speaks; the rainbow signifies, the eclipse is a sign.

The animistic personification of natural objects may be difficult for us to accept in any "literal" way. Yet, judged solely on intellectual grounds, "primitive" animism might be credited with a more sophisticated perception of physicality than we would have found in Western science through the nineteenth century. Tribal folk are apt to believe that matter has a depth and complexity that does far greater justice to what we now know of its inherent system-building tendency. Far from regarding it as dead stuff, they perceive it as infused with mind, will, and intention. We will see in later chapters, that, taken as a basis for understanding the deep self-organizing intricacy of matter, animism may provide a better initial model than Newtonian atomism ever did. Some might go further, granting animism a proven ecological utility: it disciplines the relationship of humans to their environment, imposing an ethical restraint upon exploitation and abuse. But at some point one must face a greater issue. For traditional people, animism is not merely a "model," nor is its justification purely utilitarian. It is how they truly see the world. Our ancestors evolved into human intelligence carrying something like that sensibility with them.

Is it possible that the loss of this sensibility accounts not only for our ecological crisis, but for our crazy-making discontent?

A FRAGMENT OF HISTORIC TRUTH

Freud was convinced that the "progress" of civilization would bring with it an ever-deepening neurosis. In making that morose assessment, he focused on the myriad ways in which civilized life restricts what he took to be the most powerful instinctual drives: sexuality and aggression. Most Freudians still believe that the Oedipal dilemma lies somewhere at the core of neurotic suffering, a complex that Freud fancifully traced back to the father–son conflicts of the primal horde. "There is not only *method* in madness," he felt, "but also *a fragment of historic truth.*" But what if that fragment of truth derives not from the distant ancestral past but from something more recent: the beginning of civilized life, the social and economic transition that rooted our species out of its original environment and relocated it to the city? The "primal crime" may not have been the prehistoric betrayal of the father, but the act of breaking faith with the mother: Mother Earth—or whatever characterization we might wish to make of the planetary biosphere as a vital, self-regulating system.

Let us press the Freudian interpretation of neurosis a bit farther. Indulging in his own psychoanalytical myth-making, Freud conjectured that totemism represents the displacement upon some arbitrarily selected plant or animal of the love-hate ambivalence that savage sons once felt toward their murdered father. The role of the totem was to commemorate the father, using his remembered authority to enforce various tribal taboos, especially those that relate to "the horror of incest."

> If the totem animal is the father, then the two taboo prohibitions which constitute its core—not to kill the totem and not to have sexual relations with a woman of the same totem—coincide in their content with the two crimes of Oedipus.[6]

As dramatic as the idea is, there has always been something far-fetched about it; certainly few anthropologists have been persuaded of its validity. Nor have they been willing to accept the universal applicability of the peculiarly Victorian ideas about sexuality that so often colored Freud's theories. In effect, Freud was reading the qualities of the nineteenth century bourgeois family into prehistoric tribal life, and in so doing overlooking values and priorities that mean much more to precivilized cultures than parent–child antagonism.

Freud believed he was being brutally literal in his reading of totemism and therefore brutally candid about its underlying meaning. But there may be a far more obvious meaning to totemism, namely, that it is exactly what it purports to be: a display of reverent respect for the animals who are the constant companions of tribal folk. Out of admiration, the authority of their images is appropriated for the august purpose of defining clan-membership and for various social functions. The totemic rituals, which often involve playful imitations of the animals, are symbolic gestures, but not as Freud interpreted them to be. They do not symbolize expiation for a supposed patricidal guilt; rather they express esteem for one's fellow creatures. They honor the cunning of the raven, the courage of the bear, the majesty of the eagle. They are acts of communion with the animal spirits that dwell within these remarkable beasts. To understand these creatures, to move knowledgeably within their consciousness, is a necessity of life for tribal people. The Pawnees of North America, for example, grouped themselves in animal cults that held ecstatic rites in which the various beasts were consulted about the medicinal value of herbs and roots. The animals were understood to dwell together in a great lodge that could only be entered in a state of trance. Those who found their way there were granted secret instructions in healing.[7] What are we to make of a mythology that credits the animals with such deep knowledge? Perhaps what tribal people see in them and seek to recapture—an instinctual solidarity with nature, the graceful use of one's habitat—is what human beings can just barely remember of their own evolutionary origins. The animals remain part of an undivided world where reciprocity with the elements of nature is immediate and unshakable. Honoring them is an effort to recapitulate that quality of experience. The "great lodge" might be seen as the evolutionary memory of our species; we return there with the permission of the beasts who still reside within it.

Understandably, it would be difficult for a citified intellectual like Freud to appreciate so simple and candid an offering of homage; he might have regarded it as childlike. And so it is, in the best sense of the word: an expression of the capacity for wonder in the presence of things that are wonderful. But Freud insisted upon a more convoluted interpretation, something that was more accessible to his patients and colleagues and of greater importance to them, namely, the sexual frustration that attended child-rearing in middle-class homes of the time. In our day, the relations between parent and child have greatly changed. In those industrial societies that have achieved a more affluent phase, the prudish restrictions with which psychoanalysis once had to deal so exclusively have somewhat eased. In the more permissive climate we inhabit today, we can look for other, more enduring meanings in the cultural practices of our ancestors.

Let us try to summarize this highly speculative exploration of stone-age psychiatry. Picture the matter like this: the individual psyche surrounded by a series of concentric rings.

At the center, the very core of our identity, we find the Freudian id, a modern version of human nature after the Fall: willful, rebellious, perverse. In Christian theology, this unruly element in human nature was quaintly called the "Old Adam" or "the natural man." This is also the Hobbesian brute, the "each" that wages war against "all."

Surrounding this dangerous collection of untamed instincts, caging it, *denaturing* it, we have the embattled ego, our socially defined identity negotiating our fate with the "outside" world—which it must deeply "introject" into us as the admonishing parental superego. Beginning with once severely punitive forms of toilet-training, the ego teaches us good manners, respectability, the necessary social disciplines. Superego is the phantom family within us drawing its force from the actual parents on whom we depend for sustenance and instruction.

In turn, surrounding the family is the society, which defines and enforces parental authority. Most immediately and intimidatingly this takes the form of laws, judges, courts, cops, the threat of physical punishment. If the introjection of the superego succeeds in penetrating sufficiently deep, there is also, on the part of both parents and legal authority, the emotional threat of disapproval, social disgrace, the withdrawal of love. Social beings that we are, the weapon of dis-recognition—turning the face away, driving into exile as the Lord God drove his disobedient children from Eden—can be more fearful than physical retribution. Franz Kafka made much of just this chronically psychotic aspect of modern life in his fiction. His meek antiheroes move cowering through a world that threatens disapprobation on all sides. Even when the disapproval comes from faceless officials, it cuts to the quick like a whiplash.

This is as far out from the psyche as most modern, scientific psychiatric systems go. They intend to be "interpersonal," but only insofar as "persons" are understood to be other people: parents, public officials, teachers, priests. All these function in the psychic economy as the agents of repressive guilt, forcing upon us the assigned identities that large-scale social organization demands. As we have seen, when Freud sought to widen the psychiatric context to include the cosmos, he found there only the all-devouring entropic abyss from which his successors understandably recoiled. But now, what if we were to introduce that greater circle that encompasses society and culture: the global environment, the living body of the Earth from which all life springs, the ultimate source of our individual and social being? How can so ancient and intimate a part of our organic development not have a role to play in determining our psychic balance?

Sudhir Kakar observes that modern psychiatry, at least in its classic Freudian form, differs from traditional therapies in emphasizing "text" over "context." By "text" he means the private life of the patient treated as the self-contained story of an autonomous individual. This sense of heroically embattled identity is strongly embedded in Western society's commitment to the reality of the personal soul, originally understood to be a special creation of God that has been placed in the world to work out its own salvation. This Judeo-Christian teaching underpins our culture's fascination with autobiography and portraiture, with introspective art and poetry, and with the puritanical guilt that is the core of so much confessional literature. As a basis for psychotherapy, this tight focus upon the self-as-text makes the healing of the wounded soul a lonely, purely intrapsychic struggle. The patient reports to the doctor for a private session, reclines on the couch in the quiet, darkened room and turns inward to review his or her life. Only the largely unspeaking psychiatrist is there to assist either as a nonjudgmental, sympathetic presence or as a blank screen on which the patient's anguish can be projected.

Kakar points out that traditional therapy gives little attention to personal text; rather it has always been practiced within a larger social context, on the assumption that "faith and surrender to a power beyond the individual are better than individual effort and struggle, . . . that the source of human strengths lies in a harmonious integration with one's group." In rural villages and tribal societies, the family is invariably on hand to assist in the healing; possibly the community as a whole becomes part of the process. Since the 1930s, a growing number of Western psychiatrists have come to agree that the isolation of Freudian psychoanalysis may make the reliving of the repressed far more of an ordeal than it need be. The privacy of the psychiatric session, like the privacy of the Catholic confessional, may only serve to accentuate the sense of guilty secrecy and furtiveness. So we have many new forms of family and group therapy that place the intrapsychic struggle within a supportive setting that may include parents, relatives, employers, and fellow workers who have played some significant role in the patient's life.

Even so there remains a difference between traditional and modern group psychiatry; it has to do with the number of elements that are included in the greater context. In traditional therapy, the circle widens beyond family and the immediate social group; ancestors are apt to be invoked, a powerful conservative influence that would compromise our ideal of the autonomous individual. In the tribal setting, personal problems become densely relational, involving obligations to distant, long-dead forebears. Traditional therapy is built upon a powerful sense of social and genealogical connectedness.

There are significant issues here. What would any reference to "ancestors" mean in our changeful and footloose urban-industrial society, where so few can recall relations that extend back farther than grandparents, and where earlier generations are rarely regarded as sources of enduring wisdom? Moreover, Western society's image of the autonomous and morally responsible person is surely the basis of our culture's dynamism, part of what freedom and the struggle for self-fulfillment mean to us. Much of what we honor as "the rights of man" derives from the individualism so deeply ingrained in our political philosophy. Could we bring ourselves to see our obsession with the self-as-text as more diseased than "normal"? Would we be willing to relinquish it in favor of the security that comes of surrender to the expectations of the community? What would then become of the Radical Therapist's conviction that the "mad" may represent society's best hope for defining a higher sanity? There are aspects of traditional therapy that we may find it not only impossible to recover, but undesirable as well.

On the other hand, ancestry may be susceptible to a challenging new interpretation in the modern world. We might envisage our "elders" as being the undivided family of mankind whose culture we know so fully, thanks to generations of exploration and ethnographic scholarship. In this great and rewarding sense, those of us who live in the seemingly rootless modern metropolis might yet reclaim a universal ancestry that opens the myths, traditions, and teachings of the entire race to us.

THE ENVIRONMENTAL CONTEXT

Beyond the dense social context that it invokes, traditional therapy, in its search for psychic balance, reaches out still further to include the gods and the habitat. In his study of the Pawnee, Gene Weltfish describes the elaborate days-long preparation that once ushered in the buffalo hunt. It included tribal rites of purification that invoked deities of the Earth, the waters, the stars. The hunt focused upon a figure called the *taxpiku,* a holy man who was chosen to embody the tribe's sacred obligations to the land and to the buffalo that the hunters were now preparing to slaughter. During the weeks of the hunt, the *taxpiku* was surrounded with rigid taboos that were meant to preserve the purity and worthiness of the people. He was entrusted with the role of making offerings to the powers above in return for their favor.[8] Rites like these deal with the psychology of guilt and expiation, not on a narrow personal basis, but as collective experience reflected on a cosmic scale.

Among the Navajo, animals and the great forces of nature are frequently invoked as healing agents. The medicine men of the tribe know the animal spirits from their own vision quest, in the course of which they meet the familiars that will empower them. The sand paintings that play a central role in healing ceremonies are thickly populated with the Wind People, Buffalo People, Cactus People, Snake People, Coyote People. The most powerful Navajo rite is the Blessing Way, often used to restore mental balance in the mad. Its chants and prayers call up the life-giving corn and pollen deities. Donald Sandner describes the ritual as "an orderly but mystical penetration into the mysteries of fertility and healing."[9] At the heart of the two-day ceremony lies the act of communion with the "inner form" of the Earth, which is the spiritual principle of life. The Navajo have a subtle natural philosophy. They regard all physical objects as "dead"; only their inner form enlivens them. Of all these vital principles, none is greater than the form of the Earth, in which all the forces of nature are concentrated. With Western psychiatry, the Navajo medicine man shares processes of confession and transference; but these experiences are contained within an intricate symbol system that is used to create "a new, reconstructed universe" where the ailing soul can feel securely at home.

The Eskimo shamans provide a special insight into the importance of the ecological context in traditional psychotherapy. Perhaps because these healers live within one of the most unstructured of human societies, there is a thinner shell of customs and institutions to separate them from the immediate natural environment; they work right up against the elements. Even the ancestors of the tribes receive less recognition as factors in psychosis than do the nature spirits, especially those of the animals whose life must be taken by the hunters. The fish, the seals, the walrus are understood to be fully sentient and ensouled beings. An early student of the tribes learned from one of the shamans

> the greatest peril of life lies in the fact that human food consists entirely of souls. All creatures which we have to kill and eat, all those that we have to strike down and destroy to make clothes for ourselves, have souls as we have, souls that do not perish with the body and which therefore must be propitiated lest they revenge themselves on us for taking away their bodies.[10]

This intense awareness that a life-and-death reciprocity binds the tribe to its habitat leads to long and grueling ceremonies of purification, where penance and expiation are vehemently released. The shamanic séance might be viewed as the original group therapy session. The shaman, usually drawing upon an animal spirit to lend him authority and insight, probes the souls of the community as part of a collective catharsis. Offenses of all kinds against one's fellows and against tribal taboos are brought into the open, all seen as elements of disharmony. In response to this purgation, the animals on whom the society depends for survival agree—through the shaman—to let their lives be taken.

The result, as Jane Murphy records it, is both an enforcement of the rules that defend the ecosystem and a powerful emotional cleansing.

> The St. Lawrence Eskimos believe that, if the proper acts of respect and consideration for animals are not carried out, then animal spirits will be offended and will cause the animals to withdraw from the island so that they no longer offer themselves to humans as meat for subsistence. Thus the behavior defined as sinful enough to result in disease or death was that considered threatening to the survival of the group as a whole or as an infringement of the laws about individual rights and social sharing relating to the administration of the most vital sources of food supply.[11]

Long before modern biology formulated its theories about the descent of man, traditional therapies were instinctively drawing upon an evolutionary priority older than family and society, rooted in the foundations of life itself: the claim of the nurturing planet upon our loyalty. Where our society seeks to gain security by domination and conquest, tribal societies have relied on trust, expecting their loyalty to be fairly requited. Whether we, in the long run, will prove to be the more justified in our expectations than they have been in theirs is yet to be seen. If our greedy and heedless industrial culture should meet the bad end some ecologists predict, then our choice will have been a foolish one that brought us neither peace of mind nor long-term prosperity—perhaps not even a humanly creditable stance in the world.

ECOLOGICAL MADNESS

Yet even if we admit to finding something of value in the long-lost animistic worldview, what chance is there that it can be recaptured by those of us who live in an industrial culture? Paul Shepard, in a provocative interpretation of "ecological madness," suggests the possibility may be closer at hand than we realize. He offers an evolutionary explanation for the harmony that once existed between precivilized people and their habitat. During the long hunting and gathering stage of human culture, a pattern of psychological development that responded to the intimately enveloping environment may have been favored by selective pressures. Perhaps the imprinting originated in the experience of childbirth, which, among traditional people, is practiced in a quiet, natural setting. The young are born to the sky, the songs of birds, the textures and odors of the wild. "The outdoors is also in some sense another inside," he observes, "a kind of enlivenment of that fetal landscape which is not so constant as once supposed. . . . The experience of such a world is initially that the mother is always there." An infancy that begins like this flows gracefully into a lifelong sense of kinship with the natural world. But then starting with the practice of agriculture some ten thousand years ago, human beings suffered what Shepard calls an "ontogenetic crippling." They had begun to manhandle their environment in ways that broke the bond that had for so long kept them connected to nature. The result has been "chronic madness." As grim as this sounds, Shepard believes that traces of our original ecological harmony may remain latent within us, "an inherited possession . . . a legacy of the evolutionary past in which human and nonhuman achieved a healthy rapport."[12]

While Shepard's formulation has a Lamarckian ring to it that most biologists are apt to reject (it seems to assert the inheritance of acquired characteristics), there is nonetheless a certain persuasiveness to his thesis. We know that at an advanced stage in human evolution, our highly developed intelligence took over much that was once left to the raw instinctual drives that govern the behavior of other creatures. From there forward, culture becomes a "second nature" that acts upon us by way of education and social discipline. But until the human race reached that stage, the evolutionary process had been working directly on the psyche for a long while, making it ready for this great transition. It is reasonable to assume that the protohuman psyche possessed the same spontaneous environmental rapport we find in other creatures, the capacity to live receptively and acceptively in their habitat alert to its every signal, obedient to its every demand. The brainstem in which the most primitive impulses and reflexes reside is still a physical component of the human brain. The boundary between protohuman and human is surely a hazy zone spread out over generations; yet where it is finally crossed, this instinctual repertory survives, but now assuming an intellectually self-aware character. It loses the immediate responsiveness we find in animals; instead it comes to be expressed in rite, ritual, myth, symbol—teachings and images that embody what was once instinctual. What simpler creatures understand unreflectively by way of an odor, a color, a physical hunger, we must learn by way of discursive intelligence from a folk tale or a religious ceremony. Perhaps this is what art originally was: an act of collective imagination meant to recapture the memory of instinctual union. The naivete and clarity of primitive art may stem from this primordial function. In traditional societies, a simple chant, a ritual gesture even awkwardly performed often has greater emotional force than the most polished work of civilized artists; the work stands closer to the true source of aesthetic power.

Consider, for example, the artwork of the Cro-Magnon people, as we find it preserved in the famous paintings at Lascaux. It remains a mystery why these painstaking images were placed in the recesses of dark caves where the difficulty of creating them must have been extreme. We can only speculate. Does the cave recapture the darkness of the psyche in whose depths the old instinctual wisdom still resided? This homage to the great beasts may be that memory externalized in art, yet still meant to retain the inwardness and secrecy of the psychological contents. The cave then becomes a reminder of the tribal mind, now undergoing radical transformation as individual intelligence takes over from collective instinct.

THE SENSE SUBLIME

When I read the surviving poetry of tribal people or view their art, I discover I have no experiential sense of what they meant when they addressed the animals and the elements as if they were friends, brothers, sentient beings. For that matter, I have no vivid knowledge of what the ancient Greeks were experiencing when they invoked their gods. I believe I can appreciate the plays of Sophocles, but I come away empty when I seek to grasp what filled his mind or that of his audience when his chorus cries out to Apollo for pity. Nor can I understand what so urbane an artist as Praxiteles intended when he shaped the god in marble as a gorgeously athletic youth. Of one thing I feel certain: the worship of the pagans, whether as civilized as Aristotle or as primitive as Neanderthal man, was never as childish or perversely stupid as hostile Jewish and Christian observers have supposed it to be since the time of the prophets. Obviously, the Athenians did not believe the deities to whom they appealed for guidance, mercy, and wisdom were so many oversized, well-fleshed men and women walking about the sky. So, too, I doubt that native Americans conceived of the eagle or the buffalo to whom they offered their prayers as human beings dressed up in feathers or hide.

"The heathen in his blindness bows down to wood and stone." The words, redolent with centuries of arrogance, are from a hymn written by a British missionary stationed in Calcutta at the time the first cotton mills were beginning to fill the sky above Manchester with soot. With the benefit of hindsight, realizing what a ruin we are making of the world in our times, I can no longer believe the worship of the "heathen" was ever "blindness." The blindness is ours. No people, regardless of the simplicity of their culture, ever took a stone carving to be divine. Modern anthropological scholarship now tells us as much. We have lost some quality of experience that would allow us to see the world as they did—or rather to see *through* it as they did. I take the animist worldview to be just that: things were once *transparent* to the human eye; greater realities moved behind and within them, were seen in this and that, here and there as if through a lens. This is where the concept of "spirit" comes from, this once-homely, utterly normal sense that something other than matter moves behind matter, animates it, sustains it. Of that "something," tribal people stood in awe, as Wordsworth still did when he reached back to salvage the remnants of a visionary childhood in language that can still speak to us.

> *And I have felt* [he tells us]
> *A presence that disturbs me with the joy*
> *Of elevated thoughts; a sense sublime*
> *Of something far more deeply interfused,*
> *Whose dwelling is the light of setting suns,*
> *And the round ocean and the living air,*
> *And the blue sky, and in the mind of man;*
> *A motion and a spirit, that impels*
> *All thinking things, all objects of all thought,*
> *And rolls through all things.*

That "sense sublime" was enough; it was a knowledge pure and potent of how the world truly is. But then, inevitably, the imagination, seeking to give that sense a shape, conceives of it as entities mentally and physically like ourselves. Such images symbolize what could not otherwise be put into words: the disembodied, ubiquitous will and intelligence that acts powerfully all about us.

At least, this is what I *think* the world of animist sensibility was like. I realize I must say cautiously little about it. For me, that same world that once pulsed with spiritual vitality has lost its transparency; it has grown densely opaque. To that degree, it has been *reduced*. That eclipse of sacramental consciousness is the beginning of "modern civilization." The poet Robert Bly puts it well:

> When we deny there is consciousness in nature, we also deny consciousness to the worlds we find by going *through* nature; and we end with only one world, the world of McDonald's, and that is exploitable.[13]

Some of us are coming to realize how great the cost of that denial is. But how are we to repair the damage?

SCIENCE AND THE SACRED

In later chapters we will review some recent efforts by various ecological, neo-pagan, and ecofeminist movements to resurrect the animist worldview. These are a commendable act of homage by some of the powerful many who dwell in the industrial heartland to all the perishing few who cling to its margins. They remind us how much we have sacrificed along the way in becoming civilized and industrialized. They make the best possible use of the great global convergence of our time, sampling the historical variety, salvaging the cultural wealth that science and scholarship have placed before us.

But in and of themselves, I think these efforts will not be enough. For us the way *back* in time is not the way *out* of our environmental crisis. If any part of an animist sensibility is to be reclaimed, the project will have to integrate with modern science. Nothing else will qualify as an honest intellectual effort. The work of the scientists, as psychologically underdimensioned as it may be when it comes to experiences of a nonlogical, nonmathematical kind, is too firmly grounded in empirical verification to be lightly dismissed. Moreover, along the lines of its own meticulous methods, science has produced a wealth of astonishments, investigations of the big and small that vastly enrich our understanding of the universe. If human conduct were governed by reason alone, what science has taught us about the great ecological patterns and cycles of the planet might be enough to reform our bad environmental habits.

Science permeates the lives of people everywhere in the modern world. It is the closest our species has come to a universal culture since the days of the hunters and gatherers. Even those, like the Christian Evangelicals who struggle to preserve the old-time religion from the dreaded "secular humanists," quite casually appropriate the benefits of the science they despise every time they switch on an electric light bulb or whenever a new video ministry takes to the air. So, too, the Islamic fundamentalists who rebel violently against Western values, nevertheless borrow the inventions of science and live off the market the modern West provides for their resources. When the ayatollahs address their followers, they do so with microphones and television cameras.

All of us use the power of science; we rely upon it as fully as primitive folk relied upon their skill at tracking game or foraging in the wild. Nothing now stands a better chance of uniting us as one human family. That promise is graphically embodied in the image science has given us of the Earth photographed from outer space, the icon of our era. This is not nature as our ancestors knew it, a local landscape intimately encountered in all its dense and jumbled detail. This is a neat technological artifact, a pattern of light and color captured on chemical emulsion, recorded as only the passengers aboard a spacecraft might view it. Viewed distantly from space, the Earth loses its "earthiness"; it becomes more coolly abstract than our ancestors knew it, an object to be studied rather than a living presence to be addressed and embraced. But this may yet become our sense of "locality" in the galactic wilderness. Each time I see this photo I am persuaded that it is still another way in which the living Earth seeks to remind us of the bond that holds us to it, a fragile blue outpost of life in the dark immensity.

Committed as they are to an impersonal rhetoric and precise measurement, scientists cannot speak of that world as our ancestors did; they cannot give it a face and a voice and pronounce its name with reverence—though it is remarkable how their descriptions of it continually slide into anthropomorphic metaphors, a curious habit we will investigate in later chapters. Nevertheless, the deeper modern science delves into the nature of things, the more it finds hints and traces of the primordial animist world: *mind in the cosmos,* as we will refer to it. In their own halting, roundabout way, scientists are fashioning a picture of the world as alive, intentional, creative—though they may be the last to admit it. The objective truth of the matter demands a revision of our natural philosophy. And I think something more comes into play: an ecological unconscious, the "savage" remnant within us, that rises up subjectively to meet the environmental need of the time. This is why new theoretical departures like the Gaia hypothesis and the Anthropic Principle, which we will examine in the chapters to come, are of such importance. They represent the first faltering steps toward a science that can deliver us from the dead and meaningless universe of the past. In its place, these theories offer the chance once again to *connect.*

Once upon a time—actually before time itself existed—the world *In-here* and the world *Out-there* existed in the unity of a creative instant: the inexpressible "singularity" from which, so the new cosmology tells us, all things were generated. After being so long divided by modern science as if by a great gulf fixed, these two worlds may at last be finding their way back to their original unity.

Part Two

COSMOLOGY

"Stone-age psychiatry" may offer an instructive contrast with modern psychotherapy, but its peculiar healing power derives from an animistic experience of nature that seems hopelessly lost to the modern world. "Lost" and not by many regretted. Hearing "tongues in trees, sermons in stones"—as anything more than poetic license—has come to be regarded as the very essence of superstition in the modern world. Orthodox science over the past three centuries has taught us that the natural world, far from being a speaking presence, is wholly other and alien. Life and mind, adrift in a galactic no-man's land, are unaccountable curiosities.

But science also has its history, and has many times revised its deepest assumptions. We are living through such a period of shifting paradigms. Convergent developments in cosmology, physics, and biology over the past century are radically altering our understanding of our place in the universe. As our sense of ethical and psychological continuity with the nonhuman world deepens, we have the chance to recapture, on our own contemporary terms, some trace of the ancestral sensibility.

Four

◆

MIND IN THE COSMOS
Agnosticism and the Anthropic Principle

Today there is a wide measure of agreement, which on the physical side of science approaches to unanimity, that the stream of knowledge is heading toward a non-mechanical reality; the universe begins to look more like a great thought than like a great machine. Mind no longer appears as an accidental intruder into the realm of matter; we are beginning to suspect that we ought rather to hail it as the creator and governor of the realm of matter.

JAMES JEANS, *The Mysterious Universe*

THE POLITICS OF GODLESSNESS

When I took my first philosophy course in college, the principal text was Bertrand Russell's *A Free Man's Worship*. Though the essay dated back to 1903, it was still a favorite freshman assignment—and not for its historical value. The work spoke for a point of view widely represented in the philosophy departments of American and British universities, a defense of the life of reason, which seemed to have taken on special relevance in the wake of World War II. As many liberal intellectuals saw it, any deviation from the strict logic and clear thinking for which Russell spoke would lead straight to fascist hysteria. My teacher, a doctrinaire Logical Positivist who had studied with Russell, laid his mentor's words before us with an unmistakably proselytizing fervor, seeking to win his class over to the great man's heroic stoicism. He succeeded with me. Having only recently cast aside the Roman Catholic dogmatism of my childhood, I was on the lookout for a new creed. For the next several years, I proudly and somewhat pugnaciously carried Russell's words with me in my memory as a sort of agnostic manifesto.

> That man is the product of causes which had no prevision of the end they were achieving; that his origin, his growth, his hopes and fears, his loves and his beliefs, are but the outcome of accidental collocations of atoms; that no fire, no heroism, no intensity of thought and feeling can preserve an individual life beyond the grave; that all the labors of the ages, all the devotion, all the inspirations, all the noonday brightness of human genius, are destined to extinction in the vast death of the solar system, and that the temple of Man's achievement must inevitably be buried beneath the debris of the universe in ruins—all these things, if not beyond dispute, are yet so nearly certain, that no philosophy which rejects them can hope to stand. Only within the scaffolding of these truths, only on the firm foundation of unyielding despair can the soul's habitation henceforth be safely built.[1]

From Positivism, which was at its height when he wrote these words, Russell gained a fiercely lucid perception of the role of philosophy. Philosophy was the faithful handmaiden of science, entrusted with keeping its master's methodological instruments well oiled and highly polished. Its future would have more and more to do with the esoteric intricacies of logic, mathematics, and linguistic analysis. Philosophers were technicians, the sanitary engineers of the intellectual world charged with cleaning up a culture still sunk in superstition and emotional drivel. If they did their job well, they would someday be mercifully relieved of having to deal with messy issues of metaphysics, morality, or theology. All these would have been driven off like so many noxious vapors. In this respect, Russell, a man of great conscience who continued to address ethical and political issues with zest and compassion, was far from being the most rigorous of Positivists.

In the pages that follow we will be examining how this clear, crusading vision of philosophy has come to be clouded with doubts and reservations. The "firm [if cheerless] foundation" that science once provided for courageous spirits like Russell has significantly shifted—to the point that those who wish to make some greater philosophical sense of the emerging worldview of our day will have to address questions of a frankly religious character. Can we continue to regard the world as the result of blind chance? Or is there some essential element of design in nature that intimates the presence of intelligence? Are life and mind still to be seen as the accidental epiphenomena that Russell, like Freud, took them to be? Or does the cosmology whose outlines are taking shape in the late twentieth century point toward a new human-centeredness that will require us to reevaluate our place in the universe? We may be on the brink of a rapprochement between science and religion, or at least between science and certain religious categories of thought that have long been exiled from our secular culture.

As appealing as it might be to some to find an alternative to Russell's "unyielding despair," I suspect there are few scientists, few in the intellectual community generally, who would welcome such a détente. It is important to understand why this resistance exists, since it may needlessly obstruct serious efforts at intellectual synthesis. Once again, as in many other cases, in order to understand the nature of science, we must step outside of science into its surrounding culture.

In one of the memorable, if blood-chilling pronouncements of the great age of democratic revolution, Louis de Saint-Just, the French political leader who helped administer the Reign of Terror, declared that mankind could never be truly free until "the last king lies strangled in the entrails of the last priest." The inveterate anticlericalism of that era rapidly elevated godlessness to a principled political stance. Accordingly, zealous agnostics of the Enlightenment set about ousting God from the universe as a means of driving his ecclesiastical henchmen from positions of authority. Convinced that "religion was invented when a charlatan met a fool," they lost sight of an important distinction. Anticlericalism is a matter of politics; atheism a matter of philosophy. It is one of the misfortunes of modern history that in the heat of revolutionary endeavor these two very different causes were fused into a single unwieldy program. As a result, the new science of that era, celebrated as the epitome of reason, assumed an uncompromisingly antireligious bent. The old theological categories—many of them undoubtedly defunct and riddled with obfuscation—were closed down.

The study of the universe became a wholly secular pursuit, as deeply grounded in physical determinism as possible.

At this point, let me declare an interest. I wholeheartedly endorse the political ideal of the Enlightenment as one of the splendors of the Western heritage. It may be the finest contribution our society has to offer other cultures. No question but that clerical privilege is as antithetical to democracy as aristocratic dominance, and indeed in Saint-Just's day the two stood (and fell) together. But over the years I have come to have serious doubts about the philosophical goal that came to be assimilated to the politics of revolution. I would now regard the militant secularization of liberal thought as intellectually crippling in the extreme. I say this with no doctrinal bias; by the standards of many devout people, I would surely not qualify as religious in any sense of the word they recognize. Nonetheless, there are certain concepts we inherit from theological thought—teleology, final cause, emergence— that I believe are philosophically rich, even scientifically useful.

The oblique conception of "God" I invoke here will not be negotiable with committed Christians, Jews, or Moslems; it will focus more on *mentality* than divinity, and on paternalistic authority not at all. Nor will it necessarily offer the consolation expected of a heavenly father, a deity who hears the prayers of troubled hearts and grants miraculous aid. But there is no way to pursue the line of thought I wish to take up without drawing upon elements we inherit from the world's religious traditions, especially the idea of creatively intelligent, non-physical power alive and at work within nature: mind in the cosmos. In ways they seem not to realize—and which many would shun if they heard it associated with the word "God"—scientists have been salvaging that idea for the better part of this century. It may be time for them to cease being squeamish about that fact. Throughout its history, after all, science has borrowed concepts, models, images from outside itself and then adapted them to its needs. Newtonian physics could not have bootstrapped itself into existence if it had not appropriated the image of a law-giver deity who lent nature a rational order.

Now, remarkably enough, religious concepts of a much older vintage, perceptions of spirit, creative will, intentionality inherited from the earliest animistic stages of human culture, may be playing the same role as the old clockmaker God. They may be functioning as the metaphysical scaffolding of a new cosmology. If for no other reason than that this heritage is "tainted" by elements of paganism and nature mysticism, it is apt to prove even more unpalatable to religiously conservative tastes than standard scientific agnosticism. Alien gods have always been more threatening to true believers than outright godlessness.

MATTER, CHANCE, ETERNITY

For the sake of perspective, let us review the strategy that agnostics like Russell have used since the days of Tom Paine and Baron d'Holbach to delete God from the universe. There are three gambits to the attack: materialism, chance, and infinite time.

First: one asserts that all things are made of matter, defined as tiny petrified globs of indivisibly dense primordial stuff as wholly other from life and mind as possible.

Second: one asserts that matter is acted upon by various blind, haphazard forces and energies whose impact on the tiny globs is wholly random. That is to say, these forces impinge upon matter unpredictably, heating it, cooling it, shifting it from place to place, aggregating it, blowing it apart, mixing it up in unpredictable combinations.

Finally: one asserts that given enough time—an eternity of time—this undirected interplay of inert matter and mindless force will finally produce not only the recognizable objects of the natural world, but the human mind that recognizes them as well.

Fit these three assumptions together as tightly as possible and there is no room left for creative divinity. The world just happens; it makes itself by accident. We are that accident in its self-conscious form. No God needed.

This is essentially the cosmology of the ancient Greek and Roman atomists updated by the addition of advanced mathematical formulations. In both cases, the goal was the same: to deprive the cosmos of its need for divine intervention, to account for its order in non-deistic ways. Interestingly enough, the objective of atomists like Lucretius was to spare mankind the anxiety that came of living under the shadow of fickle, omnipotent gods. Atomism meant benign, predictable order; its goal was tranquillity, including release from the dread of damnation. Doctrinaire materialism came into existence to achieve precisely the psychological consolation that stalwart atheists like to insist is the cowardly objective of religion.

The bracing, even breathtaking simplicity that marked the scientific worldview of the seventeenth century bespeaks such absolute conviction that one easily overlooks an important fact: *nothing* in it had been decisively proven at the time it was formulated. Nobody had witnessed an atom of matter, let alone tested its capacities. Nobody had ever observed any complex natural object simply falling together by accident. The known forces of nature came down to a few kinds of elementary motion, mainly gravitation. These basic motions had not yet—and never would be—successfully generalized to such phenomena as magnetism or light or the intricacy of many chemical reactions. Even the mechanistic model used to analyze nature was a fantasy, since nobody had ever built—or ever would build—the sort of machine the universe was understood to be: a perpetually revolving collection of objects driven by mutual gravitational forces. As for the duration of the universe, not only was there no proof that it was infinitely old; there was no way to measure its age whatsoever. In short, the mechanistic worldview of the Enlightenment was a compilation of *a priori* assumptions—as much so as anything the medieval schoolmen ever taught about angelic intelligences among the crystalline spheres. All it really had going for it was the brilliance of Newton's *Principia*—that and the inspiration of the great man's "mind forever voyaging through strange seas of thought, alone." That was a lot, but not nearly enough to contain the universe.

Looking back across the centuries, we can now see that the entire materialist program reads like a secular catechism based upon articles of faith. It was asserted into existence by passionate men on the grounds of their own fiery certitude. It was not a finding; it was the program of an ethical and political cause. In that capacity it served well as a way of clearing the intellectual decks for action; radical, even ruthless simplification was a way of starting afresh, eliminating the inherited clutter, trying out new ideas. But as commendably eager as materialism was to rebuild society on the foundations of pure reason, it eventually ran up against a formidable obstacle: reality. Truth is never simple, no more so in the state of nature than in human affairs.

By the early nineteenth century, it was becoming clear that Newtonian science was more limited than its disciples realized. It certainly had no sensible connection whatever with biology, which was to be the most prolific science of the period. More seriously, it would have no explanation to offer for the most advanced discoveries in the physical sciences: electricity and radiation. When Michael Faraday sought to explain the baffling phenomenon of electricity, he had to improvise a radically new, worrisomely nonphysical concept that would eventually stretch Newtonianism to the breaking point; he called it the "field." While scientists are generally reluctant to admit it, the concept of the field is as spectral as anything ever invented by the theological imagination. It has never been made clear to the general public in what sense a field is either "physical" or "mechanical" as Newton would have used these terms. The closest one can come to giving the field material substance is to fill it with some kind of subtle fluid like ether—a solution that has not proved viable. Beyond that, fields become configurations in pure space in which the once-solid atoms have dissolved into waves, vibrations, patterns of activity. Calling a field "physical" or "mechanical" is really just a way to confer upon it a reality that scientists can continue to respect. What does that "reality" come down to beyond the fact that fields can be measured and treated mathematically? But that is a reality principle more appropriate to the mystic Pythagoras than to the sort of hard-edged empiricists most "physical" scientists continue to claim they are.

By century's end, the New Physics of Planck, Bohr, Heisenberg, de Broglie was rapidly tearing down the remaining ramparts of materialism. Matter ceased to be simple and ultimate. "Things" were replaced by "events," often of an ambiguous, if not highly contradictory kind. As the dividing lines between matter, energy, and pure space evaporated, it ceased to be possible to give a coherent picture of the property that supposedly made science "physical." Matter had vanished into a mathematical formalism that measured, but could no longer render visible the elusive "something" that underlay the solid surface of everyday life. "Particles" took the place of atoms as the rudimentary substance of nature. But particles were not simply some smaller species of atom. From the outset, they were murky entities, not easily explained to the general public in ordinary language. They remain so. Whatever "particles" may be—transient bumps or charges or knots that travel in a space–time trajectory—they are not to be understood as objects. What, then, does it mean to be a "materialist" in the absence of matter?

MATTER TRANSCENDS ITSELF

The situation is ironic. By their ever more penetrating explorations of the universe over the past three centuries, scientists have made it impossible for Christians to believe that God is a bearded gentleman sitting on a golden throne at the top of the sky. No top of the sky, no golden throne, no bearded gentleman. It is a defunct idea. But now, by refining matter into immaterial fields and forces, science has dealt the same blow to materialism. It also turns out to be a defunct idea. Its basis—matter—has become a nonconcept. The tension here is not between science and religion; it is between the two great wings of science itself: *theory,* which generated materialism as a comprehensive picture of nature, and *observation,* which continues to probe deeper into the phenomena of the world, constantly uncovering angles and aspects of reality that undermine old theories and clear the stage for new paradigms. In this case, the study of the cathode ray tube, of radium and x-rays, and of black body radiation finally collected a mass of data that burst the vessel of Newtonian physicality. As Karl Popper once put it, in the new quantum universe, "matter has transcended itself."

The obsolescence of the materialist doctrine is, of course, as serious a dilemma for the religious as for the nonreligious. Both require an absolute opposition between matter and spirit. Now neither has it. We simply cannot divide the world up that way any longer. Rather, there is some kind of a continuum in nature that at one stage in cosmic time and at one level of perception assumes the solidity of matter, but in an earlier period and at a deeper level is nothing at all like the everyday world of naive empiricism. The physicist David Bohm has settled for defining matter as "that which unfolds, whatever the medium may be." Unfolds *what?* An "implicate order," which remains a realm of impenetrable mystery. If we ever find the power to search deeply enough, we may find that Spinoza was right in calling matter "God as extension." Scientists can express the behavior of matter mathematically, but we cannot say we understand its capacities or its limits. We cannot therefore say that "spirit" is other than "matter," let alone antagonistic to it. We have in our time lost a dichotomy on which centuries of both religious belief and scientific theory have relied to make their most ambitious claims.

Yet, while the New Physics was steadily discrediting classical materialism, it was not making the universe more livably human. On the contrary. By the time the atomic scientists of the early twentieth century had finished reshaping the world, it had lost all connection with common sense and ordinary experience. It had become an Alice-in-Wonderland universe where even the questing human mind might not be at home among the vast imponderables. Scientists, I sometimes think, find a certain impish amusement in teasing the lay public with outlandish descriptions of the puzzling substructure of the universe. It allows them to play with paradox and ambiguity. The playfulness shows up in the whimsical vocabulary used by theoretical physicists these days: "quarks" that have ups, downs, taste, color, and charm, "gluons" that stick things together, "wimps," "guts," "googles," "jiffies". . . . All very tongue-in-cheek; physics with a sense of humor. But—and one cannot be too emphatic about the point—*this is not what science was supposed to be all about.* Since Newton's time, it was assumed that science meant the clear, rational explanation of things: a world more accessible to human comprehension than obfuscating theologians had ever rendered it. Our place in nature was defined by intellect, the ability to understand the clear and accessible logic of the universe.

Contrast this with the way in which the physicist Richard Feynman once began a lecture series. "Nobody who comes to a science lecture expects to understand anything," he announced. But that was quite all right. When it comes to subjects like quantum electrodynamics, neither did his own students; neither did he! All he wished to do was to show his listeners "Nature as She really is. Absurd."[2] The cold void of Newton's universe had been exchanged for the queasy absurdity of Einstein's. The transition from the old to the new era in physics was in that respect no advance in human values. What Feynman was so blithely referring to is the Existenialist's void, the edge of that abyss on which Samuel Beckett's anguished dramas are played out.

The erosion of classical materialism, however, was only the beginning of the great undoing. There are two more major developments that have taken place in the course of just the past quarter century that must radically change all science-based philosophy. The first of these (which we will explore at greater length in chapters 5 and 6) is our growing appreciation of natural systems—a steady accumulation of insights that has both enriched and complicated our understanding of the world. The second is the discovery of cosmic evolution. Together, these raise troubling questions for all explanations that base themselves on chance. Chance, like matter before it, may be approaching extinction as a concept—except in its cruder usages in gambling casinos or among computer programmers.

The problem is this: among the elements of an ordered whole there is a ghostly presence. It is the enduring nonphysical pattern of the parts, a structure which is "there," but not in the same sense that the isolable physical components are there. The structure resides *between* the parts; or it is some phantom framework *surrounding* the parts. When that structure holds together as it moves through time, retaining its identity while constantly altering its physical makeup, the pattern becomes a *process* that is historical as well as spatial. Structure and process do not present themselves empirically like the simple observation of an object or a pointer-reading; they have to be recognized and explicated by the observing mind. The caterpillar knows the leaf as surely as its teeth take hold of it; but only the human mind knows the photosynthesis that takes place within it. Ervin Laszlo, one of the leading systems theorists, makes the point well. At one stage—the stage studied by science through its first three centuries—nature is "change," a simple succession of states that one measures. At another stage, which has come to occupy more and more of our attention in the twentieth century, we are drawn to study the *order of change,* which is "process." Only now are we beginning to ask about the *order of process* in the most comprehensive sense, which is "evolution." The latter two stages make up the study of "systems."

THE AMBIGUITIES OF RANDOMNESS

Where do such systemic patterns come from, how do they start, why do they endure? Can they have come about by chance? More to the point, *did* they come about by chance? For most scientists, there continues to be no question about it; their conviction in the matter can achieve an all but dogmatic certainty.

> Chance *alone* [the Nobel laureate Jacques Monod assures us] is at the source of every innovation, of all creation in the biosphere. Pure chance, absolutely free but blind, at the very root of the stupendous edifice of

evolution: this central concept of modern biology . . . is today the *sole* conceivable hypothesis . . . . And nothing warrants the supposition—or the hope—that on this score our position is likely ever to be revised.[3]

But like many words used in science, "chance" has numerous meanings both general and technical. We may ask what the "chances" are that one can roll ten consecutive sevens at the dice table. The answer is a low probability. How about a thousand sevens in a row? A much lower probability, but still a probability that can be calculated. Two dice with only so many sides: that makes a manageable problem. Similarly, the principal system known to classical physicists was a manageable one: the solar system. We now know that the "simple" mechanics of that system actually present a great number of computational complexities that were unappreciated by the early modern astronomers, not to speak of Einsteinian gravitational distortions that were unobserved until this century. Still, as natural systems go, it is among the simpler ones. Even so, most scientists of the seventeenth and eighteenth centuries were convinced it took a god to make it. Eventually, however, their more agnostic colleagues felt certain it could have fallen into place with the aid of little more than the classic Newtonian laws. No God needed.

But now ask, as we have asked about the rolling dice, "what are the chances that all the matter there is [whatever we may understand "matter" to be] can be shuffled together into the existing universe?" This is obviously a senseless question. There was only one roll of the "dice" in this game—all the debris of the cosmos blown apart in a Big Bang. That one roll produced what we have. What are the "chances" of that happening? Clearly we cannot apply the word that way here.

For that matter, it would be just as meaningless to ask what the chances are that a single protein enzyme was ever originally shuffled into existence randomly, unless we have a clear record before us of numerous combinations and recombinations that took place in the distant past. As far as we know, this also was a unique event. We may *assume* such random mixtures took place, but we do not really know that. The only argument that can be given in support of that assumption would be something like "how else could it have happened?" But that is where science is supposed to begin, not end.

"Random" is a word we can use for dealing with lottery numbers or selecting names by lot. Statisticians have designed random number machines to guarantee against bias in various operations—though some mathematicians regard these as "pseudo" random number machines because of the limitations any machine is up against in dealing with infinite operations. All forms of randomness involve certain boundary conditions. Beyond that boundary, the unpredictability may end, repetitions and patterns may begin. There are only so many names in the pool from which we draw lots, only so many tickets to be selected among in the lottery. What if there were more? What if we kept on mixing and drawing? Unless we were to run a random number machine eternally, we could not be sure that some predictable pattern might not begin unfolding just after the last number selected. The machine is random within certain practical limits. "Randomness," Heinz Pagels believes, "may be absolutely undefinable."4

Is the behavior of things in the universe "random" in some more definitive way than the action of a random number machine? Recently a new branch of science has begun studying what were once taken to be totally unpredictable, radically haphazard processes such as ocean waves and atmospheric gyrations. The field is called chaos theory. The phenomena that fall within its province include all the most tenaciously disorderly things; for example turbulence, which used to be the *bête noir* of the physical sciences due to its stubborn non-computability. The cheap and rapid calculating power of computers has made it possible to model processes that include once intractable variables—ideally (but not actually) down to the influence of a butterfly's wings on the weather. The conclusion that emerges is ambiguous. On the one hand, chaos theory has demonstrated that the sort of totally deterministic predictability once held by classical physicists to be in principle possible is, in principle, *impossible*. In chaotic systems, like global weather, the sensitivity to initial conditions is so great that computational errors are bound to grow at an accelerating rate along the way. For that matter, even a simple system like an oscillating pendulum, once thought to be fully understood, can become unpredictably chaotic, and in that sense radically "random" in its movements. Even so, the resulting chaos may assume an overall nonrandom shape, at least as modeled on a computer. It is almost as if, under extreme conditions of confusion and turbulence, matter falls back to a second line of order: the best it can do under the circumstances. Such order-of-last-resort includes "strange attractors," mysteriously favored mathematical basins toward which otherwise incalculable events want to sink. In short, if randomness underlies the superficial illusion of regularity, a still deeper order of sorts may underlie the illusion of randomness. World within world within world.

A committed materialist might still hold out against the odds, declaring that *given enough time* all the systems we know could *in principle* have blindly sorted themselves into existence. The argument assumes that even the most infinitesimal probability has some ghost of a chance of turning up over an infinity of time. In the nineteenth century, Ludwig Boltzmann, one of the pioneers in the study of gases (the word itself was derived from the Greek "chaos") took the position that chance alone accounted for the coherent structure of the universe. He even calculated the time required for chance to achieve that result. Enough time equals $10^{10^{80}}$ years. A heroic calculation indeed: ten raised to a power expressed by another ten followed by eighty zeros. There would not be enough pages in all the books in all the libraries in the world to contain that large a figure.

A number so vast seems purely fanciful, but Boltzmann was quite serious. His calculation was based on the assumption that the universe is eternal. In an eternity of time, there is a paradoxical sense in which the inexorable second law of thermodynamics can be "suspended." The law is after all a statement of probability; it tells us that any ordered arrangement of things is *likely—very* likely—to lose order in the next minute, year, millennium, eon. But if that is so, why is there any order left in the universe at all (as there obviously is) after all the time that has passed? Boltzmann's answer was: eternity is filled with endless fluctuations. As the atoms that drift through the void knock about forever, they are bound to cycle through every possible fluctuation again and again, including a return to more ordered states. This is what our present highly ordered universe is: one such fluctuation. The odds are that it will now tend toward disorder, but *in time* it will return to this state. Randomness stretched to eternity includes random states of order. Is this how our universe came into existence? That amounts to asking: have there been $10^{10^{80}}$ years of time—or anything like it?

THE HISTORY OF TIME

Obviously Boltzmann believed there had been. But now we know he was wrong. In one of its most significant discoveries, the new cosmology tells us that the universe, and with it time itself, may be in short supply. Both had a beginning and have had a measurable duration. We may not be certain whether that instant of spontaneous creation happened fifteen or twenty billion years ago, or whether we can even meaningfully say it "happened" as a moment in time. In any case, we can no longer credit the universe with that majestically eternal span of eons that Boltzmann once thought sufficient for the random accumulation of mindless matter into a coherent cosmos filed with physical and biological structures.

The new cosmology is by now familiar in its general outlines. What is often not sufficiently appreciated is the speed with which it has come into existence and the wrenching change it demands in our scientific paradigm. All the important discoveries of the new worldview can be grouped within the period between the 1920s to the 1980s, dating from Edwin Hubble's identification of the nebula in Andromeda as a galaxy, the first of the "island universes." With that discovery, infinity itself took on size. By 1930 Hubble had also announced the first solid evidence of cosmic expansion: the red shift of the galaxies. The discoveries were dramatic; but few people realize how capriciously speculative cosmology remained in the eyes of "hard" scientists. There seemed so little that could be proven about the far reaches of space, certainly not enough to discriminate between contending theories. The notion that the expansion of the universe might be due to an explosive beginning remained wholly theoretical through the 1950s. When the astronomer Fred Hoyle named that hypothetical event the "Big Bang," he did so derisively, rejecting the very idea. Not until the mid-sixties, when Arno Penzias and Robert Wilson accidentally happened upon background microwave radiation did scientists have proof that this catastrophic origin had occurred. That ghostly shell of radiation is the faint, receding aftermath of our explosive cosmic origin.

By then another astronomical novelty had been documented: the quasars, the first truly exotic heavenly bodies to be observed since the comet was sighted in Galileo's time. Quasars proved that there existed in the universe very distant entities that were also very strange, far stranger than anything theories of the past could account for. Within an expanding cosmos, the relationship between how distant quasars are and how strange they are is the important point. The discovery of the quasars, as we can now observe them billions of years after their light began its journey toward us, holds somewhat the same significance in astronomy that the discovery of fossilized dinosaur bones once had in biological theory. They are relics of an ancient universe in which matter assumed strange forms. Taken together with the Big Bang, they prove that the universe has altered radically over time. It has a *history,* a record of significant change. And since that history has to be the history of everything there is, it must include the particles that nuclear physicists have come to recognize as the constituents of matter. These too were created, have matured, and evolved. In the early seventies, nuclear physicists "discovered" cosmology and began to move in on the field. In the heat and pressure of the Big Bang they recognized the properties of a particle accelerator capable of doing what no engine of their own making could ever do: build the atoms that they had been trying to disintegrate for analysis. That unique historical event, especially what must have occurred in the first moments of creation, connected with aspects of their theories. These findings—background radiation, the quasar, the Big Bang, and later, Stephen Hawking's research on black holes—rapidly coalesced with quantum mechanics and Einstein's relativity to produce a radically new world picture. We now know that *history* is a characteristic of everything, not only living things. We know that the heavier elements we are made of were forged during that history in the deep interior of stars. We know that whatever exists, no matter how intricate, has to be accounted for within the dynamics of cosmic expansion and the framework of cosmic time.

Once we introduce the factor of duration, the discussion of randomness is radically altered. There may be a point at which probability falls to zero. Those who invoke chance to explain the order of things have never been quite candid about this. They have not distinguished between an abstract calculation about the fall of dice and the fact that in the real world a human hand must take time to throw those dice over and over again. It is one thing to calculate and jot down a million rolls of the dice, another to *make* those million rolls. In the real study of nature, it makes no sense to hold that anything is *in principle* possible when *in practice* there is not enough time in the history of time itself for the process to work through all the permutations. The history of the universe is all the time there is; when we go beyond it, that is the point at which we confront zero probability. This limit applies not only to the time it takes for the events themselves to transpire, but to our capacity as observers to prove anything about those events with mathematical certainty, including the fact that they obey the so-called basic laws of nature.

For example, while nobody would argue that a baseball game violates the laws of physics, nevertheless no scientist, using all the information technology in the world, would ever claim that every last detail of a game could be predicted with certainty, nor even what the outcome will be. There are just too many variables to chase down. It would take centuries simply to collect precise and exhaustive data about the initial conditions of the game: the state of the field and all the equipment to be used, the likely shifts of the wind and weather, the eyesight of the umpires, the judgment of the managers, the health and morale of the players, etc. By that time the game would be long over. A project like this may sound absurd; but for generations the prestige of science has been largely based on the claim that, in principle, it can do such things. If it cannot, the door may be open to some troublingly "supernatural" possibilities. There is, for example, an anecdotal study of athletics that argues that games are frequently punctuated by "psychic" events that defy scientific explanation: instances of extrasensory perception, unnatural feats of exertion, levitation, etc.[5] Is this so? We may doubt it; but the only way we could be certain about our doubt would be to see if this thesis violates a solid prediction about the course of the game. And this we cannot do. Stephen Hawking grudgingly admits to such a restriction when he tells us that *in principle* "quantum mechanics enables us to predict everything we see around us within the limits set by the uncertainty principle," but then goes on to add, "In practice, however, the calculations required for systems containing more then a few electrons are so complicated that we cannot do them."[6] This might be called the *second* uncertainty principle.

There is an important point that even this brief discussion of matter, chance, and randomness brings to light. If we agree that the traditional connotation of these terms has been all but totally dissipated, perhaps we can recognize that their true meaning was never technical or empirical. Rather, this is language that was imported into science as part of its agnostic program. All that may survive of that program in the awareness of many scientists is its underlying and now highly dubious assumption that all things in nature can be described without reference to premeditated design or purpose. No God needed. This is really all that is being said whenever people state that they are offering a "material" or "physical" explanation. It has become a rule of the scientific game to explain things on that basis. But the assumption was always a metaphysical premise, linked to a moral-political agenda.

Which does not mean the assumption has gone without some experimental exploration, especially with respect to the greatest puzzle of all: the origin of life. Ever since 1828 when Friedreich Wöhler synthesized urea, the first organic compound, scientists have been attempting to pluck the secret of life out of test-tubes by way of random mixing, heating, and electrification. Stanley L. Miller has made the most determined long-term attempt to coax life, or its rudiments, into existence in this way. He has been sparking various gases since the early 1950s, when he did succeed in producing amino acids in this way. The work continues at the University of Maryland, where a special laboratory has been devoted to the study of "chemical evolution." There, within recent years, Cyril Ponnamperuma and his colleagues have managed to produce enzyme-like molecules by shooting an electrical discharge through a model of the Earth's primordial atmosphere, proving that complex proteins may have existed before any living cells. Similarly, at MIT in 1990, Julius Rebek managed to synthesize a simple self-replicating molecule, "a primitive sign of life," as he calls it.[7] These are far from impressive results for so much experimentation. Moreover, it is difficult to say what would be proved even if the results were richer. The experiments are, after all, being carried out by thinking, planning minds with a clear goal in sight. And they are happening some fifteen billion years into the life-history of the universe at the culmination of eons of system and structure-building with no idea what the initial conditions of that lengthy cosmic process might have been.

There are still texts being written in biology that use experiments like those mentioned to explain the origin of life. One can usually expect the account to contain many slippery assumptions, plus a healthy serving of the legendary "primordial soup." For example:

Thus, it appears likely that the sea of the primitive Earth spontaneously accumulated a great variety of organic molecules. The sea became a sort of dilute organic soup . . . in which the molecules collided and reacted to form new molecules of increasing levels of complexity. Purines, pyrimidines, nucleotides, and all other constituents of protoplasm came into existence. The association of nucleic acid molecules and proteins would lead inevitably to a virus-like nucleoprotein particle capable of self-duplication or self-reproduction[8]

In the late 1970s Fred Hoyle and Chandra Wickramasinghe calculated the odds that life could have originated from just such an undirected sloshing about. Rather than trying to compute the probability for an entire organism springing into existence, they limited the problem to a sequence of twenty or thirty key amino acids in the enzymes of some hypothetical cell. The number they came up with was one chance in $10^{40,000}$. [9]

Odds like these become even more telling when we introduce the factor of time. F. B. Salisbury has attempted to do just that. He undertook to calculate the probability for the haphazard assemblage of the thousand nucleotides necessary to synthesize even a small enzyme containing a mere three hundred amino acids. His conclusion was that there would be not even a fraction of the time needed in the entire history of the universe. This left Salisbury to observe that *chance* may be the factor that has to be eliminated if the evolutionary explanation of life is to retain its cogency. An ironic proposal. Chance, previously so powerful an explanatory device, now becomes the obstacle to coherent explanation.[10]

ONE THOUSAND MONKEYS

There is a parable that was popular among militant atheists of the last century. It was meant to illustrate the omnipotent power of chance. Place one thousand monkeys in a room filled with one thousand typewriters and let the beasts bang away indefinitely. Given enough time (the monkeys are apparently immortal, the typewriters indestructible) and by the "laws of probability" the monkeys will produce the complete works of Shakespeare. No Shakespeare needed.

Maybe nobody takes this old chestnut seriously any longer. One attempt to calculate the odds for composing one line from Shakespeare by random monkey power concluded that there was one chance in 10,000 million million million million million million.[11] Within the time span such odds would require, it is easier to imagine the monkeys evolving into intelligent beings capable of creating their own literary masterpieces. But while this example has a facetious tone to it, it does allow us the opportunity to ponder the unutterable complexity of nature—and the embarrassing bravado with which scientists once confronted its study. The probabilities that must be factored when we deal with even the simplest natural phenomena are far beyond what our hypothetical monkeys confront with their typewriters. Typewriters, after all, come equipped with formed letters, ready to write words. But here beside me as I work at this word-processor sits a dot-matrix printer, which is designed to print letters on a page of paper. The letters are composed of tiny dots, rather like little atoms of ink. Suppose we removed from this machine the program that shapes the dots into alphabetical and numerical symbols. Suppose it was reduced to the point of simply spitting ink at the page. How long would we have to wait for the randomized dots to become an alphabet or a numerical system, for the letters and numbers to fall into the shape of words or equations, the words into sentences and literary works, the equations into mathematical theories?

The proposition is by now absurd, but let us loiter over it a bit longer to notice an assumption that frequently passes unnoticed in statements about probability. The question raised here makes reference to time twice. Once in the obvious form "how long?" But again in another less obvious way. The difference between random dots, formed letters, meaningful words, coherent sentences, reflective works of literature is also a question of time, in this instance *cultural time*. What a dot-matrix printer does is time-bound in this second deeper sense; it draws upon a singular progression in the course of which alphabets and number systems were laboriously created, vocabularies assembled, grammars refined. This we call *a history*. There are thousands of years of *unique and unrepeatable* cultural history embedded in this machine at my side. Even if the printer should, by chance, spray out the entire alphabet, it would not be recapitulating the history from which the alphabet derives. In that sense, it would not produce the "real" alphabet. The same is true, but even more dramatically, when we come to the constituent elements of nature at large; these too are time-bound creations that stand in the same sort of hierarchical relationship to one another that letters stand to words, words to grammar. The confidence scientists have in the creative and coordinative power of probability when it comes to complex systems and their evolution is really an article of faith, something one asserts despite the absence of any reasonable or even conceivable proof. The claims made for randomness are rhetorical devices, uttered in a tone intended to persuade us that it is supremely rational to believe in the possibility of anything to which the least quantum of probability can be assigned.

Some have suggested that once we reach the biological level, a new factor enters the scene that contributes to the creativity of blind chance: selection.[12] The argument runs like this: in the process of biological evolution, the randomness of genetic variation is disciplined by the selective force of the surrounding, ever-shifting environment, which is rather like the all-shaping invisible hand Adam Smith erroneously thought he saw working in the marketplace. Smith's economics was in fact the source from which Darwin drew his conviction in the powers of mindless selection. Creatures fit their environmental niche because, over the generations, those that did not were weeded out just as the market weeds out the incompetent and inferior. This again is taken to be an illustration of how nature can produce results that look designed but are not.

There is a problem here. Biological selection emerges some three-quarters of the way through the history of time. By then, there is a great deal more coherence to account for than the natural selection of flora and fauna on Earth. There are structures and systems, elements obeying regularities: laws of nature all in place. Though some scientists have toyed with the possibility that there might be some form of prebiotic evolution based on a nonbiological selective process, the notion approaches the preposterous. The idea of evolutionary selection is inextricably biological; it requires reproduction, adaptation, survival, extinction. None of the preconditions of natural selection can be accounted for by any sort of nonorganic selection; nonorganic things have no need to survive in order to continue being there. Selection in the state of nature can only act upon living organisms by way of competitive proliferation. There are no nonbiotic replicators other than mathematical simulations invented for computer programs. These are, of course, premeditated artifacts that were carefully designed to demonstrate that premeditated design does not exist in nature. Certainly there is no form of natural selection that resulted in the presence of such life-supporting necessities as the water on this globe or the operation of the carbon cycle.

Finally, the very process we call evolution by natural selection is in itself a system. It is exactly the way life might be installed on Earth with an eye to its survival by variation and adaptation. The element of indeterminacy involved in the random shuffling of genetic characteristics makes sense as part of such a system. As John Polkinghorne observes, the full potentiality of matter requires an element of built-in randomness in nature for its realization.

> To some . . . the role of chance is evidence of meaninglessness in the process of the world. To others of us it has seemed that the potentiality thereby exhibited as being inherent in the properties of matter—a potentiality which is explored through the shuffling operations of chance—is so remarkable as to constitute an insight of design present in the structure of the world.[13]

All of this is not to say that conventionally religious thinkers who state that God guides evolution (which is the predominant position taken by theologians since Darwin's day) are right; it is simply that they are not ludicrously wrong. They are asserting the possibility that something like intelligence seems to be involved in the evolutionary process. Similarly, the weakening position of materialism does not imply that the Vitalists, holists, organicists, etc., have always been right—simply that they may not have been as wholly wrong as their critics once thought.

While no new synthesis has yet arisen that can fill the many-sided role once played by mechanistic science, here is where contemporary science and all science-based philosophies would seem to stand as of the end of the twentieth century:

All discoveries in theoretical physics since the time of Planck, Curie, Bohr, Einstein, and Heisenberg have rendered the traditional concept of "matter" meaningless.

All discoveries related to the age of the universe and the rapidity with which matter, life, and mind have risen into existence have rendered large-scale references to randomness in nature meaningless.

All attempts to find some irreducibly simple "thing" that will serve as the building block of all other more complex things have failed. There are no simple things, even at the deep subatomic level.

Suppose then we are confronted with the following statement:

> In principle, I feel it should ultimately be possible to explain the abstract functions of the mind in terms of processes organized by the material substance of the brain.[14]

A generation ago, a remark like this would have passed as standard scientific parlance. Today, though the words were written in 1990, they are empty; the key terms ("explain," "organized," "material substance") have lost their once-unambiguous meaning.

If this does not define a philosophical crisis, then there has never been one.

Simply by raising these uncomfortable issues, we may have decisively parted company with mainstream science, which remains committed to the premise of a mindless universe. Old orthodoxies die hard. And yet mind does exist in that universe: the human mind. And in some sense science cannot fully express, that possibility was there from the outset. It was as much a part of the Big Bang as the first hydrogen atom, or the galactic clusters, or any enzyme. By its very commitment to the universality and comprehensiveness of its laws and principles, science must grant us continuity with that creative instant.

COSMIC COINCIDENCES AND THE FITNESS OF THE ENVIRONMENT

> We are only capable of understanding a universe in which beings capable of understanding it could evolve.
>
> The only kind of universe that is understandable is one that is able to evolve beings capable of understanding it.
>
> Fang Lizhi[15]

The closest that mainstream science has yet approached to granting life and mentality a transcendently qualitative distinction takes the form of the Anthropic Principle. A much-debated idea subject to a number of contrasting readings, all versions of the Anthropic Principle stem from a few basic, seemingly irrefutable premises. The quotation from physicist Fang Lizhi captures the paradoxical, yet common sensible flavor of the concept. Another way to state it might be:

A question cannot be answered until it has been asked.

A question cannot be asked until there is someone to ask it.

The words "until" and "someone" are carefully chosen. "Until" rather than "unless," because time is of the essence in the Anthropic Principle. There has come a time in the history of the universe when questions about the origin and nature of things can be asked: *our* time. And the questioning is being done not by a hypothetical agent, but by a "someone," namely ourselves, the result of a specific evolutionary unfolding. Simply by raising questions—any questions—we assert the existence of intelligence in the universe. The question may be a great one—"Why is everything the way it is?" But even greater than the question is the statement we make by the act of inquiry itself. *"We are here."* And our presence is based upon an astonishing number of delicately balanced physical coincidences.

Consider, for example, the all-important density parameter, which expresses the rate at which the universe must have expanded at the time of the Big Bang to achieve the present estimated density of matter. John Gribbin has called this the "finest of finely tuned cosmic coincidences"; he calculates that if the parameter had been different by the merest fraction ("a decimal point followed by sixty zeroes and a one"), galaxies could never have formed, and within them the stars that have generated every element besides hydrogen and helium.[16] But for just the "right" rate of expansion, life could never have come into existence on Earth and had the chance to evolve toward intelligence.

Among the first scientists to catalogue and ponder coincidences like these was the Harvard biochemist Lawrence Henderson. In two remarkable books written about the time of the First World War, Henderson mapped out the facts and laid the theoretical groundwork for the Anthropic Principle.[17] It is interesting to review his thought because of the clear sense of intellectual struggle it reflects. This is the work of a respected mainstream scientist who is groping his way beyond the prevailing paradigm into controversial territory. He was drawn to do so by what his science had taught him about the intricacy of living things. Henderson could no longer believe that complexity of this order had simply fallen into place by chance. While he never doubted that Darwinian natural selection plays its role in shaping species to their environment, he was convinced that there was a far greater factor at work. He called it "the fitness of the environment." Once it appears, life evolves within a set of complex physical and chemical parameters that seem *prepared* to receive it, support it, and nurture its further development. By way of natural selection, living things may fit themselves into their various habitats; but all the habitats are contained within a planetary environment that is already fit to sustain life. Henderson was especially impressed by the peculiar physical characteristics of water and of the elements that constitute the basis of organic chemistry. These are as delicately adapted to supporting life as any creature is to the environment those elements compose. Water, for example, has a number of unique qualities: its power to dissolve so many substances, its thermal conductivity, its surface tension, its capacity to expand when it reaches the point of freezing and so float in the form of ice on the surface of watery bodies. In all this, Henderson could not help but see a teleological factor at work that was oriented toward the goal of maintaining life.

Henderson was willing to range far afield in tracing this "preparation for the process of physical evolution." This is the point at which he broaches the Anthropic Principle. He implies that all time and all matter are implicated in the creation of life. In space, "an examination of the relationship between life and the environment . . . should rest upon a physico-chemical description of the whole universe"; and in time, "we must assume that the origin of environmental fitness lies at least as far back as the phenomena of the periodic system, at least as far back as the evolution of the elements, if they were ever evolved." This is a remarkable feat of theoretical anticipation. In Henderson's day, nothing was yet known of an expanding universe, let alone of the Big Bang and cosmic evolution. Still, he grounded his theory in the possibility that physical substance itself had a history that accounted for its birth and development. And from the beginning of that history matter was weaving the fitness of the total environment in which at some distant point life would arise to make a home in the cosmos—and perhaps not only on this planet. Henderson was convinced that many other organically evolved planets must exist.

So great was the harmony Henderson saw between the demands of life and the readiness of its environment to supply them that he was certain the result could not be accidental. There must be a "law capable of explaining such fitness of the very nature of things." That law, as he formulated it, is a "natural formative tendency" that acts on both "the organic and cosmic evolutionary processes." No sooner did Henderson produce the idea, however, than he hastened to designate it "metaphysical teleology" and to place it outside the boundaries of science. His respect for scientific orthodoxy was still so strong that it led him to segregate the teleological aspect of nature into a separate, transcendent realm that lies beyond mechanism. His solution is a kind of intellectual apartheid. He carefully sets aside everything that *results* from the formative tendency to be studied by conventional physical and chemical analysis. The tendency itself belongs "at the very origin of things, just before mechanism begins to act."

> In short, our new teleology cannot have originated in or through mechanism, but it is a necessary and preestablished associate of mechanism. Matter and energy have an original property, assuredly not by chance, which organizes the universe in space and time. . . . For the whole evolutionary process both cosmic and organic is one, and the biologist may now rightly regard the universe in its very essence as biocentric.

The "original property" that makes the universe biocentric at last retreats to the status of an Aristotelian prime mover forever beyond empirical investigation. But in contrast to older versions of the first cause, Henderson's variant draws upon everything he had learned about the complexity of natural systems. If it is a metaphysical premise, it is one that arises from the close scrutiny of physical nature.

Though Henderson struggled to make his theory compatible with scientific objectivity, he was perfectly aware that there was another, far more cautious way to view all the facts he had gathered. The fitness of the environment might be dismissed as nothing more than a *selection effect* taking place on a cosmic scale. Selection effects in science can be of many kinds. The apparatus can have a selective influence: study the world through rose-tinted glasses, and all will appear rosy. In the social sciences, the personality of the researcher may "select" for certain results. A sexist male psychologist who intimidates, infuriates, or alienates his female subjects may conclude that all women are man-haters. The very act of observation may bias the outcome. A biologist who keeps the lights on and sits staring constantly at a shy nocturnal creature may conclude that these animals never eat, move, or mate.

The same kinked result may occur in cosmology. One might contend that if physical-chemical conditions were not just as they are, nobody would be here to ask the question *why* in the first place. As far as we can say, this is the only possible configuration of things that permits inquiring, intelligent life to emerge. *Things simply happen to have turned out that way.* The only significance to the question "why are things as they are?" is that it tells us there is a kind of self-conscious matter that can ask it. Formulated in this way, the fitness of the environment becomes the "Weak" Anthropic Principle, as it has been called. "Weak" because it is devoid of teleology or any hint of guiding intelligence.

Or one can push the matter even further in the direction of paradox. Suppose there has been (or is now in some bafflingly parallel fashion) an infinite number of universes exhausting every possible arrangement of initial states, basic particles, fundamental force, and universal law: an infinite number of rolls of an infinite number of dice over an infinite amount of time. One version of this idea imagines this and other coexisting universes having the character of bubbles in some imaginary cosmic foam, each with its own configuration of forces. In this one bubble, the numbers came up as they did, and here we have intelligent observers, ourselves, to ask why things are as they are. But in some parallel or previous state of things, whatever universes might have existed were void of life, and so the question never arose. The cosmos next door is uninhabited; nobody at home.

Phrased in this way, the Anthropic Principle might be seen as the ultimate and irrefutable appeal to blind chance. It postulates that sooner or later, somewhere or another, our lucky number was bound to come up in much the same way that the thousand monkeys were bound to produce Shakespeare's works. It finds "enough time" for chance to work its nonmiraculous wonders by postulating an infinity of "other" universes, or other parts of the universe so hidden from our horizon of knowledge that the seeming specialness of the universe we know is irretrievably lost in the unimaginable vastness. The astrophysicist James Gunn has called this possibility "the ultimate Copernican idea": "not only are *we* of no conceivable consequence, but even our *universe* is of no conceivable consequence."[18] Speculation like this obviously takes the argument beyond all possibility of demonstration, and even beyond sensible discourse. What does it mean to say there have been an infinite number of universes? Would not all such universes be contained within a single, greater superuniverse? If that is the case, we are back at square one, faced with our own existence as a special, highly improbable event.

Such ideas have about them the character of a Zen Buddhist koan; they boggle the mind with contradiction. They seem to say, at one and the same time, we reside in a unique condition that is nothing special. Yet even in this almost flippant formulation, the Anthropic Principle echoes a certain subdued amazement at the very fact of intelligent being. It loiters to wonder at the fact that the universe has generated self-conscious life that survives within such a narrow zone of probabilities. If it took countless billions of Big Bangs and Big Crunches to produce this result, does that make the result any less remarkable? Could one not say that this was the point of it all? Brandon Carter (who first formulated the "Strong" Anthropic Principle) captures the paradox of the matter when he observes, "If our biological evolution had proceeded more slowly by a mere factor of two compared with the rate of thermonuclear evolution of the Sun, we would never have come into existence at all before it was too late."[19]

The Anthropic Principle has been called "sterile" and "far-fetched" by those who find they can accept it only in its weak version. But at least a few scientists cling to Henderson's conviction that there is more to the cosmic coincidences that support life than a mere selection effect. "The universe," as John Wheeler puts it, "is adapted to man."

Imagine a universe in which one or another of the fundamental dimensionless constants of physics is altered by a few percent one way or the other. Man could never come into being in such a universe. That is the central point of the Anthropic Principle. According to this principle, a life-giving factor lies at the center of the whole machinery and design of the world.[20]

Paul Davies also believes that "a hidden principle seems to be at work organizing the cosmos in a coherent way."

It is hard to resist the impression of something—some influence capable of transcending spacetime and the confinements of relativistic causality—possessing an overview of the entire cosmos at the instant of its creation, and manipulating all the causally disconnected parts to go bang with almost exactly the same vigor at the same time, and yet not so exactly coordinated as to preclude the small scale, slight irregularities that eventually formed the galaxies, and us.[21]

From this point of view, all the coincidences on which the Anthropic Principle is based would have had to be accounted for uniquely and precisely by the initial states following the Big Bang. We live not only off the thin layer of biosphere that clings like a film to this planet but off a precisely organized combination of cosmic conditions that has unfolded in just the right way over the past fifteen to twenty billion years. Life is rooted all the way down into the subtle continuum of matter-energy as it has developed since the beginning of time: rooted there as a seed is in the soil that brings it to fruition. George Seielstad has gone so far as to work a variation on the Anthropic Principle that brings to mind Bishop Berkeley's familiar conundrum. Is there sound without an ear to hear or an object without eyes to see, hands to touch? Seielstad gives the query a cosmic extension. He asks if conscious life might not be as fundamentally physical a feature of the universe as time or space. In its absence, nothing might exist; hence, the goal of a universe in search of reality is to generate observership. It is the presence of mind that "rescues a universe from nonentity by recognizing that universe's existence." In this sense, Seielstad suggests, nature has a "use" for us.[22]

The connection suggested here between life, mind, and matter is not the same as the conventional materialist position, which grants matter no history, no potentiality, but simply an ongoing, eternal sameness within which only accidental combinations are possible. The Anthropic Principle operates within a "postphysical" physics in which matter has been dematerialized to the point of taking on certain attributes of mind, for example the capacity to mature, to accumulate experience, to remember. In an Anthropic universe the material substance of nature is granted a narrative quality, a biographical dynamic that elevates substance to its present most complex state of expression in us—and in any other conscious life-forms that may exist in the universe. What is original in the Anthropic Principle is the fact that it places life and mind at the center of cosmology as matters to be accounted for and reckoned with. This inevitably leads, even on the part of those who would say it was merely a rhetorical convention, to a teleological mode of discourse: things are as they are *because* at the instant of creation they had to get *here,* to *us.* There was only one very restricted set of initial states that could do that, only one slender strain of conditions that could reach this end.

If the Anthropic Principle has done nothing more, it has freed some scientists to confess their honest amazement at the extraordinary combination of factors that lie at the basis of physical reality—and to ask, quite candidly, if these should in fact be regarded as "coincidences." This is the point at which science bridges with theology, or at least comes close to that without resorting to Sunday school language. Fred Hoyle, who has spoken of the improbabilities of organic chemistry as "a put-on job," observes that "a commonsense interpretation of the facts suggests that a superintellect has monkeyed with physics, as well as chemistry and biology."[23] His remark stems from his own remarkable contribution to the Anthropic Principle, a rare example of the principle being used predictively. In 1954, Hoyle made a calculation about the energy levels necessary for heavy nuclei to be amalgamated at the center of stars. His curiosity focused on carbon-12, without which life would not exist. But since life *does* exist, carbon-12 *must* have a certain chemical "resonance," which had not at the time been detected. Experiments were conducted that proved Hoyle's hypothesis to be correct. From that finding flows all later research in stellar nucleosynthesis: the creation of heavy elements in the interior of stars. The experiments also revealed that the existence of carbon in the universe is based on some finely tuned, highly surprising chemical conditions—coincidences of which Hoyle was prepared to say

> I do not believe that any scientist who examined the evidence would fail to draw the inference that the laws of nuclear physics have been deliberately designed with regard to the consequences they produce inside the stars. If this is so, then my apparently random quirks have become part of a deep-laid scheme. If not, then we are back again at a monstrous sequence of accidents.[24]

The Anthropic Principle still lacks a secure place in scientific theory; it may never find one. The science of Aristotle was comfortable with introducing "final cause" into its explanations, asking what things were *for* as well as how they behaved. Aristotle could deal in final causes without even giving much prominence to a creator god. But as Stephen Hawking points out, to speak this way "runs against the tide of the whole history of science." The Anthropic Principle in its strongest formulation "would claim that this whole vast construction exists simply for our sake. This is very hard to believe."[25] This is especially so when the principle is pressed to the verge of science fiction—as it has been by John Barrow and Frank Tipler in their Final Anthropic Principle. This holds that intelligent life, once it appears, has the destiny of surviving eternally, using its powers to reshape the entire universe. At the extreme, some more speculative cosmologists have toyed with the possibility of linking the Anthropic Principle with Teilhard de Chardin's "Omega point"—the culmination of the evolutionary process. In that grand climactic moment, Barrow and Tipler speculate:

> Life will have gained control of *all* matter and forces not only in a single universe, but in all the universes whose existence is logically possible; life will have spread into *all* spatial regions in all universes which could logically exist, and will have stored an infinite amount of information, including *all* bits of knowledge which it is logically possible to know. And this is the end. . . . A modern-day theologian might wish to say that the totality of life at the Omega Point is omnipotent, omnipresent, and omniscient![26]

Barrow and Tipler may only be flirting with such intoxicating teleological fantasies; yet their words are a telling measure of how far into the metaphysical twilight zone the Anthropic Principle invites the questing mind. Others are far from persuaded that such high spiritual hopes can be based on so flimsy a foundation.

Since the days of David Hume, philosophers have assembled an arsenal of weapons to refute the venerable argument from design. Hume himself, incidentally, intended that arsenal to be used not so much to disprove the existence of design as to refute the doctrines that Christians had built upon it. But as skillfully as Hume's arguments have been used to embarrass conventional Christian theology, those refutations have always had to fall back on some other, better way of explaining the order that science itself discovers in nature. That, as we have suggested here, has become more and more difficult to do as the appeal to chance has lost its cogency. Not unreasonably, then, some (like Hoyle, Wheeler, Barrow, and Tipler quoted here) have sought to salvage at least this much of the religious position: that the universe appears more and more as if it is grounded upon a nonphysical and ideational act of creation.

THE CREDULITY INDEX

At the heart of the issue we raise here there lies a question that the Anthropic Principle will not answer for us. It is an issue neither of fact nor of theory, but of *the will to believe.* "Blind faith" is a category we usually associate with religion, where it has been exercised to the point of affirming the absurd—and doing so proudly as a measure of one's devotion. But believing—whether in general principles, guiding values, or the statements of respected authorities—is one of the chief ways in which all of us find meaning in the world. Beliefs are frames of reference that help all of us, the pious and the skeptical alike, to sort through conflicting information and arrange what we take to be valid in a meaningful pattern.

Normally, on a wide range of matters, we share a consensus with others that relieves us of having to "believe" in any very strenuous meaning of the word. We trust to common sense or we accept what trusted experts tell us. At times, this reliable consensus may be called into question; at that point we realize that even what we once took to be reliable matters of fact may also be based on some underlying set of presumed truths. Does the sun go around the Earth or the Earth around the sun? Are aristocrats born with better blood than commoners? Is the papacy infallible in matters of faith and morals? Questions like these force us to ask why we believe what we believe. We may then discover that the roots of conviction lie buried in emotional needs, psychic quirks, intellectual pride and prejudice. Even disbelief can become a matter of impassioned ideological principle. People can develop just as arrogant a commitment to skepticism as to religious dogma. Though it sounds paradoxical, one can "believe" in *not* believing, in being militantly skeptical—at least toward other people's beliefs. And yet the skeptic who rejects religious faith may display no less a willingness to assent to nontheistic explanations that reach the point of absurdity. When it comes to the role of pure chance in nature, scientists have shown as great a capacity as the pious to become true believers, granting accident and coincidence a creative power once reserved only to God.

In science as well as religion there is a factor at work that might be called the "Credulity Index." Let us suppose we are seeking to understand how the apparent design of a natural phenomenon might have come into existence by pure chance. Science can make undirected randomness seem like a perfectly satisfactory explanation for some problems. For example, how are we to account for the fact that among mammalian species, the number of males and females born into the population remains in the long run exactly equal? Does this remarkably reliable result need to be explained by some sort of divine supervision? Once one understands the behavior of chromosomes in the genetic process, an explanation presents itself that allows chance alone to provide the result. We see that each newborn has a built-in fifty-fifty chance of turning out male or female.

But now take more complex matters. How did the intricate genetic coding that governs such matters as sexual physiology come into existence in the first place? How are we to account for the process of development by which all the parts of the fetus, whether male or female, grow in the right place at the right rate? Can we imagine so intricate a system arising from random chemical shuffling? When we turn to the study of any natural process that achieves this order of complexity, we find ourselves faced with a range of compounding improbabilities. Along a scale that stretches from the position taken by, say, a Christian teleologist like John Polkinghorne at one end to, say, an inveterate atheist like Jacques Monod at the other, at what point would you declare "I can't believe that"?

For those who care about such things, the Credulity Index might even be quantified. As we have seen in the previous pages, several scientists like Fred Hoyle and B. F. Salisbury have offered the sort of calculations we might use for the purpose. Their conclusions amount to astronomical levels of improbability. Similarly, when it comes to the spontaneous origin of life, Christian De Duve has worked out the combined probability of a series of hypothetical but necessary "biogenic steps" taking place in exactly the right order. The numbers that result "border on the miraculous: 10^{-300} for as few as one thousand consecutive steps." He concludes that "a multiple-step process that relies on one improbable event's following another is sure to abort sooner or later."[27]

But some would take issue with the word "sure." They would insist on saying that the series is "likely" to abort, but not certain; there is always some slender probability that things will turn out as in fact they have. Using much the same logic as the Anthropic Principle draws upon, believers like Monod might argue from first atheist principles: since there is no God, the existence of complex structures, life, and mind only goes to prove what randomness can produce. There is no way to reply to such a position; rather, what we are seeking here is that measure of personal conviction that is elicited when we find ourselves confronted with the complexity of natural systems as science has revealed them to us. Do we find it credible that what we see could be the result of chance? Those who can answer yes will see nothing more in the Anthropic Principle than its weak version. Those who cannot give that answer will choose the stronger versions of the principle.

Even the philosopher John Earman, who dismisses the Anthropic Principle as "an empty tease" and "muddled speculation," acknowledges the key role that is played in the hypothesis by simple "amazement at how 'finely tuned' the laws of nature are in favor of life." He recognizes that the principle was born of that amazement. Still, he rejects the Anthropic Principle as essentially an overblown selection effect. He asks us to "imagine the wonderment of a species of mud worms who discover that if the constant of thermometric conductivity of mud were different by a small percentage they would not be able to survive."[28]

But that objection misses the point. *Mind* is of the essence of the Anthropic Principle; it assumes the existence of rational self-consciousness. Mud worms may indeed have no idea how remarkable they are as a feature of the cosmos; they lack what it takes, which is self-awareness, curiosity, deductive intelligence. Nevertheless, the existence of any life-form deserves to be a subject of wonderment, even if the species in question is incapable of the emotion. The Anthropic Principle is based on the fact that *we* are here to supply precisely that capacity, and can stretch it even farther to marvel at our own ability to marvel. For some, including a growing number of scientists, the extraordinary "coincidences" that make the existence of that wondering species possible seem far beyond what undirected randomness can account for.

At this point in the history of the new cosmology, most scientists continue to rank high on the Credulity Index when it comes to believing that blind chance can be credited with the fact that there is "something rather than nothing" in the universe. Even so, in candid recognition of how marvelously structured that "something" is, their professional caution may be tinged with an abstract sort of astonishment. Charles Misner, who regards the question of design in the universe as a purely religious assumption, nevertheless agrees that "one should have some kind of respect and awe for the whole business. . . . It's very magnificent and shouldn't be taken for granted."[29]

". . . the whole business . . . very magnificent." The admission is so touchingly sincere, yet so heartbreakingly feeble. It is typical of a science that is trapped between old agnostic commitments and new-found wonders. Still, it represents a shift of the sensibilities. Over the past two decades, as its full implications have made themselves felt, the new cosmology has stimulated enormous outpouring of theologically tinged speculation, much of it by scientists. The word "God"—usually invoked as a tongue-in-cheek "ultimate"—has probably not appeared so frequently in the literature of science since the days of Newton and Voltaire.* But this opening toward religion is not the rule. Most scientists maintain a somewhat macho orthodoxy, still clinging to Russell's "unyielding despair," even pressing it toward unyielding hostility. Dennis Sciama's words are revealing . . . and saddening.

> Roughly speaking, what I like to say is that the universe is enormous—it is much stronger than you are—and your only way of hitting back at it is to understand it.[30]

Lawrence Henderson wisely recognized how great a part sensibility plays in science when he first speculated upon the fitness of the environment. He finished his study with the words of his friend and colleague, the evolutionary philosopher Josiah Royce.

---

*For a sampling of recent literature dealing with the interplay of science and religion, see the Appendix "God and Modern Cosmology" in this volume.

Look upon all these things descriptively, and you shall see nothing but matter moving instant after instant, each containing in its full description the necessity of passing over into the next. . . . But look at the whole appreciatively, historically, synthetically, as a musician listens to a symphony, as a spectator watches a drama. Now you shall seem to have seen in phenomenal form a story.

The capacity—or at least the willingness—to view nature with such an aesthetic eye remains as rare in science today as it was in Henderson's time. But, if anything, cosmology in the twentieth century has joined forces with Henderson's biochemistry to make the "drama" of life in the universe more convincing than ever for those who cannot believe in the omnipotence of chance.

There are those in the sciences who continue to question the findings and ideas to which the Anthropic Principle would seem to be inextricably bound: the Big Bang, cosmic evolution, cold dark matter, even the standard interpretation of the Doppler shift and background microwave radiation.[31] If any of these major pillars of the new cosmology should be seriously shaken, the Anthropic Principle might have to be scrapped. Science is, at last, an empirical pursuit. On the other hand, Errol Harris makes the point that, as long as the universe continues to reveal itself to careful scientific study as an emerging hierarchy of interlocking systems ("a scale of forms"), it will possess an order that challenges any paradigm grounded in chance, randomness, or accident.[32]

Only those who rank high on the Credulity Index will believe that mind in the cosmos results from the mindless shuffling of primordial stuff. Of course such credulity would be strengthened if the theory of the Big Bang should prove wrong and time should once again become available in a limitless supply. In an eternal or steady-state universe anything might eventually happen; as Ludwig Boltzmann once believed, every atom in the entire universe might finally fall into place with nothing more than gravitation at work in the process. Even then there would still be those who felt certain "there must be more to it than that."

As long as time is understood to have had a start, then in some sense that science cannot yet find the language to clarify, the mind I use to write these words, the mind you use to read them, have always been *there*, enfolded in the first radiation that bulged into nothingness to create space. The laws and patterns of development were there, the structure-making thrust of time was there to yield this end. Now when we look back across cosmic history to study the background radiation of deep space or the outrushing expansion of the farthest astronomical bodies, we draw upon a consciousness that was born out of that very process, and we take in what we see as an idea: the idea of the cosmos. It is there and we think it. We are that inherent possibility of mind realized at this horizon of time. Far from a marginal quirk in a dead void, mind has been there all along taking shape.

It was one of Plato's teachings that we are rational beings because we share some small, imperfect piece of the greater mind that shapes the cosmos. While this may still seem an odd way to view the scientific project, it is no longer quite so far-fetched. Perhaps all that stands in the way of such a concept is our lingering sense that intelligence must have a physical organ in which to reside. But this may be no more warranted than the notion, once so indubitable, that a wave cannot exist unless it acts within a material medium—water or ether. After all, the only waves human beings knew anything about until the late nineteenth century rode the ocean or the air. The word was taken from that commonplace experience as a metaphor and finally liberated from its physical matrix. Can we do the same with thought?

In the early years of this century, the physicist and philosopher James Jeans remarked that the universe looked to him a great deal "more like a great thought than like a great machine." Arthur Eddington, among the more pious of modern scientists, seconded the idea, suggesting that "the stuff of the world is mind-stuff." These were precocious insights. As our knowledge of system, structure, and process has advanced, the universe has taken on a quality that is more ideational than mechanistic. While anthropomorphic images of ideation may no longer serve for us, we are more and more coming to see nature as mind-like in its higher operations. Where materialism settled for simple interactions among disparate units, we now perceive a depth of organization and self-regulation, systems that were potentially there at the beginning of time and that reach so deep into nature that we may yet discover them functioning among the seemingly most chaotic phenomena. Where reductionism and materialism could find continuity between the human and the natural only at the physical level, we can now imagine a higher connection at the level of mentality. Mind-within and "Mind At Large" (to use Aldous Huxley's phrase) overlap in the perception of form and order. Science may soon be seen as the effort to think as the universe thinks.

For the general public, as well most scientists, the Anthropic Principle is apt to remain an abstract epistemological conundrum, intellectually intriguing but not the least emotionally engaging. It may embody a great deal of what is most exciting in contemporary cosmological thought; it stretches the mind ambitiously across the grand vista of cosmic evolution. But the fact that it can be assigned a "weak" interpretation and then dismissed as a curiosity undermines its place in both science and philosophy. We can, however, find an equally engaging scientific discovery closer to home, one that also holds great philosophical promise. The Gaia hypothesis, which we turn to next, opens the possibility of a new relationship between the human and nonhuman worlds—but does so with a great deal more mythological and aesthetic resonance than the Anthropic Principle. It invites us to see ourselves, not as "strangers and afraid in a world we never made," but as coevolutionary partners in the fate of a planet that life has helped create.

Five

◆

ANIMA MUNDI:
THE SEARCH FOR GAIA

THE MANY FACES OF MOTHER EARTH

Here are three texts widely separated in time and place. Read them as you might listen to variations on a musical theme. Taken together, they describe the long, strange career of the *anima mundi,* the great mothering soul of the world, as she has been celebrated in folklore, philosophy, and science.

> *Behold! Our Mother Earth is lying here.*
> *Behold! She gives of her fruitfulness.*
> *Truly her power she gives us.*
> *Give thanks to Mother Earth who lies here.*
>
> *Behold on Mother Earth the growing fields!*
> *Behold the promise of her fruitfulness!*
> *Truly her power she gives us.*
> *Give thanks to Mother Earth who lies here.*
>
> *(Pawnee tribal hymn, prehistoric)*

When the whole fabric of the World Soul had been finished to its maker's mind, he next began to fashion within the soul all that is bodily and brought the two together, fitting them center to center. And the soul being everywhere inwoven from the center to the outermost heaven and enveloping the heaven all round on the outside, revolving within its own limit, made a divine beginning of ceaseless and intelligent life for all time. (Plato, *The Timaeus*, 4th century B.C.)

The Earth holds together, its tissues cohere, and it has the look of a structure that really would make comprehensible sense if we only knew enough about it. From a little way off, photographed from, say, a satellite, it seems to be a kind of organism. Moreover, looked at over geologic time, it is plainly in the process of developing like an immense embryo. It is, for all its stupendous size and the numberless units and infinite variety of its life forms, coherent. Every tissue is dependent for its existence on other tissues. It is a creature, or if you want a more conventional, but less interesting term, it is a system. (Lewis Thomas, in *The New England Journal of Medicine*, 1978)

Myths like the *anima mundi* never die. They have the immortality of the phoenix. Reduced to ashes, they undergo miraculous transformations, returning to life with their essence intact. They might be described as a sort of ethereal gene passed from mind to mind across the centuries, mingling along the way, as all genetic traits do, with other cultural strains and intellectual mutations. Some myths have sufficient vitality to transcend the boundaries of history and ethnicity, finally to be absorbed into a permanent pool of images and teachings that become the common property of the human family. These are perhaps what Jung called "archetypes," the ageless furniture of the collective unconscious.

In the case of the *anima mundi,* we may be dealing with one of the oldest experiences of mankind, the spontaneous sense of dread and wonder primitive humans once felt in the presence of the Earth's majestic power. When they were no more than the first few representatives of a timid, scurrying new species in the world, these early humans must have greeted the immense creativity of nature with an awe that has since been lost to all but the poetic minority among us in the modern world. The Earth does go so powerfully and competently about her work, bringing forth the crops, ushering in the seasons, nurturing the many species that find their home in her vast body. She can, of course, also be a menacing giant; that too is remembered in myth and folklore. Many of the oldest rituals are acts of propitiation offered to a sometimes fierce and punishing divinity, an Earth who can be an angry mother as well as a bountiful one.

One of the oldest and best-known depictions we have of the Mother Goddess is a lumpy little carving nicknamed by anthropologists the Venus of Willensdorf. A blatantly sexual image, all breasts and buttocks, she was intended to embody female divinity as our hunting and gathering ancestors understood it. It is difficult to imagine that so primeval an image could outlast the culture of the hunting camp and the agrarian village, but so she did. Mother Earth is as universal a symbol as our race possesses, at home even in those societies that have moved on to more civilized ways. But at that point in her long history, as she leaves the land to enter the city, a significant change takes place. Her further adventures proceed along two contrasting, often conflicting routes, one religious, the other philosophical and eventually scientific. This bifurcation mirrors a deep psychological split that segregates emotion from intellect. And, as we will see, this dichotomy also corresponds to the masculine and feminine stereotypes that divide every culture. Along these lines, the transformations of the mother goddess underlie many tangled issues of sexual politics that have had to wait until our own time to be brought to the surface for discussion.

As late as the age of Plato and Aristotle, when Athens was the cosmopolitan hub of the ancient world, the Great Mother was still being worshipped in the groves and forests of Greece; but by then, her rites had become a religion of the oppressed, and principally of women, the notorious Bacchae who sought frenzied union with the mother deity through sacrificial ceremonies that were rumored to be obscene and bloody. Later still in the Roman–Hellenistic period, cults of Isis and *Magna Mater* flourished in the great cities. The urbanized versions of age-old agricultural rituals offered by the cults may have been tamer, but their promise was the same: the expiation of sin, the renewal of life, the merciful love of the divine mother. Once again the main adherents of these cults were women, who apparently found little gratification in the official, male-dominated pantheon of the civil religion. The worship of the mystery cults was more emotional and personal; there they could be in the presence of a divine woman who knew a mortal woman's needs.

All the while, subtler, or at least more circumspect minds were seeking a more sophisticated conception of the Earth Mother than such ecstatic mysteries rites provided. These were primarily male philosophers in whose speculation the image of the ancient fertility goddess was dissolving more and more into a metaphysical abstraction. She was becoming the *anima mundi,* the World Soul, who was understood to be the governing intelligence of the physical universe. We first meet her in this new identity in the works of Plato and his followers.[1]

THE COSMIC HOUSEKEEPER

Platonic cosmology begins in the realm of the incorporeal forms. The forms, like the theories of modern science, provide the intellectual substructure of reality. At their highest expression, they possess a mathematical (for Plato a specifically geometrical) purity. In this state of self-evident perfection, they stand as Plato's model for all knowledge. Logical, eternal, universal, the forms may be older than any of the gods. Without them, matter would be unintelligible if not wholly nonexistent, a realm of unrealized possibility.

It was inconceivable to Plato that the forms, in their pristine transcendence, could have any connection with the impermanent material world. How then do they take effect in nature? It was by way of answering this question that Plato conceived of the *anima mundi.* It—or rather "she" (the *anima* is always female)—serves as intermediary between the changeless being of the forms and the grubby turbulence of this lower world. *Anima mundi* is mentality embedded in physicality, that which bestows rational shape upon what would otherwise be chaos. She might be seen as the cosmic housekeeper performing a woman's traditional chores—cleaning, straightening up, arranging— on the largest scale.

One must look closely to find any recognizable trace of the voluptuous old Earth Mother in Plato's urbane metaphysical theories. In language and spirit, Plato takes us a long way from the vulgar, often savage rites with which the Great Goddess was still being honored by the bacchantes of his own day. But even in his philosophy, something of the ancient fertility mysteries survives. It can be found in his conviction that the whole of the cosmos is a single great organism, which, like all organisms, must be vitalized by a soul—an all-mothering female soul. For all his metaphysical elegance, Plato still clings to the animistic assumption that the order and purposiveness of nature must derive from the indwelling action of an intelligent being.

If Plato would have been loath to associate his philosophical abstractions with anything as grossly sensuous as the Mother Earth, I suspect modern scientists would be even more reluctant to see their work connected with an outlandish metaphysical construction like the *anima mundi*. Science prefers to keep its metaphysics muted, pretending that it works exclusively from physical facts and objective measurements. Nevertheless, it has borrowed heavily from this particular bit of Platonic cosmology. Without it, science as we know it may have never come to be. Why is there any point at all in trying to make sense of the world? Because we assume there is sense there to be found, an order that responds to the inquiring habits of the human mind. Our questions will be answered if they are properly formulated. It is the *anima mundi* that lays the foundations of all theory, teaching us that nature is a cosmos, an ordered whole. Behind its turbulent surface, it possesses a constant and intelligible structure. We inherit that premise from the Greek philosophers, and among them most importantly from Plato, who was one of the first to identify and elaborate mathematical precision as the golden key to the natural order of things.

Since Plato's time, the *anima mundi* has had a long and varied career in Western thought. Many of the richest speculations in our culture were first spun around this image. For example, Plato's disciple, the fourth century A.D. philosopher Plotinus, attributed the existence of time to the *anima mundi*. Plotinus was certain that the *anima mundi,* because she works below the level of pure, disembodied reason, cannot grasp eternity whole; she is too greatly burdened by the gross matter that she is charged with overseeing. So she does the best she can. She reads the all-at-onceness of the forms sequentially, spreading them out as one thing after another. By her mediation they become that succession of events we experience as time passing. Like Plato, Plotinus believed that time was "the moving image of eternity," the *anima mundi's* attempt to manifest the divine at a lower level of reality. There are at least a few lines of speculation in contemporary physics—theories of parallel universes—that echo this intriguing notion.

During the medieval period, the *anima mundi* was often forced to travel *incognita* through Christian Europe. She carried rather too much heretical luggage with her to be wholly respectable: memories of the old pagan deities, implications of animism. In the official view of the Church, nature was desacralized territory, created by God but apart from and wholly other than God. The *anima mundi* threatened to impart some aura of divinity to that profane and fallen realm. Some have seen in mainstream Christianity's entrenched hostility to nature worship one of the deep roots of our environmental crisis.[2] But while orthodoxy proscribed teachings that compromised the uniqueness and transcendence of God, many medieval philosophers entertained the possibility that the cosmos was populated by numerous intermediary beings—at the very least the angels and devils. Among these supernatural intelligences, one might still find the *anima mundi* who remained an especially lively concept for those who filtered their Christianity through Plato or Plotinus. Some Christian Platonists cautiously allowed her the status of a lesser deity, God's handmaiden in the running of the universe. Others assimilated her to the study of astrology, a subject not altogether banned by the Church of the Middle Ages. The *anima mundi* was frequently entrusted with mediating the influence of the stars in human affairs. The word "influence" is of astrological origin, designating what Newton and his mechanistic heirs could never fully endorse: action at a distance. In a universe that was understood to be mindless, how could such action be possible? No such problem presented itself in the quasi-animistic world of the *anima mundi*. There Mind At Large qualified as a force of nature.

At the same time, the split that had developed in Plato's time between the religious and philosophical identities of the Great Mother continued and deepened. While medieval theologians pondered the *anima mundi* as a metaphysical principle, cults of Hecate and the Earth Mother, sometimes assimilated to the Virgin Mary, continued to flourish in the countryside and in the remote villages, and once again primarily among women. In these surviving traces of the pagan mysteries, we can see the earliest adumbrations of European witchcraft, later to become a prime target for religious persecution.

THE ALCHEMICAL MISTRESS

But it was the alchemists, working along the shadowy fringes of medieval culture, who made the most consequential use of the *anima mundi*. For the "chemical philosophers," she became the reigning mistress of all natural forces. While all alchemists shared the goal of penetrating her secrets so that they might share her powers, they differed markedly about how this might best be done. One school, the spiritual alchemists, believed a harmonious communion with the *anima mundi* might only be achieved by prayerful purification of the soul. Their practice of the Great Work may have been a quasi-Christian, quasi-gnostic form of nature mysticism in which, it is worth noting, femininity played a significant if secondary role. In their quest for the mysterious philosopher's stone, those who regarded themselves as "high alchemists" frequently employed a female assistant, the *soror mystica* (the mystic sister) kept close at hand to remind them of "the eternal feminine."

But there was a second kind of alchemy—vulgar alchemy—from which we inherit the stereotype of the scruffy sorcerer in his dank and smoke-filled workshop, surrounded by bizarre apparatus, brewing up evil-smelling concoctions in bubbling vats and convoluted retorts, seeking the secrets of the material world in mixtures of mercury and mare's dung. There were such shady characters on the scene, some of them, like the uncanny Elizabethan magus John Dee, serving at the royal courts of Europe as astrologers or wizards promising godlike power and much gold to gullible potentates. Their ways with the *anima mundi* were very different. Their hope was that by occult means, they might harness the forces of the universe. High and vulgar alchemy represent two divergent approaches to the natural world, one based on respectful communion, the other on brute force. Of the two, it was vulgar alchemy that was destined to inherit the future, though in a highly unpredictable way. As comically antiquated as these alchemical "puffers" may seem to us now, in a crucial sense their activities foreshadow the coming scientific era. Those who identify alchemy as a kind of primitive forerunner of chemistry have vulgar alchemy in mind. And when it comes to underlying intentions, they are not far off the mark in seeing a connection between the two.

By the later Middle Ages, this profane species of alchemy had spun off into a school of "natural magic," which sought and often claimed to have acquired miraculous powers. Natural magic survived among learned men until the age of Newton, who was himself more than a merely dilettante alchemist; at his death, he left behind more unpublished papers dealing with alchemy and astrology than with physics. Natural magic was always careful to distinguish itself from demonic magic, which was prepared to traffic with devils and other unclean spirits. The latter was the magic of Doctor Faustus, a dangerous and forbidden pursuit. Natural magic worked more respectfully with the *anima mundi,* whose power was understood to be derived from God. This was the model that Francis Bacon adopted in the seventeenth century for what he called his "New Philosophy," the intellectual forerunner of modern science. In the eyes of the Renaissance Hermetic philosopher Cornelius Agrippa, natural magic may have been the "lowest realm of magic," but it was not for that reason to be despised, since it "teacheth the nature of those things which are in the world, searching and enquiring into their Causes, Effects, Times, Places, Fashions, Events, their whole, and Parts, also."[3]

This association of the *anima mundi* with alchemy and magic is a significant departure in Western history. Here we have pursuits aimed at mastering or at least effectively manipulating natural forces. The enterprise is pursued with conviction because it is based on the assumption that there is a responsive mind on the "other side" of nature whose sympathy we can elicit and whose secrets we can probe. For Plato, the *anima mundi* was an object of contemplation, there to be studied and described; but as the alchemists saw it, she is capable of being *used*— either gently by persuasion or forcibly. In either case, these are ways to tap her power. This represents an entirely new relationship between mankind and nature. It is not Plato's passive meditation, nor is it the supplication of folk religion. It is a willful act based upon the assumption of human superiority over all natural things and empowered by a form of knowledge that gives the ability to manipulate and exploit for immediate human purposes. Today we would refer to that knowledge as "know-how," the basis of technology. For the followers of Francis Bacon, this would soon become the only kind of knowledge worth pursuing. Bacon's writings bristle with references to nature that reveal suspicion, distrust, hostility. Nature, always portrayed as female, becomes an elusive antagonist who must be vexed, prodded, tortured into confessing her secrets. She must be stretched "on the rack" in "relentless interrogation." Mere figures of speech perhaps, but they come all too close to the persecution that church and state were literally visiting upon the Great Goddess's last disciples in Christian Europe: the witches (eighty percent of them estimated to be women) who were being hunted down and exterminated at the same time that modern science was being born.[4]

The sixteenth and seventeenth centuries are the watershed in the long life-story of the *anima mundi*. Educated minds of that era still took her existence seriously; in the many microcosmic diagrams that were drawn in that period, she is always prominently stationed just below God, just above the Earth, a regal and imposing presence in the cosmos (see Figure 2 in chapter 7). Prominent scientists still featured her in their theories. The English natural philosopher William Gilbert based his research into magnetism on the assumption that the lodestone was a piece of the *anima mundi* exerting her occult attraction on the metals of the Earth. Gilbert was among the most organic and anthropomorphic of the early scientists. He speaks defensively of the Earth against all who would dismiss her as lowly and brutish. For him, she is "the mother of us all"; her magnetic field is referred to as a "mind"; its attractive power is a form of "coition."[5] As late as the end of the eighteenth century, the pioneering geologist James Hutton was prepared to speak of the Earth as an organism possessing a metabolism.

But by that time, such notions had become quaint; the poetic metaphors and symbolic imagery that sustained the Great Goddess were wearing thin. A new metaphor was displacing her, that of the machine; and a new symbolism—mathematics—had become the principal language of science. For the next two centuries, she would go into deep eclipse in our culture. When she appeared once again, it would be in a very different guise—as a hypothesis developed out of abstruse studies in gas chromatography in a distinctly high tech setting. The language that ushered her back into the world would be that of modern chemistry and would involve many refined calculations; but she would retain one of her traditional names: Gaia.

THE GODDESS GOES HIGH TECH

In the mid-sixties, the chemist James Lovelock found himself part of a team at the Jet Propulsion Laboratory (JPL) whose assignment was to search for life on Mars. While the lab was committed to carrying out this project by way of robotic landing-craft, Lovelock came to the conclusion that this was not necessary. Life could be detected remotely and far more cheaply by long-range scrutiny of the planetary atmosphere, whether on Mars or on any other world. This thesis was connected with Lovelock's earlier invention of a technique called electron capture detection, which was able to identify faint traces of specified chemical substances. It is worth noting that this bit of technology was to have a significant though unforeseen political result. It allowed Lovelock to document the existence of faint toxic residues in the environment that could be traced back to the widespread use of agricultural pesticides. This discovery was the basis of Rachel Carson's research in *Silent Spring,* the book usually credited with launching the environmental movement. From the outset, Lovelock's work has been freighted with ecological significance.

Lovelock's assignment at JPL quickly flowered into an ambitious hypothesis regarding the relationship of atmosphere to biosphere. His contention was that living things, once they appeared on our planet, took charge of the global environment in a creative way. They became full-fledged partners in the shaping of the Earth, its rocks and water and soil. At that time, the orthodox view in the Earth sciences was that life was a passive dependent riding the planet, just fortunate enough to find a niche and survive. While it was recognized that biological systems might alter their immediate ecosystem in ways that produced significant local effects, such changes were not prominently regarded as globally significant, nor were they measured on a time-scale that comprehended the whole of geological history. Lovelock's hypothesis was a departure. It held that all species in the planetary biomass act symbiotically to enhance the total life-giving potentiality of its planet. The goal of life is global homeostasis, and toward this end it transforms the planet into what might be viewed as a single self-regulating organism. He summarized his thesis in this way:

> The Earth has remained a comfortable place for living organisms for the whole 3.5 billion years since life began, despite a 25 percent increase in the output of heat from the Sun. The atmosphere is an unstable mixture of reactive gases, yet its composition remains constant and breathable for long periods and for whoever happen to be the inhabitants. . . . living organisms have always, and actively, kept their planet fit for life. In contrast, conventional wisdom saw life as adapting to the otherwise inescapable physical and chemical changes of its environment. . . . The theory sees the evolution of the species of living organisms so closely coupled with the evolution of their physical and chemical environment that together they constitute a single and indivisible evolutionary process.[6]

This, in essence, is the hypothesis that Lovelock and his close collaborator Lynn Margulis were to call "Gaia." The idea significantly modifies the central Darwinian paradigm of modern biology. Competition—natural selection at the species level—becomes much less important than the overall integration of living things within a symbiotic global network. The basic unit of evolutionary survival becomes the biomass as a whole, which may select species for their capacity to enhance the liveability of the planet.

Gaia has been a suspicious character since Lovelock and Margulis first introduced her to the scientific community. For one thing, Gaia is a big hypothesis, an attempt to synthesize several disciplines—always a risky enterprise in the highly territorial academic world. But more provocatively, the theory is saturated with teleological and anthropomorphic implications. If there is one signal that will raise the collective hackles (and the guard) of professional science, it is any hint of intentionality. The great commandment of the guild is "Thou shalt not endow nature with goals, purposes, sentience, values," except where human beings are concerned—though the more extreme Behaviorists might refuse even that minimal concession. Nothing makes modern science more distinctively *modern* than its commitment to the image of a mindless and impersonal universe. The whole sport in science since the days of Galileo and Newton has been to find clever ways to dispel the illusion of purpose in nature.

Yet in Gaia we have a hypothesis that, for all its mathematical precision, seems bent on smuggling a barely disguised version of the *anima mundi* back into polite scientific society. The effort has met strong opposition. In a typical response, one critic characterized Gaia as "pseudoscientific myth-making," an "almost medieval" idea that rings of "obscurantism, wishful thinking and mysticism."7 The charge is largely valid. The hypothesis does echo elements of mysticism and medieval thought. For that very reason no one proved to be more uneasy with this seeming indiscretion than Lovelock and Margulis themselves. Initially, Lovelock was at great pains to explain that Gaia is *merely* a metaphor—as if metaphor were not a powerful agency of the mind, one of our most precious ways of understanding the world, and therefore perhaps related to whatever we take the "truth" to be. Challenged or stung by the criticism of his colleagues, he sought to find some chance-based, nonintentional mechanism to explain the actions of Gaia. The effort was an understandable bid to stay in the good graces of the scientific community; but what Lovelock was up against is a profound issue in the rhetoric, and ultimately the metaphysics of science. The issue has to do with the increasingly large role that *systems* have come to play in our understanding of the universe.

"MERE" METAPHORS, "REAL" MECHANISMS

In later chapters we will have more to say about the place of systems in nature and in scientific theory. Here let us simply note that systems, and especially a system as vast as Gaia, are all but impossible to discuss without employing purposive language. One asks *why* something behaves as it does within a system, and the answer automatically comes out "in order to." The parts within a system act as if they had a sense of the whole. We have no other intelligible way to discuss such matters. Critics might argue that we are committing the empathic fallacy by reading intentionality into nature. They overlook the possibility that, first of all, nature has read intentionality into us. We see what it was given to us to see.

Scientists often betray their awareness of this issue by affecting a self-consciously flippant tone when they resort to an intentional mode of discourse—a sort of wised-up wink and nod that is meant to dispel any assumption that they mean what they seem to be saying. At a certain level of description it might seem there is often nothing more to the matter than rhetorical convenience. For example, my doctor once explained a blood test for cholesterol to me by describing some lipids (the HDLs) as "the good guys" and others (the LDLs) as "the bad guys." He was clearly joking. Yet if he had sought to describe the body's remarkable system for regulating its need for cholesterol, he might have found himself just as immersed in purposive references, but with less awareness of the fact. That is what we see in this passage from a standard survey of the New Biology of the mid-sixties. I choose the book because its overall orientation is highly mechanistic and reductionistic, brimming with the newly adopted imagery of data-processing—flow-charts, feedback loops, information transfer—that has since become commonplace in the field of genetics.

So before it can even begin to act on its external environment, the cell, or the living animal, *has to provide* the mechanisms whereby, first, *it can protect itself* against dissolution and destruction by the outside world, and, second, *it can continuously resynthesize its more complex parts* from much simpler molecules. . . . How does *the cell set about achieving* the large number of highly complex chemical reactions necessary for the synthesis of macromolecules? [italics added][8]

The cell must "provide," it "protects itself," it "resynthesizes its more complex parts," "it sets about." . . . In later passages, the author speaks of enzymes that "choose," "require," "recognize," "discriminate," "refuse." "Other enzymes are slightly more choosey," he tells us, "and demand that at least one half of the molecules they act on be determined." Even in an essay whose specific purpose is to refute the existence of designing intelligence in nature, one comes upon phrases like "evolution . . . is a tinkerer, banging into shape, with minimal change, anything that works."[9] No doubt a scientist asked to explain this curiously anthropomorphic choice of words would pass it off as another "mere" metaphor. Very well, eliminate the metaphors. What other words will do the job? And how do scientists themselves, in the privacy of their own imagination, really make sense of what the enzyme is observed to be doing?

At times it is almost comic to see scientists struggling with the problem of purposiveness in nature, trying to pretend it is not there even while it infuses every word they say. Nobody could be more militant in this regard than the English biologist Richard Dawkins, who must be the last crusading village atheist left in the scientific community. Dawkins has made a career of defending Darwinian orthodoxy against a host of unspecified religious antagonists. But how does he go about it? By inventing the surrealistic notion that there exist "selfish genes" that drive the evolutionary process forward. His thesis teems with anthropomorphic characterizations of genes in action that even old Bishop Wilberforce would have blushed to employ in taking issue with Charles Darwin himself. At various points, Dawkins likens his personified genes to gamblers, rivals, companions, architects, oarsmen, master programmers, even Chicago gangsters. They "instruct," "anticipate," "give advice"; they are said to be "gregarious," "struggling," and of course "selfish." A presentation meant to eradicate the "apparent purposiveness" of evolutionary adaptation and genetic structure brims with phrases like "building a leg is a multi-gene cooperative activity." Finally Dawkins reminds us that "we must not think of genes as conscious, purposeful agents"; all this has been a "convenient short-hand," a mere "fruitful metaphor." Yet remove the metaphors and there is no thesis.[10]

Or consider a passage like this, which personifies pieces and parts of the human brain:

> The amygdala scrutinizes information perceived for its emotional weight. It notes that a growl may spell danger. If an emotional response is warranted, the amygdala sends signals along the numerous nerve cell pathways that connect it to other brain structures, which can then generate the gamut of emotional reactions such as fear, anxiety or joy.[11]

Why do we sense that there is something misconceived in statements like this—as there is in Dawkins's fantasy about gangster genes? Only because the explanation, having necessarily invoked purpose to make sense of the process being studied, then locates it at the wrong level: in the parts rather than in the whole. The description fails to recognize the comprehensive system (the whole organism, the whole person) within which the gene or the brain structure functions and to which the activity of the constituent parts is subordinated. A sensible intro-duction of purpose must relate to the correct context; that is where we would expect to find the intentional act that coordinates the parts toward some end. For some processes, like the nucleosynthesis of heavy elements in the interior of stars, that governing context may be as large as the universe—or at least, as we have seen, that is how the matter would be viewed by those who choose the "strong" interpreta-tion of the Anthropic Principle.

The inconsistency one sees in efforts like those of Dawkins that both assert and deny the existence of purpose in nature, goes back to Dar-win's own day. At the time there were many biologists who saw natural selection as (in the words of one contemporary) "one of the greatest advances in the world of thought" precisely because it brought closer "the possibility, ever so distant, of banishing from nature its seeming purpose, and putting a blind necessity everywhere in place of final cause." How mercifully this would ease "the torment of the intellect" that comes of having to speak of "functions, performances, actions, and purposes of the organs."[12] Yet Darwin himself again and again resorted to intentional metaphors to explain his theory. His hope was always that he could wave aside the implications of his language. "For brevity's sake I sometimes speak of natural selection as an intelligent power. . . . I have, also, often personified the word Nature; for I have found it difficult to avoid this ambiguity."[13] Darwin was especially hard-pressed to find his way around personification when it came to what he called "organs of extreme perfection" like the eye. Here is the curious way he addressed the problem.

> To suppose that the eye with all its inimitable contrivances for adjusting the focus to different distances, for admitting different amounts of light, and for the correction of spherical and chromatic aberration, could have been formed by natural selection, seems, I freely confess, absurd in the highest degree.

Still, he perseveres in the effort, suggesting that

> we must suppose that there is a power, represented by natural selection always intently watching each slight alteration in the transparent layers [of the primitive eye] and carefully preserving each which, in any way or degree, tends to produce a distincter image. Let this process go on for millions of years; and during each year on millions of individuals of many kinds; and may we not believe that a living optical instrument might thus be formed as superior to one of glass, as the works of the Creator are to those of man?[14]

"A power . . . always intently watching. . . ." The anthropomorphic reference and the only partially rhetorical question at the end of the passage are clear signs that the theory is straining to find a suitably impersonal explanation for a central fact of nature: the seemingly designed character of organic forms.

In choosing the name "Gaia" for their theory, Lovelock and Margulis were only giving full-blown theoretical imagery to a rhetorical habit that remains as entrenched as ever in biology. But for a long while, Lovelock was far from comfortable about that choice. He suggested the name Gaia was chosen merely as a device for communicating with the lay public without the need to employ "precise but esoteric language." As of 1979 he was at great pains to say of one of his books there are passages . . . which may read as if infected with the twin blights of anthropomorphism and teleology. . . . I have frequently used Gaia as a shorthand for the hypothesis itself. . . . Occasionally it has been difficult, without excessive circumlocution, to avoid talking of Gaia as if she were known to be sentient. This is meant no more seriously than is the appellation "she" when given to a ship by those who sail in her.[15]

Despite these disclaimers, not even Lovelock and Margulis could possibly make sense of their own theory, let alone communicate it to anybody else, without reference to goals, purposes, intentions. Nothing that is taken to be "self-regulating" can be freed of these attributes. Gaia seen as an active intelligence is emphatically *not* a metaphor. She is the very substance of the idea. A metaphor, let us remember, is a word that stands for other words. It should be possible to say what the other words are; and those words, once given, should communicate our meaning as clearly or even more so. Phrases like "body politic" and "head of state" are easily replaced by any number of possibilities. But when Margulis quite casually tells us that "prokaryotes tapped into an energy source" or that "life regulates the temperature of the planet," what "other words" could she use that conveyed her meaning more directly and clearly?[16] Would she substitute chemical formulae? She is discussing a process that serves to achieve a result; even if the process involves trial and error or flailing about—as our own human activities often do—the result connects sensibly with the activity *only* if we assume some purposive link between them. The one language we have for that is based on intentional action.

Rather than reading purposiveness *out* of Gaia, we might better try to find ways to read purposiveness *beyond* human conduct. Scientists could then avoid the "blight" of anthropomorphism (or more properly in this case *gynemorphism*, since Gaia continues to be seen as female) by conceiving of intelligence in something other than anthropomorphic terms. Their real problem is that they have found no place to locate mind in the cosmos except inside a human skull. Is it not odd that everything science finds inside the human frame, all the molecular building blocks, all the electrochemical vibrations, all the energy fields, are understood to penetrate us and extend beyond the boundaries of the body? They got "in" from "outside." Everything that is, except the mind. That exists nowhere but in the gray matter we carry about in our heads.

There are many fascinating issues connected with the question of scientific rhetoric that Lovelock raises. Why, for example, is the commonplace use of the word "mechanism" in science not also seen as *merely* metaphorical? There are after all no "mechanisms" in nature, not as we know them from the devices that this word was created to designate. And insofar as we think there are, why are mechanisms not "blighted" by implications of anthropomorphism and teleology? We know of no machines that were not created by human beings and endowed by their makers with purposes. It would seem that by invoking the connotation of hardware, nuts and bolts, engines and motors, the word "mechanism" sounds more securely physical and so has been granted a special nonmetaphorical status. Yet, if anything, a metaphor like mechanism simply places the same problems that a personified Gaia raises at one remove. It leaves us to ask, Who made the mechanisms that account for the coherence of the universe?

AN AUTOPOIETIC GAIAN WORLD

Gaia is a big system. Unless we discover life on other worlds, she is as large a superorganism as we will ever know. But the symbiotic tendency she displays in maintaining global homeostasis may extend to life on the smallest scale. We now have good reason to believe that symbiosis is one of the original and most successful strategies of evolution. Lynn Margulis has suggested that, like the planetary patina at large, every living thing may be a biological composite made up of many symbiotic entities that have joined together over the eons. All organisms are, in her view, "metabolically complex communities of a multitude of tightly organized beings." Even the ancient bacteria, once regarded as the simplest of living things, are now thought to have become systems within systems. A similar confederation of preexisting organisms may be the origin of the plastids and mitochondria in our cells. They are the descendants of bacteria that were once independent entities, but which relinquished that status in a way that allowed subsequent living things to become complex autopoietic (self-regulating) oxygen-breathing creatures. As Margulis puts it, resorting to unabashedly political personification, the first protists "cooperated and centralized, and in doing so formed a new kind of cellular government."[17]

There seems no other way to explain the suddenness with which evolution made the transition from the unicellular to the eukaryotic (many-celled) level and beyond.

Although Margulis has been as professionally cautious as Lovelock in endorsing any teleological readings of Gaia that might challenge Darwinian orthodoxy, she sees her research in "microbial community biology" as a significant theoretical departure. Standard biology regards evolution as largely a matter of passive adaptation by lucky individuals that are selected by the ever-shifting environment. From the symbiotic point of view, there are no "individuals"—except perhaps the bacteria. All beings are "intrinsically communities."[18]

At the basis of the controversy between neo-Darwinism and what Margulis calls the "autopoietic Gaian" view of nature, there lies a bone of theoretical contention that dates well back into the nineteenth century. There were always biologists and philosophers who believed that the evolutionary process was more intricate than Darwinian natural selection allowed for. Darwin, reviewing the origins of his theory, identified Thomas Malthus's law of population as the catalyst that had acted upon his years of observation in the field to produce the idea of natural selection. Malthus's famous essay was not a biological treatise at all, but an item of economic theory (if not social propaganda) written under the influence of the new school of classical economics. Malthus sought to delineate the mechanism that governed the growth and decline of population as a factor in the marketplace. His not-so-hidden agenda included his dismal moral views on sexuality. Writing as a clergyman, he took the occasion to lash out at the "vice" of the working class (meaning too much sex) and the promiscuity of women. In a treatise that was destined to label classical economics the "gloomy science," Malthus concluded that the proletariat had nobody but itself to blame for its misery. By the laws of the free market, only hard work, thrift, and abstinence could improve the condition of the poor.

All the harsh, competitive assumptions of Malthus and the Manchester School got mixed into the foundations of Darwinian biology. Far from reading the ethos of the jungle into civilized society, Darwin read the ethos of industrial capitalism into the jungle, concluding that all life had to be what it had become in the early milltowns: a vicious "struggle for existence."

Those who clung to a more romantically sentimental and holistic view of nature were never comfortable with this bellicose model of the organic world. They were more impressed by the spontaneous harmony one also sees in nature, none more so than the Russian naturalist and political philosopher Prince Peter Kropotkin, who concluded that there is at least as much cooperation within and between species as bloody conflict. Kropotkin was among the foremost critics of Darwinism at the height of its intellectual dominance. He was convinced that evolution had more to do with complex systems of cooperation within and between species—"mutual aid" as he called it—than with competition between individuals. Such systems were good for society, good for the land, and good for the soul. For that matter, even the action of predators like the wolf and lion can be seen as a ruggedly efficient way of culling and strengthening their prey. The contribution that Kropotkin made to evolutionary theory by this emphasis upon intraspecies cooperation is now generally recognized. Kropotkin would have considered Margulis's research in cellular symbiosis and the coevolution of microbial communities as a vindication of his theory of animal sociability carried to the primordial level of life. Darwin himself eventually recognized that factors like beauty among the birds may play as great a part in enhancing the prospects of proliferation as ruthless predation. Now it appears that even individual beings may be, in their genetic constitution, what Margulis calls "diversities of co-evolving associates."

To be sure, symbiotic evolutionary processes can, with enough effort, be assimilated to natural selection as the sort of advantage that favors survival and becomes part of inheritance. But all the images and metaphors that surround such a perception are bound to be different from those that have for so long characterized standard biology. As is so often the case in science, the tone of the observation, the rhetorical texture of the theory, make all the difference. Neo-Darwinism emphasizes a mechanistic simplicity in which life is passive and for the most part in peril, caught between the random shuffling of genes and fortuitous changes in the environment. One tracks the evolutionary course by way of discrete units of adaptive advantage or disadvantage. The overall, cooperative upbuilding of ecosystems, some within the cell itself, is absent. On the other hand, the autopoietic Gaian view requires a shift from the chaotic, random clashing of atomized individuals and "selfish genes" to intricate and subtle forms of balance, harmony, cooperation. The evolutionary process becomes deeply systematic; on a global scale, it becomes the creatively teleological adjustment of Gaia, nurturing all her children, weaving them into the community of life.[19]

LEARNING FROM GAIA

We will return to the greater philosophical questions raised by Gaian biology in the next chapter, especially those that have to do with the place of systems in our understanding of nature. Here, let us simply conclude by taking the hypothesis at its most cautious, minimal level. Let us define it as nonmythologically as possible as a natural cybernetic system that maintains a life-supporting condition of homeostasis on the planet. Lovelock tells us that if he had not fancifully called his hypothesis Gaia, he might have come up with something like "Biocybernetic Universal System Tendency"—a title whose acronym (BUST) preserves a certain motherly connotation. By any other name, it still remains a superorganic system, and within it our species finds its place.

But what exactly is that place? Presumably we remain as subject to its techniques of adjustment and control as the rest of nature—animal, vegetable, and mineral. Yet we are left to wonder, how does that system cope with an organism like us? How does it monitor and maneuver our conduct? It cannot be through the simple tropisms, chemical signals, and instinctual ties that suffice to influence other creatures. With us these would not be a reliable means of communication. Between us and our surviving instincts there intervenes the ambivalent barrier of culture, the product of our free-wheeling intelligence, the glory and the curse of our species. Our very survival has come to depend upon our ability to delay, even ignore the promptings of immediate impulse and physical necessity. Before we act or react, we mull things over, entertain alternatives, shuffle through a selection of scenarios. We catch the world in a net of language and play with the many possibilities the future may hold in store.

Then, perhaps, where human beings are concerned, the great biocybernetic system works through that very intelligence, relying on the fact that we are the one creature within the global feedback loop that can analyze its conditions of life. Is it possible that Lovelock and Margulis, endowing their research with an urgency that has brought so much timely attention to the plight of the biosphere, have drawn the inspiration and the imagery of their hypothesis from the subtle prompting of Gaia? But again, a connection that works through scientific intellect, while important, is unreliable. For our species as a whole, it would require a collective expertise and unanimous certainty about the environmental facts that may take too long coming. Intelligence—the habit of wait-and-see, think-it-over, look-before-you-leap—may actually work against us at the fateful moment, influencing us to argue the facts, pick at details, debate the way forward until it is too late. Moreover, there is an obvious lack of dependable rapport between our rationality and our emotional energy; the latter does not always "listen to reason." Not infrequently, psychotic distortions intervene to play their part, at times driving individuals to suicide and societies toward calamity.

How then does the great biospheric feedback system instruct and counsel us, its uniquely culture-bound, uniquely psychological species?

The answer may lie in a development that has not been entirely welcomed by Gaia's strictly scientific proponents. Lovelock and Margulis may have managed to raise the hackles of many of their colleagues; but they have found an avid audience among environmentalists and other political activists outside the scientific community. This has sometimes been more troubling for them than critical resistance within their profession. The world environmental movement is a varied affair; many contingents march beneath its banner. Among these are groups that are prepared to embrace Gaia as the rebirth of paganism in our time; others who take her as a basis for nature mysticism, others who see her as an ally in the politics of ecofeminism. The pronouncements and activities of these followers, to which we will return in later chapters, may be a long way from anything a practicing scientist had in mind. Yet here are those who have given the hypothesis, or at least their understanding of it, the emotional and moral force it may need to become politically relevant.

The situation is not without precedent. This is exactly what happened to Newtonian physics in the eighteenth century when it became identified with the politics of liberal democracy; it is what happened to Darwinian biology when it was adopted by Social Darwinists and by Marxists as proof of the value of historical struggle. Was Thomas Jefferson violating true science when he construed the laws of nature as a sanction for natural rights? Was he undermining mathematical rationality when he invoked the self-evident character of the right to life and liberty? Or were these essentially defensible efforts to connect the natural and human worlds in a way that prescribes value? Scientists may feel anguished to see their carefully defined work taken up by rank amateurs and applied to the political realm; yet it is all but inevitable that this will happen. It is one of the glories of science that it can give back to the culture from which it grows.

This is not to say that anything goes. While every extension of a scientific idea into ethics or politics may bend the idea a bit, there is a difference between reasonably knowledgeable interpretations and gross distortions. In my own view, the decisive factor in any adoption of a scientific idea for political purposes is the moral quality of the effort. The use Voltaire, Jefferson, Paine made of Newtonian science was humane and liberating. It used science to ennoble. The use imperialists and fascists made of Darwin was brutal and murderous. It degraded the idea.

In the case of Gaia's environmental crusaders, the cause and the methods have by and large struck me as brave, compassionate, and life-enhancing. There is often a poetry to ecological politics, a humble and loving appeal to the great and lordly beasts, to the beauty of the land, to the magnificence of this planet. There has even been an effort to rescue the endangered aboriginal cultures of mankind whose teachings can be construed as the original hymn to Gaia. "Green religion" builds community; it embraces variety; it teaches the solidarity of living things. It would seem little short of churlish to reject all this because it rhapsodizes certain aspects of the hypothesis.

While Lovelock has not endorsed the many poetic and religious extensions that have grown up around Gaia, he has in later writings somewhat mellowed toward those who take these liberties. He describes his own outlook as a "positive agnosticism" that prefers to keep the hypothesis modest and "manageable." Though he cannot see Gaia as "sentient," he admits to finding it "satisfying" that the theory has found a spiritual as well as a scientific reading. A generous concession for a professional scientist to make. There may, however, be more to these developments than he recognizes. A hypothesis that contends that the great biofeedback system of planet Earth acts upon all its cargo of life in ways that seek homeostasis must at some point weigh the possibility that *Gaian politics, including its ecofeminist and mystic "extremes," is among the ways such action finds expression in our species.* The poetic license and religious fervor of these efforts may even be among the planet's most effective means of self-defense—more effective than the cold edge of mathematics or the weight of fact. Gaia was after all born of wonder and ecstasy.

On the other hand, what may have been overlooked by the Gaians in their often sentimental depiction of the Goddess is the dark side of the matriarchal tradition. Not all Earth Mothers are endowed with loving kindness and mercy; some, like Kali and Hecate, are hard, often chastising parents. Sekhmet, the terrible lion-headed goddess of Egypt, once sought to devour the entire human race for its disobedience. Lovelock has warned of that. Gaia is, in his view, "stern and tough, always keeping the world warm and comfortable for those who obey the rules, but ruthless in her destruction of those who transgress."[20]

The Nobel laureate Joshua Lederberg warns us of much the same thing when he observes that we have no guarantee evolution will balance out in our favor. It is, in fact, an almost species chauvinist pride that blinds us to a more dire possibility.

> Human intelligence, culture, and technology have left all other plant and animal species out of the competition. . . . But we have too many illusions that we can, by writ, govern the remaining kingdoms, the microbes, that remain our competitors of last resort for dominion of the planet. The bacteria and viruses know nothing of national sovereignties. In that natural evolutionary competition, there is no guarantee that we will find ourselves the survivor.[21]

If the Earth is a self-adjusting organism, its adaptive power may be that of a metabolic system: efficient, impersonal, crushingly powerful. That is frequently the picture I form when I try to give some mythical embodiment to the Gaia hypothesis. If there is an integrating intelligence at work in the planet all around me, I sense it is not a human intelligence. It is at once something greater and more primal, a wisdom like that of the body in its stubborn will to pursue the tasks that physical survival demands. In the classic metaphysical use of the word, this is what "soul" meant: the principle of bodily life that only God could create, but which functioned at some lower level than the demands of mind or spirit. In Latin *anima* suggests a closer connection with "animality" (instinct) than intellect.

That may be what Gaia, the World Soul, is in her relationship to her most highly evolved creation. If so, in her brute determination to defend the variety and quantity of life she carries, she may at some point decide that this so-clever human species is too troublesome a hazard to maintain. The adjustment she may then see fit to make will be far from gentle.

Six

———◆———

WHERE GOD USED TO BE
Deep Systems and the New Deism

"But is there something where God used to be?"

Iris Murdoch, *The Message to the Planet*

THE WHOLE IS EQUAL TO . . . ?

In their more adventurous interpretations, the Gaia hypothesis and the Anthropic Principle are unlikely to find acceptance in the scientific mainstream anytime in the near future. Not many scientists are apt to agree that the Earth is a superorganism in anything more than a metaphorical sense; as we have seen, some find even the metaphor troubling. As for the Anthropic Principle, it is likely to remain an epistemological curiosity in astronomy textbooks. If it is noted at all, it will probably be in its weakest version. And even then, it may be cited only for cautionary purposes as the ultimate example of the selection effect in action: astronomers should not be surprised to discover that they live in a universe that makes the existence of astronomers possible.

Yet, whatever the fate of these two ideas, both stem from an indisputably solid and irreversible development in modern science. Both are efforts to do ambitious theoretical justice to the astonishing interplay of improbable conditions and forces that support life and mind in the universe. Thanks to the ingenious techniques and instruments of science, we now know that the biography of the universe is written in the language of ordered complexity. Insofar as we express our wonder at the magnificence of nature by speaking of "miracles" and "mysteries," our religious tradition—at least in its mainstream—pales beside what modern science has taught us such terms can mean

Given what we now know about the many-layered complexity of nature, it is startling to realize how embarrassingly primitive the explanatory devices of Western science were only as recently as the turn of the twentieth century. In seeking to understand the universe, biologists as well as physicists were making do with a pitifully small collection of objects and principles. Writing in 1900, the influential scientist-philosopher Ernest Haeckel thought he needed only two items to furnish the universe: atoms and ether. Atoms were then still defined as "homogeneous, infinitesimal, distinct particles, which are incapable of further analysis." The ether that surrounded the atoms was an equally irreducible, equally physical substance. Ether was "imponderable matter . . . an extremely attenuated medium filling the whole of space." The interaction of these two entities explained all things. In so simple a universe there was no need to deal with systemic self-regulation, let alone to invoke creative intelligence. Chemistry was a linear extension of physics; biology was a combination of the two. Even the soul was nothing more than a cluster of "psychoplasm . . . a body of the group we call protoplasmic bodies, the albuminoid, carbon-combinations which are at the root of all vital processes."

The economy of this worldview was, in Haeckel's eyes, its principal validation. It stripped the world down to its bare philosophical essentials. "Our monistic view . . . marks the highest intellectual progress, in that it definitely rules out the three central dogmas of metaphysics: God, freedom, and immortality. In assigning mechanical causes to phenomena everywhere, the law of substance comes into line with the universal law of causality." This, Haeckel was convinced, is "the steady, immovable pole-star whose light falls on our path through the dark labyrinth of the countless separate phenomena."[1]

Haeckel's barebones cosmology drew its inspiration from Darwin, who, he felt, had taken the last great step in science; he had liberated "rational anthropology" from "the fetters of tradition and superstition." But for Darwin himself things were never quite so simple. As we saw in earlier chapters, he struggled with the problem of explaining "organs of extreme perfection." Though he did his best to bring biological complexity within the province of natural selection, the effort often seems half-hearted. Darwin was a great scientist, and like every great scientist, in the presence of nature, he was struck with true wonder. "We cannot fathom the marvelous complexity of an organic being," he concluded. Each of them "must be looked at as a microcosm—a little universe formed of a host of self-propagating organisms, inconceivably minute and as numerous as the stars in heaven."[2]

He could not have guessed how crowded with complexity that "little universe" would soon become—crowded enough to call his own theory into question.

As school children in our first geometry class we learned the well-known Euclidian axiom: "The whole is equal to the sum of its parts." It is one of those statements that seems too obvious for words—until one thinks about it a second time. Then one sees that every word of this innocent precept is slippery. What does "whole" mean, or "equal," or "sum"? Is a "whole" the same as a "collection"? "Equal" in what sense, by what criterion? Suppose we were offered a choice. On a table before us lie the parts of a disassembled watch collected in a heap; beside them lies the exact same number of parts but arranged into the fully functioning timepiece. Which would one choose? Obviously, the assembled watch is preferable to a pile of loose pieces. Every organized, functioning whole is worth more, and in that sense is more than "equal."

But suppose, instead of introducing "subjective" considerations of utility and economic value, we stick strictly to measurements of quantity, which is what Euclid seems to have had in mind. What becomes of the axiom then? Now things get a bit trickier and more interesting. Is the assembled watch, even quantitatively speaking, still "equal" to the sum of its parts? Or does the assemblage have something more to it than counting or weighing would reveal? Are all sums equal? Or is the "sum" of the parts, once the parts have been organized within the whole, in some sense "greater"? Is the *form* of the assembled watch a "part" that can be counted as being *there* in the watch? Is the intangible relationship *between* all the functioning parts something that is *there* and which must be enumerated as part of the whole?

All these questions grow more baffling when we move from humanly contrived systems to natural systems. The metaphorical "clockwork" that Western science once believed it saw in nature has far less chance of being treated as an isolated, fully analytical object than a literal timepiece. How does one separate a tree from the soil and air that sustain it? Or a star from the galaxy that envelops it? Where then does any natural system *end?* There is an even more interesting question: where do natural systems *begin?* How deep in the nature of things is structure rooted? In the nineteenth century, the nascent science of thermodynamics began with the convenient assumption that the seeming order of the macroscopic world around us was a mere pause in the inevitable drift toward maximum entropy. The most familiar image of entropy (and the one that still appears in most basic physics texts) depicted the random behavior of gas molecules wandering here and there in a box or perhaps in the great "box" of the universe, becoming more spread out and cooler with the passage of time until they reached the condition called "heat death."

Is this what chaos looks like? Hardly. Now we know that these drifting molecules are already highly structured systems; so too the atoms from which they are built. Spatially speaking, they embody a high degree of order. Even if one analyzes to the level of the particles or wavicles from which atoms are made, we are dealing with structures of activity as old as the history of time. Granted that at this level quantum indeterminacy appears; but the indeterminacy is caged within highly durable structures like atoms and galaxies. Does God play dice with the universe? Quantum mechanics tells us yes; but the game is played out in the basement of the universe behind the locked doors of a well-constructed building. As Errol Harris observes, "Random activity is always parasitic on some sort of order and cannot have ultimate priority."[3]

On both the infinitely large and infinitely small scale, nature opens out before us like a Chinese box puzzle: a seemingly endless nesting of systems within systems. Every system appears to be cradled within other, bigger systems. The cells that make up the tissues of the body are systems; the tissues are clearly contained within the larger system of the body as a whole. But the body, in turn, inhabits an ecosystem filled with plants, animals, microbes, natural forces. It also inhabits a society and a culture, both the immaterial creations of the mind that draws upon the body. If we accept the Gaia hypothesis, we must locate all ecosystems within a biospheric system as big as the planet. The Anthropic Principle extends the web of complexity even farther; it suggests the cosmos as a whole might be regarded as one all-embracing system maturing through a vast evolutionary history that was dictated by the "initial conditions" of the Big Bang. Were those mysterious initial conditions, in turn, a "system," a complex of forces and principles that worked harmoniously together to produce just this universe?

Where can we leave off the study of any system, saying we know *enough* about it? The answer seems to be the same that scientists must often give in making measurements. At a certain, always arbitrary point, one simply "rounds off" the calculation on the grounds of practicality. So too with systems. One rounds off the study, hoping nothing immediately relevant has been left out. But that is a rough, pragmatic compromise; a true philosophy of systems requires global comprehension.

THE ART AND SCIENCE OF SYSTEMS

Systems, whether humanly made or naturally given, stem from the most intricately creative of impulses. Yet, ironically, their formal academic study came into its own as an adjunct of war, the most ruinous of human activities. During the Second World War, systems analysis flourished as a means of dealing with vastly complicated military operations. How to coordinate the weapons (by then called "weapons *systems*"), ballistics, targeting priorities, troop movements, command structures, supply lines, intelligence, logistics that war calls into existence? Systems analysts were entrusted with deploying radar and refining the techniques of aerial bombardment. The most famous of the early computer scientists, Alan Turing, was part of the British systems team assigned to cracking Nazi secret codes. After the war, systems analysts went on to become the original strategists of thermonuclear war. The first deep investigations of systems in our time had to do primarily with engines of destruction and with the social units and command structures that make use of them. This did much to lend the discipline a certain coldly cerebral, rigorously utilitarian image.

The study of systems has never recovered from certain characteristics that stem from this origin. The field remains crowded with thinkers of a predominantly mathematical, logical, engineering mentality. The word "system" has itself taken on a chilly, metallic ring—which is doubtlessly why it has survived so long and so prominently as part of the scientific vocabulary. First adopted in the age of Galileo to describe the heliocentric harmony of the "new world system," later to designate the Newtonian vision of nature (the mechanistic or corpuscular system), it has gone on to enjoy even more currency in the age of high tech where it has assumed a special luster. There hovers about it the connotation of something more highly engineered than the ordinary machines of yesteryear. These days every least commodity on the market has become some kind of "system." A jar of face cream is a "skin protection and rejuvenation system"; a vacuum cleaner is a "sanitary dust disposal system." If one comes upon a toothbrush packaged with a tube of toothpaste in the supermarket, it is apt to be called a "dental hygiene system." The word gives the feel of sleek efficiency, implying state-of-the-art precision. But with the image comes a style of thought that easily shades off into technocratic managerialism.

Ludwig Von Bertalanffy, the creator of General Systems Theory, sought to free his science from this prevailing military and technological association. "The systems approach," he warned, "can be used for the further mechanization, enslavement, and alienation of man. It has up till now mainly applied to the benefit of the industrial–commercial–military complex." This was, he laments, an expression of the ambivalence that surrounds every field of science. In the service of an appropriate theory of human nature, however, he hoped that systems theory might overcome "the robot model of man."[4]

Von Bertalanffy's protest reminds us that, as cold-blooded as systems analysis has become, its essential insight stems from an aesthetic perception. In the distant historical background, behind the hard-headed technicians of our day, stand the Romantic artists and philosophers—Goethe, Coleridge, Hegel. From such sources in the late eighteenth century, there descends a school of *Naturphilosophie* that has long taken issue with the "mechanistic" approach of the Newtonians and Darwinians. For Romantic naturalists, the *form* of things—especially organic things—took precedence over the study of the parts. Form, as Goethe saw it, is the "primal phenomenon"; it must be grasped as a morphological totality within which the function and identity of the parts is determined by their relationship to the whole.

Holistic thinkers, always deeply imbued with an artistic appreciation for the subtle, the mysterious, the incommensurable, were stubbornly hostile toward the mathematical and analytical habits that had for so long dominated the scientific mainstream. Reductionists seek always to understand by atomizing things into their component parts. Perhaps a machine or a purely physical phenomenon (like chemical reactions or the collision of inert particles) can be dealt with so brutally—take it apart, examine the pieces, see how they fit together—but not a living being or a social entity. Reductionists, it was argued, failed to see the forest for the trees. Worse still, as Wordsworth lamented, they "murder to dissect." Holistic biology, at least in its early formulations, seemed to imply that the study of nature is inherently bifurcated. It assigned the physical and mechanical to one realm of study; the vital, the human and social to another. At the extreme the argument was pushed to the point of insisting that the study of holistic phenomena requires the use of a totally different faculty, something that is other and more than the rational mind. Intuition, aesthetic sensibility, visionary powers have to be brought into play if nature is to be rightly understood.

Most scientists have treated such arguments with impatience, if not contempt. They regard *Naturphilosophie* as the twittering of flagrant amateurs: obfuscating poets or metaphysicians who are intent on submerging science in the Cloud of Unknowing. Conventional science has been prepared to agree that there is a dichotomy involved in the study of nature; but the dividing line falls between those who are professionally qualified to undertake the job and those who are not. As one nineteenth century biologist insisted:

> Poetry and science are two regions distinct in their inmost essence, which both lose their value when they are intermingled. . . . A poetical treatment of science . . . is as repugnant and distasteful to the clearly educated mind as if one should strike a bargain, order a coat, or call a servant [as part of] a poetical speech. . . . poetical science is the troubled mysticism of a cloudy fanatic.[5]

At times, seeking to vindicate their method, reductionists have affected a brusque, coldblooded air that makes much use of the dismissive phrase "nothing but." At the rhetorical level, relations between the two camps could become strained enough to cloud the values (and the shortcomings) that exist on both sides.

The debate was to become all the more vehement when it got mixed into political ideology and nationalist antagonism. While Romanticism swept through the whole of European society, the movement cast a special charm over the Germans, who identified it as peculiarly theirs and infused it with a deep sense of ethnic pride that eventually spilled over into the politics of two world wars. In nineteenth century Germany, holistic thought generated a school of Idealist legal and political theory that conceived of the state as a metaphorical organism, the mystic community of the *Volk* and their leaders, which could not be properly understood by purely functional or utilitarian analysis. Late German Romantic thinkers saw themselves as the guardians of a precious cultural heritage that was under threat by the frigidly geometric French and the brutally positivistic British. Nothing less than the German soul was at stake in the dispute. Unhappily, some champions of holistic thought weakened toward totalitarianism in ways that eventually associated their philosophy, especially in its more lumpen-intellectual formulations, with fascism, Nazism, and other perversely irrational political movements. "Think with your blood!" Hitler, himself a failed painter, advised his frenzied followers. In the face of such blatant mass-hysteria, his enemies found it only too easy to believe that both their predominantly empirical and analytical philosophical traditions as well as their political cause represented all that was humane and progressive: the defense of reason against naked barbarism.

THE HIGHER REDUCTIONISM

These days, with the political heat fortunately gone out of the issue, the debate between holists and reductionists is apt to seem a bit musty. A great deal has changed over the last hundred years of scientific research; concessions have had to be made on both sides. Reductionistic analysis has continued to discover more and more about the inner-workings of nature. Its productivity as a method of research cannot be denied. Things that the holists and Vitalists once considered too radically mysterious ever to be explained by callous analysis—such as the chemistry of organic life—are now understood in great detail and can often be reproduced in laboratories. At the same time, by way of that very analysis, science has found its way into more and more intricate realms of structure. The stripped-down simplicity of classical Newtonianism has given way to such undreamt-of levels of complexity as the cellular symbiosis we mentioned in the previous chapter. And not only in the life sciences. The complexity of atomic structure very nearly rivals that of biological systems. Alfred North Whitehead was not wide of the mark when he described physics as the study of "the smaller organisms."

With analysis now so deeply infused with an appreciation of systems in nature, we might wonder if there is anything left to the old argument between reductionists and holists. Are we perhaps at the point of achieving a new, humane unity among the physical, biological, and social sciences that puts to rest the issues of the past? The answer to that question has everything to do with how we conceive of the systematic character of nature. Once having recognized the prominence of systems, what model will we choose to do them justice?

At least one of the new schools of systems research, Norbert Wiener's Cybernetics, has managed to sound a provocative new variation on the old debate. Wiener asserted the proposition that *all* systems, living or inert, biological or mechanical, physical or mental are governed by a common set of principles. Cybernetics is defined as the study of "control and communication in the animal and the machine."[6] Wiener was convinced that once cybernation had produced a sufficiently advanced apparatus, "the over-all system will correspond to the complete animal with sense organs, effectors and proprioceptors, and not, as in the ultra-rapid computing machine, to an isolated brain." We should then be able to include everything living and dead within the same theory, *provided* one treats things *as systems,* granting them a complexity that old-fashioned mechanistic science never would. But what Wiener had in mind as a model for such a grand unifying system was a newer and better machine: the computer. What he was able to explain by reference to the computer—for example, the phenomenon of feedback—seemed to him a characteristic of all living things. The secret of organic self-regulation was information-processing. The telling point is the continued prominence that Cybernetics bestowed upon entropy. Entropy, as Wiener interpreted the term, may have received a new, broader meaning as part of mental activity, social intercourse, culture—all understood as forms of information-transfer. But there was no question in his mind that harnessing the secret of feedback in computerized systems granted us only a partial and temporary escape from the inexorable advance of the second law of thermo-dynamics. Though machines might "also contribute to a local and temporary building up of information,

> it is a foregone conclusion that the lucky accident which permits the continuation of life in any form on this Earth, even without restricting life to something like human life, is bound to come to a complete and disastrous end. . . . In a very real sense we are shipwrecked passengers on a doomed planet.[7]

The words, here spoken by one of the founders of systems theory, echo the stark pessimism that Freud and Bertrand Russell derived from their vision of a dead and hostile universe. If anything, the study of systems as Wiener conceived of it reaffirmed the same sense of cosmic alienation, granting it a new lease on life and an even greater place in the life sciences. By a fateful coincidence, at the same time Wiener was working out the principles of Cybernetics, geneticists were eagerly mapping out a "New Biology." In need of some model to guide their research into the intricate structure of DNA, they quickly adopted Wiener's imagery, reading cybernation into their study of the gene. Was not the stuff of life itself a sort of "biocomputer," processing information along various microscopic tapes and loops and coils? Following Wiener's lead, there would soon be computer scientists on the scene asserting that human beings were "nothing but" information-processing instruments, perhaps one day to be replaced by superior forms of artificial intelligence.

In this way, by a new route starting within the study of systems, we arrive at a higher order of reductionism. Mechanism once again enters the scene as the basic model of life, mind, and nature—only now it is the mechanism of the computer, so very much more complicated than the clockwork imagery of the past. Wiener's great hope was that Cybernetics might contribute to "the human use of human beings" by relieving them of subintellectual drudgery in the workplace. Yet his formulation of the new science of systems is as grave an assault upon holistic principles as Newtonian atomism. Worse still, it lends itself to a "robot image of man" that easily leads to the sort of managerial authoritarianism Kurt Vonnegut foresaw in his anti-Utopian novel *Player Piano*.

A hypothesis like Wiener's quickly runs into many of the same difficulties as reductionism Old Style. However closely one may feel that a computer and a living thing resemble one another, there are plaguing differences, among them one of the classic holistic observations. A machine, including the computer, can be taken apart and put back together losing nothing in the process. Not so an organism. Take it apart and something special happens. It dies. Interrupt its vital processes for any length of time by pulling it to pieces and it loses something that must have been there hidden away in the relationship between the parts and which cannot be restored. *Lived* time is radically different from clock time. Living things are systems to which history is indispensable.

This distinction shows up nowhere so markedly as in the faculty that is frequently and casually associated with the computer: memory. Insofar as machines have "memories," they function very differently from memory in the organic realm. Organic memory is a record of *experience,* an intricate, highly selective blending of emotion, sensuous stimulation, existential crisis. In plants and animals, the experience may be that collective embodiment of evolutionary history we refer to as instinct. At the human level, it is connected with the psyche, a true mind that grows from a personal as well as an evolutionary history. This in turn connects with another great difference between organic and mechanical systems, one that also has to do with time. In the history of the universe, organic systems precede mechanical systems. No machine existed until a human being made one upon this planet. And as yet, no human being has succeeded in making a machine that matches the complexity of our own mind or body. This is why the mechanistic hypothesis has always been deeply flawed; it has chosen the lesser system as a model of the more complex.

THE GHOST IN THE MACHINE

Yet, Wiener's Cybernetics, if freely elaborated, might provide us with a rather different perspective on systems than he intended, one that arises from the remarkably subtle character of information technology.

Anyone who has ever worked with a computer soon learns the distinction between hardware and software. Hardware is readily recognized as machinery; it comes in the form of boxy objects, electrical conduits, keyboards, terminals. But software is a different matter. Microscopically etched into silicon chips or finely drawn on sheets of cardboard, its very delicacy of appearance suggests that we are dealing with a fragile pattern of interlocking logical premises and inferences whose relationship to the physical materials it uses—transistors, circuits, motherboards—is highly tenuous. What we see so elegantly sketched into the tiny chips of the memory and the central processing unit of a computer is a manifestation of mind.

This is of course true of every machine; all are infused with a "system" that determines their purpose. The phrase "a ghost in the machine" may have been coined to contrast the spiritual element in human nature with the physical body that is so often referred to as a mechanism. But the words might actually be better applied in just the opposite direction. Every machine is haunted by the ghost of the human intention that animates it. This is what Tracy Kidder had in mind when he spoke of a machine as having a "soul."[8] In the past, however, the "souls" of machines were anything but subtle. They were brutally apparent in the ponderous linkage between gears, levers, cams, shafts, pistons: physical things pushing or pulling physical things.

In contrast, the systems we call "software," while they must use a machine to do their job, are not themselves mechanical in any conventional and familiar way. As programs, they are the repositories of symbols that stand for logical, mathematical, and verbal relationships. They remind us that systems are not machines; rather machines are systems. And the best way to model any system, including natural systems, is to regard them as *ideas*. The systems we see around us in nature are the cosmologically given archetypes of what rises to articulate self-awareness in us as "thoughts." We think because, in some sense that blends the literal and the figurative, the universe "thinks." It generates structure and pattern and process the way the brain conjures up ideas. The historical and hierarchical progression is from natural systems, as old perhaps as the initial cosmological conditions, through the human mind toward the social, cultural, technological systems that make up our portion of life on Earth. At which point, reflecting upon the nature of things, we mirror the ideas that were our progenitors—the great system of the universe that encompasses all the rest.

Are we discussing anything more than metaphors here, mere models of the world around us? R. D. Laing once characterized science as "knowledge adequate to its subject." It is one of the trickiest questions in science to decide at what point a model becomes so fully "adequate," that it becomes an acceptable representation of reality: a mirror held up to nature reflecting what is *really* there. But even if we insist on maintaining the distinction between models and reality, the model we choose can make a great deal of difference. Conceive of nature as a machine—any machine, even a "thinking" machine—and you assume one relationship to the world. Conceive of it as sentient mentality, and you take another stance. To see the world as a realm of interrelated ideas places us in a condition of dialogue; it connects In-here with Out-there as a continuum. It places us on "speaking terms" with the universe.

DEEP SYSTEMS

These days all scientists acknowledge the complexity of natural systems. For most, systems remain a secondary feature of the universe that can still be explained (at least "in principle") by physical reduction and possibly mechanical simulation. But for others, systems are "deep"; they are primary and radical structures that cannot be reduced to anything simpler without losing something essential to the phenomenon under study. Here again, as in the case of Lawrence Henderson's approach to the fitness of the environment, the sensibility of the individual scientist may be the decisive quality. What is "essential," and when has it been "lost"?

Issues like these sound one of the main themes in the study of deep systems: *emergence*. Emergence is what happens when we move across the boundary that defines hierarchical levels; we encounter authentic novelty. Possibilities arise that were not there before and could not have been predicted. In a universe of deep systems, *surprise* is a basic category of experience. This can be seen even at the "lowest" levels of physical reality. The structure of the atom, together with all the most basic forces that give it permanence, could not be fully predicted from the most thorough analysis of the elusive quarks and other particles that compose it. The material unit we call an atom, the enduring assemblage that arises when waves, vibrations, fields are packaged together just so, is radically undeducible; it would have come as a surprise to any observer who could have been on hand to see it rise into existence. Suddenly, where there was streaming energy, there came to be compaction, stability, opacity: persisting *things* instead of transient *events*. So too the "wateriness" of water, so commonplace that it is nearly impossible to describe: its capacity to shape itself into drops, trickles, streams, to feel "wet," to be loosely coherent, to achieve a temporarily binding tension at its surface, to expand at the freezing point—none of these familiar qualities and properties could have been deduced from an analysis of the two gases that combine to create the water molecule. As Niels Bohr once remarked to the biologist Ernst Mayr, systemic complexity is no longer the monopoly of living things; the properties of the chemical elements "could not have been predicted in detail on the basis of a knowledge of isolated protons, neutrons, and electrons."[9] Systems theory pays attention to qualities, as much so as the science of Aristotle and the alchemists; rather than hastening to reduce qualities to quantity, systems theorists take the form, texture, feel, appearance of things to be independently important.

While there is as yet no consensus among the systems theorists upon the names and number of levels that must be included in a complete inventory, there are certain broad areas of agreement. All theories of deep systems are *hierarchical*. They map the universe as a pyramid of systems ranked from lesser to greater, lower to higher, simpler to more complex. Invariably, the physical stuff of the world (particles, atoms, molecules) is classified as lesser and lower. Complex structures (life, consciousness, mind, culture) are classed as greater and higher. Mario Bunge, for example, offers an eleven-level scale of systems; each level compounds into the next as we move up the scale of complexity. Though each level subsumes the subsystems below it, no higher level can be fully explained by the levels below, nor could it have been deduced from the lower levels. "Every concrete thing is either a system or a component of a system, i.e., a thing composed of interconnected things. . . . at every level some properties (in particular laws) are gained (or emerge) while others are lost (or submerge)."[10] (Figure 1.)

While concepts like hierarchy and emergence can be formulated as abstruse metaphorical distinctions, they also have a homely reality that is as close at hand as our everyday experience. Consider the commonplace fact that an automobile mechanic who knows nothing about

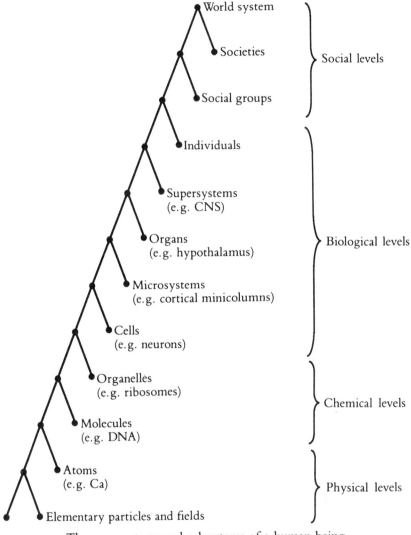

The supersystems and subsystems of a human being.
FIGURE I

basic physics—quanta, quarks, thermodynamics—is quite capable of repairing a car, and doing an excellent job of it. Every piece and part he handles, every process he manipulates is subject to profound physical analysis and could be expressed in sophisticated mathematical formulations. The mechanic needs to know none of this; he works within a system—the automobile—which is pragmatically self-contained, elevated above its components and principles. On the other hand, the physicist who studies the atomic foundations of metal, combustion, electricity may have no idea how to fix a car. The mechanic and the physicist work within an obvious continuity, but between their areas of expertise there is a radical disjuncture that allows them to pursue their goals separately and autonomously.

Heinz Pagels has a name for this: he calls it "causally decoupling." Where we cross "the barrier of complexity" between a higher and lower system, each takes on an autonomy.[11] All specialization in science is based on this astonishing process by which each structural level is not only elevated above, but in a significant sense is *liberated* from the governance of the next level down, and so can be understood in its own terms. Each level both depends upon and yet transcends the level below. The pattern holds all along the line. Biologists would never question the fact that the physical organs and processes they study are constituted of atoms; but their professional interest in those atoms need not require a complete mastery of theoretical physics. It may not go beyond a practical knowledge of organic chemistry. So too anthropologists need know nothing whatever about the chemistry of cells in order to study the culture and customs of the people who are made of those cells. In what sense, then, is reductionism from higher to lower levels an "explanation" of anything? If it were, how could such autonomous fields of study be possible?

Richard Feynman, commenting on the same problem, offers a succession of ascendingly complex levels reaching from fundamental laws of heat and pressure up through human affairs and philosophical concepts like justice, evil, and beauty. "We cannot, and it is no use making believe," he tells us, "that we can draw a line all the way from one end of this thing to the other, because we have only just begun to see that there is this relative hierarchy." Nor can we be certain "which end is nearer to God, if I may use a religious metaphor."[12]

Of course, it is important to be aware of the continuities that weave the natural world together; science begins with the assumption of universal law. But the decoupling and reconfiguration of qualities that occur spontaneously as we move from level to level within the hierarchy of systems is as real as any symmetry or invariance and perhaps more philosophically significant. Things do not simply collide or mix or compile; they radically alter their form and their behavior. Again, to use a reference drawn from mentality rather then physicality, at the point of juncture between the levels, it is as if a new *Gestalt* appears, as unforeseen as the *Gestalt* that the human eye or ear create from scattered perceptual stimuli or the mind from disjointed intellectual material.

THE OLD DEISM AND THE NEW

But how does inert stuff become transformed into a hierarchical arrangement of systems so complex that our science still struggles to find a model that will match its subtlety? How does mindless matter become the mind that struggles with the task of understanding matter? Scientists can be remarkably casual in dealing with such questions; at times so off-handed that they seem not to recognize the questions at all. "In the beginning, life assembled itself," one scientist writes. Another coins the phrase "spontaneous self-organization" to supplement Darwin's theory of evolution by natural selection. Still another speaks of life "bootstrapping itself into existence from a soup of amino acids."[13] Such formulations mean to sound smoothly automatic, but not far behind them hovers the implication of primordial directive intelligence. And the name our culture gives us for that is "God." Though systems theory may be based on the latest findings of the laboratory and the observatory, in one important respect it reaches back to the earliest days of modern science before natural philosophy had parted company with theology.

In the era of Galileo, Kepler, and Newton, the prevailing worldview of most advanced Western intellectuals was that curious blend of reason and faith called Deism. Also known as "natural religion," Deism was the theology that seemed most compatible with the Newtonian universe. The leading figures of the Enlightenment—Voltaire, Jefferson, Locke, Doctor Johnson—were Deists, convinced that it was the highest calling of reason to "read God's Mind in the Works of Nature." For men like these, Deist Christianity, purged of its miracles and prophetic tremors, was a thoroughly civilized religion, a simple belief in the First Cause and the rule of reason that was intended to stand as a barrier against every form of fanaticism and at the same time as a bridge between people of good will everywhere. It was also a politically potent ideology holding for self-evident and universal human rights.

Deism may have been the religion of scholars, scientists, and gentlemen of good conversation, but it was no match for merciless skeptics like David Hume, who came to believe they could do very nicely without a Supreme Being. Hume's attack on natural religion was on two levels: one logical, the other factual. At the level of logic, he took issue with those few fond remnants of Judeo-Christianity that Deists were nostalgically determined to preserve. Deism continued to view God the Creator as he is pictured in the first two chapters of Genesis, and it was committed to preserving the status of Jesus as the best and wisest man who ever lived. Deism may have reduced its relations with the inherited religious tradition to a minimum, but in the eyes of more fanatically secular thinkers, it suffered for the few tenuous connections that remained. Somewhere in the background there was the lingering memory of bearded Jehovah on his mountaintop handing down the tables of the law. The old gentleman may have become more of a celestial bureaucrat (some Deists referred to him as "the Great Manager"); the tablets of the laws may have become logarithmic tables; but the imagery remained illogically anthropomorphic. God was still a "He" (or for Doctor Johnson a "Sir") somewhere in the distant heavens, an assumption that became more and more intolerably superstitious.

Even more telling, the Deists tried, against all logic, to preserve the traditional idea of the Prime Mover as a caring father to his children. This lingering affection for the consolations of Sunday school catechism came in for withering analysis. Where was the evidence, Hume demanded, for the goodness and loving-kindness of God in this troubled world? By what right do we regard the universe as "designed" from the viewpoint of human happiness? If anything, the vale of tears we inhabit suggests a malicious deity, or at the least a bumbling and negligent one.

At the factual level, Deism faded into obsolescence because the sort of shallow systems it set out to explain came to be seen as needing no supernatural explanation. The clockwork universe that the Supreme Being watched over was so predictably law-abiding, it became possible to imagine it running by itself forever. In a famous boast, the French physicist Laplace once claimed that his science no longer required the "hypothesis" of God; the implication was that the cosmos might have simply fallen into place by accident. After an eternity of bouncing around at random, the tiny billiard ball atoms had finally slipped into the ruts of a few simple laws of motion and, thanks to an absolute determinism, stayed put in an endless stability. The simplicity of such a universe left little room in nature for any form of mentality beyond the original blueprint that God might have drawn up. By the early nineteenth century, few scientists felt the need for blueprints; instead, as their research became constantly more specialized, they had less interest in the integrative form of inquiry that theology demands. Careers were built upon findings, not faith. Stephen Toulmin speaks of the "disciplinary abstraction" that came to characterize professional science in the course of the century. With the advent of professionalism, scientists sought a "productive" approach to knowledge that guaranteed solid results and, not incidentally, a rewarding career. Almost necessarily, the division of intellectual labor secularizes thought by drawing it away from great questions of "cosmic interrelatedness."[14]

Deism had one more significant vulnerability, a weakness that was the other side of its strength. The religion of civilized and reasonable people, it was chillingly cerebral. There was neither visionary splendor nor prophetic fire to it. "Enthusiasts" like the Wesleyans, who longed for a religion of the heart, found it a bloodless bore and boisterously dissented from it. Their unbecoming behavior—camp meetings featuring lively hymns, soul-wracking confessions, ecstatic seizures—only strengthened the resolve of sincere Deists to assert the virtues of reasonable conduct all the more insistently. As a matter of principle and of taste, natural religion left the passions unengaged and unexplored. In this respect, it contributed to that repressive rationality of nineteenth century European culture that the Romantics found intolerable and that, eventually, modern psychiatry would be created to heal.

In its view of both nature and human nature, Deism Old Style lacked depth. The science on which it was based saw nothing more to the world around it than the endless, law-abiding interaction of atoms, nothing more to the human mind that it cared to dignify than cool logic. No deep systems, no deep feelings. Deism had no taste for mysteries Out-there or In-here. Rather, it preferred clarity and good manners. When, at last, Freud developed psychoanalysis to delve into the unconscious, the neuroses he found festering there were wounds inflicted by the underdimensioned psychology of the very science he so admired.

Looking back, we can now see that Deism in its original formulation sought to straddle an impossible divide in the study of nature. It found design in the universe at two levels, both of which it conveniently assimilated to the category of "order." Though it was not fully understood until the twentieth century, these levels are distinct and in some ways incompatible. Both exist in nature, but each requires a different mode of understanding.

There was first of all the level of general physical laws, mainly the Newtonian laws of motion and gravitation. These were admired for their simplicity and universality. From this there arose the image of God as a mathematician and clockmaker. Second, there was the perception of order in the complex adaption of things to one another in the world around us. This was seen primarily in the neat fit between organisms and their environment. The flower seemed designed for the bee, the bee for the flower. Order in this sense is far from simple and may not be mathematical at all. Rather, it is the very intricacy of the arrangements that elicits wonder. Newton's formulas are succinct and easily stated. In a sense, they are final within a certain realm of observation and discourse: namely the three-dimensional world of large bodies moving more slowly than the speed of light. On the other hand, one can write whole books on the marvelous complexity of the termite colony or the physiology of the tree, knowing that there will always be more to see, more to discuss. There is "order" here, but not the sort that can once and for all be wrapped up in a mathematical formula.

To some degree, these two forms of order appeal to different tastes and sensibilities. One is abstruse, almost reclusive in temperament; it is a labor of the mind working among numbers and logical relations, needing perhaps nothing more than pen and paper. The other is profoundly observational and relishes a wealth of enmeshed detail. One must go walking through the world to seek it out. The first few generations of Deist philosophers assumed that somehow the simple mathematical order that characterized astronomy and physics had given rise to the complexity of biological phenomena and would ultimately explain it. Someday the connection between the two would be found. But when that connection was finally made by Darwin in the late nineteenth century, it proved devastating to the argument from design.

Darwin's natural selection, while not mathematical in its formulation, had all the simplicity Deists admired in Newton's laws. It included, however, one lethal element. Chance. Darwin argued that variation, selection, and adaptation can, by purely random combinations, produce the order of the biological world—if given enough time.

At the time the argument seemed absolutely conclusive, especially to those who were willing to use any convenient stick to beat the pious. Yet it was badly flawed in two directions. There was no firm connection between the physical and biological, only the assumption that, once again by chance, living things had arisen from inert matter. Second, as we have seen, the intricacy of natural systems is far greater than the science of Darwin's day allowed for. As that complexity came to be more and more appreciated, it required a higher and higher Credulity Index (as we have called it) to believe that so much order could be generated within the timespan that modern cosmology offers us. It is at this point that the age-old argument from design took on a new life.

The new Deism, whose shadowed outlines one can see throughout deep systems theory, has a much firmer intellectual and psychological foundation beneath it. It harbors no lingering loyalty to Judeo-Christian theology, no need to prop up a personal God. It is not called upon to trace the intelligence it finds reflected in nature back to a divine and fatherly law-giver. The evidence it discovers for Mind At Large is solidly grounded in good science. Ordered complexity exists; its discovery, system by system, system *within* system, marks the greatest chapter in the history of science. That complexity can be approached by way of mathematical abstraction, but it also requires indispensably that empirical phenomena be studied fully. Errol Harris puts the point well: "The argument from design in modern dress" is not "a resort to God as a cloak to cover our ignorance, but is the logical consequence of the very nature of our knowledge and of the structure of the universe as discovered by empirical science."[15]

Without dismissing the role of reason in the investigation of nature, the new Deism opens itself to intuitive insight and aesthetic experience and so sounds more levels of the psyche than conventional rationality can. Its strong sympathetic connection with deep ecology, ecofeminism, neo-paganism also lends psychological breadth. Along many lines, deep systems theory might be seen as the expository prose version of nature mysticism. Most important, systems theory offers the unique promise of achieving what science has always posed as its goal: a unified worldview that seeks to do justice to the mental, the cultural, the spiritual as much as to the mathematical and physical.

There is a subtle but insistent continuity between the study of deep systems in nature and the system and structure-making habits of the human imagination. The experience is not unknown even in the most exact sciences where aesthetic pleasure has often opened the gates of knowledge. James Watson, reducing the "secret of life" to chemical formulae, was drawn to the double helix as much by its beauty as its explanatory power. It was, as he said, an "idea too beautiful not to be true."

Lancelot Law Whyte, one of the pioneering theorists of form in the sciences and among the first to designate the morphic tendency in nature as a special subject of study, once described his fascination with hierarchal structures in this way:

> To understand hierarchy is one way to understand ourselves. Each of us is a hierarchically constructed organism; our anatomy, physiology, thoughts, and actions are all organized in a sequence of levels. When not pathological the human person is, like all viable organisms, a differentiated hierarchy, a superbly coordinated system of hierarchies. . . . When we are ill there is a failure of coordination at one or more levels in these hierarchies, and the clarification of the relation of body to mind and psychosomatic illness requires a hierarchical approach. Guilt, hypocrisy, heartbreak, and so on, are lesions in the hierarchy. *Hierarchical structure is the basic feature common to matter and mind.*[16]

The study of deep systems lies at the intersection between form as we find it in nature and form as we create it in culture. Form in the world calls out to form in the perceiving mind. How can any Theory of Everything be complete if it leaves out the imagination that created it?

Seven

◆

THE HUMAN FRONTIER
The Meaning of Omega

I believe the first living cell
Had echoes of the future in it, and felt
Direction and the great animals, the deep green forest
And the whale's-track sea; I believe this globed earth
Not all by chance and fortune brings forth her broods,
But feels and chooses. And the Galaxy, the firewheel
On which we are pinned, the whirlwind of stars in which
   our sun is one dust-grain, one electron, this
   giant atom of the universe
Is not blind force, but fulfills its life and intends its course.

Robinson Jeffers, De Rerum Virtute

THE BILLIONS AND THE BILLIONTHS

Nothing is more impressive about the worldview of modern science than the magnitudes in which it deals: the tininess of the atom, the vastness of the galaxies. These are the first cosmological facts every schoolchild learns, the constant theme of every popular science documentary. Astronomers explore distances in space that overwhelm the imagination. At the other end of the scale, atomic physicists dazzle us with the minutiae of the world, leaving us with the knowledge that we move each day through a ghostly mesh of invisible entities. We have learned that between the realms of the billions and the billionths, there is no limit to how small or how large the works of nature can become. The result is a mystique of quantity that simultaneously disorients and disenchants us. We seem to live sandwiched between magnitudes that have no human proportion.

The historian of science Alexandre Koyré suggests that the transition from "closed world to infinite universe" in the age of Galileo was the most wrenching intellectual experience of the modern Western world.[1] Infinite is not simply very big; it is *meaninglessly* big, an immensity that seems to devour every value and virtue within it. In the early history of the infinite universe, there were only two quantities that had philosophical importance: inconceivably tiny us and inconceivably big *It*. Only faith in a creator God filled the void between. When God faded from the minds of thoughtful skeptics, nothing remained to bridge the gap. Infinity became a wilderness in which the Earth wandered without guiding direction, without merciful witness. It may well be that the most nagging, existentially wounding knowledge we carry through the day—even the most religious among us—is the numbing anxiety of being sunk in the abyss of endless space. We may not speak of it, but the question is there at the back of our minds. What living sense can we make of our lives in the presence of that annihilating immensity?

The twin infinities great and small take on a wholly different aspect, however, when we introduce the factor of *time* as it functions in the new cosmology. In both the Newtonian and Einsteinian universes, time, understood as eternity, was little more than so much gray cosmic wallpaper, a purely neutral background endlessly there for no better purpose than to allow matter and chance to play out their mindless game of random interaction. But in the new cosmology, time becomes history. And in historical time, both space and matter take on a quality that restores their human significance; their vastness becomes the precondition of life.

The Anthropic Principle tells us that life could have come into existence only within a certain interval of cosmic history. Lacking an inventory of heavy elements to build with, no life could be possible. But heavy elements can come into existence in the necessary abundance only after at least two generations of stars have lived, died, and poured their substance into the void of space. The appearance of life demands a certain period of cosmic expansion during which the universe can cool and the galaxies achieve stability. "If the birth of life requires a gestation of many billion years," Hubert Reeves observes, "the expanding universe must consistently spread over billions of light-years."[2] The two aspects of our modern worldpicture that have often seemed so humbling—the size and age of the cosmos—now prove to be life-sustaining. They must be exactly what they are to make life possible. Just as the womb shelters and nurtures the newly fertilized cell it so vastly overwhelms in size, so too these intimidating immensities sustain the life that seems lost within their magnitude.

Furthermore, in historical time, the universe takes on a narrative direction; it relates the story of a well-defined evolution toward higher and higher levels of ordered complexity. Consider once again Mario Bunge's hierarchy of emergent and submergent structures referred to in the previous chapter. The pyramid of ordered forms he describes is not static; time unfolds between the levels. No matter how modestly one cares to construe the Anthropic Principle, it is grounded in this one important cosmological insight: that time, matter, life, and mind are twined together historically. The universe down to its most infinitesimal particles has a biography in which there is a significant "before" and a significant "after." We now know that the structures studied by astronomy and physics (the atom, the stars, the galaxies) are early creations of the universe, dating back to the first few billions of years after the Big Bang—or, in the case of the basic particles, to the first few moments. The new cosmology begins with the first split seconds in the history of time, intervals that have no readily conceivable meaning since they actually predate the existence of time as we know it.[3] After that, for eons, we have the generations of stars whose role it was to forge the inventory of heavier elements that would eventually form the planets we know in our own solar system and which some believe may exist throughout space. Within the last few billion years, at least on this one planet warmed by a main sequence star about halfway through its life span, organic life appears. Finally, emerging in the latest chapter of the history of time, we find our own human species, the culminating level of complexity. All the systems that have come before are either subsystems of our biological structure or the supersystems (galaxies and galactic clusters) that account for the cosmological structure within which life has uniquely had the chance to develop.

In this sense, as the emergent form at the outer edge of cosmic evolution, our species assumes a strange, new centrality in that history. As vast as all the universe may be in its sheer quantities, *qualitatively speaking* there is a specialness to life and to mind that makes it more than a marginal accident in some dark corner of infinity. Seeing things this way is simply a matter of disengaging sufficiently from the mystique of size to recognize that the universe is not essentially in the business of producing bigness, but of elaborating complexity. That is what it uses distance and matter for: *to embody its ideas of things.* Sizes both big and small are governed by these complexities, each level shaped by the needs of the next level up—or at least this is one reading that systems theory would offer within the assumptions of the Anthropic Principle. There must be atoms of a certain size and character, durable galactic structure, space of a certain expansive magnitude—all there to cope with the primary forces of nature if more complex levels of organization are to appear. This is what the universe has been doing in all the long while since the atom and the galaxy rose into existence. It has been reaching forward toward finer orders of complexity, toward realms so subtle and complex that they can be fabricated only out of the delicate dynamics of the human imagination. And what stands at the crest of the hierarchy holds a crowning position. It embodies the full potentiality of all that has gone before, realizing it, expressing it. It occupies the *frontier* of the cosmos.

How can this not be a significant fact?

TIME'S NEW ARROW

As we have seen, nothing more firmly anchored the heroic fatalism of Freudian psychoanalysis than the concept of entropy. With so many others of his generation, Freud shared an absolute conviction in the heat death of the cosmos. This willingness to endorse so pessimistic a vision of life deserves a closer reading, especially in light of what systems theory and the new cosmology now offer as an alternative worldview.

Along with evolution, entropy was the crowning achievement of nineteenth century science. Beginning its career as a technical problem in the study of heat engines, the idea was destined to spread well beyond the perimeters of science to touch every area of surrounding culture. By the end of the century, as a "law" of thermodynamics, it was being widely touted as mankind's supreme insight into the nature of the universe. *Law* in quotation marks, because this was a new and strange kind of law: the first statistical generalization in modern science to gain that status. Entropy is, after all, a statement not of absolute regularity, but of probable tendency. Newton's laws might be said to express God's power; the second law of thermodynamics expresses human impotence. "It seems odd," the historian of science Charles Gillispie observes, "that a fundamental law of nature should rest upon the exclusion of what man cannot do, namely create perpetual motion."⁴ Entropy might almost be seen as a cosmic projection of the helplessness many people of the period felt before the vast, inexorable forces that the industrial revolution had released in the world. There is a deep psychological link between the withering desperation of the characters we find in Franz Kafka's novels and the entropic worldview of the early twentieth century.

One might have expected more caution on the part of those who so eagerly read the operations of heat engines into the universe as a whole, especially when so very much about the culture of science was at stake. In an earlier period, the materialism and atheism associated with the advance of science had been forces of liberation, intended to sweep away the accumulated superstition of the past. Godlessness was regarded as a precondition of progress. By the late nineteenth century, a darker prospect of the industrial future prevailed. The dislocation and suffering of the system seemed insurmountable. Optimism was no longer the vogue. Instead, the impending thermal demise of the universe was now thought to define the very direction of time, a problem that had been left unresolved by Newton's time-reversible formulas for motion.

Curiously enough, even Freud, a student of the inner life, never asked why the direction of time should have been any sort of "problem" in the first place. However ambiguous Newton's equations may be when it comes to the observation of recoiling and gravitating bodies, human consciousness spontaneously records time as directional, moving from birth to death, from thought to deed, from actions to their results. Reverse a movie film, and we have no difficulty recognizing that it is running backward—unless the movie shows nothing more than billiard balls careening across a table. Even then, include the billiard players in the picture, and we can tell at once whether the action is moving forward or back. The human experience of time stems from memory, which is the foundation of personality. Memory tells me who I am; it is the register of growth, maturity, and moral responsibility. The recollection of things past is the raw material from which psychoanalysis would presumably shape self-knowledge and wisdom. Yet in the great age of materialism, even a psychologist was reluctant to introduce such "subjective" considerations into the study of nature. Instead, Freud lent his authority to the belief that only a physical process could tell us the direction of "time's arrow" and that the flight of that arrow is in the mathematically measurable direction of increasing entropy.

Modern science has been curiously reluctant to let go of this dreary vision, even when it has every good reason to do so. In a remarkable book published in 1930, the astronomer Harlow Shapley listed some fifteen levels of ordered complexity ranging from subatomic particles to the distant galaxies. The universe, Shapley contended, describes "progress toward order." One of the first to study galactic structure, he was clearly not discussing some marginal and transient aspect of the universe, but a central feature of its development, in which the human mind might be seen to rank as the uppermost point of development. Though he touched upon the subject guardedly, Shapley was compelled to ask, "If Mind appears at all, might it not possibly enter every class and subclass?"[5] By which he meant, mentality might be seen as potentially "present" all along the way.

Nevertheless, the allegiance of science to entropy went unshaken. When the atomic physicist Erwin Schrödinger turned from physics to the study of biology, he had to acknowledge that living things would seem to be the very antithesis of entropy. But then, as if to censor that obvious fact out of existence, he denied the phenomenon any proper name; he gave it the shadowed reality of a negative definition. Things that do not follow where entropy points display "*negentropy*," negative entropy. This is on the level of defining love as "nonhatred" or beauty as "negative ugliness." The implication is clear: dead stuff dominates the universe. What deviates from it is abnormal.

Even more chilling is the role that Norbert Wiener saw fit to assign to entropy in laying the foundations of information theory. Wiener saw the introduction of thermodynamic probability into physics as "the first great revolution of twentieth century physics." He went on to suggest a striking parallel between entropy and Freud's discovery of the unconscious. Both, it seemed to him, were recognitions of the radically random and irrational, one inside and one outside the mind. As such, both were elements of "evil . . . the negative evil which Saint Augustine characterizes as incompleteness."[6]

Given what we now know about the prominence of systems and structure in the universe, we should be in the position to see that the once-omnipotent second law of thermodynamics was based on an eccentric interpretation of order. Like so much else in its vocabulary, science borrowed the word "order" from outside its boundaries, from fields like law and aesthetics. But in so doing, the scientists very nearly inverted the meaning of the term. As the second law would have it, there was more "order" in the earliest stages of the universe than there is now. And what was that order? An expanding flash of radiation in which nothing had shape or substance, within which (most likely) no laws of nature could govern. In what sense except the concentration of energy can this be called "order"? And in what sense can the use of that energy for the creation of all ensuing physical reality be called "disorder"?

Within limits, scientists are free to define their terms as they please. But words have a history that deserves some respect, especially where great philosophical issues are involved. Whatever we may care to say entropy is measuring, it ought not to be called "order." An artist who invests many years of life in a piece of sculpture has expended energy that can never be recovered. He has "used up" time that can never be lived again. Materials may have been irreversibly changed by his efforts. All this might be seen as a kind of "entropy." But there is also finally a work of art that meaningfully embodies the previously scattered units of time, energy, material. What was once only potentially there as an unrealized image in the artist's mind is now present for all to see and share. Has there been a loss or a gain? Is there now more or less "order" in the world?

In every traditional use of the word, the Big Bang, that initial burst of raw, unformed energy, would be regarded as the near absence of "order." Mythologically speaking, this is the "chaos" that existed before the moment of divine creation when "the Earth was without form and void." As nothing but unrealized potentiality, it would have been regarded by most schools of metaphysics as "nonbeing." For that matter, even common sense, clinging to the ordinary meaning of words, would insist that there is more "order" in a universe of galactic systems and living beings than in a barren ball of fire. From a culturally literate point of view, there is more order in the robin's wing or in the simplest nursery rhyme taught by mother to child than one can imagine in the Big Bang when it was all there was. Deep systems theory builds upon both traditional thought and common sense in interpreting the cosmos as an evolution toward increasing levels of coherent organization.

In this respect, we can say without any subjective implication that order is "in the eye of the beholder," because the beholder (ourselves) is the *inheritor* of all that has come before. We find order building toward us, generating us in all our physical, mental, social, cultural complexity. "Time's arrow," once thought to be exclusively oriented toward the heat death of the universe, points in the direction of structures and systems, and at last conscious life: the human frontier. Entropy is exhausted matter's arrow, not the living mind's.

"Somehow, after all," James Gleick observes, "as the universe ebbs toward its final equilibrium in the featureless heat death of maximum entropy, it manages to create interesting structures." The great question then is "how a purposeless flow of energy can wash life and consciousness into the world."[7]

THE PARADOX OF DISSIPATIVE CREATION

From the viewpoint of systems theory, ordered complexity, not entropy, represents the dominant theme of change in the universe. Entropy shrinks to a lesser stature, a more limited phenomenon within the structure-building cosmos at large. It becomes a characteristic of systems that exchange neither energy nor matter with their surroundings, eventually reaching equilibrium and succumbing to thermal depletion. Some scientists use the term "closed" for such systems; others call them "isolated." In either case, those systems that best display increasing entropy are all but wholly hypothetical phenomena. David Layzer states simply, "Closed systems aren't to be found in nature." On the other hand, there are innumerable "open systems" that can hold out against entropic degradation indefinitely, buying the luxury of time while they burn the animating resources of the universe. Some open systems can fluctuate further and further from equilibrium, possibly moving into that area now studied by chaos theory. In the 1940s, Ilya Prigogine and Paul Glansdorff undertook the study of such nonequilibrium systems. They discovered that such nonlinear systems have the capacity to produce new ordered structures on the far side of instability. As long as they receive a steady flow of energy from "outside," they do not degenerate into randomness, but become self-organizing. Prigogine named these "dissipative structures."[8] Life is a structure that constantly recreates itself by dissipation. For deep systems theory, it is of the essence of the new cosmology that life appears "later" rather than "earlier" in the history of the universe. Dissipative structuring is what time builds toward. Not only do we have quasars and galactic clusters extending to the far reaches of space, but on at least this one planet, we have the astonishing complexity of organic life, human culture, social life. We have science itself, a prodigious intellectual edifice.

Eventually, of course, life on Earth will deplete all the sources of energy we can now imagine; even the sun will die. But will that be the end of dissipative structures including living things everywhere? This amounts to asking whether entropy increases in a *universal* system—of which we have only one example. Clearly the universe is an exceptional system. It is everything there is drawing upon the thrust of a unique explosive or inflationary event. Does such a system ever achieve equilibrium? Or does it have some inexhaustible source of "outside" energy that makes it an all-encompassing dissipative structure? Some theorists have raised the uncanny possibility of "spacetime tunnels" that channel matter from "other universes" into ours through black holes.[9] Perhaps the universe "bounces" between Big Bangs and Big Crunches so that it is perpetually in motion, an energetic system that will never cease its creativity. We have no way of knowing. But neither do those who assign everything to the universal heat death. How can they be so confident about extending the second law of thermodynamics from here to eternity? Is this anything more than an arbitrarily morbid vision?

For the systems philosopher Erich Jantsch, dissipative structures find their highest destiny in evolution, the adventure of using time to achieve surprise.[10] Jantsch's approach vividly displays the radically new (and highly controversial) perspective that the study of systems has to offer at its most ambitious extension. Systems theory tends to be augmentative rather than reductive. While there can be exceptions (as we have seen in the case of Wiener's Cybernetics, which clings to a mechanistic model), most systems theorists "round off" toward the *next* highest level, explaining by way of direction and purpose. While no less rationally analytical than conventional science, systems theory prefers to project its analysis forward from the cause to the effect (the fully developed system), searching for intimations of that result in the cause. In the Aristotelian science of an older period, this was known as the study of "final causes," that end-state that seems to guide the process toward its completion. Inevitably, this draws some, like Jantsch, to ponder the culmination of all processes in the universe as a whole. The theme one then sees threaded through the universe from beginning to end is the evolution of consciousness, the most recent and complex of all systems. As we can see in the following figure, Jantsch's universe strives toward a true "Theory of Everything," the realm of mind as well as the realm of matter. Integrating the two is evolution. It progresses as a hierarchy of dynamic systems, all of which culminate in the human world. (See Figure 2, next page.)

Read from lower left to upper right, this matrix is meant to present the inert and simple together with the vital and intricate as a continuum. At first the juxtaposition of the physical, biological, mental, and cultural we see here is bound to be jarring—especially to more cautious scientists, whose habit is either to keep these realms separate or to assume the more complex can somehow be explained by reduction to the less complex. Yet, as a representation of the totality of scientific knowledge, such a graph might be regarded as a nonmathematical extension of Mendeleev's familiar periodic table of elements. One need only read into that table (as the new cosmology has) a temporal dimension, recognizing that at one point in the history of time there were only a few lightweight nuclei, mainly hydrogen and helium, synthesized out of the Big Bang; all the other elements arose later, each one gifted with surprising qualities that could not have been deduced from its preexisting modules. No more (or no less) remarkably, at some time later, these elements composed themselves into the universe we know today: a universe of ordered complexity that shows

FIGURE 2

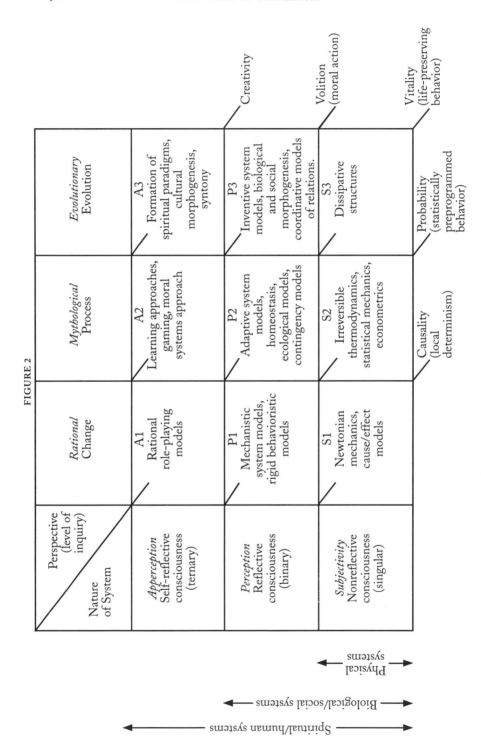

Perspective (level of inquiry) / Nature of System	Rational Change	Mythological Process	Evolutionary Evolution	
Apperception Self-reflective consciousness (ternary)	A1 Rational role-playing models	A2 Learning approaches, gaming, moral systems approach	A3 Formation of spiritual paradigms, cultural morphogenesis, syntony	Creativity
Perception Reflective consciousness (binary)	P1 Mechanistic system models, rigid behavioristic models	P2 Adaptive system models, homeostasis, ecological models, contingency models	P3 Inventive system models, biological and social morphogenesis, coordinative models of relations.	Volition (moral action)
Subjectivity Nonreflective consciousness (singular)	S1 Newtonian mechanics, cause/effect models	S2 Irreversible thermodynamics, statistical mechanics, econometrics	S3 Dissipative structures	Vitality (life-preserving behavior)
	Causality (local determinism)		Probability (statistically preprogrammed behavior)	

← Physical systems →

← Biological/social systems →

← Spiritual/human systems →

no sign of entropic demise. As an anonymous scientific quip puts it, "Hydrogen is a light, odorless gas, which, given enough time, turns into people."

Like all sciences, the study of systems often suffers from bloodless abstraction. But at times we gain an insight into the poignancy and drama of key concepts like "potentiality." Contemporary ethology offers us one. In the field of animal communication, nothing has been more hotly disputed than the study of ape language. Those who work closely with the apes come away convinced that they have a remarkable capacity to learn human language: to understand it, to generate new words, to master simple sentences. On the other hand, there are critics who insist that language is uniquely human. In their view, apes lack the "cognitive substrate" to deal with language except in the most rudimentary, mainly mimicking way. The debate seems to turn upon the inability to find a middle term between continuity and discontinuity in evolution. "Potentiality" is exactly that term. It is the zone of possibility that lies waiting to be crossed between hierarchical levels. It is there, but not there at the same time. The word allows us to say that apes have a well-developed capacity to use language, but not to invent it or to elaborate it fully as a child can. Potentiality is that nameless form-creating thrust that carries reality forward from one level of the hierarchy to the next.

The much-studied pygmy chimp Kanzi offers a glimpse of potentiality at work. Kanzi, who was born in 1980, makes his home at the Language Research Center in Atlanta, Georgia. There he has made more progress in mastering language than any ape before. His achievements are remarkable, but nothing is quite so impressive as the picture his trainer gives us of Kanzi pressing at the limits of his innate ability.

> His capacity for comprehension far outstrips his capacity to produce language using the lexigram. "He gets extremely frustrated," says Sue Savage-Rumbaugh. He often gets very vocal at these times, a kind of high-pitched squeaking. Is he trying to imitate speech? . . . "He tries very hard. He looks right at you and makes these sounds. When you talk back to him he vocalizes more and more."[11]

That high-pitched squeaking strikes a chord. Is it the anguish and the effort that comes of encountering unfulfilled potentiality? Did a cry like that sound deep inside our ancestors as they struggled to extend the range of their experience? Perhaps it can still be heard inside us whenever we find ourselves thwarted in the pursuit of an aspiration that lies beyond our grasp. Is the suffering we call "neurosis," then, significantly tied to such encounters with the greater identity we find locked away inside us?

SATAN'S ANUS

Yet even if the concept of a human frontier in the cosmos should prove to be intellectually engaging, I suspect there would remain an emotional barrier for many in accepting the idea. One no sooner raises the prospect of a human-centered universe (in any sense of the phrase) than one senses the discomfort of secular skeptics who can hear nothing more than the arrogance it seems to imply. Once again, bigness enters the discussion. How can anything as small as the Earth, as tiny as the life it carries really matter? To suggest that quality rather than size is the essence of the cosmos, that novelty, surprise, purpose are of more importance than brute magnitude, brings to mind the overweening self-importance human beings supposedly once claimed within the traditional religious worldview.

True enough: human beings once saw themselves as a special creation of God, made in the divine image, placed at the center of the universe. A psychiatrist might see nothing but infantile delusions of grandeur in that story: narcissism on a cosmic scale. But there has always been another reading of the myth of Genesis, one that emphasizes responsibility rather than presumption. Being at the center, bearing the divine stamp, represents an ideal that takes some living up to. And in the Judeo-Christian tradition, the teaching is that mankind *failed* in that assignment. In the old geocentric astronomy, after all, the center of the universe was the *bottom* of the universe, a vale of tears, a den of iniquity. Christian theology interpreted this to be the proper home of a flawed and fallen creature, one that had many sins to work off, many failures to make good. In the Christianized Ptolemaic worldsystem, heaven and the angels in their perfection were at the distant perimeter; the Earth was the cesspool of creation; it was regarded, in the words of one sixteenth-century theologian, as "so depraved and broken in all kinds of vices and abominations that it seemeth to be a place that hath received all the filthiness and purgings of all other worlds and ages."[12] The lowest level of creation lay at the core of the Earth itself; it was called hell, the point most hopelessly distant from God. In his *Divine Comedy,* Dante was even more explicit. The exact dead center of the universe was Satan's anus frozen forever into the icy foundations of perdition. Centrality was hardly a laudatory status.

It was the pre-Christian Greeks and the high-spirited humanists of the Renaissance who mustered the self-importance to assert that "man is the measure of all things." The proud claim that Pico della Mirandola put forward in his famous "Oration on the Dignity of Man" was a deliberate effort to throw off the sense of shame and unworthiness that Christian humility seemed to require. So, too, the early Copernican astronomers: they saw their cause as that of salvaging the dignity of the Earth and its human population from the slanderous ignominy that the geocentric universe entailed. The English cleric John Wilkins, writing in the mid-seventeenth century, associated himself with that goal. The old universe brought with it the assumption that "bodies must bee as farre distant in place as in Nobilitie"; this meant that "the Earth is a more ignoble substance than the other Planets, consisting of a more base and vile matter," and therefore closer to hell, which "must needs be situated in the centre of our Earth."[13] Anthropocentrism can, in short, bring with it very different attributes; it can be seen as conferring privilege, justifying conceit, imposing a duty, or raising a challenge. It can be a vain boast or a terrible burden. But in all cases it requires us to take the human adventure seriously as a major feature of the universe. It asks us to seek knowledge of nature not only beyond ourselves, but *in* ourselves and *through* ourselves.

The concept of the human frontier poses great problems even for those who are willing to endorse it. A frontier is unknown territory apt to be filled with hazards, a place where one easily loses one's way. If the human mind marks the beginning of that frontier, we should remember that it is an instrument that can sound many modulations. Intelligence, as we know from our own daily experience, assumes any number of forms. We possess a rich inventory of mental faculties to describe the range of the mind: wisdom, judgment, intuition, reason, insight. Which of these is the essence of mind, the faculty that brings us closest to Mind At Large in the cosmos? More challengingly, we have the various psychopathologies to take into account: the mind warped, bent, gone wrong. A brilliant mind can be deranged, slow wits can be gifted with compassion, rationality can be cold and twisted. Does mind in the cosmos share any of these traits? Science fiction tells tales of alien intelligences that are hostile; ancient mythologies speak of gods who are malevolent, even mad. If there is an ordering principle like mentality at work in the universe, does it attach to a personality? Can it offer warmth, sympathy, consolation? If mind evolves, does it necessarily progress toward wisdom?

NOOSPHERE OR NEUROSISPHERE?

> By the very nature of Omega, there can only be one possible point of definitive emersion—that point at which, under the synthesizing action of personalizing union, the noosphere (furling its elements upon themselves as it too furls upon itself) will reach collectively its point of convergence—at the "end of the world."
>
> PIERRE TEILHARD DE CHARDIN, *The Phenomenon of Man*.

The place of mind in evolution has been a conundrum since the theory was first expounded. Though Darwin himself was reluctant to speculate on the question beyond the narrow limits of selective advantage, the cofounder of evolutionary theory, Alfred Russel Wallace, pondered the greater issues raised by human intelligence. Wallace was frankly bewildered by the exaggerated dimensions that mind has attained in our species. There is simply so much there! A surplus of intellective, creative, imaginative capacity. Why should this be so? How can a theory based on natural selection cope with what would seem to be a massive exception to its own principles? It is not difficult for Darwinian biology to account for small, incremental advances in intelligence. A creature sharing the same habitat with others that manages to "think" a little better—for example, the chimpanzee competing for resources with its own kind or closely related types—may survive better thanks to a bit more cunning, quicker judgment, the ability to take up a stick in self-defense, the capacity to find its way to fruit in a high tree. But once that level of superiority has been reached, why should the brain grow the least bit more cunning, let alone creative? Where does art fit in, or religion, or dreams? Where does science itself belong? Being able to calculate the orbit of Mars or to explain the photosynthesis of leaves clearly confers no selective advantage.

There does exist a biological category called "hypertrophy"—overdevelopment, a good thing that has gone too far. One can see evidence of such evolutionary liabilities in the remains of extinct species: antlers, fangs, talons that grew too large to be of use. It was once thought the dinosaurs, specializing in size, outgrew their food supply. Is that how human intelligence is to be classified? If so, science would have to designate its own best instrument as a biological mistake. As Wallace saw, when we come to our own species, brains have gone far beyond anything necessary for mere survival. With that recognition, a philosophy of mind becomes especially pertinent.

The issue can be taken up from a different, more ominous angle. Not every aspect of human mental development is easily seen as an advantage. Humans have the ability to frighten themselves with ghastly fantasies, to invent cruel gods, to anticipate dire fate. They can also become the victims of hallucinations, nightmares, false beliefs, superstition. They can lie—to others and themselves. What contribution does such perverse conduct make to our biological condition? Hard-headed evolutionary theorists have never quite faced up to this dilemma. If intelligence is a selective advantage, does that advantage include all that comes with it? Does it include neurosis, which seems to be the constant companion of intelligence?

Among the most ambitious efforts made to integrate mind into the evolutionary process is that of the French paleontologist–priest Pierre Teilhard de Chardin. Teilhard argues that atop all the other physical spheres of our planet (the lithosphere, biosphere, stratosphere) there is the "noosphere," the culminating realm of mind. The noosphere is the greatest system of all and the most pregnant. It leads forward toward the climactic sphere of supermentality called "Omega Point." Evolution moves toward that level, building from primitive sentience to high philosophy and mysticism. At the summit of development, all individual human minds will coalesce into what a student of Teilhard describes as "one single, hyper-complex and conscious arch-molecule coextensive with the planet itself."[14]

But Teilhard's treatment of mind suffers from obvious idealization. It leaves out whole levels of pathological deviation at the human level. If we grant the legitimacy of the noosphere as an evolutionary phase, it might still be the case that its selective advantage ends with the higher primates, the placid gorillas for example, whose intelligence allows them to live reasonably contented lives, or with aquatic mammals like the whales and dolphins. With mankind, we may move beyond the noosphere into what might better be called the "neurosisphere": the realm of psychiatric disease. If it were the case that our species managed to kill itself off and take most of the biosphere with it, would we not have to judge our experiment in intelligence as a failure?

Teilhard de Chardin is only one of those who have developed a philosophy based on the reflexive character of evolution: the possibility that the universe attains self-consciousness in the human mind. He was himself much under the influence of the Vitalist philosophy of Henri Bergson, who surveyed the same ground in his theory of "creative evolution." Bergson's philosophy postulated the existence of an *élan vital* a sort of *anima mundi* in progress. The *élan vital,* shaping itself along the way, guides the evolutionary process forward. At its highest level of creativity, it generates human intelligence. But for Bergson this was not the end of the story. The mind that mattered was that of the artist and saint, the mind gifted with intuition. Below that level, consciousness is flawed in ways that produce suffering and carnage.

Most philosophies that deal in the evolution of consciousness place more value on the creative and spiritual than the merely clever. They remind us that the mind is a universe in its own right divided into many sectors, many levels. Even if we were to agree that the cosmos is mind-like in character, we would still have to discriminate among the varieties of mentality, asking which represents the way forward in the history of time. At what point does our mind most parallel that greater mind in which the galaxies whirl like so many magnificent ideas?

ECOLOGICAL HIERARCHY

Teilhard's speculation takes us to an apocalyptic extreme where anybody's guess is as good as his. But by brainstorming the concept of hierarchy on such an ambitious scale, he raises significant ethical and political questions. Hierarchy is a rich idea; it is also a risky one. It needs to be handled with care. In spelling out the importance of hierarchy in systems theory, we must be careful to distinguish organic and ecological from political and social structures. Every form of despotism has, after all, grounded itself in some version of the metaphorical body politic, reducing its citizens to the status of cellular units within a greater whole.

Teilhard's Omega, culminating in a single static and transcendent point, is reminiscent of Dante's vision of the great, glowing heavenly rose at the end of *The Divine Comedy*. There, at the height of paradise, every living presence has become a depersonalized petal in that fiery bouquet. The light is dazzlingly brilliant, but it washes away all individual features. The angels are interchangeable entities immersed forever in a solid celestial collectivity. Nothing changes, nothing moves, nothing happens. Teilhard patterns Omega on Dante's image of ultimate beatitude, but with an evolutionary dimension added. Time progresses toward this point, species by species, until, with the ecstatic apotheosis of humanity, all individual minds coalesce into one unified planetary consciousness, a mental singularity that is the final ethereal counterpart of the physical singularity from which the Big Bang erupted at the beginning of time. "At the world's Omega, as at its Alpha, lies the Impersonal." There are no longer people in view, but only "a harmonized collectivity of consciousnesses equivalent to a sort of superconsciousness."[15] One has the picture of a single and eternal compacted intelligence left to think one thought forever. Teilhard speaks of this condition as "hyperpersonal," but it is difficult to see that the personal soul, the most distinctive feature of Christian psychology, survives in the all-embracing divine persona. We have arrived at the highest stage of theocratic totalitarianism, an image of our destiny that might be used to sanction lower, secular forms of regimentation.

Everything Teilhard says about Omega tends to melt away into scientized mysticism. But the metaphors seem to draw a consistent picture. "Involution . . . implosion . . . unification . . . convergence . . . mega-synthesis . . . unanimity . . . centeredness." This is the language of authoritarian centralization. In the history of life on Earth, hierarchy of this kind is a recent human invention, dating back no farther than the despotic monarchies of the early River Valley civilizations. Its pattern is the Egyptian pyramid topped by a single capstone that represents the divine omnipotence of the pharaoh. It authorizes a monolithic style of politics born of fear, greed, and ambition. Societies like this can be welded together only by terror, mystification, and violence. In later industrial terms, this would be the society of Orwell's Big Brother.

If deep systems ecology has anything of value to teach us, it is that Teilhard's Omega is a bad idea about life raised to the highest power. Hierarchy, as he wields the term, is an invention of the human neurosisphere. Natural hierarchies (like our own bodies) arise spontaneously out of the evolutionary process; once selected, the constituent entities (cells and organs) hold together symbiotically. They do not need to be whipped and driven into existence by brute force. They do not cost their component parts some unrealized potentiality. In contrast, once the members of a species have attained a sufficient degree of individuation, they become participating partners within ecosystems where diversity, not unity is the basis of health. As we can see from the extravagant proliferation of life-forms, variety characterizes the evolutionary process. Evolution works out and away from its once safely stable and utterly uniform microbial origin, showing no sign of reconverging toward a single point. It does not contract; it flowers.

Yes, there are ant-heaps and beehives, herds and flocks; but there is also the human community, based upon voluntary belonging and mutual aid. The human mind makes all the difference. Far from being a cellular subunit of the body politic, it is a universe in its own right. At the human frontier, the proper ecology of mind takes us in the direction of personal growth and democratic rights.

Some deep systems theorists have great reservations about the concept of hierarchy. Viewing it as another form of anthropocentric arrogance, they fear it encourages the sort of "human chauvinism" that, in the words of the ecophilosopher Warwick Fox, results in an "unwarranted differential treatment of other beings on the basis of the fact that they are not human."[16] The concern is justified. Hierarchy is one of those ideas that can intoxicate. Teilhard was among the first to recognize that the process of evolution confers a new centrality upon the human species. "Man," he observes, "is not the center of the universe as once we thought in our simplicity, but something much more wonderful—the arrow pointing the way to the final unification of the world in terms of life. Man alone constitutes the last-born, the freshest, the most complicated, the most subtle of all the successive layers of life." Unfortunately, Teilhard shows us how such rhapsodic self-congratulations can lead to absurd conclusions, as when he decides that insects display "psychic inferiority" because they are "too small."[17] Poor things! They have reached a "morphological dead end." Only mammals are the right size.

Anybody who wants to explore the philosophy of evolution would do well to start with Teilhard; from the viewpoint of standard biology as well as Deep Ecology, he goes wrong in every way imaginable.

There is no question but that anthropocentrism can lead to claims of human supremacy over nature that lie at the root of our ecological problems. To state the possibility is to issue the warning, and to invite a different reading. We should remember that the worst environmental depredation has taken place in the modern period within a rigorously nonanthropocentric cosmology, one that reduces human existence to an inconsequential cipher in the universe. The thesis of this book has been that such a sweepingly devaluation of human life may only serve to starve our need for meaning until it produces a pathological infatuation with power. If so, it is our despairing flight from nothingness more so than any sort of anthropocentric pretension that encourages the willful assertion of human dominance.

Insofar as the evolution of the cosmos can be seen as an unfolding of ordered complexity, the human mind holds an advanced position in that process. It deserves as much admiration as all that came before. It should be possible to say this without staking out inordinate claims to superiority. More appropriate in my view would be a pride tempered by a sense of responsibility and above all curiosity. Our role is not to play pharaoh to the universe. If only we could depend upon our sense of humor to show us the comedy of such megalomania. Unfortunately, our species has too often allowed ludicrously cosmic pretensions to go to its head and has behaved accordingly.

Robinson Jeffers, perhaps the greatest English-speaking nature poet of our time, spent a lifetime of art and thought pondering the place of human life in the universe. He at last found his way to a richly ambivalent philosophical position. He described it as "Inhumanism: a shifting of emphasis and significance from man to not-man."

> It seems time that our race began to think as an adult does, rather than like an egocentric baby or insane person. This manner of thought and feeling is neither misanthropic nor pessimist. . . . It involves no false-

hoods, and is a means of maintaining sanity in slippery times; it has objective truth and human value. It offers a reasonable detachment as a rule of conduct, instead of love, hate and envy. It neutralizes fanaticism and wild hopes; but it provides magnificence for the religious instinct, and satisfies our need to admire greatness and rejoice in beauty.[18]

In the service of Inhumanism, Jeffers became a voice raised in celebration of "the transhuman magnificence." That voice, that singing voice, bearing unsentimental witness in its unique way to all that cannot know its own grandeur—"star-fire and rock-strength, the sea's cold flow and man's dark soul"—comes close to defining all that I would name as the glory of the human frontier.

IMAGO MUNDI

Through the seventeenth century in the Western world, there existed an artistic genre that combined cosmology and psychology. It was the art of the microcosm, the "little cosmos" as it might be graphically depicted. Until the universe came to be seen as a mathematical artifact best understood by numbers and formulas, natural philosophers freely employed religious symbols, myths, and poetic metaphors to depict and explain the world they lived in. The depiction *was* the explanation. Human forms, the signs of the zodiac, mythical beasts, esoteric emblems were intermingled to illustrate the shape and nature of the cosmos. Numbers were also prominent, a treasured legacy of Pythagoras and Plato, who taught the primacy of mathematics in the representation of knowledge. But the mathematics of the time was almost exclusively geometry, which lends itself to graphic art. Without exception the geometric forms of the planets, the celestial spheres, the crystals, the seasonal cycles shaded off into a mystic numerology that embraced astrology, alchemy, the music of the spheres, the transcendent harmonies of nature.

Invariably human beings and the Earth found their place at the center of the *imago mundi,* richly surrounded by all the stuff of nature and culture. Through deep self-knowledge, human beings might each ideally become microcosms in their own right, distillations in body, mind, and spirit of all the universe around them. In this sense, a microcosm was a sort of mandala, the symbolic circle used in Eastern cultures to concentrate the mind during meditation. The microcosm, like the mandala, is a contemplative domain where the soul finds its proper place.

A fully elaborated microcosm might become hopelessly congested in its attempt to tie all things together by way of esoteric correspondences: the planets of the heavens with the metals of the Earth, the anatomy

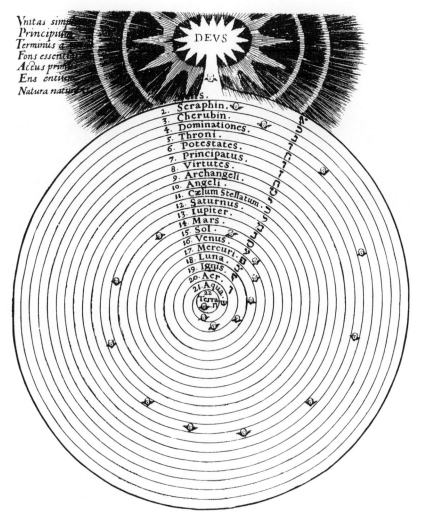

FIGURE 3: *Typical Ptolemaic microcosm c. 1540.*

of the body with the musical intervals, sexual symbols with astronomical images. This was the ancient and medieval world's effort to create in an artistic mode what scientists today seek in a Grand Unified Theory. As late as the mid-seventeenth century, leading thinkers in the Western world were convinced that the forces of nature, the principles of art, poetry and music, medicine, biblical lore, and high theology might all be harmonized into a unitary system.

Although the traditional Ptolemaic cosmos pictured here managed to hold its place in the religious doctrines of the Western world for some two thousand years, it was, from a certain point of view, inherently "materialistic." It defined the relationships between all things (the Great Chain of Being) spatially. God, heaven, and the choirs of angels were at the "top" presumably occupying some remote, circumambient location; man and the Earth were at the axis, which was also, ambiguously, the "bottom" of the cosmos. Subtler minds might also read a symbolic meaning into the geometry of the system; but the spatial arrangement of the heavenly bodies and the central location of the Earth were also understood to be literally true. The universe *looked* this way both to the observing eye and the contemplative imagination. The anthropocentrism of this cosmology was thus embedded in physical locations: things found their order and value on the basis of their distances and proximities in space.

In the pre-Copernican cosmos as depicted by Robert Fludd (see Figure 4), the *anima mundi* mediates between God and physical nature. She stands astride the heavenly and terrestrial spheres. Fludd, an alchemical philosopher, was among the most prolific microcosmic artists of the seventeenth century. Careful to stay on the right side of Christian orthodoxy, he says of Dame Nature in this depiction, "She is not a goddess, but the proximate minister of God at whose behest she governs the subcelestial worlds." Notice the Great Chain of Being that runs from the hand of God through her grasp to the Earth below. It is meant to represent the ranked order of things throughout the universe. The monkey to whom she is connected by the chain is the symbol of human culture, the "ape of nature," an image that nicely expresses the way in which the creative power of human thought was understood to mirror divine power. Once again, the imagery expresses anthropocentrism spatially, ordering things by their place.

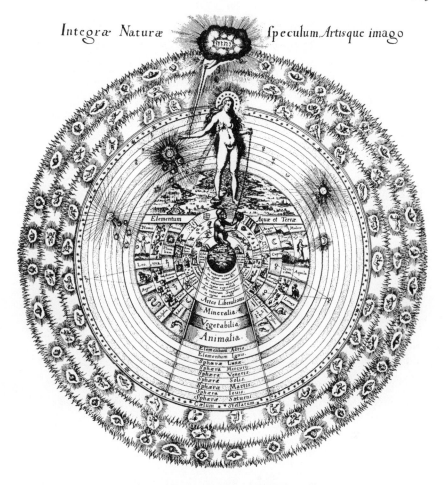

FIGURE 4: *Microcosm including* Anima Mundi

THE MICROCOSM REDRAWN

The new cosmology is not quite done with certain elements of physical centrality for our world. It is among the more striking cosmic coincidences that the dimensions of physical bodies in the infinite universe are not, as one might expect, random and erratic. Things do not come in all sizes; rather everything appears to lie within a fairly restricted zone of possibilities. "Suppose," John Barrow asks, "we were to commission a survey of all the different types of objects in the universe from the scale of elementary particles to the highest clusters of galaxies." He then shows us what that assignment might produce on a size–mass diagram (Figure 5).[19]

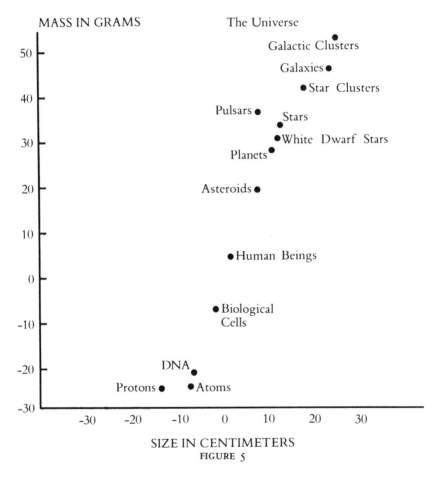

SIZE IN CENTIMETERS
FIGURE 5

While we might have expected Figure 5 to reveal a senseless scattering of objects, it clearly does not. There is a systematic clustering in one sector of the plane, leaving large areas empty. What to make of this? George Seielstad, working with a similar diagram, draws a thought-provoking conclusion. After roughly arranging all there is in the universe—from the bacterium to the galaxy—along the two axes of size (in centimeters) and mass (in grams) he concludes that "not too far from the middle of this enormous span of sizes and masses lies the one configuration of matter that has pushed the investigation in both directions."[20] In this curious statistical spread, "humans are a rough mean between the near-infinitesimal and the near-infinite. . . . For the mathematically minded, a human's size is the approximate geometric mean of the sizes of a planet and an atom, that is,

$$\text{human's size} \simeq (\text{planet's size} \times \text{atom's size})^{1/2}$$

His or her mass is the approximate geometric mean of the masses of a planet and a proton:

$$\text{human's mass} \simeq (\text{planet's mass} \times \text{proton's mass})^{1/2}"$$

Here, in a version by John Gribbin and Martin Rees, is much the same idea, this time using a somewhat more traditional iconography: the tail-biting serpent Oeroborous, the alchemical symbol of wholeness (Figure 6).[21] The depiction is meant to show "the linkages between micro and macro scales," the great and small of the cosmos. Once again mankind is centrally positioned. The scientists postulate that the smallest of things, "the dominant dark matter may be subnuclear particles surviving from the Big Bang. The ultimate unified theory . . . may relate quantum gravitational effects (on scales of the Planck length, 10^{-33} cm) to the properties of the entire observable universe (10^{28} cm)."

How seriously should one take this sort of numbers game in the philosophical reconstruction of modern science? As far as mere statistical novelties and highly speculative correlations are concerned, perhaps not very. Barrow believes some of the curiosities referred to here may be among the lesser selection effects of the Anthropic Principle. Then, too, numbers—even the seemingly exact quantities of physicists—lend themselves to many arbitrary permutations. With the aid of a small computer, one could probably generate all sorts of coincidences and correlations. But when Sir Arthur Eddington tried to make some ambitious epistemological sense of the many dimensionless constants on which modern science is based, he was accused of indulging in numerology. Still, it is of some interest to note that there are scientists these days who take time to play such games.

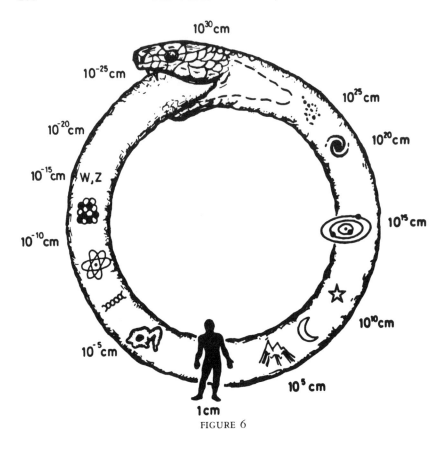

FIGURE 6

On the other hand, the relationship between the size, mass, or structure of things and the *history* of the universe is another matter. That time and matter have a parallel history is a solid fact in modern science, one that ties together a growing body of knowledge in both physics and astronomy. There is, of course, always the chance that everything about the new cosmology—the Big Bang, cosmic inflation, background radiation, the general theory of relativity—might come unstrung by new evidence. But if the theory holds, it places life and mind in a temporal-developmental position that is distinctly new and provocative as a frontier phenomenon. The microcosms presented here may lack the artistic resonance and rich symbolism that once characterized natural philosophy; but behind these graphs and charts—which could not have been drawn as recently as two generations ago—there lie ideas about the cosmos that bring with them a new interpretation of human centrality.

In the new cosmology of the late twentieth century, human centrality is defined historically, rather than spatially. Life and mind emerge at the culminating "now" of a hierarchically evolving universe. Their place is as unique as that of humanity in the ancient Ptolemaic cosmos, but the expression of that uniqueness has become more scientifically sophisticated and more ethereal—in the sense that it depends upon the nonmaterial medium of time. In this case, the Chain of Being becomes the temporal progression of complex systems emerging and maturing since the Big Bang, from the most primitive atomic configurations through to the organization of galactic clusters and finally—within our own galaxy—the life-bearing Earth. In this depiction of "the history of the universe" by Paul Davies we see direction in time replacing position in space as the central consideration for philosophical elaboration (Figure 7).[22]

David Layzer offers a chart that illustrates the same hierarchical progression, but extends it farther into the realm of mind to include the "feedback loops" that produce social and cultural levels of exper-

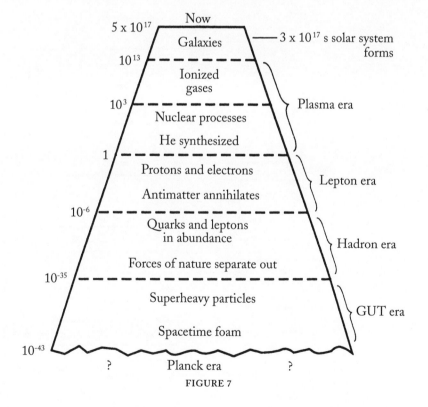

FIGURE 7

ience (Figure 8).[23] He notes that "at the beginning of the cosmic expansion, there was little or no order in the universe. As the universe expanded, chemical and structural order come into being. . . . Every process creates structures and initial conditions that make possible new processes. . . . Every level and sublevel of the hierarchy of initial conditions embodies a qualitatively distinct variety of order."

Among the most aesthetically ambitious modern microcosms is Dion Wright's "Evolution Mandala," which for all its artistic liberties is a reasonably accurate presentation of modern scientific ideas (Figure 9). It is an achievement that the natural philosophers of Robert Fludd's

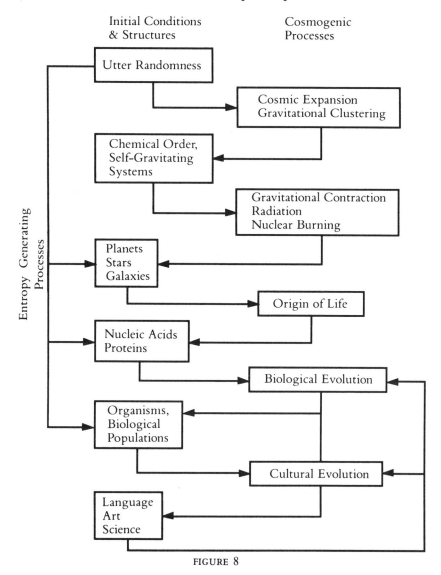

FIGURE 8

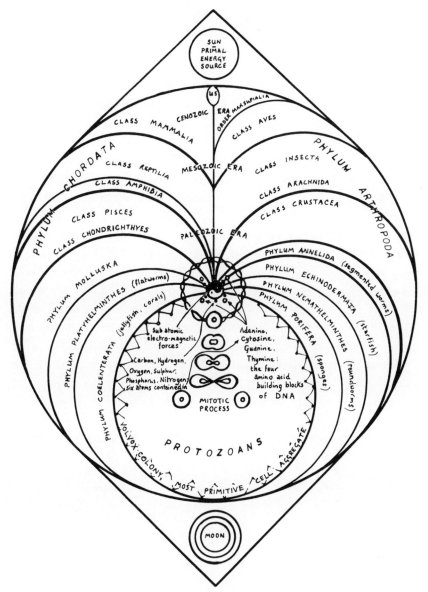

FIGURE 9: *Evolution Mandala by Dion Wright*

age would have respected. The original work, which was painted in a corncrib in Woodstock, New York, in the mid-sixties, is too large and detailed to be reproduced here. I offer a small schematic diagram that shows its overall conceptual organization. The artist admits to taking a few poetic liberties. A yin-yang, male–female polarity is introduced associating man with the sun at the top, woman with the moon at the bottom. But this is done with a cautionary note that the prominence of the human in this design is meant to imply planetary stewardship not dominance.

The overall coherence of the work is more than a matter of creative selection and embellishment, however; it draws thoughtfully upon valid astronomical, geological, and biological knowledge and arranges it in a defensible order. Most notably, Wright has found a way to avoid the stolid and misleading linearity of most evolutionary depictions, which almost inevitably use a tree-branch formation or a grid that loses the efflorescent creativity of the process. Instead, here we have a flowering pattern in which the endless organic variety at the circumference wells up from a simple core where we find the basic atomic-molecular constituents of life surrounded by the DNA double helix. In such a depiction, we have the sense of "progress" in evolution not as an orthogenic straight line, but as rich diversity with an overall increase in complexity as time goes on. We also achieve a clear sense of the magnitude of the nonhuman in the story of life, especially the enormous space taken up with Protozoans.

For all its detail and magnitude, what this depiction lacks is the dimension of cosmic time and development from the moment of the Big Bang. We would then see the biology of the Earth embraced by a still greater evolutionary framework requiring an even greater appreciation of hierarchical process and structure in the universe at large.

Part Three

◆

ECOLOGY

The New Cosmology and our deepening study of ordered complexity provide the raw intellectual material for a new understanding of human connectedness with nature. In time, with enough help from the artists and visionary philosophers, this body of fact and theory may mature into an ecologically grounded form of animism. We will find ourselves once again on speaking terms with nature. Within this greater environmental context, sanity and madness take on new meanings. We begin to see how the urban-industrial reality principle represses much that is essential to the health both of person and planet: the primitive, the organic, the feminine, the child-like, the wild.

Let us assume that the psyche, like all natural systems, retains the capacity for creative self-adjustment—at least within limits. It is, after all, an offspring of the greater Gaian system that works to enhance life on Earth. How, then, does the planet respond to the reckless monkey cunning of its troublesome human children? Is it possible that the "narcissism" we see emerging in the high industrial societies has a creative role to play in taming our Promethean delusions?

Eight

◆

CITY POX AND THE PATRIARCHAL EGO

URBANISM IN EXTREMIS

Imagine we possessed a motion picture of the planet Earth filmed from an orbiting satellite over the time span of the last million years. An animated slice of the most recent and eventful chapter in Gaia's biography. The greatest movie ever made.

Suppose we accelerated the film to compress those million years into a few hours running time.

What do we see?

For nearly the whole of that period, only the seas and deserts, the grasslands and forests, the polar ice-caps and great mountain chains show through beneath the drifting clouds. No sign of animal life is visible, certainly no trace of human existence, even though, during the last few hundred thousand years, our ancestors are there, tiny hunting and gathering bands unobtrusively roaming the woodlands and savannas, chasing down game, pulling up roots, plucking berries. For most of the movie we see just this: a floating blue-green sphere with swatches of sun-baked sand and crinkled belts of rock.

Not until we reach the final scenes—the most recent four or five millennia—do we detect a few scattered human works, mainly in the fertile valleys of the Nile, Euphrates, Indus, Yellow rivers. Fragile irrigation grids, patchwork plots and strips of cultivated soil. Possibly the Egyptian pyramids or the Great Wall of China would show up, the terraced mountain slopes of the Andes and the curious "Nazca lines," the colossal Earth-drawings of Peru. But more significant than any of these giant-sized works would be the unusual habitat in which their builders reside. It is a space of their own making: tight little clusters of homes, workshops, markets along the seacoasts or at the junctures of rivers. Around these confines, the humans build high walls; within them they cover the ground beneath their feet with paving stone, forcing the green land, the forest, and the wild things away from them—as if they wished to become a world to themselves.

We are watching the first cities come into being. There are only a few and they are small by our standards, but already we can sense a fateful change in the human condition. The townsfolk are an alert and greedy breed. They connive to draw riches to themselves from distant points; they organize armies clothed in bronze and iron that subjugate the tribal peoples nearby. They create self-congratulatory myths of their power and magnificence, tales of heroes who stamp the Earth with ruthless conquest. Kings appear among them who disport themselves like gods and organize vast collective projects: roadways, fortresses, canals that carry the water of rivers where people wish it to go. For the first time, we can see the marks of human will graven on the face of the planet, a message of mighty structures that seems to declare to the heavens, "See, we are here. Take notice of us!"

With these settlements, a daring experiment begins. We see a small fraction of our species ensconcing itself within a tiny universe of their own design, a theatrical arena that magnifies the stature of its occupants and multiplies their energy. But the towns are no more than pinpricks on the surface of the globe, none of them visible without the aid of a zoom focus. They are still massively surrounded by an invincible wilderness that mockingly dwarfs their pretensions And so they remain for another four or five thousand years . . . until we are no more than two centuries from our own time.

Then in the closing moment of the film (we must watch closely now to catch sight of this) we notice a curious change in the scene below us. It begins in the midlands of Britain, a tiny island off the western edge of the Eurasian land mass. Gray and black dots issuing smoke like strange, smoldering sores break out on the surface of the planet. The dots spread across western Europe, leap the ocean to North America, then to the other continents. They quickly increase in number and in size, becoming ugly dark blemishes. Focusing in more closely, we can see heaps of slag and rubble forming around them like weltering flesh. We see the smoke thicken into man-made clouds that block out the sky. Rivulets of oily waste and noxious fluids issue from these fuming sites, draining into nearby lakes and streams.

We are watching the rise and spread of the first industrial towns—only a few at first, but growing haphazardly in size and number. From them, railways of steel, highways of asphalt and concrete fan out to connect one with another until over sprawling sectors of landscape there is a vibrant network of racing vehicles that carries the urban rhythm over the countryside. Soon the sky is filled with the traffic of aircraft; great ships ply the seas, converging upon the cities with cargoes from distant lands. We see one more thing, and that perhaps the most ominous. By the thousands, then by the millions, people leave the countryside to stream into the cities as if they were hypnotically drawn by the hammering tempo of this new way of life. As the cities swell in size, they begin to take up a prodigious amount of open space; they dilate through stages of gargantuan growth—from metropolis to megalopolis to conurbations that stretch across continents, spreading one urban stain into another.

Gaia has been stricken with City Pox.

What we experience in our time in a thousand forms of discomfort, unsightliness, disease originates in this sudden, spreading rash of industrial cities. "Sudden" means within two centuries, since the first mill towns sprang up in England in the 1780s. Even so, in England, the cradle of industrialism, the population did not become predominantly urban until 1850; in the United States not until 1910. We are talking about the last eyeblink in the history of life on Earth. Yet within that mere instant of geological time, industrial culture has become an urban empire whose power spans oceans and continents.

For that matter, it is not enough to diagnose City Pox by the mere territorial size of cities. We must imagine the appetite for resources and political control that spreads out like so many invisible filaments from the urban centers, claiming the forests, the buried mineral deposits, the pools of oil, the deep aquifers, the most distant sources of energy. The cities own everything, govern everything, consume everything. Their pipelines and electrical power-grids cross mountains, jungles, tundra; their satellites patrol the frontiers of empty space. The subtle web of their communications wraps the planet in an electronic skin. Their artifacts rest on the surface of the moon and nearby planets. The wilderness has become their playground, recreational space for weary tourists. Wildlife survives by their sufferance upon reservations, as do the few remaining traditional societies. The culture of cities has become the planet's only culture, all others lingering on as curiosities preserved for scholarly study, or, as in the case of the Moslem fundamentalist insurgents, fighting a losing rear guard action. In the presence of the urbanites, only the vermin and the microbes thrive and multiply.

Now, in just the last few frames before our film rushes to its end, we see the megalopolitan pockmarks on the planet's surface swirl and churn themselves into so many insatiable vortices. Nothing escapes the pull of their omnivorous metabolism. They suck in the riches of the Earth and spew them back in running streams of merchandise and debris. We can see nothing below us but a vista of parasitic urban agglomerations that eat and eat at the substance of the planet, returning more garbage than the world's natural cycles can clean away.

City Pox may be approaching its terminal stage.

THE MADNESS OF CITIES

Modern psychology has always been plagued by the problem of evidence. Wishing to be more than purely speculative, it has had to find an empirical method for exploring the inaccessible interior of the psyche. By its very nature, the mind is a mystery; it cannot be laid on the table for dissection or x-rayed like the limbs and organs of the body. Wanting to know more about the meaning of human behavior than he could learn from studying muscular reflexes and physiological traces, Freud arrived at the concept of "projection." The hidden contents of the psyche must in some way be *projected* into the world for analysis.

He began modestly. The first projections were simply what he could get his patients to tell him. Psychoanalysis was "the talking cure." Patients revealed themselves by letting consciousness stream. Eventually, Freud hoped, they would get around to telling him what mattered most. The method may have borrowed indirectly from the new technology of motion pictures. At least that is what Freud seemed to have in mind when he described the analyst as a "blank screen" on which the troubled psyche can be freely projected. Cleverly used, the technique can be reasonably productive, but there are obvious pitfalls. Repression distorts and misleads. Memory is not always the most reliable register of motivation, affect, emotion. Patients forget, they exaggerate, they lie. Seeking a more direct route into the unconscious, Freud hit upon dreams, the symbolic landscape of the psyche. This may have been his most enduring contribution, primarily because it opened up a new vista for the study of human nature. If dreams can be read as a code that reveals hidden intentions, why stop there? Might not the whole of culture be seen as the collective dream of our species? Thanks to Freud and to Jung after him, psychiatry rapidly developed from a would-be science that had nearly nothing to work with into a philosophical inquiry that had everything to work with, all the myth, lore, art, literature, and religion of the human race.

As bold as psychiatry has become in using cultural contents to probe the unconscious, it has been less willing to use political and social institutions for that purpose. This may be because governments, corporations, political parties, armies present themselves as products of deliberation and reason, rather than free fantasy. They seem more "real" than the inventions of art and religion. It has been left to artists like Kafka and De Chirico to capture the nightmarish quality that haunts the streets, the bureaucracies, the law courts of everyday life.

And what of the city, which has grown to become the biggest of all human institutions? Nothing has absorbed more human energy; nothing projects more of our aspirations. Yet modern psychiatry has never undertaken a symbolic reading of the city. Doubtless this is because psychiatrists work from within the city on which they are totally dependent for sustenance, for recognition from their peers, for making money, and for building their careers. Nevertheless, for an ecopsychology, nothing serves as a more telling symptom of our collective state of soul than this urban habitat, which has balanced on the edge of psychopathology since its beginning. Now thoroughly rationalized and accepted as "normal," the city dates back to the fantasies of megalomaniac pharaohs and conquering god-kings. It was born of delusions of grandeur, built by disciplined violence, and dedicated to the ruthless regimentation of man and nature. The walls and towers, pyramids and ziggurats of ancient cities were declarations of a wishful biological independence from the natural environment. For many centuries that isolation was only partial; the wild environs were never far away. With the passage of time and the growth of technology, we have gained the power to reify the wish. Soon there will be no great beasts that are not in zoos or on reservations; there will be no tribal peoples who remember a different relationship to the planet than that of the urbanites. At last our delusions of omnipotence can be fully indulged; the projection of the urban fantasy is complete. We see it in every modern city, realized in glass, concrete, and metal. It is the ancient dream of a totally encapsulated existence free of disease, dependency, the dirt and discomfort of organic life—perhaps even finally of death.

As a way of life, urbanism was never intended for more than a small minority of maniacal warlords, profit-frenzied merchants, and eccentric intellectuals, people obsessed with human works and human power whose view of the world was bounded by the city walls. Industrialism, with its rapacious use of the environment as either raw material or dumping ground, has further entrenched the city's alienation from nature. It has more solidly institutionalized and rationalized urban culture's psychotic habits. Wilhelm Reich coined the phrase "body armor" for the neurotic defense mechanism that cuts us off from spontaneous vitality and sensuous intimacy. The industrial city might be seen as the collective "body armor" of our culture, a pathological effort to distance us from close contact with the natural continuum from which we evolve. Yet it is in this crazed and crazy-making context that our psychotherapeutic rites are practiced in obedience to theories that *include not a single critical reflection on that context.* Freud and the Radical Therapists may have been bold enough to float the possibility that all people participate in a "collusive madness." But even they raise the hypothesis from within cities, looking out upon the world and upon history through that warped lens. They are like astronomers who should not expect to see the heavens that lie beyond the glowing haze of the cities unless they leave those cities for distant, unpopulated places. What they would offer as therapy, even at its most compassionate, is an artifact of the same urban intellect that raised up what Lewis Mumford once called "the megamachines" of the ancient River Valleys. Their science too is indebted to the technics and politics of mass extermination.

The situation is somewhat like this.

Imagine we are watching a psychiatrist at work, a good, caring, even gifted psychiatrist. In the waiting room outside sits a throng of patients, a thriving practice. One by one they are brought in for treatment. They prove to be a demanding lot, exhibiting a veritable compendium of emotional disorders: people nearly hysterical, people weighed down by suicidal depression, people suffering hallucinations, people turned catatonic, people afflicted with horrific nightmares, people driven to desperation by paranoid delusions that they are constantly being watched by those who intend them grave harm.

Dutifully, at the psychiatrist's bidding, the patients do what they are asked to do. They rehearse their dreams, confess their fears, their hidden desires, their guilty secrets. The psychiatrist listens and ponders each case, struggling heroically to heal them, spending long, hard hours at the job. But few are cured. Their terror and tormenting delusions continue and even grow worse. The psychiatrist very nearly despairs, yet soldiers on determined to do whatever can be done by a humane doctor offering first-class care.

Now step back and view the scene from a wider perspective. The patients report for therapy to a room. The room is in a building, the building is in a place. The place has a name. Buchenwald. Just outside the doctor's window we can see the barbed wire, the whipping post, the ovens.

What would we say of a psychiatrist who undertook to heal the mad in a place that was itself the creation of madness? What would it mean to "cure" in such a place? Would it mean reconciling the inmates to their condition, soothing away their fears, talking them out of their nightmares?

Psychiatry as we know it, practiced by urbanites upon urbanites in an urban setting, is very much that sort of project. If neither doctor nor patient can see it that way, it may be that those who are born and raised in a concentration camp have no reason to believe there is any place else to be, and even less so when the camp expands to become as big as all the world.

THE DREAM OF SAVAGE WISDOM

The American Indian is the vengeful ghost lurking in the back of the troubled American mind. . . . That ghost will claim the next generation as its own. When this has happened, citizens of the USA will at last begin to be Americans, truly at home on the continent, in love with their land. The chorus of a Cheyenne Indian Ghost dance song—*"hi-niswa' vita'ki'ni"*—"We shall live again."

GARY SNYDER

Gaia is sick. In her fevered state, she dreams—through the minds of her most sensitive human children—of the simple folk who once lived lightly on her ample body, taking little, giving back in pious reciprocity, admiring and fearing her magnificence. Images of noble savagery haunt the modern Western world, a healthy sign of self-doubt.

It was, significantly, a woman, the seventeenth century English novelist Aphra Behn, who created this piece of folklore. Herself an outsider, a career woman in the densely masculine, intensely competitive intellectual community of her time, she could easily envision the dignity that might reside in those who shared her outcast status. She invented the figure of Oroonoko the Royal Slave as a critical corrective to the smug self-righteousness of the London intelligentsia through which she moved as an amusing oddity.

The myth of the noble savage has always had about it a dream-like ambiguity, an overlapping of contradictory images. In the civilized Western world, the prevailing public perception of real traditional people has long made them out to be contemptible heathens, cultural failures bordering on the subhuman. Even anthropologists of the early twentieth century tended to regard their uncivilized subjects of study as woefully retarded, therefore deservedly obsolescent. On these grounds of arrogant ethnocentrism, popular and scholarly opinion converged. Savages were backward because superstitious, superstitious because backward, therefore much in need of Christianizing, civilizing, and development. (Or more likely, eligible for outright extermination at the hands of their white Western conquerors.) Hostility to the primitive and traditional was the party line of revolutionaries as well as colonial profiteers. From Marx's viewpoint, the goal of progressive politics was to abolish "the idiocy of rural life" and all that predated it in favor of industrial progress. Among the political philosophers of the industrial period, only sentimental anarchists like William Morris or Peter Kropotkin held out against this ideological consensus, harking back like the Romantics before them to a legendary state of nature when village democracy and tribal egalitarianism reigned.

At the same time, in each generation, some version of primitive innocence has returned in fiction to challenge our confidence in the rightness and rationality of civilized ways. Figures like Oroonoko, Uncas (the last of the Mohicans), Robinson Crusoe's Friday, and Tarzan (who combined both European whiteness and jungle savagery) have enjoyed widespread popularity, betraying a fascination with virtues that we sense civilization endangers.

Through the nineteenth century, the nobility of savages was understood to reside in their moral excellence. They were pristine and pure, the children of Eden untouched by original sin. That image remains with us today. In the early 1980s a South African movie called *The Gods Must Be Crazy* attained a cult status in the United States, in many cities setting records for the length of its run. A slender effort that had little to offer except some zany slapstick comedy, its totally unexpected popularity apparently had to do with the picture of life it offered among the Bushman natives of the Kalahari. Audiences, especially in college towns and upscale neighborhoods, found them charmingly naive, trusting, the perfect foil for the mad antics of the civilized whites around them. Of course, these Bushmen were appearing in a movie; some of them may have been professional actors. In any case, they were playing a part—and a very clichéd part: the noble children of nature all over again. But the public loved it.

Implicit in this image has always been the assumption that living close to untamed nature accounts for the superiority of uncivilized people. Often the wilderness was credited with little more than the capacity to isolate the savage from the vices of the city. At different times different heroic qualities were understood to prosper among savage folk in their seclusion. Their inherent honor and freedom proved most appealing during the Enlightenment and through the Romantic period. Or sometimes it was their child-like innocence that drew a more condescending admiration. "The savage," as Shelley put it, "is to the ages what the child is to years." Later among the Social Darwinists and Nietzscheans, it was their hardihood and toughness that won acclaim, the virtues of the warrior. The savage was more self-denyingly rugged, lived more abstemiously, possessed more valor than what the chauvinistic Teddy Roosevelt called "the over-civilized man." (Though, by a nice contradiction, T.R. also regarded a "war against savages" as the "most ultimately righteous.") Later still, after Freud, who envisaged prehistoric people as dominated by "heedless sexual and primitive egotistic motives," writers like D. H. Lawrence imagined that savages were gifted with greater erotic prowess and a guiltless disregard for middle-class inhibitions; they lived closer to the instinctual drives, went proudly naked in the world, and fornicated without shame.

What none of these flattering, largely fantastic images granted to savages was intellectual competence, the ability to understand the world better than their civilized counterparts and use its resources to greater advantage. Primitive folk were, by definition, underdeveloped. They had no true science; they possessed no technological proficiency. This might contribute to their moral health, but not their economic well-being. Savages were noble *in spite of* their ignorance, backwardness, poverty. Only now, as the empire of cities crowds the wilderness toward obsolescence and threatens all traditional societies with extinction, does an intriguing new variation on the old theme emerge: *savagery as ecological wisdom,* the secret of survival and permanent well-being. It is precisely the technological simplicity and the absence of science that create the environmental harmony in which traditional people supposedly live. Their "superstition" emerges as an alternative worldview possessing its own dignity and practicality.

We know now that the durability of traditional societies had much to do with the moral reciprocity between human beings and their environment that characterizes the animistic worldview. Some anthropologists have come to see the value of "ritually regulated ecosystems" that impose religious constraints on human depredation. There are some remarkable examples of these still in existence. In some cases, they look enough like viable solutions to contemporary economic problems to attract the attention of experts. Perhaps these traditional ways offer solutions where more sophisticated methods have failed. For example, in the Colombian Amazon, native peoples have proved so successful at sustaining the integrity of the rainforests, that it became official policy in the late eighties to restore them to the land from which they had been driven by rubber companies and other industrial vandals. Their religious lore plays an indispensable role in their discriminating use of the jungle's rich but imperiled resources. One student of these societies (they number more than fifty ethnic groups totaling some 70,000 people) calls the shaman who stands at the center of their hallucinogenic rites, "an ecologist by culture," one who negotiates with "the guardians of the plants and animals" to determine the hunting and gathering privileges of the tribes.[1]

Similarly, in Bali, the potentially disastrous impact of Western "green revolution" agriculture has been mollified by the influence of an American anthropologist. Steven Lansing took the care to study the traditional water control system of the island. He used an ingenious computer simulation to analyze the operations of the age-old water temples of Bali, each the shrine of a water goddess attended by a priest. He discovered that centuries ago the rice farmers had achieved a remarkably efficient system of water-sharing that also serves as a form of pest control.[2] In another part of the world, hydraulic engineers are now rethinking many of the ambitious irrigation and drainage projects planned by African nations where the scarcity of water is often the greatest barrier to development. Some of the grandiose dams built in Nigeria, Egypt, and Zambia over the past few generations have turned out to be expensive failures. The alternative to such Western-inspired "engineering megalomania" may be a return to traditional techniques of trapping rainfall by means of tunnels, walls, dikes, and microcatchments. These cheap, durable, and flexible methods derive from generations of experience living in barren terrain. In a recent study of archaic water-collecting techniques, archaeologist David Gilbertson concludes that "the wisdom of the ancients in managing these harsh landscapes was more substantive than our own."[3]

One of the oldest and most effective ritual-based ecosystems can be found in the Bolivian Andes. Anthropologist Joseph Bastien has studied what might be called the "metaphorical economics" of the villages that survive on the severely vertical terrain of Mount Kaata. In Inca times the indigenous people worked out an elaborate image of their mountain as a vast human body. Each subgroup has its place within the geo-anatomical design of the region. There are the pastoral folk who inhabit the largely barren highlands on the "head" of the mountain; the central fields around the village of Kaata are the "belly" and the "heart"; farther down the slope in the lower corn fields, the families think of themselves as the "toenails" of the mountain–body. The anatomical paradigm cements the economic interdependence of the villages; but more than that, it expresses basic religious teachings. Wholeness is understood to be sacred among the Andean people; the integrity of the region is the chief focus of rites carried out by tribal diviners who understand the sacrifices they conduct as the spiritual metabolism of the mountain. The role of the ritualist is "to circulate life and energy throughout the social and ecological levels. He sets in motion vital principles which unite the mountain into a social and metaphorical whole."[4]

How markedly different from our own response to the environment is the reverence we see displayed in these examples. Yet the use of ritual and metaphor works in ways that even the most utilitarian observer would find commendable. Each also reflects the personal rapport with the natural world that we found at the core of traditional psychotherapy. Far from assigning economy and psyche to separate compartments of life, these cultures blend them in ways that allow the physical and spiritual to enhance one another. Even if we find little here that we can directly borrow and use, a renewed appreciation of the primitive and the traditional may be one of our most useful resources in dealing with our environmental emergency. Granted that one can find instances of tribal societies that have abused and even ruined their habitat. In prehistoric times, the tribal and nomadic people of the Mediterranean basin overcut and overgrazed the land so severely that the scars of the resulting erosion can still be seen. Their sacramental sense of nature did not offset their ignorance of the long-range damage they were doing to their habitat.

Even so, one finds nothing in the historical record to compare with the wanton assault upon the global environment we witness in our own time—and this on the part of developed industrial societies that arrogantly claim to know better. When it comes to understanding nature in all its complexity, knowledge—the sort of knowledge modern biology, geography, geology make available—is surely essential. But just as surely, when it comes to preserving the environment, knowledge is not sufficient. Something else is needed, at the very least, a properly nonethnocentric humility and a willingness to admit the error of our collective ways. And beyond that, the greatness of soul to seek instruction wherever it can be found, even from nonliterate, nonurban societies. These are not virtues the civilized have practiced in their relations with the primitive—until very recently.

NEOLITHIC CONSERVATISM AND THE ETHICAL UNCONSCIOUS

The reappraisal of the primitive—especially for its ecological wisdom—has come along many routes, in some cases heavily freighted with political as well as environmental priorities. This can be seen vividly in the Utopian anarchism that Paul Goodman brought to prominence in the sixties. Goodman liked to refer to himself, somewhat impishly, as a conservative, one who cared most of all

> for green grass and clean rivers, children with bright eyes and good color whatever the color, people safe from being pushed around so they can be themselves. Conservatives at present seem to want to go back to conditions that obtained in the administration of McKinley. But when people are subject to universal social engineering and the biosphere itself is in danger, we need a more neolithic conservatism.[5]

In contrast to the "phony conservatives" who continue to care more for the welfare of high rollers in the marketplace and the baronial corporations, Goodman took as his historical baseline the tribal simplicities of the prehistoric past. The result was a conservatism that reached so far beyond the empire of cities that it became the basis for a new radicalism. Goodman was through and through a New Yorker of intensely sophisticated tastes; yet like many romantic anarchists before him, he nursed a sincere if somewhat sentimentalized allegiance to bucolic folkways. His goal was to recapture these ancestral values within the context of the modern metropolis. Like E. F. Schumacher, he sought to achieve the "small" that is "beautiful" within the context of the big by way of decentralization and internal diversification. He felt this would be the cure not only for many of our political ills but for the crippling sense of powerlessness that is the peculiar psychopathology of industrial society. For Goodman, the ideal village for modern times would be something like Greenwich Village in its heyday, a colorful, lively community of artists and intellectuals blessed with cultural distinction and a decent amount of neighborhood autonomy within the otherwise suffocating bulk of greater New York.

In his effort to recapture the spirit of the neolithic within a high industrial order, Goodman was following the trail blazed by Prince Peter Kropotkin, whose discovery of intraspecies cooperation we have mentioned in chapter 5. Kropotkin's place as one of the founders of modern ecology is widely acknowledged; he is among those who created the concept of the ecosystem. What is less recognized is the psychological theory that Kropotkin deduced from his studies and that qualifies him as among the first ecopsychologists.

Kropotkin was always careful to insist that the mutual aid he discerned among all living things was not primarily an altruistic virtue. It went much deeper. It was an instinctual, utterly spontaneous impulse welded into the foundations of animal consciousness and evolving throughout the history of life on Earth. The contrast with Freud could not be more dramatic. Based on his close, lifelong study of animals in the wild and the tribal societies of Siberia and Manchuria (a larger body of evidence than Freud ever accumulated in his consulting room), Kropotkin concluded that human nature was fundamentally ethical; kinship and moral concern come to it as naturally as the song comes to the bird. At the foundations of the unconscious one finds *conscience,* the moral energy of the personality as firmly rooted in the psyche as patricidal jealousy or the death instinct—or possibly more so.

> It is not love and not even sympathy upon which society is based in mankind. It is the conscience—be it only at the stage of an instinct—of human solidarity. It is the unconscious recognition of the force that is borrowed by each man from the practice of mutual aid; of the close dependency of every one's happiness upon the happiness of all; and of the sense of justice, or equity, which brings the individual to consider the rights of every other individual as equal to his own. Upon this broad and necessary foundation the still higher moral feelings are developed.[6]

For Kropotkin, the factor of innate conscience makes human community a great deal more than an agglomeration of people held together by a social contract. It is a biologically deep and intricate system. In contrast to the totalitarian regimentation that treats the populace as so many subordinate cellular units of the body politic, Kropotkin would have a society of autonomous persons, each linked to each by ethical caring. Nothing more is needed, no police force, no bureaucratic apparatus. But of course we *have* police and bureaucracy; we have had them for a very long time. Why? What is the need if there is an ethical unconscious that provides a reliable social bond? Anarchists have never produced a good answer to the question; they are no better at explaining the origin of evil than anybody else. But it is nonetheless clear that if an ethical unconscious did *not* exist, no amount of police force or bureaucracy could hold any society together. We form ourselves spontaneously into family, clan, band, tribe, guild, village, town. This is social ecology in action. The anarchist asks: how far can this instinctual sociability be used to solve the social evils that beset us?

Freud, dealing with the psychic casualties of bourgeois industrial Europe, could find nothing in nature with which to connect the psyche but vindictive selfishness—and beyond that the alien void of a dead universe. Kropotkin, dealing with healthy animals in the wild and ruggedly independent peasant folk, asserted an ethical unconscious derived from biological symbiosis. Goodman, in his turn drawing on the same fine faith in human nature to create his neolithic conservatism, broadened the analysis. He was among the first to connect decentralism and healthy ecology with the Taoist tradition. In the Tao, at least as he understood it, he found the principle of organic self-regulation whether of the body, the community, or the environment. The homely mysticism of Lao Tzu, the Chinese peasant sage, became the basis of Goodman's Gestalt psychology, a significant departure from Freudian orthodoxy that involved trusting the body, the senses, and the natural environment to solve their problems in their own spontaneous way.

Gestalt began in the 1920s as a divergent approach to the psychology of perception. In contrast to the Behaviorists, who saw perception as essentially passive and receptive, the Gestaltists Wolfgang Köhler and Kurt Koffka fixed upon the remarkable capacity of the sensory organs to create meaningful patterns ("Gestalts") even when confronted with seeming chaos. The mind makes meaning, even when it has little to work with. This finding raised intriguing questions. How far can this formative tendency be extended beyond the eye, ear, touch? Can it be found throughout the organism in all parts of mind and body? Can it be found in our relation to other people and external nature as a whole? In the late forties, Goodman and the Freudian maverick Fritz Perls, starting with these questions, elaborated Gestalt into a new school of psychiatry, the first therapy to use the word "ecology" to describe the spontaneous adjustive power of the organism within its environment. Gestalt assumed innate healthy functioning. Where there was neurosis, then, the therapeutically pertinent question became: *what is getting in the way?*[7]

The distinguishing feature of these early efforts to combine psychology and ecology is optimism. Both Kropotkin and Goodman credit human nature with native innocence. Neither force nor the threats of a father god are necessary to make people behave as convivial beings. The politics of domination begins when some people teach other people that the body, the psyche, the community, and nature at large are unreliable, incompetent, hostile, therefore in need of top-down supervision. Authoritarian politics roots itself in the guilty conscience. It begins by convincing people they cannot trust one another, that they cannot trust themselves. The Zen poet Gary Snyder summarizes the critique nicely. His poetry is meant to invoke "the Great Subculture" that "runs without break from Paleo-Siberian Shamanism and Magdalenian cave-painting; through megaliths and Mysteries, astronomers, ritualists, alchemists . . . right down to Golden Gate Park," the scene of many a gathering of the San Francisco tribes during the 1960s.

> All this [he tells us] is subversive to civilization: for civilization is built on hierarchy and specialization. A ruling class, to survive, must propose a Law: a law to work must have a hook into the social psyche—*and the most effective way to achieve this is to make people doubt their natural worth and instincts, especially sexual.* To make "human nature" suspect is also to make Nature—the wilderness—the adversary. Hence the ecological crisis of today. [Italics added][8]

From a scholarly viewpoint, Kropotkin, Goodman, and Snyder may take great liberties in their generalizations about "primary people" (Snyder's name for tribal and peasant societies), though I would say less so than Freud. They are nonetheless offering us the founding principles of a new psychology, one that seeks to do justice to the whole of our cultural experience, the tribal as well as the civilized. The result is a significant critique of the basic sanity of urban-industrial society. In this respect, the myth of savage nobility as neolithic conservatives have elaborated it is a *good* myth, one that counsels tolerance and provokes self-criticism—always the highest virtues of civilized life.

The reappraisal of primary people as a basis for contemporary politics and personal sanity is no small achievement. It is a rare act of cultural renunciation. After all, the cultural life of the modern world, whatever its national, ethnic, or ideological variations, belongs to citified intellectuals, an international class that shares a common commitment to urban ways. They monopolize the critical dialogue. Whatever questions of justice may divide the classes, races, and sexes of the urban-industrial world, those questions are raised within the culture of cities and between members of that culture. For this reason, those who speak in behalf of nonurban or preurban people—like those who protest for the endangered species—reveal a unique sense of the universal.

DEEP SYSTEMS, DEEP ECOLOGY

Neolithic conservatism is among the most important tributaries flowing into contemporary environmental politics. It is the basis of "Deep Ecology," the mystical–religious–feminist wing of environmentalism. The Deep Ecologists remind us of the unsettling fact that many of the cultures that white Western Europeans have for so long been pleased to dismiss as backward and deservedly defunct possessed one quality that may yet elude us: *survival* . . . at least up the point at which *we* rendered them extinct. Gary Snyder's "Great Subculture" lasted the better part of ten millennia and may at times—as among the Pacific Northwest tribes and still today the Bushman–Hottentots—have achieved a comfortable, if modest standard of living with much leisure left over for cultural creativity. The anthropologist Marshall Sahlins, writing on "Stone Age economics," even suggests that the hunters and gatherers might be regarded as "the original affluent society."

> The world's most primitive people have few possessions, *but they are not poor.* Poverty is not a certain amount of goods, nor is it just a relation between means and ends; above all it is a relation between people. Poverty is a social status. As such it is the invention of civilization.[9]

Plato observed that "poverty consists not so much in small property as in large desires." A poor man is one with many needs; a rich man one with few. In that wise sense of the word, at least in contrast with our own limitlessly needy high-consumption society, primary people who live within their environmental means might be called "wealthy."

The Deep Ecologists have taken facts like this seriously enough to divide the environmental movement into two often heatedly contentious camps. They reject the premise that most of our ecological problems can be solved by a legislative agenda that settles for improved resource budgeting and better global management. Deep Ecology contends that our environmental crisis is more than a random catalogue of mistakes, miscalculations, and false starts that can easily be made good with a bit more expertise in the right places. Nothing less than an altered sensibility is needed, a radically new standard of sanity that undercuts scientific rationality and uproots the fundamental assumptions of industrial life.

The Norwegian "ecosopher" Arne Naess, one of the founders of Deep Ecology, described his goal in a seminal article in 1973 as "rejection of the man-in-environment image in favor of the relational, total-field image. Organisms as knots in the biospherical net or field of intrinsic relations." What he meant by this terse formulation is, within the context of the social and biological sciences, little short of revolutionary. It was a call for "biospherical egalitarianism" among all species. (Or at least "in principle," since, as Naess admits, "any realistic praxis necessitates some killing.")

> The ecological field-worker acquires a deep-seated respect, even a veneration for the ways and forms of life. He reaches an understanding from within, a kind of understanding that others reserve for fellow men. . . . To the ecological field-worker, the equal right to live and blossom is an intuitively clear and obvious value axiom. Its restriction to humans is an anthropocentrism with detrimental effects upon the life quality of humans themselves.[10]

"An understanding from within . . . " Naess is saying that there is a deep system in nature that contains *us* as a species, if only we can open ourselves to the knowledge. Deep Ecology was from the outset the academic and political expression of nature mysticism, based on an alternate, essentially animistic mode of experience rather than a different set of theoretical principles. It found the root cause of our environmental ills in our inveterate belief that human beings stand apart from nature and above it, whether as master or steward. Many major environmental organizations (the "shallow" ecologists) continue to regard the planet as *ours* to do with as we see fit; their methods are essentially managerial. That assumption, Deep Ecology argues, poisons all we try to do. It endorses our self-proclaimed superiority over nature and with it our isolation from all the beings with whom we ought properly to share the planet in biocentric fellowship.

A question we might well ponder: when human beings unilaterally declare their superiority to all other species, who do they think is paying attention?

The contrast between deep and shallow ecologies is revealed in the difference between those conservationists who would deal with the possible extinction of the great whale herds by setting international quotas upon their kill, and organizations like Greenpeace or Earth First, which would set the quota at zero—on the basis that no species, or at least no large, fully sentient species (there continues to be some disagreement on where one draws the defending line, if at all) may be denied its right to life. In a biocentric democracy, the "rights of man" belong to all species. Natural rights have at last been extended to nature at large.[11]

PALEOLITHIC CONSERVATISM AND FEMINIST SPIRITUALITY

Having staked out the radical wing of the environmental cause, the Deep Ecologists could hardly have expected to find themselves outflanked by a movement that had even more acute cultural and psychological insights to offer. But this is exactly what happened. A new form of feminism—ecofeminism—emerged from a landmark conference on "Women and the Environment" held at the University of California at Berkeley in 1973. It was destined to unsettle both Deep Ecology and the women's movement itself.

No one could have predicted when Women's Liberation began in the middle sixties that it would, within a decade, become a principal force in environmental politics. The initial issue raised by feminists was the conventional democratic demand for political and social equality that dates back to the suffragettes of the Victorian period. Votes, jobs, education for women. Betty Friedan's *The Feminine Mystique* (1963) was a straightforward critical attack on the discriminatory stereotyping that kept middle-class women locked away in a split-level, suburban ghetto cut off from the educational and employment opportunities that would allow them to compete fairly for careers. Even when the movement broadened to include Third World women and women of color, the political agenda remained essentially integrationist, aimed at gaining admission to male-dominated privileges for women both rich and poor alike.

In the past two decades this aspect of the movement has achieved a reasonable degree of success, more so than anybody might have imagined from the vantage point of the Eisenhower fifties. One need only watch some reruns of family situation comedies from that period to register the contrasting images of women then and now. Yet, all through this early phase of the movement, there were socialist feminists who insisted that the true goal of Women's Liberation ought to be a radical change in property rights and class relations—the familiar program of social democracy. The socialist critique held that all institutions within a capitalist economy are morally tainted, no matter how racially or sexually integrated they may become.

What came as a surprise to both liberal and socialist feminists was the turn the women's movement took in the early seventies. One might say the socialist analysis was pressed so far to the "left" that it carried beyond the edge of the ideological spectrum.

For by then there were women who had come to believe that the "taint" in question runs deeper than the vices of the capitalist marketplace. The root of the problem lies in prehistoric sociology. Modern institutions, whether socialist or capitalist, have been corrupted to their core by patriarchal values that vastly predate the modern property system and all other class relations; it is the prototypical form of social domination. In order to find a culture free of its distorting influence, one may have to reach back in history to that early neolithic, village-based, agrarian culture that the archaeologist Marija Gimbutas calls "Old Europe." What we know of this pre-Indo-European culture that once spanned Europe can only be reconstructed speculatively from its physical artifacts. These suggest a matrilineal, relatively egalitarian, nonmilitaristic way of life based on the cult of the goddess.

Speculating still more ambitiously, some feminists came to see this as the original and once universal human culture, a matrifocal golden age which lasted until the time of the big-game hunters. Their politics became a paleolithic conservatism whose insights were at once political, psychological, and ecological.[12] They recognized the severe personal price they might have to pay if "progress" meant they must accept the status of honorary men. A false consciousness was being forced upon them, even by their own political leaders. They were being asked to imitate the very male stereotype that had for so long oppressed and restricted them.

From the outset, Women's Liberation had been a searchingly psychological movement, grounded in consciousness raising and confessional introspection. Now that style revealed a subliminal level of oppression that was more radical than discussions of marriage, family, and career had touched. Along lines of myth, metaphor, symbol, theological doctrine as well as social mechanics and political structure, women were finding their fate linked to the fate of the "Earthbody" of the planet. Gender identity in all but a few exceptional cultures of the world stems from the assumption that "women [in Sherry Ortner's classic formulation] are to nature as man is to culture." Most decisively for purposes of environmental politics, even modern science, in the tough-minded, aggressively probing, emotionally detached objectivity of its method, has been "genderized" into a kind of all-purpose intellectual gynecology. The traditional imagery of Mother Earth and Dame Nature is far from a mere poetic simile. It embodies an age-old association between women and the natural world that has transformed both into alien and contemptible targets of male domination.

Return for a moment to the origins of the city in history. There are myths that commemorate this great transition in human culture. They are shot through with sexual politics. The great Babylonian father god Marduk is remembered as the creator of the civilized world. His achievement came at the expense of the monstrous sea-goddess Tiamat, the female embodiment of chaos who had ruled the Earth before him. As we have seen in an earlier discussion of thermodynamics, the distinction between order and chaos is very much a matter of taste. "Order" is something we expect or prefer; "chaos" may only be another kind of order, one not anticipated or appreciated. In the Babylonian creation myth, Tiamat's so-called chaos represents the old culture where females played a greater role, perhaps at times a dominant role. Recent archaeological finds suggest that in the time of the village cultures that predate the city, women were socially and spiritually potent enough to keep the warlike, reckless male in a condition of partnership and to defend the land as if it were their own mothering bodies. In Marija Gimbutas's influential formulation, it was the Indo-European incursion of warlike Indo-European nomadic tribes, worshippers of masculine sky gods, that replaced the matricentric cultures of Old Europe with an "androcratic warrior" society and that henceforth claimed all the virtues of "civilization" for itself. But before that there had been a "civilization of the goddess" marked by peace and high art. Under the spell of this original version of Gaia, there was even a different kind of "city," one that honored the Earth and rested lightly upon it.[13]

The women's movement has created a speculative history (her-story) of its own to explore that remote, all but forgotten period. If it existed, its demise is remembered as a battle of the sexes on a cosmic scale. Marduk, the great male deity, ousts Tiamat from power, tears her body to shreds and uses the pieces to construct a new world order more to his liking. It will be the order of warlords and patriarchal masters. It will also be the order of science; Marduk measures and bounds the world he creates, establishing the fixed rhythms of seasons and stars. He is the first astronomer, geographer, and surveyor. After him, god-kings rule the river valley by force and by law. Though female deities survive in the pantheon (associated more and more exclusively with fertility and childbearing), they are consigned to strictly subordinate positions; even mortal men can be their superiors. The great hero Gilgamesh spurns the love of the cruel and devious goddess Ishtar, the Babylonian Venus; he is permitted to defy and defeat her. Her love is treated as something treacherous and enfeebling. For that matter, all the male rivals he faces in battle are ridiculed as "women"; they are overthrown with unpitying contempt.

A dream of human omnipotence lies at the foundation of the city. But it is a male dream, realized at the expense of women's values, women's ways. Reflecting on the sexual undercurrent of this historical episode, ecofeminists make the following argument: Deep Ecology finds anthropocentrism at the root of our environmental troubles. But if the "anthropos" in *anthropocentric* refers to such character traits as domination, aggressiveness, intellectual detachment, the lust to subjugate and exploit, then "anthropos" does not refer to *all* human beings.

It refers to *some* human beings. They are called "men." Other human beings (called "women") lack those traits—generally speaking. They are *expected* to lack them. They are reared and conditioned to lack them; they are expected to bear great social disadvantages because they lack them. And perhaps (the point is subject to great dispute) they really do lack them as a matter of genetics. In any case, women have been raised to take their place in the world among those many "others" (enemy peoples, social inferiors, savages, the beasts of the hunt, nature in general) against which masculinity pits itself in the struggle for mastery.

Ecofeminists insist that a distinction needs to be made. *Androcentrism,* not anthropocentrism, is the cause of our environmental problem. *Men* are the problem—at least in the person and planet-crushing role they have assigned themselves to play in history. "The hatred of women and the hatred of nature are intimately connected and mutually reinforcing," Ynestra King laments. And yet,

> Ecologists, with their concern for nonhuman nature, have yet to understand that they have a particular stake in ending the domination of women. They do not understand that a central reason for women's oppression is her association with the despised nature they are so concerned about.[14]

Viewed from this angle, even Deep Ecology comes to be seen as "shockingly sexist," in Sharon Doubiago's words. And this due to some of its most distinctive traits. In a typically high-handed male way, Doubiago charges, the Deep Ecologists have appropriated "woman consciousness" without crediting its source. They pay homage to traditional American Indian cultures, to Buddhism, to the new physics, to mystics and transcendentalists, to everything "exotic, removed, and masculine," when in fact

> as you, male ecologists, will have to admit upon any reflection, your bed partners and the person who most likely dominated your childhood has been sharing this consciousness with you all your lives.[15]

Doubiago's remarks raise issues that divide feminists themselves. Is there a "woman consciousness"? If so, is it innate or inculcated? Many ecofeminists have been inclined to say that there is indeed a peculiar and inherent bond between women and nature, a viewpoint that comes close to agreeing with misogynists down through the ages who have insisted that woman's biology is her destiny. For some, those involved in Feminist Spirituality, that destiny is proudly embraced. In true loyalty to Gaia, it involves honoring some version of the "Goddess culture," the matriarchal golden age of natural harmony that predates extensive irrigation systems and the rise of the city. These efforts to revive the prehistoric cult of the goddess can at times approach a new wave of stereotyping on the part of women themselves, some of whom would claim intuition, sensitivity, mystical rapport with nature as exclusive female qualities. There are significant issues here that feminists, social ecologists, and ecofeminists have yet to sort out. They are well summarized by Betty Roszak:

> The crucial question has to be raised. Are women once more to be identified with the archetypal mother, or Mother Nature? Do women have a special calling to save humanity and the Earth through a superior compassion and wisdom? Or is this just another repetition of the old stereotyping we have tried so hard to break? Are we not being used again subtly in the service of male power? By acknowledging a special relationship between women and nature, do we not reinforce the projection of male responsibility onto women as saviors of the world? . . .
>
> As feminists we need to guard as much against a new sentimentalized interpretation of women as against the romanticization of nature. . . . Until every man accepts and expresses what has been called "the feminine" in his own nature and every woman is allowed to express what has been called the "masculine" in her own nature, we must be wary of setting ourselves apart as women in a new version of the Noble Savage who bears all wisdom and will redress the wrongs and injustices of the world.[16]

THE TROUBLE WITH MEN

No political movement on the contemporary scene has achieved the astonishing range of feminism. Since its inception in the sixties as a liberal reform program essentially skewed toward the interests of educated middle-class women, the movement has generously grown to embrace issues of race, poverty, sexual preference, child abuse, war, the Third World, religion, endangered cultures, endangered species, the global environment. Women have come to see their exploited "otherness" reflected in all forms of victimization. The patriarchal ego has been found at work everywhere from the worship of the warlike Father God of the Old Testament to the bellicose videogames and movies that treat adolescent boys to the thrill of world-shattering violence.

The better to understand the origins and power of patriarchy, the women's movement has had to immerse itself in issues of psychological theory, asking why men are what they are, why women are what they are, how far back differences of gender go in personal life and in the history of our species. Feminists soon discovered that, as vital as these questions are, orthodox psychiatry is of little help in providing answers. In many ways, it is among the bastions of sexism. In Freud's view and that of his followers (including the women analysts among them[17]), men were the official representatives of the human race; the male psyche was normative. The problems of women were frequently introduced as an afterthought or a minor qualification. Feminists have not been alone is seeing such culture-bound notions of male–female child development as little short of ludicrous. Penis envy, in particular, so central to Freudian analysis, has come to be seen by both sexes as material for one-line comedy rather than serious psychiatry.

Jung was little better than Freud when it came to giving women fair representation in psychiatric theory. Though he recognized the existence of a feminized *anima* in men as well as women, much of what he wrote on the subject remains heavily swaddled in German-Romantic *Schwärmerei* about "the eternal feminine"—a pedestal that feminists have learned better than to mount. In the Jungian psyche, character traits like tenderness, ambition, heroic endeavor remain sex-identified; repackaged as *anima* and *animus,* the old stereotypes continue in force. Jung, like Freud, held dismally conventional ideas about a woman's place. He was prepared to warn any career-minded woman who consulted him that she was doing something "directly injurious to her feminine nature." Moreover, as feminist critics now equipped with more accurate historical scholarship have observed, many of the Jungian archetypes that are meant to relate to women—and to relate to them inspirationally—are permeated with the sexist bias of the Olympian pantheon, a later patriarchal reinterpretation that usually subordinates the goddesses to the gods. The pre-Hellenic and paleolithic goddesses, so much more potent and robust, are given much less prominence.[18]

With so little to draw upon that was free of sexual preconceptions, the women's movement has very nearly had to reinvent psychotherapy, its methods, theories, and values. Ecological implications lurk in the background at every step along the way in that project. The Gestalt analyst Dorothy Dinnerstein was among the first to recognize how the patriarchal ego violates the environment as well as women's nature. She takes it to be a central role of therapy to mobilize "our protective filial concern for Earthly nature." The main way she would bring about "new uses of gender" seems modest enough, if not downright homely: men should do approximately half the world's childrearing, the better to enjoy the nurturant satisfactions of the job. The result would be a world of "relational individuals" gifted with the best possible combination of the stereotypical masculine and feminine traits. At that point it might be possible to stop identifying human characteristics by gender and allow a free choice by each sex. Dinnerstein puts it this way:

> When men start participating as deeply as women in the initiation of infants into the human estate, when both male and female parents come to carry for all of us the special meanings of early childhood, the trouble we have reconciling these meanings with person-ness will finally be faced. The consequence, of course, will be a fuller and more realistic, a kinder and at the same time more demanding definition of person-ness.[19]

Object Relations is the post-Freudian school to which many feminist psychiatrists have turned for a more constructive approach to child development. Object Relations theory pays particular attention to the pre-Oedipal period in which children begin to separate themselves from a "mother figure" that has come to seem "all-powerful"—especially in societies like our own where breadwinning usually takes the father away from the home. Supposedly, the experience of separation differs markedly for boys and for girls. Feminist Object Relationists believe boys disengage from the mother in ways that leave them emotionally isolated within hard-edged ego boundaries. Growing up to be a manly man entails censoring all traces of femininity within themselves in order to make that separation secure. "The self-identity of the boy child," Marti Kheel observes, "is thus founded upon the negation and objectification of an other."[20] Pitted against this alienated other, the male grows up to be sharply and competitively differentiated. The result may be more than a matter of personal psychology; it may bleed over into the natural philosophy of the culture. Catherine Keller makes a telling observation:

> It would seem that the sense of self inflicted upon males bears a startling resemblance to the Newtonian atom! It is separate, impenetrable, and only extrinsically and accidentally related to the others it bumps into in its void. . . . The more fully does a male incarnate this sense of separateness, the more efficiently has he conformed to the machine-economy of modern patriarchy.[21]

Girls, on the other hand, generally preserve a warmer, more "intersubjective" quality about their mature personality. If they grow up to be good, stereotypic females, they will become the docile and nurturing mothers a patriarchal society expects them to be. But they will also be less publicly assertive and more dependent.

If this sexual asymmetry in the early experience of individuation can be taken as universal, it may explain why nature in myth and metaphor has come to be perceived as feminine. As a network of intricately related systems, it possesses the more relational quality that has been inculcated upon females. Men have read into the world around them the caring warmth they insist on having from women and hope to find in nature. The insight is a valuable one, but given just the right twist, it could have a far from beneficial result for the feminist cause. It can make the job of mothering so "apocalyptic" (as Nancy Chodorow puts it) that women might wind up bearing the full responsibility for the warped development of their sons. In their own minds they can allow themselves to be victimized by the "myth of the perfect mother."

Still, in its tight focus on early mothering, Object Relations may have something of value to offer the women's movement. All the more unfortunate then that so much of its literature comes off sounding stilted and abstract. Common enough vices of the academic style, perhaps, but exactly the qualities that feminists themselves have perceptively identified as official patriarchal prose: words drained of their emotional juice. After all, what is one to make of a name like "Object Relations"—especially where the "object" in question means mothers?

Despite the best efforts of ecofeminists, the ecology-psychology connection still waits to be spelled out by psychiatrists at the professional level and is long overdue. By now we have all the historical and anthropological perspective on sexual stereotypes we could possibly need. We also have the long chronicle of injustice and suffering that women have endured as (in the eyes of the emotionally crippled adjacent sex) living embodiments of nature. All that may be lacking is a female and feminist Freud to weave the heartbreak and the theory together. The need is urgent. There is no question but that the way the world shapes the minds of its male children lies somewhere close to the root of our environmental dilemma. As long as the men who run the media keep feeding the minds of the boys they seem to think are their only audience on a steady diet of *Terminators* and *Liquidators* and *Annihilators* and *Die Hards* and *Top Guns,* we cannot expect to free ourselves from the morals of extermination. We are tied to it by the psyches of twelve-year-old boys who will grow up to become thirty-year-old corporation executives and forty-year-old colonels and fifty-year-old politicians. Consider for a moment the *Robocop* movies that have enjoyed such popularity among males between the ages of ten and twenty-five. What do we have here as an ideal of manly prowess? The corpse of a cop reanimated by science, equipped with an indestructible metal physique and an electronic brain, sent into the streets with an armory of hair-trigger phallic weaponry to perpetrate instantaneous mass annihilation. The bodies fly, the buildings explode, the vehicles collide, the blood gushes. All the kindest appeals and gentlest gestures on the part of ecofeminism and Feminist Spirituality pale before the virulent power of images like these that tempt but do not assuage the most violent appetites of the death instinct.

Habits as old as gender discrimination put down deep roots, so deep that we cannot tell with certainty where culture leaves off and nature begins. Currently even some of the most sensitive men around seem rather too desperately intent on retrieving a few sad remnants of their insecure gender-identity. Responding to the uppity women around them, they fall back on salvaging some version of the "warrior" qualities. No matter how metaphorical a reading they may give the word, they are working with a tradition that will not easily have the blood wiped from it. That makes their task both pathetic and threatening. In the best of hands, recent efforts at male consciousness-raising veer fearfully close to expressing a fiercely resentful backlash. They sound a little too much like the old "white power" movement responding to the cause of civil rights. The poet Robert Bly, who has emerged as the major spokesman for imperiled males, is convinced that "the deep masculine" need not preclude gentleness, sensitivity, and nurturing warmth. Let us hope he is right. But if he is, he ought to know better than to believe he is talking about specifically male attributes. He sometimes seems to acknowledge as much. Thus, he distinguishes the "wild man" he would have men liberate within themselves from the "savage man." Wild man, unlike savage man, accepts "the feminine side" of his personality, having no desire to exploit or do violence. But why then name these "men"? There will be no peace in the battle of the sexes and no ecological sanity until we finally have done with the nonsense of sorting human virtues into masculine and feminine bins.[22]

RECAPTURING THE PRIMITIVE

Generalizations about "the nature of man" and "the nature of woman" turn out to be generalizations about the entire human race—always a risky exercise. A moment's reflection on one's own personal experience is usually sufficient to produce scores of exceptions. Perhaps that is what human nature is: countless exceptions to all the rules. But while people are many, role models are few; and there is no question but that gender has been more heavily freighted with stereotypes than any other human distinction. Suppose we were to grant, then, that at least within the realm of stereotypes, the ecological sensibility the planet needs can be found sheltering in "woman consciousness." We are left to ask if it is to be found *exclusively* there? And if not, how long must we wait to see it evoked in males as well? Are mothers themselves, rearing their young in a still male-biased culture, proud enough of these nurturing virtues to want to see them flourish in their sons as much as in their daughters? If our environmental crisis is as ingrained in the childrearing habits of the human race as the Object Relationists believe, we may be a long while waiting for the patriarchal ego to yield its cultural dominance to the relational psyche.

And in the meanwhile . . . ? How long can we expect women, now that they have a far greater choice of careers in the male world, to carry on as the long-suffering exemplars of virtues that men must emulate? Perhaps this is the importance of ecofeminism and Feminist Spirituality in our time. As a visible, outspoken movement it dignifies and champions the human qualities that must be saved if the planet is to be healed. In the process, ecofeminists have made some of the most dramatic efforts to recapture the age and ethos of the goddess experientially. Precisely because they have found the daring to throw off conventional academic restrictions, ecofeminists have, through the arts and through ritual practices, discovered new ways to recreate the animist sensibility.

As bizarre as these efforts may seem when viewed from the outside, they represent a serious archaeological dig back through the collective consciousness. For who can say what might still survive there though buried alive? Perhaps some small part of our ancestral worldview still holds out within the reluctantly civilized id. If we are to develop an ecopsychology, finding our way back to some at least rough approximation of our species' oldest natural philosophy will have to be part of the search.

I recall an event of this kind that I attended: a ritual staged by a group of California "ceremonialists" who treat their calling as a cross between research and performance art. There was no pretense of historical accuracy surrounding the occasion. Everyone was aware that we were a gathering of modern Western men and women; we had arrived by car and valued the indoor plumbing we had left behind us at home. The goal of the evening was to honor, and just possibly come closer to the vital core of another people's vision of nature than words alone might bring us. The result becomes a sort of freely fashioned anthropological composite of (in this case) a winter solstice ceremony. Selections are read from Native American mythology; there is music and chanting; artifacts are passed around; gifts are exchanged, food shared; a fire is lit, people move solemnly about it in a made-up dance.

To take another example: the Council of All Beings is a "re-earthing" ritual that has been performed in a variety of locations from wilderness settings like the Grand Canyon to student lounges at universities. Created in the mid-eighties by John Seed, the director of the Rainforest Information Centre in Australia, and Joanna Macy, the American therapist and writer, the event begins with a period of solitary meditation in which participants are asked to imagine their way into a nonhuman identity. The inspiration for the exercise traces back to the American naturalist Aldo Leopold, whose "land ethic" of the 1930s is usually taken to be one of the first statements of Deep Ecology. Leopold held that no one can fully understand an ecosystem until they try to "think like a mountain." Accordingly, those who gather as part of the Council of All Beings don masks of their own making and speak as Rainforest, Wombat, Wild Goose, Slug, Dead Leaf, Mountain. Thus, Dolphin says:

> I love to roll and leap and play. Yes, humans, to play with you too, when I can trust you, for we feel great affinity with you. But in the gill nets you use we tangle and drown. Taking cruel advantage of your friendliness, you use us for military experiments, fix monitors and transmitters on our backs. You wall us into your sea parks for show. . . . I speak for all captive beings. Find your own freedom in honoring ours.

Along the way there are ceremonies that draw on the traditional rites of the Medicine Wheel, but the pervasive spirit of the occasion is distinctly modern and Western, a braiding together of folklore, environmental research, and the news of the day. In distinctly contemporary terms, one and all are asked to "remember our bio-ecological history, as our species and its forebears evolved through four and a half billion years of this planet's life."[23]

If it were not for the undeniable sincerity and unpretentious good humor that animate them, events like these might be cynically dismissed as New Age fun and games. Yet give them a chance to take effect, and at the very least one comes away wishing our society still celebrated the seasonal rite like that of the reborn sun with some more dignified, emotionally engaging gesture than the annual Christmas shopping orgy and Hallmark greeting cards. One has surely gained the sense of *something* there to be experienced, a rhythm of the Earth that "normally" (among us) passes with less recognition than the annual Superbowl game. And for what better reason have we surrendered that experience than because once upon a time the fathers of the early church decided that such rites were a heathen transgression? And because several centuries later the fathers of modern science, who were no less hostile to the animist sensibility, decided that the seasons are nothing more than a certain measurable tilt in the rotational axis of a small planet orbiting a dead ball of burning gas?

We are not any emotionally richer for following such dictates, nor any closer to the secret of a healthy ecology, which must at some point draw upon love and wonder as much as upon scientific precision.

Exercises like the Council of All Beings bear little resemblance to the techniques of conventional psychiatry. They are communal; they are participative; they involve drama, song, dance; they draw upon non-verbal powers of expression and catharsis. There is no commanding professional presence, no *doctor* who knows better and takes charge. But then perhaps an ecopsychology must break new ground, as much so in practice as in theory.

Nine

◆

THE NEON TELEPHONE
The Moral Equivalent of Wretched Excess

A PRODUCT IS A PRODUCT IS A PRODUCT

It was one of those stores you find in all the malls these days, a cornucopia of glitzy novelties and "adult toys" fashioned in the image of a Las Vegas casino. They sport names like Razzle-Dazzle, Gizmo Heaven, Electric Dreams. Upscale franchise versions like The Sharper Image have been called "a Woolworth for the millionaire kid in all of us." At The Sharper Image, a personalized, programmed, digital voice-read-out scale can cost up to $450. Step on the platform and it intones your weight, reminding you (with a cheery "Congratulations!") how many pounds you've lost or (with a sincerely concerned "I'm sorry to tell you") how many you've gained. You have your choice of either male or female vocalizations.

This place was called Headlines, a garish, middle-scale operation whose decor and merchandise tilted toward riotous bad taste. And there occupying center floor space was this month's featured astonishment.

The neon telephone.

Not one model, but a dozen, some winking and blinking, some spiraling colored lights, some bubbling and perking. Most were designed in see-through acrylic, revealing a fake inner circuitry sizzling with rainbow-tinted sparks. One was fashioned in the likeness of the old giant Wurlitzer; another lit up like a picture palace marquee when it rang, the colored lights flashing "Ring-a-ding!!!" They were without doubt the ugliest commercial objects I had seen in years.

I picked one up, turned it over. "Made in Taiwan."

Some inspired entrepreneur had set out eight thousand miles across the sea to have this high-tech monstrosity manufactured. Someone else had labored to design it, dredging up every fluorescent bend and curl out of the depths of an aesthetic nightmare; hundreds of others had toiled, no doubt at a rock-bottom wage, to assemble its thousand microscopic parts. Perhaps some dedicated minister of overseas trade had spent months in delicate negotiations to position the object so that it might earn his nation the maximum foreign exchange. Reportedly, Taiwan is among the Third World economies that is proving itself good at this sort of thing: a hard-charging rapid developer, a member in good-standing of the Pacific Rim boom. This was the evidence of that boom. The neon telephone.

In the nineteenth century, anticapitalist critics like Marx insisted that economics must be contained within an ethical context; social justice counted for more than industrial efficiency or private profit. In the late twentieth century, the environmental movement is trying to teach us that both economics and ethics must be contained within an ecological context. In our own enlightened self-interest, if for no better reason, our conception of distributive justice has to include the whales, the redwood trees, and the ozone layer. Whatever wealth there is to share must be ecologically as well as socially affordable. But the neon telephone underscores a terrible dilemma in everybody's bookkeeping, whether Marxist or capitalist. All over the Third World today, investors are investing, workers are working, planners are planning with a view to making the great leap forward into industrial affluence. For the assembly-line worker in Singapore or Mexico, a novelty like the neon telephone means a job that pays enough to feed the family, maybe someday to emigrate to a richer country. For the ambitious entrepreneur, it means the chance to usher himself and his nation into the corporate major leagues, perhaps to be bought out and taken over by a Japanese or German or American conglomerate that will invest more capital and employ more people to build the next generation of bigger, gaudier neon telephones. For governments that struggle to consummate the long-delayed revolution of rising expectations, a salable product means money to pay off the World Bank in time to hit the International Monetary Fund for another loan.

Some of what comes of this maniacal rush toward development is defensible enough by the going industrial standard of living: automobiles, television sets, aircraft, computers . . . though even these may soon be among the items that will have to be cut back by any country that embarks upon environmentally sustainable policies. Much the rest of what the developing economies produce—cheap fashions, gimmicky appliances, Sega and Nintendo computer games—is obvious waste. But then, is the distinction even worth raising? All that registers on the ledgers of orthodox economic accounting is the fact of production, the fact of selling. As long as the item moves in the marketplace, it does not matter that societies lacking the bare essentials may be lavishing their capital, their resources, their muscle and brains on the prolific production of tomorrow's garbage. This, after all, is *their* way into the modern world—or so they hope. Find a product; make it cheaper; sell it in St. Louis or Stockholm or Sydney. Sell lots of it, then make more. A product is a product is a product. On electronic gadgetry alone—cellular phones, answering machines, computer games, VCRs with more buttons and switches than most people can identify—Americans were spending in excess of $50 billion in the late eighties. For the practical economist, that brute monetary fact says it all. It takes us to the edge of the known intellectual world. Beyond lies outer darkness.

Within the last fifteen years a few of the more developed economies have invented a category called "environmental impact." Those undertaking large-scale operations are now expected to file a statement justifying that impact. How meaningful such statements will be wholly depends upon how honestly concerned governments are, how vigilant the public is. Usually, not very. Even given true concern and vigilance, imponderable questions remain. Where does one draw the boundaries of the assessment in space and time? Do we try to take into account cumulative global influences, as well as short-range local effects? Do we include the fate of distant generations? Which generations? The generations of the trees, the rivers, the wolves? Most economists would regard these as social values and ethical priorities that have no place in their science. The notion that the future of the human race, let alone its spiritual well-being, may be a nonrenewable resource, plays no part in serious economic analysis. Our habit has been to regard the future as the carpet under which environmental degradation gets swept. It is called "externalizing" the costs, meaning writing them off to our children's, children's, children's. . . . Out of sight, out of mind. On the other hand, the crying need of underdeveloped peoples to attain a bare subsistence before their children famish is clear cut and immediate. What is the calculus of such competing interests? There are environmental militants (like some in the animal rights movement) who assert the equal right of every species to life, a position not apt to find widespread endorsement among the hungry many where their interests clash with bird or beast.

THE AGE OF DEMOCRATIC LUXURY

Standard economics is right, however, when it reminds us that a flourishing supply implies an expanding demand. The Third World would not be producing frivolous junk if the First World did not provide so gleeful a market for it. That fact raises another, deeper issue. Ask anybody on the street if they really need a neon telephone; what answer would you expect to receive? Most likely a unanimous "not at all." But ask again after they have seen a neon telephone or two, and they might—some of them—sheepishly confess that, while they don't actually *need* such an item, it just might be "fun" to own one. "Fun" covers a great deal of economic territory in affluent societies. It sells a lot of merchandise. Fun movies, fun clothes, fun cosmetics, fun food . . . why not fun telephones? Fun—meaning impulse buying relished as much for the impulse as for the buying—delivers a sense of well-being, a small touch of luxury. It makes shopping one of the staple entertainments of our time. Always another cute little novelty, another quirky gizmo, another fad or fashion to bring home and talk about.

In times past, only the elite could afford to squander the wealth of the nation. It was done as a spectator sport for the toiling masses to see and perhaps vicariously enjoy. From a strictly environmental viewpoint, one might almost say that an aristocratic social order makes ecological sense. It limits prodigality to an affordable few. The penurious majority dare not waste lest it go to bed each night wanting. If the neon telephone were marketed only to a narrow elite, the biosphere could easily budget the excess. But what if neon telephones are to be produced and consumed by the millions? Even cut-rate luxuries may be more than the Earth can provide, if they must be provided on a democratic basis.

Lester Brown of the Worldwatch Institute has defined the goal of the environmental movement as *sustainability,* by which he means "the capacity to satisfy current needs without jeopardizing the prospects of future generations." But who is to define "current needs"? At the level of physical needs, nutritionists and medical doctors can specify the criteria of health with some assurance. But at a certain point, economics borders on psychology, and there the objective criteria are much less clear. We cross that line when we probe any consumer demand that goes beyond physical necessity. How do wants at that level become needs? The question transcends industrial societies. Among tribal groups living in far more reduced material circumstances, the potlatch provides a ceremonial opportunity to squander, even destroy wealth. The wealth has been saved up for that very reason; the act of wasting it confers social status. The occasion, a ritualized blow-out, is enjoyed by all as an experience of uproarious extravagance.

With the advent of industrialism, at least through the period of primitive accumulation, the chance to experience such extravagance was significantly diminished for working millions—but only for a few generations. Eventually, the privation became both intolerable and unnecessary. Phase two of every industrial economy is the pay-off when consumption becomes not simply a pleasure but a duty. The need to move the goods becomes so pressing that ingenious methods must be invented to enhance the hunger for more. An advertising industry is created to stimulate consumption, lest the system grind to a halt. But once our human weakness for frivolous, high-spirited expenditure comes to be joined to the massive productive power of an industrial system, we are clearly in for trouble sooner or later.

The classic imagery of early industrialism was that of sweated labor and grinding exploitation. There is no question but that the infrastructure of the capitalist economies was wrung from a powerless proletariat that was expected to function as nothing more than the "hands" of the system. But one generation after Marx died, something very different was being required of the workforce: the duty of compulsive consumption. Entrepreneurs like Henry Ford readily acknowledged that they had become dependent on the capacity of their workers to afford the tin lizzies they were producing. Today in societies where many still lack for the necessities, there is an appetite for "fun" merchandise that can make the demand for neon telephones as fierce as the demand for bare subsistence ever was. There are no wretched of the Earth any longer who live so remote from a movie theater, a television set, a VCR that they have not been treated to scenes of people like themselves in the developed societies wallowing in abundance. They see it, they want it, they need it. Amenities that were unimaginable for the workhouse rabble of Marx's day have become commonplace priorities around the world.

The passion to have, to own, indeed to waste is more than mindless extravagance. Consumer egalitarianism is clearly the inevitable adjunct of political equality. In the modern world, an inalienable right to the pursuit of happiness has come to include a universal claim upon discretionary income. Emphasize the "discretionary." That has become the crucial distinction between equality as an individual political right and uniformity as a collective economic condition. Even in prosperous societies like Britain and the Scandinavian countries, taxation at a level that eliminates a certain margin of discretionary spending, no matter how capricious, has led to middle-class taxpayer revolts against the welfare establishment. Not, in all cases, because of simple greed, but because the ability to pick and choose in an open market, to buy a luxury or two brings with it a sense of freedom and dignity.

Of necessity, a democratic social order must be an ecological order; and the truer the democracy (meaning the more authentically accessible the power and the goods) the more real must the collective ecological intelligence of the society be. The standards of consumption set by aristocrats and the early industrial bourgeoisie simply cannot be extended to societies *en masse*. Rather, the desires that undergird those standards—the craving for specialness, distinction, personal worth— must be uncovered, examined, reshaped. The aspiration must be peeled down to its essence. In practical environmental terms, what does it mean (in the words of the old populist slogan) to proclaim "every man a king?"

PLENITUDE

Freud taught us that there are two ways in which a society can deal with moral vice. It can try to repress the act by some combination of intimidation and punishment. As every naughty child knows, this works but only for as long as watchful authority is on hand to enforce its dictates. If it once looks aside, the vice reemerges, possibly to be perpetrated with greater relish as a forbidden pleasure. The better course, he advised, is to find ways to divert unacceptable conduct into acceptable, even constructive forms of gratification. This he called sublimation, which might mean salvaging some residue of nobility that lies hidden in otherwise base conduct. By and large, the strategy of the environmental movement in dealing with wasteful consumption has been repression. Committed ecologists have too often been sternly censorious, meeting our human frailties with doctrinaire intolerance.

There is a strain of stern asceticism running through environmental politics that has been unwilling to recognize, let alone condone the connection between consumerism and the search for personal fulfillment. The neon telephone may be a pathetic object on which to rest that need, but scolding and shaming the public will never break the habit of waste if one fails to ask *why* humans so often waste the wealth of the planet as they do. In one sense, nobody *needs* a neon telephone; in another sense everybody does and deserves one. How do we make luxury democratically available, yet ecologically sustainable?

A century ago, when militaristic bravado was the going standard of national greatness in the Western world, the philosopher William James recognized that many of the noblest human qualities—courage, self-sacrifice, loyalty, daring—had gotten tragically confused with the blatant chauvinism of the period. James felt that while political aggression had to be eliminated, the virtues attached to it should be preserved and encouraged. We need, said James, a "moral equivalent of war." In James's lifetime nothing like this was found. But in our own day, a group like Greenpeace may have hit upon exactly the solution James wanted: an ecological substitute for warfare that summons up a kind of interspecies chivalry in defense of the biosphere.

Something like the same strategy of creative redirection needs to be applied to the problem of wasteful extravagance. Industrial power is one of the great achievements of our species, the closest we have come to building a world in which health, leisure, long life, material security, and a truly global community become possible. But we are in danger of losing all these benefits if we cannot find a moral equivalent for wretched excess.

In one of his last works, *The Pentagon of Power,* Lewis Mumford, the premier historian of industrial culture, pondered this problem, recommending a new category in economic thought: *plenitude,* a sense of "enoughness" that can only be achieved when people are encouraged to ask "wealth for *what?*"

> Under a regime of plenitude abundance is permissive, not compulsive: it allows for extravagant expenditures to satisfy man's higher needs for knowledge, beauty, or love . . . while it may exact the severest economy for less worthy purposes. Emerson's advice, to save on the low levels and spend on the high ones, lies at the very core of this conception.[1]

While Mumford believed one might find scattered economies of plenitude among tribal groups, his appeal was not backward-looking. Too often "primitive plenitude" led to "fossilization"; it was "solitary, meager, unadventurous" with a tendency to sink "into torpid penury and stupefication." For Mumford, the trick was to make industrial progress compatible with plenitude. "It is not to go back toward such a primitive plenitude, but forward to a more generous regimen . . . that the coming generations must lay their plans." Where there is true affluence, one might even afford "the luxury of turning one's back upon specious luxuries."

What Mumford had in mind might be as close at hand as challenging people to take their rewards in life in the currency of leisure (say, as sabbatical leaves from the workplace) rather than wages—free time to think, create, play, meditate. The current buzzword for the idea is "quality time"—which I doubt that anybody would suggest means shopping. To some degree the widespread practice of job-sharing might be a step in the direction of trading money for time, though often it is simply a way for families to find a second income. In any case, who will value unencumbered leisure in an economy that continues to pin its accounting to so fictitious a measure as the Gross National Product? From the viewpoint of the GNP, time off is a waste of time that might have been spent producing neon telephones.

Plenitude is not an economic calculus; it does not measure anything in the marketplace or prescribe a line of fiscal policy. Its value, like that of any good idea, lies in its Socratic provocation. It challenges us to define our real needs, at first personally, then socially. Present such a challenge to most economists and their answer is predictable. "Questions like these lie in the realm of philosophy and ethics. None of our business." But that in itself is a significant reply. It reveals the self-confessed limits of economic science, telling us we must look elsewhere for the secret of an economy of plenitude.

UTOPIAN TRANSFORMATIONS

If defining an appropriate human standard of living has seemed too subjectively slippery for the economists to pursue, it is the very substance of Utopian literature. In striking a balance between luxury and necessity, Utopias fall somewhere along a spectrum that stretches from ascetic to hedonistic. At one extreme, Plato's *Republic* and Thomas More's *Utopia* favor an abstemious standard of consumption, at least for those who embody the community's criterion of enlightenment. Plato's philosopher–kings live lives of monastic simplicity for the good of their souls; More's ideal society includes a voluntary class of public servants who live poor, do the dirty work of caring for the old and sick and cleaning up the streets for no pay, accepting as their only reward the acclaim of the community. In neither case is austerity required of the entire population; the hope is, rather, that by conferring prestige upon self-denying philosophers and saints, one will induce others to constrain their appetite for material goods. Quite a contrast with our contemporary fixation on the "lifestyles of the rich and famous," an item of popular culture that uses envy to promote high consumption.

Plato expected little in the way of intellectual endeavor from the Republic's nonphilosophical many; he assumed they would continue to value their creature comforts. Thomas More, with a greater democratic optimism, believed that life-long learning, a delight of the mind that requires only leisure and modest material support, could become the focus of society as a whole provided a dependable security was guaranteed to all. Nearly two thousand years divide More from Plato, yet both were writing under conditions of preindustrial scarcity that demanded a low consumption standard. Together, they established the basic strategy for an economics of plenitude; they place their hope for happiness in a nonmaterial wealth that diminishes the need to acquire and consume. Fulfillment at some higher level of aspiration is offered as the alternative to material self-indulgence. The psychology of the effort is clear: controlled consumption must be given a positive quality.

By way of education and persuasion, the good of the soul must be made to seem of greater appeal than the pleasures of the flesh. The monastic orders of the middle ages were wholly devoted to an economics of plenitude. The rule of life was simple. *Ora et labora*. A life of labor and prayer disciplined the appetites (especially sexuality) and incidentally produced a wealth of culture and invention.

At the height of the Renaissance, François Rabelais cleverly inverted the monastic ideal to explore the other Utopian extreme: hedonistic leisure amid inexhaustible abundance. At his fictitious Abbey of Thelème, the inhabitants comport themselves in a regal splendor that was clearly the stuff of fantasy in the early sixteenth century as a standard for society at large. But a century later, Francis Bacon decisively transformed the Utopian tradition. He raised the possibility that, given sufficient technological power over nature, the hope of a democratic abundance might not be unrealistic. Bacon's New Atlantis holds its place as the first scientific Utopia, a bold prediction of good things to come based on the assumption that the unlimited proliferation of material goods is within the realm of the possible. That vision has hovered in the background of the entire industrial process as its one justification for the privation, harsh discipline, wrenching dislocation, grime, and soot that this great adventure has cost. Combine Rabelais and Bacon, and you have the promise of aristocratic opulence for all derived from limitless mechanized productivity. With that prospect in view, the concept of plenitude went into eclipse; the foundation of our contemporary ecological crisis was laid.

It was not until the waste, drudgery, and filth of industrialism were vividly imprinted on the historical landscape that the plenitude formerly sought in the medieval monasteries became a timely topic once again. William Morris, the Victorian poet, painter, and political philosopher, was among the first to take up the discussion in his Utopian novel *News From Nowhere*. Morris, a bitter critic of both the ugliness and injustice of the industrial system, laid his hopes for a balanced economic order upon a reformation of taste. In Morris's land of Nowhere, aesthetics is the context of economic life. The sensibilities of people have been schooled to value the quality, not the quantity of goods. For Morris this meant a handicraft standard of excellence, which he took to be of benefit for the soul as well as the body. His Arts and Crafts Movement sprang from the conviction that one good item of apparel, one aesthetically pleasing personal possession counted for more than thirty pairs of shoddily made shoes in the closet, a dozen cheap and perishable appliances in the kitchen. Among Morris's Utopians, with their trained eye for "whatever is made good and thoroughly fit for its purpose," there would surely have been no market for the neon telephone.

One need not endorse Morris's doctrinaire antiindustrial stance in order to see great practical sense in his proposal. As a matter of environmental sanity, there may be a point at which industrial societies will have to revive the handicraft standard, emphasizing the value of fine design and durability as an alternative to disposability or wasteful turnover. Once the physical necessities of life have been more than met, consumption might be disciplined by seeking an aesthetic satisfaction in what one owns. The land of Nowhere is sited near a postindustrial London of the twenty-first century. Nothing is more striking about its vista than the clean air, pure water, and healthy wildlife—amenities Londoners had not enjoyed for centuries. In Morris's Utopian bookkeeping, these natural beauties are accounted the true wealth of the nation. It is also worth noting that the livelihood of the society—handicrafts—is that form of calming and balancing work universally recommended as "occupational therapy" for the distressed psyche. Morris, following his aesthetic instincts, had found his way to the outskirts of an ecopsychology.

In her ecological Utopia *Woman on the Edge of Time,* Marge Piercy proposes another approach to plenitude. In the environmentally intelligent future she envisions—a worldwide society of well-kept rural communes—there exists a global lending library of luxuries, from which jewels, *objets d'art,* fashionable clothes may be borrowed and examined by the entire population. Everybody gets the chance to handle, appreciate, admire. It is, once again, an idea worth pondering. Can the enjoyment of valued objects, like the books we share in the library, be kept separate from ownership? At the highest stage of industrial development, does environmental necessity dictate a greater public expenditure on readily accessible, neighborhood-based museums, galleries, concert halls?

In one of the most highly developed ecological Utopias, Ernest Callenbach deals with problems of necessity and luxury by imagining a "stable state" economy that redirects the gratifications of high consumption toward a variety of cheap, nonmaterial pleasures.[2] As in Morris's Nowhere, the citizens of *Ecotopia* own little, but it is elegantly handmade; beyond that, the prevailing style of housing and dress is dropped-out funky. The workweek has been pared back to twenty hours; leisure becomes a value in its own right, used for the arts and crafts, for play, for recreational sports—especially hiking, camping, climbing in the fiercely defended wilderness, which has come to be respected by one and all as Ecotopia's principal public asset. There is also much sexual dalliance in the baths and the woods and the fields—more than the staid Victorian Morris could allow for. Callenbach's version of Utopian plenitude has the feel of a human potential spa like the Esalen Institute in California. People take joy in one another's company, in the beauty of the land, in simple sensuous pleasures that cost no resources.

From the viewpoint of psychoanalytic orthodoxy, both ends of the traditional Utopian spectrum—that of excess and that of austerity—would have to be classified as "neurotic." The pursuit of luxury would be seen as a form of displaced anal-eroticism oriented toward the retention of a cherished object that was originally the child's own feces. The lust for money is that frustrated infantile goal transferred to the world's official symbol of wealth. On the other hand, asceticism is no less neurotic. As a form of instinctual renunciation, it qualifies as masochism and can have behind it only the motivation of guilt.

Plenitude, however, seeks to moderate and synthesize these Utopian ideals within a sustainable environmental context. Rather than a form of self-inflicted punishment, an economy of modest means makes possible a simplicity that allows other needs to be gratified. The goal is not cathartic suffering, but pleasure of a superior order. Freud would have seen this superiority as the "displacement upward" of an instinctual goal that must undergo sublimation. But within a broader ecological framework, this sublimation is a necessity of survival and so constitutes a psychiatric imperative.

ECOLOGY, ETHICS, AESTHETICS

If there is to be a moral equivalent of wretched excess, it will have to be designed within several parameters: the ecological, the ethical, the aesthetic, the spiritual. The general formulation might be somewhat like this: *ecology* defines the economic framework within which we decide what the planetary biosphere can afford to provide; *ethics* decides how the wealth is to be shared, especially with respect to the minimal standard that must be available to all as a matter of right; *aesthetics* and *religion* provide the values that set the upper limits to material consumption.

Mumford was right in believing that the standard of plenitude we seek for the modern world requires the abundance that only an industrial technology makes possible. But the abundance must be democratically shared before there is the chance for it to be individually squandered. This means spreading the sort of "safety net" beneath the economy that even fiscal conservatives now grudgingly regard as a legitimate public responsibility. And it must be a generously wide, dependably secure net. No advanced industrial economy need consign thousands of its members to the permanent status of homelessness and joblessness, nor to a lifetime spent below a statistical poverty line. To do so is not only inhumane but self-defeating. Unless there is guaranteed universal access to the high and healthy living standard that industrial power, sanitation, and the best medical practice make available, we will never be free of the anxious compulsion to hoard and glut. The haves will consume all the more voraciously, convinced there is not enough to go around. The have-nots, in resentful desperation, will do all they can to gain their turn at the trough. Inadequate and humiliating welfare systems do nothing to inspire a sense of environmental responsibility, either on the part of those who pay for them or those who live off them.

That much most environmentalists will grant. But frequently beyond the minimal standard, they paint a picture of the future that is oppressively frugal and self-denying. They leave no place for some margin of discretionary income, "mad money" people may save or spend freely as an expression of personal taste that diversifies an otherwise grimly uniform state-controlled system of social security. But allow for that, and you must expect that there may well be a certain amount of frivolous merchandise floating through the marketplace, perhaps even a certain number of neon telephones. The appropriate response to the wasteful mass proliferation of such inanities is to tap those deeper motivations, both aesthetic and religious, that Plato, More, and Morris placed at the foundations of their Utopias.

At the very least, that response must lead to the reevaluation of leisure as an economic good of the highest order, the chance to grow, to create, to enjoy time and the world. Leisure is what John Ruskin had in mind when he proclaimed that there is "no wealth but life"; it is what all the labor, the investment, the production are *for,* that personal sabbath in which we work out our salvation with diligence. William Morris would have known exactly what to do with that leisure. He would have invested it in the cultivation of popular taste, especially the arts and crafts. People will only cease cluttering the world with more junk than the planet can metabolize if they can recognize junk when they see it, and appreciate its absence when they walk through the untrashed landscape of the city or the open land. It would be a counsel of despair to conclude that the popular culture in our time cannot be schooled to respect excellence as it did in the days of Sophocles and of Shakespeare—both of whom wrote for *hoi polloi.* What we most need in order to set out on that great educational venture is a clear recognition that art has a vital role to play in curing our environmental ills. It is the gentle discipline of the appetite.

FOOLS OF GOD

But something more than a heightened aesthetic sensibility is needed to put plenitude to its full use. Another Utopian work rounds out the picture. In one of his last books, Aldous Huxley sought to offer his own response to the future he had predicted forty years before in *Brave New World.* His novel *Island* stands as one of the most comprehensive ecological Utopias yet to be written. It was Huxley's conviction that religion and science must ultimately be brought together in a graceful, mutually supportive synthesis. He refused to believe that the "perennial philosophy"—his name for the universal teachings one finds at the source of the great religious traditions—required that the great discoveries of modern science, especially those of biology, must be brushed aside or viewed with hostility. In his Utopia, the study of deep systems begins in kindergarten as the introduction to religion and ethics.

> Never give children a chance of imagining that anything exists in isolation. Make it plain from the very first that all living is relationship. Show them relationships in the woods, in the fields, in the ponds and streams,

in the village and the country around it. . . . always teach the science of relationship in conjunction with the ethics of relationship. . . . Elementary ecology leads straight to elementary Buddhism.

Unlike more secular Utopians, who often fail to provide a convincing motivation for the good life they would have people lead, Huxley grounded the plenitude enjoyed by his imaginary islanders in his own hybrid brand of Vedantic mysticism. The religion of the society is the secret of its sustainability as well as its sanity. For Freud, religion was an illusion, perhaps necessary but nonetheless pathetic; it was a fragile consolation that denied the body and crucified the mind. Huxley, however, imagined a religion that allowed for gratifications of mind and body Freud never dreamed of. In his ideal society, hallucinogens like LSD are discriminately used as part of a therapeutic yoga. Moreover, the islanders are expertly trained in *maithuna,* a form of Tantric sex that also doubles as the society's main contraceptive technique. Huxley outflanks Freud in his treatment of sexuality. Rather than settling for a meager sublimation of the libido, he sets out to salvage the total-body eroticism of our original instinctual impulse.

> What we experience all through infancy and childhood is a sexuality that isn't concentrated on the genitals; it's a sexuality diffused throughout the whole organism. That's the paradise we inherit. But the paradise gets lost as the child grows up. *Maithuna* is the organized attempt to regain that paradise.[3]

Given his liberal and many-faceted religious tastes, it was possible for Huxley to infuse his ideal society with an eclectic, nonascetic spirituality that works in tandem with the quest for plenitude. He draws here upon a cultural image that is well represented in the Eastern religions: the happy sage who lives at one with nature in a free and joyous simplicity, the mind alert on all its levels, the senses fully alive. Both the Taoist and Zen traditions feature such figures of crazy wisdom, good-humored monks untouched by the solemnity or long-suffering of Western monasticism. Even if their way of life is celibate and abstemious, it has nothing about it that suggests the mortification of the flesh.

It is difficult to imagine an ecological Utopia based on Christianity that would not be dismally austere. The necessary rapport with nature is not prominently there. In Christianity, the "green man" of the Middle Ages—a free spirit roaming the woodlands, living the life of Adam before the Fall—smacked too much of the pagan Pan; the figure could not blend with saint or sage. Yet something of the jovial monk managed to survive in Francis of Assisi and his zany follower Brother Juniper. Both were such fools of god, delighting in the company of the birds, the trees, the sun, and the stars. It is no coincidence that this variety of spontaneous elation is connected with the pantheistic love of nature. It is as if the body of the sage has grown to encompass the greater body of the Earth whose variety and fertility he then claims as his own. There are, here and there, a few brave and embattled Christian thinkers—like Father Matthew Fox, Father Thomas Berry, Rosemary Ruether—who are struggling to give their tradition ecological depth.

> In relation to the Earth [Thomas Berry reminds both his religious and nonreligious readers] we have been autistic for centuries. Only now have we begun to listen with some attention and with a willingness to respond to the Earth's demands that we cease our industrial assault, . . . that we renew our human participation in the grand liturgy of the universe.[4]

Experiences of this order, a nature mysticism embodying all that Deep Ecology has to teach us, belong to a higher sanity that will find in plenitude greater rewards than the machines can ever offer.

Ten

◆

NARCISSISM REVISITED

I long for a self which is continuous and permanent; which, untouched by all we acquire and all we shed, pushes a green spear through the dead leaves and through the mould, thrusts a scaled bud through years of darkness until, one day, the light discovers it and shakes the flower free—and we are alive—we are flowering for our moment upon the Earth. This is the moment which, after all, we live for.

KATHERINE MANSFIELD, *Scrapbook*

THE WALL

Historians may never find anything good to say about the American experience in Vietnam. The bastard child of ill-conceived, deeply deceptive, and badly executed policy, it is America's most morally compromised military adventure. All the society has managed to do in order to "put the war behind us" (as official Washington likes to describe its policies of induced social amnesia) is to drown the memory in the blood of another "successful" war fought a decade and a half later against a more vulnerable opponent. Yet along with its many scars, the war has left behind one ethically significant landmark.

The wall.

The Vietnam Memorial in Washington may be, aesthetically speaking, the single most understated public monument in history. For that reason it is worth pondering its one distinctive feature. It lists all the names. Rather than presenting an idealized figure or a symbolic group over the grave of a great national agony, the wall simply lists the names. And while there are only the names, the public that comes to view the wall has from the beginning sought to bestow a personal value on these names, bringing photos, mementos, flowers, messages, standing in grieving silence before the one name that matters, reaching out to touch it, to plant a kiss. These tributes have become a part of the wall; its very featurelessness invites decoration.

The names are not there as they might be on tombstones where necessity requires it. A monument is meant to express a nation's collective sense of a great event's importance. The wall does so by stripping that event of everything that has been used for that purpose in the past: the platitudes, icons, patriotic emblems. Nothing is left but the terrible reality. The names of the dead. What else would a nation so divided about the war have tolerated? Sculptor Maya Lin, interviewed in *The New York Times,* says of her monument,

> I stripped the question down to 'How are all these people going to overcome the pain of losing something?' How do you really overcome death? And that brought me to the names. It would absolutely not help them to put up something that was falsely heroic. The only way you can work with history and the only way you can overcome anything is to accept it very, very honestly.

I want to characterize the wall in a special way. I want to call it the monument to a *narcissistic* era. I use "narcissism" as we find it in the words quoted from Katherine Mansfield above, a woman close to death becoming suddenly, fiercely aware of her moment upon Earth, a moment made special by her unique presence within it. Her adventure, her opportunity, once lost, never to be repeated.

This is not the way "narcissism" is normally used. Ask what the word means and most people are likely to identify it as disease or moral failure, a synonym for conceit and antisociability carried to a pathological extreme. In psychology textbooks, one is apt to find it described pejoratively as a life of "grandiose fantasy," "obsessive self-gratification." Narcissus is, after all, the gorgeous youth who starved beside the pool, enchanted by his own beguiling reflection. The condition named after him has never had a healthy ring to it. At its extreme, the condition has been traced by some therapists to an inner sense of emptiness for which the narcissist compensates by inventing a histrionic "false self" that may be highly vulnerable to rapid deflation and inconsolable despair.

What the disparaging, popular reading of narcissism overlooks is the fact that Freud, who did the most to embed the word in our psychological vocabulary, believed there was a normally narcissistic interval in life, diseased only if it is prolonged without modification into adulthood. He did not invent the term, but borrowed it for the specific purpose of taking issue with the psychiatrist who had classified it as a perversion. It was not, in Freud's view, the same as egotism, a more disruptive adult disorder, nor was it to be equated with greed, conceit, swinish self-indulgence. It was, in the form called "primary narcissism," the child's normal preoccupation with the pleasures of the body. "It is probable [Freud reasoned] that this narcissism is the universal original condition out of which love-objects develop later without thereby necessarily effecting a disappearance of the narcissism."[1]

Taking our lead from Freud, then, we might be able to salvage an affirmative use for the word—one that explains the intensely emotional importance so many people have tried to find even in the names that line the blank facade of a war memorial. Narcissism, for all its suspect qualities, may be a necessary stage in the creation of an authentic personal identity. Even in its most frivolous forms, it can play that part in people's lives. It may represent the destination to which our long forced march through the industrial process has finally led us: the building of a social order in which the great Socratic project of self-knowledge becomes possible for one and all. Moreover, it may be that, at a certain hazardous ecological phase in the industrial process, narcissism is the compensatory balance our threatened planet needs if it is to restrain the excesses of industrial growth or even reverse them.

Narcissism in the form of auto-eroticism is the individual's first experience of physical exhilaration; it includes such lifelong delights as sex, sleep, and those varieties of gratification which Freud named "polymorphous perversity." In its initial manifestation before the infant can clearly distinguish the bodily boundaries of individual identity from the surrounding world, it embraces everything in an undifferentiated "oceanic" eroticism. In contrast to "egotism," which relates to mundane interests and social goals usually of a competitive character, narcissism aims for the private satisfaction of libidinal desires. It is the basis of that joy that world-beating egotists may spend a sullen lifetime denying themselves. For this reason, there are psychiatrists who reserve a place in their diagnostic catalogue for "healthy" or "high-level narcissism," without which, one authority tells us, "we could not invest our unique self-representations with the positive feelings necessary for self-esteem and self-assertion."[2]

THE GREAT REFUSAL

Seen in this light, narcissism may survive into later life as a legitimate concern for sensual pleasure, even as an erotic response to all of nature—as with the Romantic poets whose ecstatic embrace of the landscape was always associated with a lingering child-like innocence. In a seminal work of the nineteen fifties, the political philosopher Herbert Marcuse saw a significant political value in these possibilities. Narcissism, Freud had said, is implicated in "the backwardness of sexuality in learning to conform to the reality principle." By "reality principle" he meant the going standard of sanity. But, asked Marcuse, what if the reality principle is life-denying and plain crazy? What if it is maniacally hell-bent on the exploitation of man and nature, submerged in acquisitiveness, obsessed with violence and war? As we have seen, Freud had once raised this possibility. But Marcuse was prepared to draw the political conclusion Freud left unspoken. If reality as the world understands it is pathologically warped, might not a great deal then be said for *anything* that is prepared to "revolt against culture based on toil, domination, and renunciation" in favor of "a non-repressive erotic attitude toward reality"?[3]

For Marcuse, one of the early Marxist–Humanists, Freud's insight into primary narcissism became the basis for what he called the "Great Refusal," the rejection of a mad world's dehumanizing values. Marcuse argued that in the high industrial period, democratically shared affluence and leisure become real options. Accordingly, the "surplus repression" that makes narcissism one of the childish things we are forced to lay aside in becoming adults is substantially lightened and the onerous discipline of the "performance principle" (steady toil and deferred gratification) can be lifted. If we do not see this happening, the reasons are neither biological nor psychological but political; the situation is ripe for change.

Ideas like this, which so clearly endanger industrial discipline and the work ethic, were not without their critics. As one might have expected, the corporate community and the government, whose programs of high production, full employment, and mandatory consumption were responsible for the easing of social constraints, suddenly found themselves confronted with more free expression, irreverence, and outright rebellion than they had bargained for. During the twenty years following World War Two, while America held its place as king of the industrial mountain, we passed through a remarkable political period in which, for the first time in history, those who wielded power sought to defend their status more often by way of inducement, reward, and bribery than by brute force and the threat of privation. This was not a matter of generosity; the war-born prosperity of the period demanded a steeply rising level of consumer spending. The feasible standard of living in America was potentially so high, there was no way to bring scarcity to bear as a social control except where it might coincide with lingering forms of racial or ethnic bigotry. Even so, the nation's minorities ("the other America" as it came to be known) soon began to demand admittance to the affluent society in ways that could not be thwarted. The easiest course was to buy off the discontent on all sides. Hence, the great Society and the War on Poverty. Or at least that was the strategy until the mid- to late seventies, when later transformations in the world economy dictated less generous policies.

What political and corporate leaders expected to purchase for their largesse was, in the words of sociologist C. Wright Mills, a population of "cheerful robots." Marcuse used the phrase "one-dimensional man" to refer to a similar state of timidly acquiescent gratitude. In return for high wages and good times, the populace was expected to kowtow to authority, become obedient Organization Men (and their housewifely wives) willing to trade citizenly initiative for suburban contentment, credit cards galore, and season tickets to Disneyland for the family. There might even be a suave new level of sexual permissiveness, a big-spending, commercialized eroticism: "repressive desublimation," as Marcuse called it. In the immediate postwar period, George Orwell had seen the world headed toward the sadistic totalitarianism of 1984. But as of the Eisenhower fifties, it looked as if Aldous Huxley had made the better prediction: industrial society was on its way into a Brave New World of expertly engineered, imbecilic hedonism.

In these economic transformations there was a dialectical process at work that Marx could never have foreseen. He had expected rebellion to arise from suffering; the terrible precondition of revolution was the intolerable "immiserization" of the masses. Instead, in the course of America's first affluent generation, the possibility began to emerge that pleasure, leisure, abundance might provide the basis for political disaffiliation. What the corporate leadership of the affluent society expected was loyal employees; what the government expected was productive bomb physicists and obedient cannon fodder. They got a good deal of that; but they also got beatniks, hippies, yippies, Woodstock, the Weathermen, Kool-Aid acid tests, teach-ins, be-ins, love-ins, and far more hell-raising than they could handle. It is no wonder that they soon went sour on the strategy of manipulative permissiveness. Paul Goodman put it colorfully when in 1969 he observed of "the theoretically 'impossible' youth revolt" that it was "in the cards for the children of affluence, brought up without toilet training, freely masturbating, and with casual clothing, to be daring, disobedient, and simple-minded."[4]

SPANKING NARCISSUS

That deviant conduct like this would shock the politicians and the corporate elite was predictable enough. But there were others outside the circles of power who were no less distressed by the strange new morals and mores of the affluent society. Their reservations were more honest and cut deeper. Daniel Bell called what he saw about him "the megalomania of self-infinitization, . . . a longing for the lost gratifications of an idealized childhood." Peter Marin called it plain "solipsism . . . a retreat from the worlds of morality and history." Christopher Lasch was the most influential in labeling the new middle-class American hedonism as a "culture of narcissism" in the most damning sense of the word. For him, such developments as the "awareness movement," the human potential therapies, the "rhetoric of authenticity" thinly masked an underlying despair. It was all infantile and empty, a futile attempt to flee "the void within." Worse, it was "a retreat from politics." Unlike others who wielded the term in a disparaging way,

Lasch had a sure and discriminating grip on the clinical meaning of narcissism. He used it, nonetheless, like a heavy parental paddle to spank the narcissists of American society who, as he saw it, were unable "to lay to rest the terrors of infancy or to enjoy the consolations of adulthood."[5]

Now it is one thing for social critics to lambast well-defined groups—especially those gifted with wealth and power who can be held culpable for doing obvious harm. It is another to strike out so harshly at anonymous millions of one's fellow citizens who are at worst doing a less than brilliant job of growing up and growing wise. Surely the critics who raise the charge are making ambitious claims for their own emotional balance and ethical impeccability to position themselves on such lofty ground. What is it the antinarcissists purported to find lacking in the generation of the sixties and seventies? That so many have botched their marriages, their love affairs, their parental responsibilities, their careers and citizenly duties? That they have failed to become whole and happy elders, a model to the upcoming generation? A serious indictment, but one that could be drawn against Everyman and Everywoman down through the ages. What is the historical baseline for such a scathing attack? Where in the past do we find societies of fully mature, totally competent adults masterfully taking charge of their lives? The forties . . . the fifties . . . the seventies . . . the eighties?

Of course, we find nothing of the kind. For most of human history, the adults of the world—a handful of saints, sages, and political heroes excepted—have been overgrown children struggling to fill the shoes of equally incompetent parents, usually making the sort of mess of their world that has provided novelists and dramatists with the raw material of their art, and prophets with the object of their wrath. What are we to make of the generations that were the target of Voltaire's recrimination—or Tolstoy's or Marx's or Zola's or Ibsen's or Shaw's?

On the other hand, the eagerness to openly psychologize one's miseries and failures—"the therapeutic outlook," as Lasch called it—this *is* new. The whining and the tears, the endless revelations of anger, pain, resentment, the delicate awareness of victimization—these are new. So, too, the level of expectation that people have set for themselves in contemporary America when it comes to freedom, enjoyment, and self-expression. Even more so the capacity for hurt and disappointment when those expectations are not met. The fact that we *know* these things about people, can comment on them, ridicule or satirize them if we will, the fact that so many people are prepared to be so candid about their vulnerabilities, to "let it all hang out" demanding our attention for their grievances, all this is new. New and significant, even when it fails to find elegantly refined expression.

This is what most distinguishes the "culture of narcissism," this willingness of so many to lay bare their confusion and self-doubt before the world, to reveal themselves as the antiheroes most people have always been. Even when, for lack of better means, they resort to "psychobabble," they are telling us a great deal about weaknesses and inadequacies that may deserve more mercy than they have received from critics who would have us believe they share no such frailties.

This is what gets lost in the diatribes that have been directed against the derelictions of narcissism. Over the course of the last generation, a uniquely insistent, if frequently ungainly sense of personal identity has been developing in the popular culture of the high industrial societies. While they have not often gone about it gracefully, thousands, especially in the United States, have been in pursuit of therapeutic self-knowledge more intensively, and more inventively than one would expect to find anywhere in times past except among the artistic and contemplative few. Nor has this psychologically sensitive style been limited to the affluent middle-class. One need only think back to works like Malcolm X's memoirs or Eldridge Cleaver's *Soul on Ice*. Here we find black Americans groping through their own childhood insecurities and sexual hang-ups with an honesty that is unprecedented in the literature of political protest. Nothing is more striking than how rapidly a confessional candor that would have been shocking to our parents' generation has come to be taken for granted—to the point that it can be used as the raw material for humorists like Woody Allen, Jules Feiffer, Gary Trudeau.

This is a remarkable cultural development. And yet, liberal and radical thinkers who might at least have been expected to show some curiosity about the matter have hurried to participate in the same backlash against the political disaffiliation of the sixties and seventies that was already under way on the part of the nation's political and corporate leaders from the Johnson presidency on. Whether their approach was a scholarly application of Freudian psychiatry or a journalistic tirade against the "Me Generation," the storyline was the same:

the protest of the period was skin deep and immature; for the most part it was frivolous, an outburst by pampered adolescents whose real values turned out to be those of their parents; where alternatives to the middle-class way of life were presented, they failed because they were insincere or misconceived. In time, the "big chill" was bound to set in, the hippies would give way to the yuppies, and the great American way of life rolls on unperturbed.

Even the towering fact that these spoiled brats, wishing to make love not war, did a reasonably effective job of stopping the military machine in Vietnam, unseating a corrupt president, raising issues of justice in every mainstream American institution, and in general authoring the most sweeping indictment of the nation's moral failures since the days of the muckrakers, has not seemed sufficient to offset the exasperation that remains for remembered discourtesies and occasional aberrations. Discourtesies and aberrations there were. But then name a major political movement that ran its course with unexceptional good manners and exemplary intelligence. Lint-picking the scattered flaws and faults of a cause while ignoring the greater issues raised has always been an easy way to distract and discredit.

THE EMPOWERMENT OF INNOCENCE

One cannot help but feel there was more to this critical battering of narcissism than issues either of good taste or moral reservation. For often these objections, even when they were reasonably appropriate, were touched with an unspoken apprehension that was never fully clarified. I believe it was the astonishing *guiltlessness* of those who were labeled narcissists that offended so many and invited their belittling. For a brief period, a mere fraction of a generation, images of a joyous, antinomian life were brazenly projected on the social scene. People dared to be *interested* in themselves, and therefore claimed the right to *be* themselves and to *like* themselves, making no apologies, showing no visible shame for the affront they posed to good manners, respectable appearances, sexual morality, social duty.

Such misconduct, if it amounts to no more than the wishful and crippled gestures of an anarchic few, even if it is for the most part an illusion fabricated by the sensationalizing media, strikes at well-entrenched values. It seems to make a laughingstock of what Lionel Trilling once called "the stratum of hardness that runs through the Jewish and Christian traditions as they respond to the hardness of human destiny." Daniel Bell, fretting over the fact that "release, debauch, and total freedom" stand in danger of becoming "the democratic property of the mass," was echoing a moral horror that reaches back to the prophets of Israel. Among modern intellectuals it has long been fashionable to scoff at the Puritanism that once dominated the cultural establishment in England and America. But the scoffing was mainly a matter of clever jibes and polished literature. It was for qualified people to do, people of education, social presence, scintillating wit. That ordinary people—people unskilled in the conversational arts and without literary talent—should *act* on that criticism, should treat sexuality as a natural right and condition, talk dirty, uncover the body, even fornicate publicly, and do all this *shamelessly,* that is quite another matter. Worse still, that people should blithely mock all authority, the discipline of the workplace, intellectual rigor—this smacks of barbarism.

It runs remarkably deep in our culture, this stern conviction that freedom, pleasure, self-indulgence must be earned—and hard-earned at that. Somewhere at its foundation lies a radical sense of human unworthiness, a belief in the congenital perversity of our nature that we must struggle to redeem. Socrates believed that the goal of philosophy was self-knowledge. But the only methods of knowing one's self that Western culture has invented start from the assumption that the essence of introspection is the search for dirty secrets. Consider the techniques: the Catholic confessional, the Puritan diary, the campground testimonial. The process in each case is the rehearsal of sins, the plea for forgiveness. One finishes with acknowledging inborn demerits that must be worked off. Freud is said to have invented the psychoanalytical couch as a confessional for Protestants. He too conceived of the human heart as a den of iniquity; the object of analysis was to rake the muck. Self-knowledge in the Western world has come to mean self-castigation; it has been practiced under the wrathful eye of a lawgiver god from whom no evil can be hidden.

What happens then if, quite unpredictably, a generation appears whose rearing has softened these elements of self-loathing and denigration, leaving it equipped with what Freud would have regarded as a shamefully underdeveloped superego? People relax, they enjoy, they goof off, they make love, perhaps in public places—and (worst of all) they think well of themselves for doing it. Or at least they *try* to do all this with an air of entitlement. Of course this looks irresponsibly, self-centeredly impudent to many an astonished observer: "narcissism" in the mean and wrathful sense of the word. But from another view-point, they have also developed that prickly claim upon pleasure and freedom that makes for Marcuse's Great Refusal. In this sense, their innocence empowers them, urging them to demand more from life than any generation of the past. They take off along their peculiar path. Quoting Emerson, they assert that life is a matter of "doing your thing"—or as the even more personalized popular version of the phrase would have it, "doing your *own* thing."

THE EUPSYCHIAN VISION

Critics who pay more attention to the gracelessness and raucous tone of these defiant antics than to their substance are bound to overlook what Western psychiatry as a whole has largely ignored since its inception: that there is a bright spirit waiting to be found in each of us, a true self that needs the optimistic trust and freedom that neither social respectability nor conscience-driven politics will give it. Abraham Maslow's Humanistic Psychology is among the schools that can be credited (or blamed) for exerting this corrective pressure upon mainstream psychotherapy. Taken as a whole, this often awkward yet boldly innovative body of thought might stand as the best landmark for any evaluation of narcissism that wishes to deal with something more than journalistic anecdotes.

Maslow began writing his way out of the Behaviorist laboratory in the early fifties. His groundbreaking 1954 work, *Motivation and Personality,* is a struggling but brave effort to map out "the healthy half" of the personality that Freud had neglected. By the early sixties he and Anthony Sutich had launched the *Journal of Humanistic Psychology* to deal with such strange new subjects as "self-actualization" and "peak experiences." Maslow's thought was always cumbersome in both style and content. The "eupsychian" image of human nature he had in view did not exactly flow from his pen when he sought to depict it. His writing was wordy, over-organized and jargon-freighted. He was given to coining terms like "B-Motivations" or "D-Values" to distinguish high-level from low-level functioning and then compiling long lists of criteria to measure each. Worse still—at least from the viewpoint of the intellectual establishment—he could seem utterly boorish in his treatment of contemporary cultural idols. For example, he dismissed the European Existentialists for their "exclusive harping on dread, anguish, despair, and the like." He called their work "high IQ whining on a cosmic scale"; he preferred to emphasize "joy, ecstasy, or even normal happiness." Sartre and the rest were dismissed as "non-peakers, people who just don't experience joy." This was not the way one curried favor in the best literary journals of the fifties and sixties, where Freudian *angst* and Marxist fervor were the fashion.

As liberating an influence as Maslow proved to be for many younger academics in his profession, Humanistic Psychology might have been a long while passing over from theory to practice. But there was another, more active force on the scene that was moving rapidly to meet the still inarticulate popular need for new therapeutic outlets. The Human Potential movement was inventing what would become the "mass medium" for Maslow's thought; it was called the growth center. In the early sixties, by way of little more than a chance encounter, Maslow joined forces with the most prominent of the centers: Michael Murphy's Esalen Institute in California.[6]

At the time, Murphy and his colleagues were exploring what Aldous Huxley once called the "nonverbal humanities," an attempt to extend education beyond the jabbering forebrain to the mind and body as a whole. At Esalen, Maslow crossed paths with another psychological maverick, the Gestalt therapist Fritz Perls who, despite his Freudian training, had taken eagerly to the free-wheeling (often literally) unbuttoned atmosphere of Esalen. Though the relations between Maslow the restrained academic and Perls the priapic wildman were abrasive from the start, between the two of them they managed to give a new public visibility to "Third Force Psychology" in America. While Maslow regarded this as a "revolution in the truest, oldest sense of the word," he nevertheless looked forward to a "still higher Fourth Psychology, transpersonal, transhuman, centered in the cosmos rather than in human needs and interests, going beyond humanness, identity, self-actualization, and the like."[7] This is to ask, once again, Freud's great question about the natural foundations of sanity; but here we find that question raised by a later, far more optimistically American generation of psychologists. From that source flowed a host of new, unorthodox therapies. The techniques and theories of Gestalt, Encounter, Transactional, Psychodrama, Transpersonal differ in many ways, but all the schools are united in asserting the essential health and innocence of human nature. They are the therapies of a narcissistic culture, and unapologetically so.

The humanistic therapies differ widely in intellectual quality. Some may be easily dismissed as little more than touchy-feely parlor games: mutual admiration ("I'm O.K., You're O.K.") in the hot-tub. Others are quite bizarre, but intriguingly so. At a San Francisco Bay Area seminary, I once came across an improvisation called Bodily Theology, a species of nude encounter for nuns and priests. Exercises like this come close to sounding like the stuff of satire; but speaking from the viewpoint of my own guilt-ridden Catholic boyhood, I rather wish the clergy who were in charge of my early education had been brave enough to confront the sexual distortions that they and their predecessors in the Church had visited upon generations of children. How do people get out from under their neurotic fears? Maybe it takes more than lectures and books.

Other humanistic therapies offer unusual insights into the nature of the personality. Gestalt Psychology, a formidable mixture of Reichian sexuality and Westernized Taoism, is among the richest modern forms of introspection. Even the quirky form of bodywork called Rolfing (after Ida Rolf) tells us that our real autobiography may be engraved in our muscle fiber more deeply than in our memory. The body remembers what the head willfully forgets; Freud, I think, might have approved of such an effort to tie mind to body, though he might not have wanted to agree that the kinks and knots of old anxieties can be pummeled out of the flesh.

In any case, however one might wish to evaluate the new therapies on their intellectual merits, one and all they deserve serious attention as symptoms of a significant need in our time: the passion for self-discovery and guiltless self-assertion that we find among the most seemingly ordinary people. Even the most simplistic of these systems is grounded in a commitment to the creative potentiality in people. In our time that need makes itself felt as powerfully and infectiously as the demand for political equality once did, and where that happens people do the best they can, not always with a clear idea of what it is they seek beyond attention, appreciation, recognition. Not many in our society find their way to a great Socratic master. For most, an easy-to-do, even commercially opportunistic therapy is the best our society has to offer. If at times people go about the project of self-knowledge with less polish than a Saint Augustine or a Rousseau making their eloquent confessions to the world, what are we to say about that? At a certain point of urgency, the search for self-knowledge is neither a public performance nor a literary exercise; it is the hunger of the soul wanting to be acknowledged as a unique event in the universe. Better, then, to make the halting effort than to surrender one's claim to personhood.

I have never left a session at one of the growth centers without marveling at the candor and intensity with which the people around me searched their motives, their needs, their fears. The importance of the project was unmistakable. Critics who feel such introspective ventures do not go deep enough would do well to ask: how much better was the task performed fifty years ago, a hundred years ago? Was it *ever* undertaken before by more than a sensitive handful? Once again, what is the baseline for this negative judgment? How crushing it would be to insist that the adventure of self-discovery belongs only to the few who can carry it off with intellectual excellence in full public view. One might understand such stern elitism on the part of conservative critics out to strengthen the politics of domination. But why should purported liberals and radicals compete in enhancing the repression?

SOCRATES AND FREUD

The deepening psychological tone of late twentieth century life, however amateurishly expressed, is born of a healthy sense of unlived life and alienated power. Just as neurosis, recognized and diagnosed, can be the first step toward sanity, so a narcissistic fascination with the self can be the beginning of cultural renewal.

Let us think of the psyche as a self-regulating system that deals in emotions, passions, aspirations the way the living cell deals in proteins and energy transfers. The environment that the psyche must confront in its task of adjustment is the culture that psyches before it (those of the parents and ancestors) have created as a "second nature." Accordingly, the psyche strives to cope with the stresses and strains this cultural environment imposes upon it. Even when the demands are severely out of balance with the needs of its own internal biological economy, it struggles to conform, if need be by way of crazy distortion. At last, having gone as far as it can to accommodate the pressures, it asserts its desperate need for healthy balance.

What the modern cultural environment has required of us is an enormous extroversion of attention and energy for the purpose of reshaping the Earth into a global industrial economy. For two centuries we have been subordinating the planet and our deepest personal needs to that project. This great act of collective alienation, I have suggested, lies at the root of both the environmental crisis and individual neurosis. In some way, at some point, a change of direction, a therapeutic turning inward, had to take place within a culture as maniacally driven as ours has been by the need to achieve and conquer.

In this great and far from finished task, Socrates and Freud, philosophy and therapy, are allied as midwives of self-knowledge. But Freud was the beginning, not the end, of the project. His could not be the last word. The humanistic therapies can be credited with devising a more refined analysis of guilt than Freud had to offer. We can now see that there are two kinds of guilt. There is the guilt that legitimately attaches to acts of violence and betrayal against our fellows. But there is another guilt (some would call it "shame" to make the distinction) that is essentially society's chief means of regimenting its millions. Shame stems from our anxiety that we have failed to honor the identity that society has assigned us in life. If we are not what a man–husband–father is *supposed* to be, if we are not what a woman–wife–mother is *supposed* to be, we are made to feel ashamed. Human history has for the greater part been populated by such types and stereotypes. The false identities they wear are what William Blake called the "Mind-Forged Manacles." No society gets its work done, its taxes collected, its wars fought unless millions will accept the bondage of these chains.

But now we arrive at a point in the life-story of the planet where that discipline needs to be broken; the great industrial armies, the technological systems must be hobbled in their runaway career. I think this is how it is done. At least in part, narcissistic fascination is the way we break the manacles. Whatever Gaia may be, impersonal system or immanent divinity, she speaks to that within each of us that wishes to be known peculiarly and personally, the self that fits no mold, the "me" that cannot be made interchangeable.

This "song of myself" may be no more than a brief discordant tune. But sung by a sufficient number, it is enough to halt the rhythm of the great machine. In that moment we become what Charlie Chaplin's little victim–hero became in *Modern Times* when, falling out of synch on the assembly line, he wound up jamming the man-eating gears. In becoming even a small piece of ourselves, we become what the burdened planet needs: creatures with some more urgent calling, some greater joy than comes of waging war upon nature.

Was Montaigne a narcissist? Was Whitman? Was Rilke or Kierkegaard or Dostoyevsky? Or are they excused from the label because they possessed the talent to raise their obsessive soul-searching to the level of great art? Are the rights of self-knowledge then to be restricted to genius? It is a question intellectuals have never asked: what would an ethos of democratized self-knowledge look like? The answer may be: look around you. This is it. Or at least this is how it begins.

THE RIGHTS OF SELF-KNOWLEDGE

We might better appreciate this transformation in the light of an historical parallel that takes us back some three centuries. In the view of most historians, the modern era began with the wave of eighteenth and nineteenth century revolutions that destroyed the old feudal order and replaced it with democratic, or would-be democratic societies, which in turn set free the capital, the entrepreneurial skill, and the laboring masses to undertake industrial development. The words I quote below come from the beginning of that mighty transition in whose turbulent wake we now find ourselves. The year is 1647; the place is Putney Common in England, the nation that was destined to launch the liberal tradition and the industrial revolution; the speaker is a man we know little about, one Colonel Rainborough, who, despite his military rank, was an illiterate soldier risen from the ranks of Oliver Cromwell's revolutionary legions during the English Civil War.

Really I thinke that the poorest hee that is in England hath a life to live as the greatest hee; and therefore truly, Sir, I thinke itt's cleare, that every man that is to live under a Government ought first by his owne consent to putt himself under that Government; and I doe thinke that the poorest man in England is nott att all bound in a stricte sence to that Government that hee hath not had a voice to putt himself under . . . every man born in England cannot, ought nott, neither by the law of God nor the law of nature, to bee exempted from the choice of those who are to make lawes, for him to live under, and for him, for ought I know, to loose his life under.

These words come from one of the most remarkable documents in European history. The Putney Debates are the verbatim record of a series of impassioned discussions held around the campfires of an insurrectionary army. Colonel Rainborough emerged as the spokesman for the common soldiers in these debates, voicing their demand for a new constitution once the monarchy had been driven from power.

Most of what the man has to say should be as familiar to modern readers as the air we breathe. A century and a quarter later, in 1776, revised by a more learned hand, the ideal we find expounded here would become the text of our own Declaration of Independence. But read the words again, and as you do so, try to hear the struggle behind them, the trembling voice, the stutter of uncertainty. Hear them as the words of a common man demanding his rights of social superiors who have never heard of such rights, who regard them as an absurd, if not obscene improvisation.

Think, as you read these words: nothing like this had ever been said before in human history.

This is the beginning, the absolute beginning of democratic politics. This is where it started, in this stammered outpouring of an unlettered soldier's moral conviction. "Really I thinke . . . I thinke itt's cleare . . . and I doe thinke . . . and I am confident . . ." But he *was not* confident. How could he be, when the officers and gentlemen who gave him his marching orders and who opposed him in these debates with eloquence and learned allusion regarded him as a member of the rightless mob, one not authorized to hold a thought, to speak his piece. Fearing for their property and their privilege, the gentlemen rejected everything he said as impudent and presumptuous nonsense. The man did not speak their language. His faltering references to scripture, to theology, to law lacked erudition; his vocabulary was meager, his logic flawed. Worst of all, there was no humility in the man, no sense of shame and unworthiness. Scornful critics of the time might have dismissed his garbled efforts as "rabble-babble." Colonel Rainborough lost the debate. His "betters" prevailed.

Two generations later, these words, with their grammar corrected and their rhetoric suitably polished, were on the lips of all the keenest minds of the Enlightenment. The age of democratic revolution had found its intellectual cadres.

Here is the parallel I wish to draw.

In Colonel Rainborough's day, what was crucially at stake was the political integrity of the commonwealth. The cause that needed to be advanced was that of equal rights. The language of those rights was legal and political. The result of the revolutionary fervor those words inspired was the modern industrial world we see about us.

In our day, even before democratic rights have been universally won, what is crucially at stake is the physical integrity of the biosphere. The cause that needs to be advanced is that of biocentric community. But the endangered species, the imperilled biosphere, cannot speak for themselves. We must be their voice. We speak for them when we speak for the personhood that is endangered by the same forces that burden the planetary environment. On this historical horizon, the right to self-knowledge parallels the right to self-government. The *specialness* of people-in-particular takes its place alongside the *equality* of people-in-general. The language of this new cause, still every bit as rough-tongued and halting as Colonel Rainborough's untutored speech, is psychological, the only idiom of self-knowledge we have.

A further parallel.

In Colonel Rainborough's day, there were elites around the camp-fires at Putney who greeted the ideal of democracy with uncomprehending contempt. So, too, in our day there are elites who greet the cause of self-discovery with the same bewildered disdain. They, too, decry the presumption of innocence they hear in these struggling attempts to achieve self-knowledge. They miss the *angst* and sophistication they wish might be there. They hear "ordinary" people calling out for personal acknowledgment, and they call it "narcissism." They hear the desire to be treated as special and unique, and they call it spoiled self-indulgence. They bemoan the buzz-words on the surface, failing to attend the desperate need beneath. Shall we say they "pity the plumage, but forget the dying bird?"

A "Me Generation," "psychobabble," "self-infinitization," "the triumph of the therapeutic." . . . After the easy condemnation has been pronounced, the question remains: what shall we do in the presence of this rising popular demand for attention and recognition? Do we work with it, strive to educate it, shape it into the tool the planet needs . . . or resign the ideal? For my own part, though I wince at the frequent vulgarities, I see great political, personal, and ecological value in this change of cultural direction, too much for me to reject it out of hand. It is the brave beginning of a project that both the person and the planet require.

If this be narcissism, make the most of it.

Eleven

TOWARD AN ECOLOGICAL EGO

THE STRENGTH OF THE EGO

The separation of the ego from the id seems justifiable, is indeed forced upon us by certain findings. Yet on the other hand the ego is identical with the id, is only a specially differentiated portion of it. If in our thinking we contrast this portion with the whole, or if an actual disjunction of the two has come about, then the weakness of this ego becomes apparent. If, however, the ego remains one with the id and indistinguishable from it, then it is its strength that is apparent.[1]

This was as close as Freud came to dignifying the status of the id, granting it the role of a sort of psychic muscle that might, by drawing upon the original unity of the soul, serve to empower the embattled ego. But empower the ego against *what*—and in behalf of *what?* It remained for his followers, or at least the more adventurous among them, to spell out the possibilities of the idea.

It is implicit in Freud's concept of neurosis that parents drive their children more or less crazy by splitting ego from id and then, by virtue of the inevitably unresolved Oedipal complex, leaving these once-united sectors of the psyche forever at war. But, of course, these parents were driven more or less crazy by *their* parents. And now their children will visit the same sad condition upon the next generation of infantile victims. And on and on. Freud envisioned this state of affairs reaching back to the legendary "primal horde," with the father, a sexually acquisitive brute, bearing particular blame for the initial sundering of the psyche.

Supposedly, fathers of this kind, retrospectively modeled on the nineteenth century bourgeois *pater familias,* had been visiting psychic lesions upon their woeful sons since time immemorial, and for quite as long, the sons had been (in fact or fantasy) murdering these heavy fathers and suffering pangs of patricidal guilt. In some later schools of psychiatry, mothers have been held responsible for deforming the minds of the young. Not so Freud. He traced the original psychotic trauma to the mythic father of us all somewhere in the dim prehistoric past. In effect, the archetypal father-figure invented the repression of the instincts, first by emasculating his sons, then by becoming the focus of the remorse they felt for venting their murderous rage upon him.

Oddly enough, despite the glaring injustice of this scenario, Freud failed to draw the obvious conclusion. Nowhere does he suggest that the task of making ego and id one and inseparable again might best begin with a clear declaration that, at least in the therapist's compassionate eye, the patient's guilt is uncalled for. If there were ever fathers like this, they deserved what they got in the way of hostility, ingratitude, even perhaps a few hard knocks. Rather, Freud was persuaded to accept such toxic human relations as eternally given, an irremediable biological warp at the core of family life. Since he was himself, by all reports, just such a domineering Big Daddy both to his family and his students, it was apparently unthinkable to him that this wretched state of affairs might be altered. Freud was resigned to defining normality within the terms of the familial status quo as passable, low-grade functioning, provided all the leftover childhood anxieties and animosities were kept under control—or at least under wraps. The Oedipal remnants might leave behind some messy castration fears; but since this did not usually get in the way of "normal" genital intercourse, one must simply live with it as the best one can expect in life.

The proposition never arises in Freud's work that *all this must stop*—with the psychiatrist coming to the child's rescue. How could this be done without changing the society from top to bottom? Even the childhood memories his female patients so often laid before him of sexual abuse at the hands of their fathers failed to produce outrage. What could these shocking stories be but fantasies of the wishful unconscious? We have since learned, as Freud might have discovered with more sensitive examination and greater trust in his patients, how frequently these reports turn out to be true. He preferred to regard them as figments of the overwrought female sexual imagination. They were to be talked away in favor of saving the reputation of fathers and the stability of the family.

Similarly with the post-Freudians, we find the family and society generally but casually implicated in driving each new generation to one degree or another crazy—though usually with less emphasis on sexual repression. Once again, recognition of the parental culpability for neurosis does not lead to a revolutionary conclusion. One settles for a therapeutic fix performed on a case by case basis. This is rather as if physicians, confronted with an outbreak of cholera, undertook to treat each case individually, making no attempt to get at the source of the infection.

Among the early post-Freudians, only the eccentric Wilhelm Reich was prepared to identify the castrating father as a major political issue. The damage done in the nursery, Reich insisted, was more than personal and private. It did not stop at the front door but flowed into the streets to become totalitarian mass movements.

Reich is a thinker who must be handled with care. The latter part of his career became a notorious thicket of quackery and paranoia that is best left charitably unmentioned. But as a critic of Freudian orthodoxy in his early years, Reich produced a number of intriguing ideas. Among the most promising was his conviction that the unconscious as Freud described it is not the *true* unconscious. It is an intermediary "layer" between the ego and a still-deeper level of the psyche. Freud's unconscious is merely "the sum total of all so-called secondary drives." It is not that which is repressed; it is that which represses. Represses what? The "primary biologic urges," which might be called the id beneath the id. "If one penetrates through this second layer of perversion, deeper into the biologic substratum of the human animal, one always discovers the third deepest layer, which we call the *biologic core.*" At that core and given favorable conditions, Reich felt certain that "man is essentially honest, industrious, cooperative, loving."[2]

On the other hand, Reich saw Freud's false unconscious as the psychic force that was used by repressive ideologies to strangle "man's original biologic demands." It was the fascist within all of us. "Pleasure-anxiety (fear of pleasurable excitation) which is represented physiologically in chronic muscular spasms . . . is the soil on which the individual recreates the life-negating ideologies which are the basis of dictatorship."

Since "orgastic impotence" lies at the root of fascism, Reich argued, the struggle to achieve a healthy "sex economy" must begin by unleashing the full healing power of the thwarted instincts.

> Freud's therapeutic formula is correct but incomplete. The first prerequisite of cure is, indeed, to make the repressed sexuality conscious. However, though this alone *may* effect the cure, it *need not* of necessity do so. It does so . . . *only if the awareness of instinctual demands goes hand in hand with the capacity for full orgastic gratification.* In that case the pathological psychic growths are deprived of energy at the source.[3]

From this point of view, Reich was convinced that "even after the military victory over German fascism, the fascist human structure will continue to exist in Germany, Russia, America and everywhere else." The "supreme goal" of therapy would therefore remain "the establishment of orgiastic potency, of the ability to discharge an amount of sexual energy equal to that accumulated."

The instincts, to which Reich traces his political analysis, play a curious role in modern psychotherapy. In the hands of radical theorists, they are the supposed bedrock of depth psychology, as deep as analysis can go. Yet they are most often depicted as essentially the mammalian sexual drive. In Freud, the id, which is the source and shelter of that drive, is associated with stereotypes of wild savagery and unfettered protohuman lechery. The Darwinian reference is obvious, as is the prudish Victorian framework within which Darwin worked. The randy appetite lingers on within us, a repressed heritage of ancestral animality always in danger of breaking loose like the hairy ape that strains at the bars of its cage. For three generations, writers and artists (D. H. Lawrence, Henry Miller, Norman Mailer, as well as every pornographer on the scene) have exploited this image of the caged libido for its erotic possibilities. Few have asked whether this characterization of our mammalian forebears is at all accurate. How all-consuming a preoccupation is sexuality among the "lower" animals, and how rapaciously is it displayed? In few species is sex as constantly available as among humans, and in none (as far as we can discern) is it as subject to fantastic elaboration.

But there is a greater question. Why should this speculative exploration of the "biologic core" stop at the mammalian level, rather than probing deeper into evolutionary history? If we take Darwinism seriously as a key to human nature, we are related all the way back along the biological tree, to the fish, the reptiles, the plants. We might then expect this greater lineage to have left its residues within the id. If so, then the ego, in its search for a robust, independent identity, may have something greater to draw upon than mammalian sexuality. It may possess a Gaian birthright from which to draw strength.

THE PSYCHOLOGY OF THE REVOLUTION

The question is an important one because the hope for a revolutionary psychology has grounded itself so exclusively and for so long in the power of the sexual instincts. Consider, for example, the position taken by Reich's staunchest American disciple, Paul Goodman, and by the Gestalt school he helped to develop. Goodman clung fiercely to Reich's belief in the liberating effectiveness of "true orgiastic potency." He pressed this point with his usual flair for provocation, at times seeming to take an impish delight in shocking his more sedate colleagues. He went so far as to assert that any system of psychotherapy that diminished the role of the instinctual drives, even if it was advocated by certified left-wingers like Erich Fromm or C. Wright Mills, was simply a surrender to the various psychologies of adjustment that flourish in high industrial culture. Goodman could imagine no other source of significant social disruption and renewal than free sexual expression. "Orgiastically potent people," he argued, "will not tolerate authority or present-day industrial forms, but will instinctually create new forms." This, he believed, was "the psychology of the revolution."

As late as the Eisenhower fifties, there was something to be said for this extreme Reichian position. It did then seem that "present-day industrial forms" were committed to a priggishness that could not help but make sexuality an explosive force. In those days, the very words "pregnancy" and "virginity" were unmentionable in the mass media. There could be no open discussion of homosexuality, nor even of such elementary physiological facts of life as menstruation, masturbation, impotence, venereal disease. For this reason, as a matter of political principle, Goodman, at various stages of his life, courted scorn and physical abuse by flaunting his bisexuality. He had every reason to believe that "immediate general sex-liberation in education, morals, and marriage" was the gateway to revolutionary change. Why else was sexuality being so tightly patrolled? Why were frank talk about sex and overt displays of lust regarded as "bad taste" even by supposedly enlightened intellectuals? In a gesture that was typically both quirky and illuminating, Goodman claimed he sometimes answered phone calls from friends with the remark that he could not speak now; he was busy masturbating. He was convinced that their skittish response must mean something. Wrapped within that conviction was an article of anarchist faith, namely, that fidelity to our original nature is the only sure foundation of a just, free, and fulfilling social order. Where else was this original nature to be found but in the carnal instincts of the organism, and no place more deeply rooted than in our gonads?

History has since caught up with that assumption and revealed its limitations. Even before Goodman's death, in 1972, the sexual mores of the industrial societies had changed significantly. In part, the change was due to the widespread youthful rebellion that Goodman himself had done so much to instigate. Sex is the one front on which the countercultural insurgency of the sixties clearly won out over the parental order. But that breakthrough was itself part of a transformation that emerged as one of the spinoffs of high industrial affluence. Even the politically timid psychologies of adjustment that Reichians scorned have played a part in preparing the ground for this transformation. They ushered in a permissive style of childrearing that substantially softens parental authority, taking the pressure off toilet training and sexual curiosity. At the point when Goodman wrote, the first generation of Dr. Spock's babies was just beginning to raise hell, in large part inspired by the hunger for sexual freedom. And as it turned out, along these lines the established order was prepared to make concessions.

Let me make clear, I am not referring to the soft-core titillation of *Playboy* and *Penthouse* or to the commercial exploitation of sex by advertising and the media—though even these developments presuppose a relaxed acceptance of nudity, graphic descriptions of sexual activity, and the once unspeakable perversions that was nowhere to be found before the sixties except in Bohemian enclaves. Rather I have in mind the simple, everyday frankness one finds these days when it comes to sexuality in the best novels, films, magazines, public television documentaries, serious journalism, and sex education in the schools.

Sexuality has lost its charged allure along with its Romantic mystique. It is simply no longer taboo. I cannot think of a single sexual topic that one might not expect to find openly described and discussed on the local news, in the daily paper, in the mass circulation magazines. Surely all this has something to do with diminished repression. Has our culture, then, achieved "true orgasmic potency"? Since the words have the sound of an extremely ambitious goal—a kind of erotic satori—the answer is probably no. But on the other hand, sexual habits and values have changed remarkably over the past two decades, enough to make clear that the Reichian ideal falls well short of revolutionary significance. "Present-day industrial forms" continue to grow, to integrate, and to centralize despite the open erotic expression they now tolerate.

Goodman, who based so much of his political faith in a return to "the state of nature," had the right goal in mind but the wrong route. If we have not gone all the way down the Reichian road, we have traveled far enough to realize that it shows no sign of taking us beyond the city limits of industrial culture.

It is all to the good that the once absurd sexual constraints that burdened our society have relaxed; while they were in effect, they provided an efficient means of intimidating people or of driving them crazy. Now, sexual shame is much less available as a means of domination. That development is a necessary step toward our liberation; but it is not sufficient. A surfeit of sexual gratification—a great deal more than ever the Victorian family could have imagined—does not guarantee happiness or fulfillment, let alone citizenly engagement. There are two ways to think about this situation.

Either there is something incomplete, distorted, or illusory about the gratification—in which case, we must return to square one to redo a failed sexual revolution.

Or the sexual revolution, while adequate in its own terms and a distinct contribution to sanity, is not enough in itself to restore the ego to its full strength. If that is so, then the cure for the discontents of civilization must lie elsewhere.

My interpretation will be the latter.

THE WISDOM OF THE ID

For what shapes our lives and natures is not simply the content of our conscious mind, but in much greater degree that of our unconscious. Between the two is a sieve, and above, in the consciousness, only the coarse material is kept back; the sand for the mortar of life falls into the depths of the id; above remains only the chaff, down below the good flour for the bread of life collects, down there in the unconscious.

GEORG GRODDECK, *The Book of the It*

Let us return then to the id as we find it presented in classical psychoanalysis: a repository of unruly energy that resides at the instinctual core of our nature. Though Freud may once have credited the id with the capacity to bolster the ego, more often he saw it as the task of the ego to tame this savage self into social acceptability. In a famous image, he once characterized the ego as "a man on horseback" struggling to control a runaway bronco. The anxiety that attends the onset of neurosis is the ego's fear that the id is about to run wild. Within the highly repressive middle-class context in which Freud worked, the id was seen in narrowly moralistic terms. Its recalcitrance and assertiveness were viewed as wholly uncivil; the satisfaction it desired was regarded as mere selfish pleasure, a threat to the stability of family and society. The id, in the imagery of a classic Victorian morality tale, was Mr. Hyde plotting the overthrow of the rigorously respectable Dr. Jekyll. When Freud sought to give his theories an evolutionary foundation, he unquestioningly adopted the harsh Social Darwinism that was the fashion of his day. This only reinforced his conception of the id as a fiercely predatory beast of prey stalking the jungles of the unconscious.

But this is absurd. The id is that very protohuman psychic core that our evolution has spent millions of years molding to fit the planetary environment. Its seeming unruliness deserves a deeper understanding, if only because it grows from a long evolutionary history. In the course of that history its dominant characteristics must have been selected for some good reason.

The id is very old, therefore well-adapted; the civilized society that presumes to instruct it is the "infantile" element in the picture, the come-lately product of many false starts and compromises between ecological balance and social aspirations that, like the grandiose ambitions of the god–kings of the ancient river valleys, border on megalomania. Here, at the very outset of civilization, were warrior-autocrats who regarded themselves as divine, who sought to change the course of rivers, to raise up monuments that rivaled the mountains. They had learned their skills and proved their virtues as hunting chieftains and warlords. Transferred to the landscape of the early civilizations as an inordinate desire to control and reshape, their investment in violence and domination permeated the societies they built with a sense of antagonism to the Earth. The distrust born of that bad beginning lingers on in our relations with the environment—a "war against nature," which has finally swelled to the goal we call "the conquest of space."

The id, as Freud recognized, is a deeply conservative component of the psyche. But lacking ecological insight, he misconceived the locus of that conservatism. At one stage in his theoretical development, he connected it with the father–son rivalry of the primordial horde; at another, he reached back to connect it with the death instinct, a longing to return to the inanimate state. But between these two way-stations in the history of the cosmos there lies a broad historical-evolutionary zone during which life and mind emerged from the innate system-building tendencies of the universe. In that vast interval, all the patterns of environmental adaptation were meticulously laid down as basic properties of living things and of the planet as a whole.

Seen from this perspective, what the id conserves from its long maturing process is our treasury of ecological intelligence. Its intractability stems from its deeply ingrained resistance to all social forms that endanger the harmony of the human and the natural; its untamed "selfishness" represents a bond between psyche and cosmos whose distant origins reach back to the initial conditions of the Big Bang. Just as there is a "wisdom of the body," which often has a better sense of health than medical science, so too there may be a "wisdom of the id" that knows what sanity is better than any school of psychiatry whose standard of normality is essentially a defense of misconceived social necessity.

What are the implications of that possibility for contemporary psychotherapy?
There have been a few marginal members of the Freudian tradition who conceived of the id in comparably ambitious terms. Georg Grod-

deck, for example, attributed to the deep unconscious an autonomy and power that practically annihilated the ego. "We are lived by our unconscious," Groddeck argued.

> I am by no means "I," but a continually changing form in which the Id displays itself, and the "I"-feeling is one of its tricks to lead man astray in his self-knowledge, to render his self-deception easier, to make of him life's pliant tool.

If we are sick either mentally or physically, Groddeck believed it is because the id has so decreed. Significantly, he is one of the few Freudians to treat art in a nonreductive way. He did so because he believed "great works of art are works of nature just as truly as mountains, streams and plains." Taking his inspiration from Goethe, the one great Romantic whose influence left no mark on Freud, Groddeck almost perversely prided himself on being unscientific in his approach to psychiatry. He affected a homely literary style and preferred an organic and aesthetic model of the psyche to a mechanistic one. In this way he hoped to reconnect human beings with the natural world. "Men lose their chance of cultural development if they turn away from nature, cease to recognize their dependence upon the universal whole, and direct their love, their fear, their reverence only upon the strivings and sufferings of their fellow-men."[4] The authority of Groddeck's unconscious, however, was limited to healing the personal mind and body. Here we suggest that it may have a greater, transpersonal role as the enduring reservoir of intuitive environmental knowledge. This may be the most significant version of noble savagery: the id as the Earth's ally in the preservation of the biosphere.

But what would it mean to return the ego to its evolutionary-ecological sources in the id?

THE PERFECT ENVIRONMENT

D. W. Winnicott, a founder of the Object Relations school, once offered an intriguing formulation of the psyche's most powerful need: "The mind has a root, perhaps its most important root, in the need of the individual, at the core of the self, for a perfect environment."[5]

As we have seen, the word "environment" in Object Relations is as underdimensioned as it is in most mainstream schools of psychiatry. It is a wholly interpersonal concept, with no extension beyond social relations. In the infant state, which is most decisive for Object Relations, that environment contains a population of two. Besides the self, there is one other "object": the "primary caregiver," usually understood to be the mother. Or rather "the environment mother," not to be confused with the "object mother," who is the target of the libidinal drives. If the mother, in the tiny habitat of the newborn, does her job well, she will socialize a reasonably whole and functioning personality into the world. That will be, as Winnicott mercifully saw it, "good enough." But as often as not, she does her job poorly, since she is herself the somewhat damaged result of somewhat inadequate mothering. Then the result will be another neurotic specimen struggling to piece together the jagged fragments of a life. In this sense, Winnicott was prepared to define psychosis as "an environment deficiency disease."

The special contribution of Object Relations is to emphasize the importance of this early, pre-Oedipal phase in which the primary social relationship of mother and child exerts the single most decisive influence in human development. But while Object Relations offers a welcome escape from the intrapsychic confines of Freudian orthodoxy, some feminists within the psychiatric community have come to feel that the school unfairly assumes that the responsibility of caregiving must be restricted to women, and with it all the scapegoating that attends "bad mothering." The task is more than most women can discharge competently, especially if they must deal with many children, an outside job, a troubled marriage or no marriage at all, failing health, little money . . . in short, with real life.

As we saw in an earlier chapter, some feminist therapists, Dorothy Dinnerstein foremost among them, argue that a larger, more varied style of parenting is needed, one that includes the often remote father. In this way, if the task is shared between the parents, a more balanced gender-identity will be available to boys as well as girls. But the benefit would be more than merely social. Dinnerstein thinks such coparenting would have far-reaching ecological implications. It would dissolve the mythological association of human mother with Mother Nature that has throughout history given the male encounter with nature exploitive sexual overtones. "It is at this point that the human projects of brotherhood, of peace with nature, and of sexual liberty interpenetrate."[6]

Dinnerstein may be expecting rather too much to come of a change in parenting arrangements, as significant a reform as that might be; but her idea, pressed a bit farther, may lead us to a greater and more fruitful project.

Freud's familiar formula for the psychoanalytic goal was: "where id is, there ego shall be." Working within the ungainly vocabulary of Object Relations, the feminist psychotherapist Nancy Chodorow has suggested a revision: "where fragmented internal objects were, there shall harmoniously related objects be." But now suppose this psychiatric agenda were broadened to include something more than shared childrearing. Suppose we introduced not only feminist but *eco*feminist values into the mix. Then, granting the need for a "perfect environment," we might let it be the *real* environment of all living things: the planetary biosphere, which is everybody's "primary care-giver." We might then have "relational individuals" whose relations extend beyond family and society to embrace the natural world that sustains all living communities. Let us imagine parenting that is responsible for making *that* environment as "perfect" as possible. What, after all, do parents owe their young that is more important than a warm and trusting connection to the Earth that accounts for our evolutionary history?

Admittedly, we are taking liberties with what Winnicott and his followers meant by "environment." But bear in mind what once-shocking liberties Freud took with the ordinary meaning of sex, expanding the "normal" man–woman relationship—officially limited in his day to straight genital intercourse—to include all the perversions and polymorphous gratifications. The result was a sudden and illuminating expansion of the concept. In Winnicott's case, a great deal was brought within the therapeutic horizon by simply extending the infant's "environment" to include the paraphernalia of child care: the bottle, the bath, the blanket, the toys and teething ring. Winnicott himself, who possessed a certain Wordsworthian vision of childhood that gave him a remarkable rapport with the many children he treated, might not have objected to expanding the analytical environment to embrace the still greater planetary habitat . He had the habit of doodling his ideas into his notebooks in little line drawings that often played with such key concepts in his theory as "space" and "boundary." In his work, as in that of most mainstream psychiatrists, the lines never reach beyond an outer circle labeled "society" or "government." But suppose we stretch that circle to its maximum and label it "Earth," "cosmos." Significant insights might then come of reading such a greater meaning of "environment" into his conclusion that

> Independence is never absolute. The healthy individual does not become isolated, but becomes related to the environment in such a way that the individual and the environment can be said to be interdependent.[7]

Freud, given his dour, alienated vision of nature and of our anomalous place within it, could not have recognized the therapeutic relationship we are proposing here. There is one element of his theory, however, that leads in that direction: his conviction that the psyche is biologically grounded. The Freudian revisionists have taken fierce issue with his extreme "biologism," which was admittedly shot through with reductionistic overtones. But their adjustment works in the wrong direction; it substitutes sociology for biology, emphasizing parenting, family, the society at large. There is, however, another possibility: to read not less, but *more* biology into the psyche. Biology is, after all, the thread that leads from the wounded psyche through the body and its organic drives, and finally (if we follow the course to its end) radiates out into the true environment beyond. The body—its appetites and vital drives, its electrochemical rhythms and genetic memory, its busily scheming gray matter—is the intermediary between nature and human nature. Instead of retreating from biology, then, we might move through it toward ecology, committed to the search for an environment that is perfect because we have sought to make ourselves at home within it as a loyal species.

There is one highly original member of the Freudian school who has sought to introduce the "nonhuman environment" into the psychiatric mainstream. In a book by that title, Harold Searles undertook an ambitious study of the role of the biosphere in neurosis and child development. The book is marked throughout by a strenuously defensive stance that betrays how divergent he felt his theories to be. The prospectus for the future of psychiatry he mapped out (and which found no response in the profession as of 1960) is quite similar to the position I take in this book.

> During the past sixty years, the focus of psychiatry's attention has gradually become enlarged, from an early preoccupation with intrapsychic processes (particularly the individual's struggles with his own conflictual id, ego, and superego strivings), to include interpersonal and broad sociological-anthropological factors. It would seem, then, that a natural next phase would consist in our broadening our focus still further, to include the investigation of man's relationships with his nonhuman environment.

Searles raised the possibility of a "pre-object" stage in child development that links farther back than the connection to the pre-Oedipal mother. He identified a still earlier phase of "deeply felt kinship" with the nonhuman environment perhaps reaching as deep as the subatomic level. Successfully terminating our innate "dedifferentiation" from that phase during the early postnatal period (especially the first five months of life) may be more critical than the separation from the mother that plays so great a role in Winnicott's work. Almost amusingly, Searles, rejects the idea that the "objects" discussed in Oject Relations theory are symbolic representations of human beings like the mother. They are, rather, *real* objects: things of the nonhuman world still permeated in every infants's experience by a primordial animism. The child's consciousness recapitulates the psychic phylogeny of life on Earth, preserving the ancestral sensibility. In the modern world, Searles feels, we have not found a good way to achieve "divorcement" from the animistic stage; that failure lies at the root of schizophrenia and other disorders.

Though Searles drew freely upon literature (Wordsworth, Thoreau, the novel *Green Mansions*) to illustrate his theory, his interest was far from purely theoretical. He undertook to apply his insights to very difficult cases, especially the chronically psychotic. He even sought to work out clinical techniques that involved using natural settings, which he describes lyrically. But there is an odd twist to his pioneering efforts. As significant as the psyche's relations with the nonhuman world may be, they were, for Searles, shot through with an anxiety that arises from our fear of being swallowed back up by the "chaos" of that world. Ultimately, he believed, there must be a durable separation from the nonhuman environment; the personality must grow beyond any "regression to the primitive infantile ego" to develop a "sense of integrity and independence." There must be no "dissolution of the ego boundries." At last Searles appeals beyond psychiatry to philosophy for his model of sanity: the I-Thou relationship of Martin Buber defines the ideal nexus with the nonhuman world. "Relatedness," not unity is the goal of maturity. In this respect he sees no greater value in the "oceanic feeling" than Freud.[8]

Object Relations quite properly focuses on early infancy as the critical stage in development. But its perception of that period is skewed by the same alienating tendency we find in all schools of psychiatry that arise within urban-industrial culture. There is no real nature anywhere to be seen on its intellectual horizon. If "environment" is restricted to being used metaphorically to mean interpersonal relations (whether within the family or in the society at large), then it is no wonder that so many mothers fail in their task; and fathers too, working as they do from within an ecologically ignorant cultural setting. The assignment is wrongly defined. The "environment" that matters most is not a social construction; it is given by nature at large. Until civilized society begins to manhandle it, that environment cannot help but be "perfect," since it is all there is: the evolutionary record left behind by time and matter, a magnificence beyond words, the stuff of high art and worship. All we can seek to achieve is a perfect *response* to that environment, one that allows us to grow, move, act within it gracefully.

THE ENCHANTED CHILD

Freud was frank to admit he had taken many of his insights from the poets, especially the Romantics who were almost frenetically eager to give voice to the unconscious. Typically, the Romantics had no need to recapture the repressed; the repressed captured them—engulfed them, swallowed them whole. Among the prominent Romantic themes Freud chose to ignore was that of enchanted childhood. While the Romantic attitude toward children weakened toward sentimentality, there was more to it than that. Childhood held an epistemological significance. The Romantics were convinced by their own powerful gift for introspection that children possess a rare noetic talent. Children's innocence endows them with purity of perception. They greet life, and especially the natural world around them, with an instinctively animist response. It is alive and personal for them. It has a voice. In the lucidity of their experience, something of the old sacramental vision of nature is reborn.

The poet who most vividly expresses this special quality of child-like perception predates the Romantics by two generations. Thomas Traherne, who was born within a few years of Isaac Newton, produced one of the most astonishing bodies of verse in the English language. Much of it recounts his eidetically vivid recollection of nature as he knew it in his childhood when "som thing infinit Behind evry thing appeared." Not only did Traherne remember what he had seen, heard, and felt, but he remembered the sensory texture of the moment: the *how* of the experience as well as the *what*. He offers a perfect example of the "childish animism" that Jean Piaget believes may last through the first five years of life.

> *All mine! And seen so Easily! How Great, how Blest!*
> *How soon am I of all possest!*
> *My Infancie no Sooner Opes its Eys,*
> *But Straight the Spacious Earth*
> *Abounds with Joy Peace Glory Mirth*
> *And being Wise,*
> *The very Skies,*
> *And Stars do mine becom; being all possest*
> *Even in that Way that is the Best.*

Like Wordsworth's later exuberant memories of childhood in the wilds of England, Traherne's poetry tunnels back into the animistic foundations of the unconscious, the point at which we remain tied to the distant preverbal origins of our species: the world as we once knew it before we were taught that it is an accumulation of dead and purposeless stuff. Traherne was inclined to believe that the acquisition of speech marks the end of our innate animistic sensibility; from there forward the child grows away from inherent intimacy with nature. In his hymn to "dumnesse," he recalls the time when he experienced

> . . . *evry Stone, and Evry Star a Tongue*
> *And evry Gale of Wind a Curious Song.*
> *The Heavens were an Orakle, and spake*
> Divinity.

This was before his response to the world was caught up in language. Then the only voice was that of the Earth speaking to his childish intuition.

> . . . *the first Words mine Infancy did hear,*
> *The Things which in my Dumness did appear,*
> *Preventing all the rest, got such a root*
> *Within my Heart, and stick so close unto't*
> *It may be Trampld on, but still will grow;*
> *And nutriment to Soyl it self will owe,*
> The first Impressions are Immortal all.

As if confounded by his own experience, Traherne asked, "Is it not Strange that an Infant should be Heir of the World, and see those Mysteries which the Books of the Learned never unfold?" But stranger still is the reality principle that sees fit to root that heritage out of each child. "Growing up," at least within the Judeo-Christian and Islamic cultures, has meant throttling our joy in Traherne's natural mysteries, and replacing it with distrust of nature, if not hostility toward it. Finally, it has meant imposing a proper respect for the emotionally denatured objectivity that is the ideal of modern science. Along the way, this strange ordeal in consciousness deprivation has cost us our inherent ecological intelligence. What remains after that act of parental vandalism is the small poor residue of sexual and aggressive drives that has become the total preoccupation of modern psychiatry.

Take a modest but instructive example. For generations it has been a subject of debate among naturalists whether animals can be said to have any form of intelligence or even minimal sentience. In the early days of science, the consensus was overwhelmingly negative. The anatomists of that period indulged in the vivisection of unanesthetized animals, dismissing their howls of anguish as merely mechanical reactions, the sort of sound a spring might make when it was struck or twisted. Following Descartes and the orthodox Christian teaching that animals have no souls, the investigators compared their specimens to clocks, which feel no pain when they are taken apart. For that matter, as recently as the early years of this century, some behavioral psychologists found it methodologically unpardonable to concede that human beings, let alone animals, have minds, feelings, inner thoughts. When Jane Goodall undertook her long, arduous study of chimpanzees in the wild, eventually coming to see them as intelligent personalities, even companions, she found it no easy task to win over her colleagues to the value of her methods. Since then, however, at least a few daring zoologists and psychologists have (in the guarded words of Richard Byrne writing on "brute intellect") found it "tempting to view some animal behavior as the expression of minds—oddly limited minds, to be sure." Even so, he still finds that "the question of animal consciousness is fraught with problems."[9]

Contrast such professional caution with the fact that children everywhere are raised on a body of folklore and fairy-tales that is grounded in an intuitive admiration of animals as sentient, purposive creatures. It makes perfect sense to children to endow the beasts with intelligence, even personality; it is what the unbiased eye sees in their conduct. It is not until we "educate" them to think differently that the young surrender this naive, spontaneous perception. In short, education censors their experience in the name of making them "realistic." Yet here is a case where scientists of the current generation have learned that being "child-like" in our response to the world (as Jane Goodall had the courage to be) has salvaged an impressive body of knowledge where experts once thought there was nothing to be learned.

Some might ask, of course, how far such child-like personification of the natural world should be allowed to go. Skeptically, one thinks of the talking ducks and the mice in human clothing that populate Walt Disney cartoons. But these are not the creations of children, who know full well that the animals do not speak our language nor wear our clothes. These are the sadly condescending efforts of adults, themselves estranged from the child's real view, seeking to depict what they believe happens in the child's imagination. Perhaps the children play along; but their own experience is simply that the animals seem to be going about what they do with intelligence and intention. And so they do.

The psychologist Nicholas Humphrey has pondered the seemingly incorrigible propensity of human beings to view the world in anthropomorphic terms, a habit of mind not limited to tribal folk and children. As we have seen in earlier chapters, the literature of science brims with casual personification and intentional rhetoric. Humphrey suggests that the tendency has an evolutionary explanation. It derives from the need of early humans to solve problems requiring social rather than technical intelligence. Hence, things are treated more or less like people. "Social intelligence" inculcates the habit of envisaging all things as sentient and endowed with mentality. Humphrey believes "socio-magical" thinking once conferred such a selective advantage that it may be irrepressible.

> Through a long history, men have, I believe, explored the transactional possibilities of countless things in their environment, and sometimes, Pygmalion-like, the things have come alive. Thus many of mankind's most prized technological discoveries, from agriculture to chemistry, may have had their origin not in the deliberate application of practical intelligence but in the fortunate misapplication of social intelligence.[10]

What we have then reborn with every child is a habit of mind that has served our species well for a very long while, that communicates observations about the behavior of systems, especially biological systems, more clearly than any alternative mode of description, that appeals to common sense, that has yielded significant scientific findings in contemporary ethology, and that has produced a wealth of art and literature. This would seem to go a long way toward qualifying as "truth."

All this might seem like a minor quibble if it were not for the fact that this commonplace aspect of childrearing—encouraging children to doubt rather than build upon their inherent response to the natural world—is the first step toward a worldview that will finish by reading sentience and intentionality out of nature at every level. In this way we deprive the id of an important portion of its inborn ecological wisdom. How difficult it then becomes for well-trained scientists to make sense of the ordered complexity they find in all the natural systems they study. They are staring at the evidence of mind in the cosmos, the original mentality of which their intellect is a distant echo. But professional caution prevents seeing things that way . . . or from saying that they do.

Preserving an accessible trace of our innate animism is what Paul Shepard seems to have in mind when he speaks in praise of the way children in traditional societies are brought into the world. They take the environment in with their first breath. "The experience of such a world is initially that the mother is always there."

Along similar lines, the anthropologist and therapist Jean Liedloff concludes that the modern world's pathological suppression of our innate ecological connectedness begins from the moment of birth. It occurs in the commonplace practice of separating the infant from the mother. This act, routinely carried out in every hospital, violates the child's "evolved expectations" of the world, namely, to be held, to be made warm and secure against the mother's body. The traumatic separation breaks the physical "continuum" between mother and child, which ought to provide the newborn's transition from "the entirely alive surrounding inside of the mother's body to a partly live one outside it."

And so the civilized baby enters life crying . . . as babies born into traditional societies and kept in-arms usually do not. The crying, which is a protest, is conveniently regarded as "normal" and allowed to continue until the baby learns it is useless to cry and resigns hope. At that point the civilizing process has begun. Liedloff defines the "appropriate environment" for the newborn as the bodily intimacy provided by anyone—father, siblings, grandparents, friends, neighbors—there to hold and care. "Mothering" can be done by all members of the family.[11]

"Where the id was, there the ego shall be." But the therapeutic project will fall short of its ecological potentiality if the id we speak of has been reduced to its minimal social content. Even if, as feminists in the Object Relations school propose, we seek to strengthen and balance the "relational values" of both boys and girls, the circle of relationship will fail to encompass that greater and all-encompassing "primary care-giver" that needs most to be integrated into the mature ego.

THE ECOLOGICAL UNCONSCIOUS

Of all the theoretical apparatus we inherit from mainstream modern psychology, Jung's often elusive and always controversial notion of a collective unconscious may prove to be the most serviceable in the creation of an ecopsychology. Like the Freudian id, the collective unconscious is meant to be an essentially conservative entity, a sort of psychic ballast filled with residues of formative experience. In his original formulation, Jung intended it to be a repository for the compounded evolutionary history of our species. "Just as the body has its evolutionary history and shows clear traces of the various evolutionary stages, so too does the psyche."[12] In the reading of some analysts, it extends beyond the human farther back into the past. For the Jungian analyst Calvin Hall,

> The collective unconscious is a reservoir of latent images, usually called *primordial images* by Jung. . . . Man inherits these images from his ancestral past, a past that includes all of his human ancestors as well as his prehuman or animal ancestors. . . . they are predispositions or potentialities for experiencing and responding to the world in the same ways that his ancestors did.

The deepest and most influential substratum of the collective unconscious is our archaic prehuman experience: "man's basic animal nature . . . the most dangerous of all the archetypes."[13]

This is the material that coalesces into the Jungian archetype of the shadow, a constellation of unruly animal vitality Freud could easily associate with the id. For a time Freud also entertained the possibility of a "collective mind." This, he felt, might be the physical locus of a "psychical continuity in the sequence of generations," which has communicated the drama of the primal horde and the sin of the murdering sons down through the ages.[14]

But while Freud was willing to allow for the preservation of a few prehistoric memory traces somewhere in the brain, Jung went on to expand the collective unconscious to a far larger size and importance, making it more and more exclusively human and more and more rarefied. It became a massive cultural storehouse, especially suited to housing the great religious symbols of the human race. In its most elaborated form, it came to resemble a psychologized version of Plato's world of eternal forms, the realm of true being. Its contents were no longer evolutionary episodes or prehistoric incidents; they were grand spiritual themes on which human experience became so many minor, transient variations. The mortal flesh began to diminish in comparison to these transcendent symbols. The mother's womb, whatever its psychological importance to the individual, was only a particular instance of the archetypal womb of the Mother Goddess and seemingly less "real" in comparison.

Jung's thought was always suffused with a certain Platonic-Gnostic aversion to the physical, a legitimate concern insofar as Freud's theories tended to assume a narrow sexual emphasis. He wanted urgently to find a place to shelter the religious needs within the cruelly reductionistic and materialistic paradigm that prevailed in the sciences. His was one of the "soft" psychologies, prepared to sacrifice scientific rigor in order to save the spiritual values. His solution was to make the collective unconscious increasingly more incorporeal and strictly cultural, a realm of art, myth, and piety lifted safely above the brute matter of the cosmos, elevated as well above the primitive instincts of our physical evolution. The psyche seemed to need such a lofty status to preserve a modicum of sanctity in a godless culture.

Within recent years, some Jungians have sought to grant the body a more central place in analytical theory and practice. The archetype has, for example, been interpreted as a "psychosomatic entity having two aspects," one of which is "linked closely with the physical organs."[15]

Jung might not have felt so passionately intent upon transporting the collective unconscious beyond the physical had he taken greater advantage of his association with Wolfgang Pauli and recognized that the New Physics of his time was already dissipating matter into an incorporeal enigma. Add to that development, as we have sought to do in this book, our deepening awareness of the hierarchical systems into which matter organizes itself, and we have the possibility of radically reinterpreting the collective unconscious. It might then be regarded as the repository of an evolutionary record that ties the psyche to the full sweep of cosmic history. Mind, far from being a belated and aberrant development in a universe of dead matter, *connects* with that universe as the latest emergent stage on its unfolding frontier.

In a famous formulation, William James, one of the first psychologists to explore religious experience with the goal of salvaging its values, concluded that "if there be higher powers able to impress us, they may get access to us only through the subliminal door."[16] Drawing upon the most recent findings of science, we might now say that

Gaia—however we might want to envisage the life-creating and enhancing potentiality of our planet—gains access to us through the door of the id. The voice of the Earth is that close by. If we are, as the Romantic poets believed, born with the gift of hearing that voice, then turning a deaf ear to her appeal must be a wrenching effort, and a painful one to maintain, just as all efforts to hide from the truth of our identity must be painful. Repression hurts. We call that pain "neurosis."

Strict Freudians used to argue that any form of psychiatry that did less than engage the instincts is merely adjustive. It will end as an ego psychology that may relieve the immediate suffering, but leaves the core of the neurosis untouched: a wound still needing to be probed and cauterized. Might not the same be said of any psychiatry that limits itself to sex, parenting, family, social relations, but fails to engage the ecological level of the unconscious? It, too, is merely adjustive. It leaves the underlying neurosis—which is our estrangement from Gaia—untreated. Worse, by somewhat assuaging the anxiety (a result that is more and more achieved these days by medication) and assuring us that we have indeed been healed, it may return us to our bad old habits of urban-industrial life with the energies of annihilation renewed and ready to do more damage.

All psychologies turn to the unconscious to find the root of neurosis, as well as the powers that will heal the troubled psyche. Like detectives investigating a mystery, therapists work through the tangled contents of the submerged mind seeking clues to our true identity. Freudians find there fantasies of incest and murder, Jungians the remnants of myth, ritual, religious symbolism, Reichians a backlog of thwarted orgasmic energy, Object Relationists the ragged termination of the mother–child nexus, Existentialist analysis the anguish of an *Eigenwelt* adrift in the void of meaninglessness. Only the Gestalt school has introduced a larger, more fully biological context for therapy that seeks to unite figure with ground, organism with environment; it is the only school that uses the concept of ecology in its theories. What I propose here builds upon that beginning. The collective unconscious, at its deepest level, shelters the compacted ecological intelligence of our species, the source from which culture finally unfolds as the self-conscious reflection of nature's own steadily emergent mindlikeness. The survival of life and of our species would not have been possible without such a self-adjusting, system-building wisdom. It was there to guide that development by trial and error, selection and extinction, as it was there in the instant of the Big Bang to congeal the first flash of radiation into the rudiments of durable matter. It is *this* id with which the ego must unite if we are to become a sane species capable of greater evolutionary adventures.

Twelve

◆

ATTENDING THE PLANET

THE PROMETHEAN INTERVAL

Psychology, like theology, must eventually come to terms with original sin. Both madness and sin presuppose a preexisting state of grace. At some point, the healthy animals we once were, if only for some split second of prenatal or postnatal time, lost that primal sanity and grew up to become the bad mothers and fathers who made all the bad institutions. Within the framework of an ecopsychology, we raise the question: how did a psyche that was once symbiotically rooted in the planetary ecosystem produce the environmental crisis we now confront?

Blaming the trauma on parents or on society in general is no real answer; it simply moves the problem a step farther back. Systems theory, especially the work of Ilya Prigogine, which plays so great a role in Deep Ecology, may offer a better answer. Prigogine focuses on those systems that elude entropy by oscillating through and out of equilibrium. Their order is not that of dead rest but of constant fluctuation, a sort of dialectic of dissipative structures. Their episodic oscillations are as natural as the compensatory equilibrium toward which they tend to return. All organisms—and in the case of human beings, the social structures they create—are examples of such "nonequilibrium thermodynamics." Evolution through symmetry breaking is their normal mode. Extending Prigogine's theory to the study of society and culture, Erich Jantsch suggests,

Human systems with all their tangible and intangible aspects might then perhaps be regarded as dissipative structures, arising from the interaction of strong and highly nonequilibrium flows of ideas and actions. . . . This organization would be physical as well as psychic. Indeed, the borderline between both becomes blurred in the light of the emerging insight that information itself may have a self-organizing capacity.[1]

This approach to our ecological condition possesses a rich ambivalence. In the tiny slice of cosmic time that represents the history of human life on Earth, we may imagine consciousness evolving through a series of creative oscillations. Various distortions and exaggerations occur. With hindsight, we can now identify these as various cultural styles of the past playing in and around the equilibrium of sanity. The balance point would be the "perfect environment" understood as a state of solid harmony with our habitat, the sort of unquestioning stasis that prehuman organisms have presumably attained. But we are the species that is uniquely capable of becoming "unbalanced"; the capacity to flirt with imbalance makes us such an interesting experiment. Following Prigogine, we might assign, if only metaphorically, an intriguing new thermodynamic meaning to this familiar term for madness. Human intelligence oscillates like every open system. Developed far beyond what competitive advantage requires, it takes off on flights of creative fancy, high art, religious and scientific speculation. It has created a universe within the universe, a realm of wild, spinning, and magnificent ideas that, from time to time, take hold of entire populations and become a culture. The tension between neurotic distortion and sane equilibrium is what we call "history."

Currently, we find ourselves somewhere at the outer limit of a particularly exaggerated oscillation. It is called urban-industrialism, the willful withdrawal of our species from the natural habitat in which it evolved. The modern city represents our most daring attempt to live "beyond" nature as its detached observer and master. As we approach the giddy extremity of that distortion, modern science comes to play the most energetic and decisive role in our history, producing the one culture that the entire human race has come closest to sharing since the Paleolithic period. By tapping and trapping the forces of nature, Western science has made it possible to knit the disparate cultures of the world together into the urban industrial complex we inhabit today.

This has been a prodigious accomplishment; it places at our disposal all the genius of our species to be mined and reworked. But it is also a risky venture. It allows us, like the defiant Titan Prometheus, to steal the fire of the gods, and in turn to play god to the planet, transforming it to suit the often whimsical and profligate tastes of an urban population no longer in vital touch with the true conditions of its survival. As of the late twentieth century, we are somewhere near the culmination of this Promethean interval, at a point where its powers have to be renounced.

But in favor of what?

WHERE SHALL WE HEAR THE VOICE?

The environmental crisis has become the news of the day everyday. There is, as the journalists put it, a "hole" saved for it in every edition of the papers, every newscast. That is all to the good. But it is a story without a center, a formless flurry of incidents and events. There are endless accounts of disaster, menace, impending doom; but the scattered reports come at us like gunshots fired by a sniper in the night. Our life is at stake, but the danger seems accidental, a stroke of bad luck. There are facts and figures about the threat, more than most of us can take in. At a certain point we may even grow numb and turn off in confusion or resignation.

Our argument here has been that the environmental predicament is a great deal more than this—more personal, more threatening, more radical. It may well be that more and more of what people bring before doctors and therapists for treatment—agonies of body and spirit—are symptoms of the biospheric emergency registering at the most intimate level of life. The Earth hurts, and we hurt with it. If we could still accept the imagery of a Mother Earth, we might say that the planet's umbilical cord links to us at the root of the unconscious mind.

Our culture gives us little opportunity to stop and to honor that great truth. There are no deep seasonal celebrations left that have not become media fictions and merchandising gambits. We give more attention to the Dow of the marketplace than to the Tao of the universe. But sometimes the voice of the Earth breaks through to us in an instant of realization that flashes back across the eons, reminding us of who we are, where we came from, what we are made of. For an instant we touch the great cosmic continuity that is easily lost in the frenzied affairs of the day. Here is a candid and moving example of such a moment, a recollection by Charlene Spretnak, one of the leading voices of the ecofeminist movement.

In thinking about ecofeminism recently, I remembered an event that took place sixteen years ago, which I had nearly lost from memory. When my daughter was about three days old and we were still in the hospital, I wrapped her up one evening and slipped outside to a little garden in the warmth of late June. I introduced her to the pine trees and the plants and the flowers, and they to her, and finally to the pearly moon wrapped in a soft haze and to the stars. I, knowing nothing then of nature-based religious ritual or ecofeminist theory, had felt an impulse for my wondrous little child to meet the rest of cosmic society. The interesting thing is that experience, although lovely and rich, was so disconnected from life in a modern, technocratic society that I soon forgot all about it.[2]

A small private ceremony to welcome the newborn. But how furtively undertaken and how soon forgotten. And yet, unless the Earth can speak to us of our dependence in ways like this that engage the heart, what will all the knowledge of all the experts count for? It will remain a chaos of information without an integrating theme. That theme, if we have the courage to face it, is our entire way of life, the pattern and the power of an industrial culture that cuts us off from the natural continuum.

A feminist psychotherapist has suggested that the clinical setting for analysis might be changed in ways that seek to dissolve the masculine/ feminine dichotomy with which so many patients are burdened. A more "feminized" encounter might set a different tone for the examination of the self. Instead of the conventionally silent, detached and "blank wall" stance of the (usually) male analyst, there might be an effort to achieve "real relationship" and "cognitive exchange" between the two participants. The objective would be to introduce more of the "empathy and nurturance" that is stereotypically attributed to women.[3] No doubt such a change would contribute to a warmer dialogue. Many practitioners over the years have felt the need for a different doctor-patient, therapist-client relationship, something more empathic and unstructured. But this more humane setting would still be surrounded by the same alienated urban-industrial context in which all therapy takes place in our society. It would happen in an office or a clinic. On the other side of the door would be the waiting room and the receptionist. Outside would be the parking lot, the street, the city, the suburb. The patient would leave to see more telephone poles than trees, more high-rise buildings than mountains, more storm drains than rivers. And overhead perhaps no sun or stars to be seen for the grime in the air.

While James Hillman has proposed "prescribing nature" as part of therapy, therapists, tied to the city by their careers and their bank accounts, cannot be expected to treat their clients anywhere but in the city. We have no psychiatry that requires doctor and patient to abscond to a place apart from human works and urban rhythms, not even for as long as a single therapeutic session. Therapy makes no demand for clean air, the songs of birds, the presence of trees or sea, mountain or stream. The troubled soul locked in a tortured ego will never be coaxed to look out and around at something greater, more lordly, more enno-bling: a state of nature that invites the mind to contemplate eternal things. Yet common experience tells us that a solitary walk by the river or ocean, a few calm hours in the woods restore the spirit and may produce more insight into our motives and goals than the best labors of the professional analyst. The quiet contemplation of the night sky before one turns to sleep and dreams might do more to touch the mind with a healing grandeur than weeks, months, years of obsessive autobi-ographical excavation.

My guess would be that by the time most clients have fought their way home on the freeway, whatever good was achieved during their $100-per-fifty-minute-psychiatric-hour has been undone. They are sunk once more in the collusive madness that they never left behind.

The issue I raise here about the practice of psychotherapy might, of course, be asked of everything that gets done within the confines of the urban empire, including my own work in the university and in the literary marketplace. What are my needs as professor and writer? Li-braries, bookstores, university campuses, museums, art galleries, the media, and at last the money and means of the publishing industry. Even the most conscience-driven ecologists are beholden to the culture of cities to make their message known. The environmental philosopher Anthony Weston puts the point with admirable candor.

I think it not surprising . . . that much of the environmental ethics offered by contemporary philosophers is very often the most abstract, wholly intellectual construction. . . . How many times I have walked to my evening classes watching the blazing Long Island sunset, only to lose sight and thought of it as I am pulled into our windowless lecture building—even as I plan to discuss the values of nature! But what the literature offers fits the building, not the sky the building hides.[4]

THE QUESTION OF SCALE

The way out of our collusive madness cannot, in any case, be by way of individual therapy. We have neither the time nor the medical resources to place our hope in such an approach. Nor do we have the professional consensus to get on with the job. While we need a psychology that is ecologically grounded, we cannot look to psychiatrists to make the institutional changes that a life-sustaining biosphere requires. The therapist's role is primarily a heuristic one, that of raising questions about our standard of sanity. That is an extremely important role, as much for what it might serve to downplay (careerist pressures, money, and status) as for what it might emphasize (our abiding need for wilderness, tranquility, or animal companions). But the energy that will put that standard to work as a political force must come from other, more widespread and spontaneous sources. The direction in which that force will have to work is clear enough. Both the therapists and the ecologists offer us a common political agenda for the good of the planet, for the good of the person. It is simply stated:

Scale down.

Slow down.

Democratize.

Decentralize.

Ecological goals that can heal the psyche; psychological values that can heal the planet.

This convergence of inner and outer needs cannot be purely coincidental. It is the Hermetic philosopher's old dictum—"As above, so below"—come back to us as the shared prescription of psychiatry and science.

If there is one generalization about traditional people that holds true, it is that they lived on a smaller scale than civilized societies have known since the days of the pharaoh. It is easy to overlook this obvious fact. We too easily assume it to be a law of historical development that because big things start small, all small things are meant to get big. But the small scale has enduring virtues all its own. It may be essential to the survival of our species, the secret of what E. F. Schumacher called "an economics of permanence." Even those traditional societies that failed and perished did not, thanks to their limited dominion, drag down the rest of the species with them. Their relations with the Earth were mediated by modestly scaled tribal systems; that, as much as their nature worship, accounts for their frequently surprising endurance. Or, rather, the two factors worked in tandem, modest scale and animist sensibility reinforcing one another. The intimate rapport they sought with nature was only possible in societies that could know the wild things as companions. And the better they knew them, the more likely they were to respect and admire them.

I think how warmly, often wistfully many people, though hopelessly enmeshed in our industrial society, continue to respond to the wild things of the world as if some deeply submerged loyalty bound them in fellowship to these creatures. The response is surely there in children whose fascination with the animals lives on irrepressibly. Even when "untamed" nature can be contacted only in pathetically contrived ways—by way of packaged tours to African game parks or National Geographic documentaries on television—still honest curiosity and affection are there. And yet so warped have our relations with the planetary environment become that these very gestures, a small, sad reaching out to our endangered companions, often distort or destroy more than they help. Jane Goodall has warned that safaris into the wildlife reserves of Africa now threaten to drive the anxious chimpanzees crazy; so too the intrusions of well-intentioned wildlife photographers and documentary filmmakers can reach the point of menacing saturation. These days even the Antarctic wilderness is being staked out as a tourist attraction; reportedly, the scientists who visit there to explore its long-remote splendors are the worst polluters of the region, leaving it littered with everything from beer cans to radioactive waste.

If some genetically ingrained vestige of the animist sensibility remains buried within us mercifully nurtured and preserved by the evolutionary process, it will surely not have the chance to unfold until it once again has something more than tourist outings and media facsimiles to connect with. An instinctive camaraderie with nature needs the living presence of nature—as autonomously there before us as we would want any loved one to be. That means scaling back the urban-industrial dominance in order that the wild things may have the autonomy they need to survive with us in biocentric community.

How do we regain that scale from within the empire of cities that now holds the entire planet in its grip?

I think not by the sort of direct frontal assault that more militant environmentalists have attempted. Neither fear nor guilt will do the job, nor stringent demands for puritanical self-denial. The motivation for change on a planetary scale must arise from within, a genuinely personal need for a new quality of life. If she has her wits about her, Gaia, I suspect, is working along these lines. Let us see if we can turn to her for guidance, if only as a speculative exercise.

A CONGRESS OF UNAUTHORIZED IDENTITIES

If we evolve in body and mind within some greater sentient and self-adjusting system, we might expect the ultimate goal of our animal intelligence, whatever its wild periodic fluctuations, to be life-sustaining and enhancing. It is one of the primary insights of ecology that stability is grounded in variety. The dynamics of evolution also emphasize the importance of plentiful variation, many types bidding to colonize many habitats. As Darwin observed with an awe that was touched with dread when he saw how spendthrift nature was in weeding out her multitudes, excess is the basis of evolutionary development. If we apply this tendency toward proliferation to the realm of thought, we have, instead of the DNA helix, the human personality as the generative factor. But where thought and value are concerned, there is no need for competition. Play might be more appropriate than struggle. The habitat of mind is infinite in its capacity. Ideas and values are born of individual minds, each a microcosm all its own; style, taste, insight grow from within personalities. If we are to have a rich harvest of ideas, we must have whole, free, and inspired people and between them a respectful dialogue.

Diversity is the health of ecosystems. Every new species, every least variation within a species, represents a heightened chance of survival under unpredictable conditions. Diversity matters to the species itself; it matters to us—who may make unforeseeable uses of things that variation and selection bring us. As advanced as our best laboratories may be, we continually discover substances in the plants and animals around us that heal and nourish: a toad or moth here, an orchid or a fungus there. In only the last few weeks, as I complete this manuscript, there have been reports of a chemical isolated from the bark of a rare yew tree that provides the promise of a cancer cure; and another of a new class of drugs extracted from a nondescript garden spider that will help treat stroke and epilepsy. This is why the steadily accelerating rate of extinction we witness today impoverishes us even if it is in ways we may never realize. How much more important it is, then, to protect the diversity of talent and intelligence we find among our own kind.

Where we address the role of mind in the cosmos, what is at stake is not simply a matter of mere survival but of our greater destiny on this planet. Who can say what mix of intellectual and aesthetic gifts we may need to make us as fully human as we can become? As we have seen, a philosopher like Henri Bergson, a theologian like Teilhard de Chardin might be inclined to nominate the sages and saints as the most valuable minds among us. It is understandable that they should do so in a materialistic and pragmatic era, suggesting that these more spiritual endowments point the way forward in the evolution of consciousness. But there are so many great and ennobling human virtues, too many by far to limit our choices to a single human type. The Renaissance philosopher Pico della Mirandola came closer to the mark when he described mankind as a species of chameleon whose role it was to explore all the possibilities of experience. If nothing else, the efflorescence of human personalities makes for a delightful existence. We need the clowns as well as the sages, the athletes as well as the aesthetes, the logicians as well as the mystics. We may even need the villains as much as the saints.

Freud spoke of sanity as the reclamation of the repressed. He never thought of the project in political terms, yet repression, which divides the soul, can also unite oppressed people in the cause of liberation. Since the end of World War Two, like so many restive tribes, the outcast and dispossessed have been making their unofficial presence shamelessly known. The cosmopolitan openness and affluence of high industrialism makes such boisterous self-expression possible. For a time, this opening up of the system took the form of highly visible "liberation" movements—not simply among formerly colonized people in the Third World, but among the *internal* colonials: the excluded minorities most obviously (the black, the Native American, the Asian, the Hispanic), but also the women, the gays, the old, the disabled, the fat, the mad. These days public campaigning along the liberation front may be less obstreperous, but the cause is ingrained and has become intricately refined. Every least nuance of specialness demands a hearing. Women are no longer simply "women"; they are Third World women, lesbians, lesbian mothers, battered wives, daughters of alcoholic mothers, mothers of drug-dependent daughters, women with AIDS, women ex-cons, hookers. A flyer I come upon in a local bookstore invites "wounded daughters of remote fathers" to meet for support. The identities are not always those of victims, but victimization is often the first step toward self-knowledge. And the next is coming together with others who have the same song to sing. Ask any public agency, any personnel manager, any boss anywhere trying to make a big bureaucratic system work, and they can give you a listing yards long of the social variety they must—but cannot—deal with each day. The pressure of the divergent many can be felt within every institution, an insistent demand for respect, fairness, freedom.

Because those who join together in this congress of unauthorized identities speak for what they are, proudly and endlessly, they are (incorrectly) labeled self-indulgent and spoiled, and they are scolded by critics who are fortunate enough to need no such platform. Because they demand attention and concessions, they are (correctly) seen as an obstacle to the technocratic order and are badgered, hassled, beaten back as often as possible, though never for long. The powers that run the urban-industrial world are well advised to see the personalistic style of the times as threatening. No well-oiled, efficient system can coexist with such a riot of personal improvisations. Self-discovery is the death of the industrial megamachine in the same way that democracy was the death of feudalism. But the disintegration we see impending is a *creative* disintegration, one that opens a generous place for difference and diversity. Political equality was the beginning of this historical current; personal uniqueness is its destination. And both—the demand for equality, the demand for uniqueness—began *inside,* in the depths of the private psyche before either became a revolutionary movement in the world. Long before there was a political cause, there were people secretly hurting, needing, wanting.

For the first time in human history, every odd and outcast member of our race will be able to step forward without shame and tell his or her story. If we are a culture of narcissists, we seem to find everybody's narcissism as fascinating as our own. Images of the outlandish and bizarre fill the media of modern times. The daily audience participation and talk shows on television probe every kink and twist of human nature. Pausing at the checkout counter of the supermarket, I come upon a small library of tawdry newspapers, each vying with the other to lay a more grotesque freak show before its readers. Yet even these exercises in tasteless sensationalism tell us something important. They reveal how very *interested* in one another we have become, how we crave to learn of the oddness and eccentricity of people everywhere. Simple animal curiosity may finally come to our rescue; there may be a saving wisdom hidden in this fascination with everyman's and every-woman's story. We will need all these personal histories to do even minimal justice to whatever the *rerum natura* is. Ecologically speaking, the music of the spheres is neither a solo nor a massed chorus carrying a single melody, but a jazz improvisation where each player has a riff.

There is something more we can learn from basic ecology besides the value of variety. The urban revolution was the beginning of the interval of disequilibrium in whose latter days we now live. By human standards, the five thousand years of that interval may seem enormously long; but in the Gaian chronicles of the planet it is a minor, recent fluctuation still playing out its full implications. Now we begin to see with benefit of historical perspective how very ruthless this experiment has been in the regimentation of mental and physical energy. In the industrial period, machines of metal and chemical fuels have taken the place of muscle and animal metabolism, but the massification of people that began with the pharaoh's work-gang continues in the form of the assembly line, the white collar office force, the consumer market, the conscript army.

Industrialism demands massification for its extraordinary power over nature: mass production, mass media, mass marketing. Our complex global economy is built upon millions of small, private acts of psycho-logical surrender, the willingness of people to acquiesce in playing their assigned parts as cogs in the great social machine that encompasses all other machines. They must shape themselves to the prefabricated identities that make efficient coordination possible. If Gaia is to moderate the planet-punishing thrust of world industrialism, that capacity for self-enslavement must be broken. And the rock on which it founders is self-discovery, your conviction and mine that we are each a remarkable, unrepeatable event in the universe, a life shaped around an idea that happens only once and never again. The ecological ego is born of a narcissism that boldly asserts love and fascination with the self, not as a competitive agent, but as a freely created being demanding attention, recognition, respect.

Is this not exactly what we see happening throughout the major industrial societies today? Most surprisingly we see it in the socialist countries where for so long it seemed that collectivist pressure had crushed the personality. For two generations the anticommunist propaganda of the capitalist West has been filled with images of robotized millions obediently serving the will of Big Brother, all the while ignoring the degree to which market economics, advertising, and political propaganda have done a subtler but no less effective violence to the rights of the person in our own society. But now we see that the autonomous personality remains alive even in the most restrictive conditions. We place the rebellions of Eastern Europe and China in the category of politics; but it may be that these revolutionary currents serve a greater purpose. In league with a heightened ecological awareness, they may also represent the first steps toward a postindustrial culture in which both the person and the planet at last receive the loyalty they deserve.

What the political and economic leaders of East and West have in view for our future is doubtless another chapter in the dreary, soul-squelching history of industrial progress: bigger systems, bigger markets, more getting, more spending. Those who govern the market economies of the world see this as their moment of triumph and opportunity. Armed with tempting investments and intoxicating plans to scale still dizzier heights of industrial development, they are poised for the economic invasion of Russia, Eastern Europe, and China.

But what Gaia has in mind may be something very different. Her needs lie with that worldwide congress of unauthorized identities we see all around us groping fitfully toward another kind of wealth. At the height of the industrial epoch, she summons us back to the oldest of philosophical tasks: *know thyself.*

Epilogue

ECOPSYCHOLOGY—THE PRINCIPLES

Our scientists seek a Grand Unified Theory that will embrace all things, all forces, all time and matter. In the past they have found no place for themselves in that unity. But their painstaking study of nature over the generations—a labor of honest inquiry and intellectual passion—has finally given the questing mind a significant status in the universe. What unity ultimately requires is closure. The circle of scientific theory comes round like the alchemical snake that bites its tail. What *is* must at last be *known*. Perhaps that is what underlies the eager unfolding of the natural hierarchy from the Big Bang to the human frontier: substance reaching out hungrily toward sentience.

Oddly, this seems to have been better known by prescientific humans who worked from myth, image, ritual. If ecopsychology has anything to add to the Socratic–Freudian project of self-knowledge, it is to remind us of what our ancestors took to be common knowledge: there is more to know about the self, or rather *more self* to know, than our personal history reveals. Making a personality, the task that Jung called "individuation," may be the adventure of a lifetime. But the person is anchored within a greater, universal identity. Salt remnants of ancient oceans flow through our veins, ashes of expired stars rekindle in our genetic chemistry. The oldest of the atoms, hydrogen—whose primacy among the elements should have gained it a more poetically resonant name—is a cosmic theme; mysteriously elaborated billionsfold, it has created from Nothing the Everything that includes us.

When we look out into the night sky, the stars we see in the chill, receding distance may seem crushingly vast in size and number. But the swelling emptiness that contains them is, precisely by virtue of its magnitude, the physical matrix that makes living intelligence possible. Those who believed we were cradled in the hands of God have not been so very wrong.

All this belongs to the principles of ecopsychology, but not in any doctrinaire or purely clinical way. Psychiatry is best played by ear. It is after all a matter of listening to the whole person, all that is submerged, unborn, in hiding: the infant, the shadow, the savage. The list of principles we finish with here is merely a guide, suggesting how deep that listening must go to hear the Self that speaks through the self.

1. The core of the mind is the ecological unconscious. For ecopsychology, repression of the ecological unconscious is the deepest root of collusive madness in industrial society; open access to the ecological unconscious is the path to sanity.

2. The contents of the ecological unconscious represent, in some degree, at some level of mentality, the living record of cosmic evolution, tracing back to distant initial conditions in the history of time. Contemporary studies in the ordered complexity of nature tell us that life and mind emerge from this evolutionary tale as culminating natural systems within the unfolding sequence of physical, biological, mental, and cultural systems we know as "the universe." Ecopsychology draws upon these findings of the new cosmology, striving to make them real to experience.

3. Just as it has been the goal of previous therapies to recover the repressed contents of the unconscious, so the goal of ecopsychology is to awaken the inherent sense of environmental reciprocity that lies within the ecological unconscious. Other therapies seek to heal the alienation between person and person, person and family, person and society. Ecopsychology seeks to heal the more fundamental alienation between the person and the natural environment.

4. For ecopsychology, as for other therapies, the crucial stage of development is the life of the child. The ecological unconscious is regenerated, as if it were a gift, in the newborn's enchanted sense of the world. Ecopsychology seeks to recover the child's innately animistic quality of experience in functionally "sane" adults. To do this, it turns to many sources, among them the traditional healing techniques of

primary people, nature mysticism as expressed in religion and art, the experience of wilderness, the insights of Deep Ecology. It adapts these to the goal of creating the ecological ego.

5. The ecological ego matures toward a sense of ethical responsibility with the planet that is as vividly experienced as our ethical responsibility to other people. It seeks to weave that responsibility into the fabric of social relations and political decisions.

6. Among the therapeutic projects most important to ecopsychology is the re-evaluation of certain compulsively "masculine" character traits that permeate our structures of political power and which drive us to dominate nature as if it were an alien and rightless realm. In this regard, ecopsychology draws significantly on some (not all) of the insights of ecofeminism and Feminist Spirituality with a view to demystifying the sexual stereotypes.

7. Whatever contributes to small scale social forms and personal empowerment nourishes the ecological ego. Whatever strives for large-scale domination and the suppression of personhood undermines the ecological ego. Ecopsychology therefore deeply questions the essential sanity of our gargantuan urban-industrial culture, whether capitalistic or collectivistic in its organization. But it does so without necessarily rejecting the technological genius of our species or some life-enhancing measure of the industrial power we have assembled. Ecopsychology is *post*industrial not *anti*-industrial in its social orientation.

8. Ecopsychology holds that there is a synergistic interplay between planetary and personal well-being. The term "synergy" is chosen deliberately for its traditional theological connotation, which once taught that the human and divine are cooperatively linked in the quest for salvation. The contemporary ecological translation of the term might be: the needs of the planet are the needs of the person, the rights of the person are the rights of the planet.

Afterword

ECOPSYCHOLOGY SINCE 1992

As far as I am aware, the term "ecopsychology" was coined in the pages of *The Voice of the Earth* in 1992. That was the year of the Earth Summit in Rio when the air was filled with debate about the future of the environmental movement. *The Voice of the Earth* offered the concept of ecopsychology as an appeal to environmentalists and psychologists for a dialogue that would enrich both fields and play a significant role in public policy. The catch phrase that encapsulated the proposal was "ecology needs psychology, psychology needs ecology." At the time, there were various efforts around the fringes of professional psychotherapy to achieve that goal. They bore names like "green psychology," "nature-based therapy," or "ecotherapy." Each was some one therapist's idea about how to include the more-than-human world in their work with clients whose problems seemed to transcend the social context that delimits conventional psychology. There was also the well-developed field called "environmental psychology," but that has to do with the harmonious design of rooms, buildings, and landscape—the architectural environment of urban life, which is more the problem than the solution when it comes to our alienation from nature.

It is hardly unusual for fields of study to work out the sort of alliance ecopsychology seeks. All interdisciplinary efforts arise from the fact that the demarcations dividing specialists are wholly artificial and may at some point limit our understanding. For example, where does one sensibly draw a hard and fast line between economics and political science, or between geography and geology? Or consider sociobiology, a much-publicized effort to bring sociology, evolutionary biology, and psychology together in support of some highly controversial conclusions about human nature. In much the same spirit of intellectual adventure, ecopsychology suggests that what psychologists have learned about human behavior may have much to tell us about our bad environmental habits. Since environmentalists seek to change those habits, would it not be helpful for them to draw on what psychologists can tell them? This would seem to be especially important where the human behavior in question is wholly irrational, even to the point of self-destruction.

I began to wonder about this possibility several years before I wrote *The Voice of the Earth*. I was struck by how often people characterize the environmental behavior of our species as "crazy." It is "crazy" to destroy the ozone layer in order to enjoy the convenience of spray cans. It is "crazy" to wipe out magnificent wilderness areas to build shopping malls and parking lots. It is "crazy" to keep filling the atmosphere with automobile exhaust in order to drive around in sport utility vehicles. In all these cases, people have been given the facts of the matter, but most of them continue doing irreparable damage to the planetary ecology as if they cannot help themselves. Environmentalists scold them, but that does no more good than scolding a pyromaniac for setting fires.

Many environmentalists believe they have an adequate answer to the question of irrational environmental conduct. They believe there are profiteers at work acting against the public interest. There are real estate interests out to make money at the expense of polluting rivers; there are conscienceless marketers whose bottom line depends on selling things that waste resources. True enough. But that only removes the problem by another step. At some point environmental activists have to recognize that the relentless pursuit of money is among the most widespread kinds of craziness in our world. There are fabulously wealthy CEOs who are literally killing themselves on the job to make another million—and taking down whole rainforests with them. Had there been some greater environmental awareness in their time, would Freud or Jung, Sullivan or Horney agree that behavior like this is "sane" because it leads to greater profits for Exxon or Monsanto?

Like everybody who speaks to the world about the environmental crisis, I was once in the habit of scolding people about the stupidly destructive things we do to the planetary ecology. I would, for example, show them a plastic six-pack holder and tell them with blood in my eye how these silly objects find their way out of the landfill where we bury them into the lakes and oceans where they have been known to strangle water fowl. Or I would call attention to the styrofoam cups they had brought to the lecture, then bawl them out for adding to the CFCs that are eating away the ozone. I was good at that kind of tongue lashing. I had a hundred examples of thoughtlessly harmful behavior to unload on my audience. It made me feel virtuous to stand before them predicting the environmental doom our way of life would soon bring down on us. But I also recognized that presentations like this were making less and less of a difference, and indeed I was growing weary with spreading gloom. The public that responded to scare tactics and guilt trips had been used up, and it was not the vast majority. Too many others were either not paying attention or just did not care.

And then I began doing something unusual for anybody in the environmental movement. I stopped scolding and began listening. I asked people why they did the environmentally destructive things they did, and gave them a chance to talk. The answers were jarring. They had nothing to do with ignorance, greed, or indifference. There were few people I met who were not aware of our troubled relations with the planet. Some confessed to having dreams about the failing state of the world, dreams about forests and rivers and animals that made them sad. They spoke of a favorite tree or a lovely landscape they recalled from their childhood that was now gone. Deep inside some were grieving about the natural beauties they had seen vanish in their lifetime. No psychologist had ever asked them about those dreams, but they were having them just the same. I was reminded of the opening scene in the movie *sex, lies, and videotapes*. The woman tells her shrink that she is seriously anxious about all the garbage that is piling up in the world. She wishes she could do something about it. Her therapist responds, "Tell me more about your marriage."

I discovered that, far from being underinformed, people are often overwhelmed by the magnitude of the environmental crisis. The situation seems so far gone that they assume there is nothing they can do. Every day they see reports of environmental disaster in the news; everyday they receive mail from groups announcing the immanent death of another species, another dire prediction of global famine or drought. Which are they to save first, the whale or the tiger, the rivers or the valleys? What can they do to stop the devastation of an old growth forest they were told ten years ago could not survive another decade? Hasn't time run out? At last they withdraw with a sense of helplessness. But ironically, their despair is the direct result of bad psychology on the part of the very people who want to enlist them in the environmental cause. The environmental movement would seem to have invented a problem so big that there is no way to solve it.

Another common response I elicited was the sense of being trapped. People inherit a way of life; everything about that way of life is interconnected. Tell them that they have to throw out the whole social order by next Monday morning, and they cannot help but to be stunned. If they stop using their automobile, they will lose their jobs . . . and their homes. If everything on sale in the supermarket is toxic or environmentally incorrect, what will they eat? Even if the situation is that bad, it is fruitless to ask people to change too much too fast, and worse than useless to blame them for global catastrophe. In some cases I discovered such accusations make people both angry and stubborn. They respond by reviling the grieving greenies and stop listening.

I learned that people are especially interested in talking about their consumption habits—as good a place as any to begin. At the Rio Earth Summit, President George Bush, attending with great reluctance, made a speech in which he announced that he had not come to Rio to undermine the American way of life—by which he meant getting and spending without limit. So I asked people to tell me about how and why they consume. I don't know if I expected them to confess to swinish greed, but what they did tell me was as pathetic as it was illuminating. "When I feel really depressed, I go shopping." Scores of people gave me that answer. "I like to be where there are lots of happy people. So I go to the mall . . . and I end up buying something I don't need." "Every time I break up with a guy, I throw out all my clothes and jewelry and use up my credit card buying a new wardrobe." Several women admitted to that. Other people said they enjoyed the experience of power they gained by deciding which product to buy; it made them feel they had some control over their lives.

Or consider another remarkable finding. When asked why they continued to commute one-to-a-car when they knew that car pooling makes more sense, some people confessed that the hour or two they spent in their car was the only chance they found in the course of the day to be on their own and reflect on their lives. So here we have two bad environmental habits, one that turns out to be a flight from depression, the other a search for solitude. At least to me, it made a difference to see those habits as something more than blind ignorance or selfish aquisitiveness.

And finally, most revealing of all, there were many who admitted that they experienced shopping as a form of "addiction." They felt ashamed to admit it, but they simply could not control themselves. Going out and buying something—*anything*—relieved some terrible agony within.

That became a major insight for me. Addiction is, after all, an irresistible compulsion to do something that one knows is harmful, demeaning, or destructive. I talked that over with some psychologist friends who were quick to tell me that the worst thing to do with addicts is to shame them. Shame is what brought them into therapy in the first place; they don't need more of it. Making them feel guiltier may only make things worse. As one therapist put it, "If you shame them more, you lose them."

I found myself asking how many of our bad environmental habits stem from compulsive behavior people do not understand and cannot stop. In short, crazy behavior, but crazy behavior by now so well-rationalized that it passes for realistic public policy and practical economics. If that is so, then reason and logic on their own cannot solve our dilemma. Some greater force within us, some instinctive loyalty to the living planet, will have to be invoked.

Thinking along these lines, I soon found myself dealing with deeper and darker questions than the shopping habits of the modern world. I eventually had to agree with the environmental philosopher Paul Shepard that our total orientation toward nature in the modern world is a form of madness. Shepard was the first ecopsychologist, the first thinker in the environmental movement to apply psychological categories to our treatment of the planet. "Why do men persist in destroying their environment?" he asked at the beginning of his classic work *Nature and Madness*. And he did mean "men," for his answer was that men are "ontogenetically crippled" by childish fantasies of power. "The West," he believed, "is a vast testimony to childhood botched to serve its own purposes, where history, masquerading as myth, authorizes men of action to alter the world to match their regressive moods of omnipotence and insecurity."

Working along much the same lines, I have also come to believe that, at its deepest level, the environmental crisis traces to the twisted dynamics of male gender identity. *The Voice of the Earth* touches on this, and even more so my novel *The Memoirs of Elizabeth Frankenstein* and my essay on the sexual psychology of science, *The Gendered Atom*.

When we speak of costs and benefits, we are using an economic category; when we speak of resource depletion, we invoke an ecological category. But "crazy" is a psychological category. Ecologists and economists are not at home dealing with craziness. Psychologists are. They try to understand the crazy things people do. They have developed a rich fund of ideas about irrational conduct. I began *The Voice of the Earth* with a question. If environmental abuse has become the psychopathology of everyday life in our time, might psychologists not have something of value to offer environmentalists who are seeking to change people's behavior? I naively assumed that both psychologists and environmentalists would find such a dialogue worthwhile.

I was wrong.

I discovered that few psychologist have any interest in relationships that reach beyond couples, families, and maybe the workplace. The fact that all these relationships are contained and sustained by the natural environment goes totally unrecognized, something not worth mentioning. The guiding light of the profession, the *Diagnostic and Statistical Manual*, mentions nature in only one respect: seasonal major depressive episodes, feeling blue when the weather turns rainy. The *DSM* offers scores of refined categories for sexual disorders, substance abuse, and antisocial behavior. It never asks about the quality of people's relationship with the natural world in which our species spent ninety-nine percent of its evolutionary history.

Ecopsychology could go a long way toward correcting the self-defeating public relations that underlie environmental politics. But there is a great deal more the field has to offer. Indeed, in the century ahead as the science of ecology matures, psychologists may come to see that our sympathetic bond with the natural world—the "ecological unconscious," as I call it—is a defining feature of human nature, the one aspect of the psyche that has been most cruelly repressed by urban industrial culture. It may assume the place that sexuality holds in Freudian psychology, religious archetypes hold in Jung's psychology, and family relations hold in several more recent schools.

At a conference dealing with ecopsychology in 1994, I was approached by the psychology editor of the *New York Times*, a reasonably well-informed authority. He had heard about ecopsychology, but he was skeptical. (After all, I was from California.) He was curious about this idea that human beings have some kind of emotional rapport with nature that might be worth serious psychological attention. Were there any "hard data" for that?

Hard data? What could he possibly mean? Might Wordsworth and Shelley qualify as hard data? Would generations of landscape painting qualify? Would Taoism and other forms of nature mysticism qualify? What about the myth, folklore, and fairy tale of countless centuries past to which every child still seems to respond with spontaneous fascination? My principal interest in *The Voice of the Earth* had been material of that kind. Would that qualify? No. The editor wanted quantification. After all, psychology is a science. And science assumes numbers are more real than experience. I did find numbers for him, and he then did a report on this odd new direction in psychology.

I found the numbers by logging on to *Psychological Abstracts* and searching for descriptors like "nature," "wilderness," "mental health," "trees," "animals," "therapy," "experience" . . . I stopped when I had printed out eighty single-spaced pages of titles and abstracts. The titles were all rather like this: "The Effects of a Wilderness Therapy Program on Changes in Self-esteem and Teacher-rated Behavior of Youth at Risk," "The Effects of Wilderness Camping and Hiking on the Self-Concept and Environmental Attitudes and Knowledge of Twelfth Graders," "The Impact of a Wilderness Experience on the Social Interactions and Social Expectations of Behaviorally Disordered Adolescents."

As for the abstracts, they read something like this: "This study provides empirical confirmation of the limited research that reports positive effects of wilderness therapy on changes in self and behavior of youth at risk." "Results indicated that participating adolescents showed a significant increase in cooperative behaviors and that direct observation procedures were more sensitive to behavior changes than were standardized measures." It was only after I submitted the results of my search that the *Times* editor felt secure enough to run a story on ecopsychology.

I remain bewildered that so large a body of research has had so little influence among professional psychologists. I am just as bewildered that environmentalists have made nothing of this evidence for the healing value of wilderness. I assume this body of work has simply been ignored in favor of more important matters. Almost everything psychologists say about money, sex, or eating gets attention. If a therapist delivers a paper at a professional conference dealing with the anxieties that result from making a killing on the stock market or ending a love affair, it is almost certain to be reported in the media.

It was not only the quantity of published research on the psychological benefits of nature I found impressive, but even more so the uniformity of the findings. Take a group of battered wives, abused kids, cocaine addicts, terminal cancer patients, convicts, depressed junior executives, suicidal adolescents for a walk in the woods, a canoeing trip, a seashore retreat, a hike in the desert . . . and they feel better. As every Romantic poet once knew, viewed against the background of an Alpine landscape, a stormy sea, a lovely sunset, personal problems take on a distinctly lesser scale. When it comes to getting out of one's own, self-obsessed world of money worries, broken love affairs, or office politics, there is no tranquillizer more effective than standing under a starry sky at night and breathing in the wonder. There were even hard data on these matters, statistics that read something like: "after climbing a mountain, alcoholic housewives achieved an eighty-seven percent improvement in self-image as measured by the XYZ index; this effect degraded by fifteen percent over the next twenty-two weeks." As far as I could tell by reviewing all the testing and all the numbers, nobody came back from any kind of exposure to open space and grand vistas feeling worse. Some felt they had come close to God.

And yet, the environmental crisis remains of little interest to practicing psychologists. I suspect things will remain that way until environmental craziness is given a numbered heading in the *Diagnostic and Statistical Manual.* Until that happens, no therapist will be able to bill for his or her services. A major barrier. Even more threatening may be the fact that resorting to the healing powers of nature—getting away from it all as we often seek to do when we take a vacation, going into deep retreat, standing in the presence of natural magnificence—requires little intervention from professionals. Again, a financial loss to the profession.

Beyond these purely mercenary considerations, there is a more formidable problem. If, as I suggest in *The Voice of the Earth*, our culture is profoundly invested in an anti-environmental ethos, then psychologists may find challenging that ethos is simply too much to take on. After all, they too are residents of our urban industrial society, well-embedded in its values and assumptions. They earn from urban *angst.* Most therapists I know are content to tinker, adjust, and above all prescribe; it is all their clients seem to expect. Going deeper takes longer and hurts more. As long as there is Prozac, who needs environmental sanity? The courage with which Freud faced the radical madness of modern life in *Civilization and its Discontents* is rare. He was prepared to psychoanalyze our entire culture. Few have followed in his footsteps.

Nevertheless, it is my conviction that ecopsychology has a promising role to play in environmental policy. One of its more well-defined initiatives impinges upon environmental law. Suppose the *Diagnostic and Statistical Manual* contained an ecologically-oriented definition of mental health, something with an impressively clinical name like "dysfunctional environmental relations syndrome." It might then be possible for lawyers to bring cases based on the damage done to the mental health of a community by environmental destruction. That would be even more feasible if the Wilderness Act, the legal foundation for most environmental cases, were amended to include the psychological benefits people gain from untamed nature.

The environmental lawyer Christopher Stone has written a classic essay titled "Should Trees Have Standing?" by which he means should a forest, a pristine wilderness area, a species have rights at law? Stone believes they should. But he admits this would require a "shift of consciousness." It would require people to overcome the "sense of separateness" that makes them believe nature is the "dominion" of humankind. Obviously few people, especially in government and business, are ready for such a change. For better or worse, in the modern world, transformations of consciousness have been staked out by professional psychologists as their province. What, then, does ecopsychology ask of them? That they offer us an environmentally-based criterion of mental health that reconnects us with the living planet that mothered the troubled human psyche into existence.

—THEODORE ROSZAK
Berkeley, 2001

Appendix

◆

GOD AND MODERN COSMOLOGY

Over the past generation, new developments in cosmology and in the study of ordered complexity have forced scientists, philosophers, and theologians to rethink the place of life and mind in the universe. While there is as yet no consensus on these matters, the agnostic orthodoxy that dominated the sciences during the early years of this century has been called significantly into question. Ideas about teleology and design that were once regarded as little more than pious wishful thinking are now finding a new, more scientifically based status. The "new Deism," as we have called it, perhaps precisely because it is no longer tied to Christian apologetics, restores a traditional relationship between religious thought and natural philosophy that was broken off at the end of the Enlightenment. It has been the thesis of this work that there are significant ecological implications to be found in this renewed exchange.

This bibliography, collected and annotated by Paul Fayter, Lecturer in the History of Sciences and Humanities at York University, Canada, illustrates the scope and variety of literature dealing with cosmology and natural theology. It is limited to materials that have appeared since the 1980s and does not include works that, like Fritjof Capra's *Tao of Physics* or Gary Zukov's *Dancing Wu-Li Masters*, draw primarily upon Asian religion or philosophy. It might be seen as an extended footnote to chapters 4, 6, and 7, indicating how rich and lively the dialogue has become.

Adair, Robert K., *The Great Design: Particles, Fields, and Creation*, New York, Oxford University Press, 1987.

Adler, Mortimer J., *How to Think About God*, New York, Collier Macmillan, 1980.
A philosophically lucid and cogent (though theologically problematic) revision of the cosmological argument for God in light of modern science.

Ambrose, E. J., *The Mirror of Creation,* Edinburgh, Scottish Academic Press, 1990.
The "fine-tuned," ordered, and evolutionary universe as God's creation. Ambrose is an English cell biologist.

Barbour, Ian, *Religion in An Age of Science,* The Gifford Lectures, 1989–91, vol 1. San Francisco, Harper & Row, 1990.
Method in theology and science; physics, cosmology, evolution, and theological implications; process theism. One of the most respected science-and-religion scholars offers a clear, critical exposition of the issues.

Barrow, John D., *The World Within the World,* Oxford and New York, Oxford University Press, 1988.
Quantum theory and the "laws of nature." Concludes that the Anthropic Principle is not an argument for God's existence, though it is compatible with natural theology.

Barrow, John D., *Theories of Everything: The Quest for Ultimate Explanation,* New York, Oxford University Press, 1991.
The theologian's role is being preempted by a new generation of mathematical physicists. Barrow is skeptical that any scientific formula or theory can ever deliver the whole truth about the universe.

Barrow, John D., and Frank J. Tipler, *The Anthropic Cosmological Principle,* Oxford and New York, Oxford University Press, 1988.
Corrected paperback edition of a 700-page treatise.
Raises questions of design, purpose, and human meaning from the physical structure and invariant constants of the world. Barrow is an astronomer; Tipler is a mathematical physicist.

Bartholomew, David J., *God of Chance,* London, SCM Press, 1984.
Science, chance, and God's providential activity. Bartholomew is an English mathematician.

Bartusiak, Marcia, *Thursday's Universe: A Report from the Frontier on the Origin, Nature, and Destiny of the Universe,* New York, Times Books, 1986.
A good, popular survey of recent theories and personalities in cosmology.

Betty, L. S., and B. Cordell, "God and Modern Science, New Life for the Teleological Argument," *International Philosophical Quarterly,* 27, 1987, pp. 409–435.

Birch, Charles, William Eakin, and Jay B. McDaniel, eds., *Liberating Life: Contemporary Approaches to Ecological Theology,* Maryknoll, New York, Orbis, 1990.
Toward a new theology of nature and environmental ethics. Essays by Habgood, Birch, Regan, Haught, Cobb, et al.

Bohm, David, *Wholeness and the Implicate Order*, London, Routledge & Kegan Paul, 1980.

Note: See also Russell, 1985, Griffin, ed., 1986, and Sharpe, 1987.

Bohm, along with Prigogine and Stapp, is one of a group of eminent physicists whose work is seen (especially by Whiteheadian process philosophers and theologians) as having significant metaphysical and theistic implications.

Briggs, John, and F. David Peat, *The Turbulent Mirror: An Illustrated Guide to Chaos Theory and the Science of Wholeness*, New York, Harper & Row, 1989. A popular, lucid, and visually stunning account.

Bruck, H. A., G. V. Coyne, and M. S. Longair, eds., *Astrophysical Cosmology*, Vatican City, Pontifical Academy of Sciences, 1982.

Collection of technical papers. Coyne is a Jesuit priest, cosmologist, and head of the Vatican Observatory.

Carvin, W. P., *Creation and Scientific Explanation*, Edinburgh, Scottish Academic Press, 1988.

Historical and philosophical analysis of creation ex nihilo, natural theology, and cosmology.

Cornell, James, ed., *Bumps, Voids, and Bubbles in Time: The New Cosmology*, Cambridge, Cambridge University Press, 1988.

The discovery of ultra-large structures in the universe has provoked revisions to the Big Bang model. Accessible articles by cutting edge cosmologists, including Geller, Guth, and Lightman.

Coyne, George V., Michael Heller, J. Zycinski, eds., *Newton and the New Direction in Science*, Vatican City, Vatican Observatory, 1988.

The new cosmology and its implications.

Davies, Paul, *The Accidental Universe*, New York, Cambridge University Press, 1982.

Davies, Paul, "The Anthropic Principle," *Particle and Nuclear Physics*, 10, 1983, pp. 1–38.

Davies, Paul, *God and the New Physics*, London, J. M. Dent & Sons, 1983. Argues that "science offers a surer path to God than religion." As a theologian, Davies makes a good theoretical physicist.

Davies, Paul, *The Cosmic Blueprint: New Discoveries in Nature's Creative Ability to Order the Universe*, New York, Simon & Schuster, 1988.

The universe is unfolding as it was designed to do. Finds "powerful evidence" of "something going on" behind the laws of physics and biology.

Davies, Paul, and John Gribbin, *The Matter Myth: Toward 21st Century Science*, London, Viking, 1991.

Traces paradigm shift in modern science from Newtonian determinism to a "cosmic network" characterized by "self-organizational complexity."

Davies, Paul, *The Mind of God*, New York, Simon & Schuster, 1992.

Earman, John, "The SAP Also Rises: A Critical Examination of the Anthropic Principle," *American Philosophical Quarterly*, 24, 4, October 1987, p. 314. Severely skeptical critique of Anthropic Principle as "muddled speculation." But see Harris (1991) for an unmuddled, sympathetic analysis.

Fennema, Jan, and Iain Paul, eds., *Science and Religion: One World*, Dordrecht, Kluwer, 1990.

Ford, Adam, *Universe: God, Science, and the Human Person*, Mystic, Connecticut, Twenty-third Publications, 1987. Reflections on the religious meaning of physics, cosmology, and evolution.

Gerhart, Mary, and Allen M. Russell, *Metaphoric Process: The Creation of Scientific and Religious Understanding*, Fort Worth, Texas Christian University Press, 1984.

Glieck, James, *Chaos Theory: Making a New Science*, New York, Viking, 1987. A sound introductory discussion.

Greenstein, George, *The Symbiotic Universe*, New York, William Morrow, 1988. Appendix offers useful summary of main "cosmic coincidences."

Gribbin, John, and Martin Rees, *Cosmic Coincidences: Dark Matter, Mankind, and Anthropic Cosmology*, New York, Bantam, 1989.

Griffin, David Ray, ed., *Physics and the Ultimate Significance of Time: Bohm, Prigogine and Process Philosophy*, Albany, SUNY Press, 1986. Includes paper by Stapp on time in Einstein and in process thought.

Griffin, David Ray, ed., *The Reenchantment of Science: Postmodern Proposals*, Albany, SUNY Press, 1988. Essays by Griffin, Bohm, Birch, Sheldrake, Cobb, et al.

Halliwell, Jonathan J., "Quantum Cosmology and the Creation of the Universe," *Scientific American*, 265, December 1991, pp. 76–79, 82–85. Perhaps the universe appeared from a "quantum fuzz," having "tunneled" into existence from "nothing" in "imaginary time," followed by real time "inflation" and the hot Big Bang. It should be noted that, given the nature of quantum fluctuating vacua, "nothing" is a misnomer.

Halliwell, Jonathan J., *Quantum Cosmology*, Cambridge, Cambridge University Press, 1992. Toward a scientific, naturalistic, and "complete" account of creation, following Hawking's quest for what happened "before" the Big Bang. Theology is rarely as confident and arcane as Halliwell's science.

Harris, Errol E., *Cosmos and Anthropos: A Philosophical Interpretation of the Anthropic Cosmological Principle*, Atlantic Highlands, New Jersey, Humanities Press International, 1991.

A fine study, informed by process theism and postmodern biology, of new developments in cosmological, quantum, and chaos theory. Discusses the implications arising from our natural knowledge of the intricate and interdependent structure of the world. Offers a new argument from design based on "the unity of the universe as a necessarily self-differentiating and self-explicating whole."

Harris, Errol E., *Cosmos and Theos: Ethical and Theological Implications of the Anthropic Cosmological Principle,* Atlantic Highlands, New Jersey, Humanities Press International, 1992.

A critical and constructive review of new developments in physics and cosmology that opens up room for revisions of the traditional arguments (ontological, cosmological, teleological, and moral) for the existence of God.

Hartshorne, Charles, "God and Nature," *Anticipation,* 125, 1979, pp. 58–64.

A contribution to the large literature on science and theology sponsored by the World Council of Churches. Hartshorne, along with Whitehead and Cobb, is a key architect of process metaphysics. He is also an ornithologist.

Hartshorne, Charles, *Omnipotence and Other Theological Mistakes,* Albany, SUNY Press, 1984.

Haught, John F., *The Cosmic Adventure: Science, Religion and the Quest For Purpose,* Ramsey, Paulist Press, 1984.

Theology, cosmology and evolution. Haught is a Catholic Whiteheadian.

Haught, John F, "The Emergent Environment and the Problem of Cosmic Purpose," *Environmental Ethics,* 8, 1986, pp. 139–150.

Hawking, Stephen, *A Brief History of Time: From the Big Bang to Black Holes,* New York, Bantam Books, 1988.

Reviews recent changes to the Big Bang model, including quantum cosmology and inflationary theory. Though he raises all the ultimate questions, Hawking is no theist; he is confident that science will one day "know the mind of God," by which he means achieve a complete theory of the what, how, *and why* of "creation."

Houghton, John, *Does God Play Dice? A Look at the Story of the Universe,* Leicester, InterVarsity Press, 1988.

Reflections on cosmology and God by an English atmospheric physicist.

Houghton, John, "New Ideas of Chaos in Physics," *Science and Christian Belief,* 1, 1989, pp. 41–51.

Jahn, Robert, and Brenda Dunn, *Margins of Reality: The Role of Consciousness in the Physical World,* San Diego, Harcourt Brace Jovanovich, 1989.

Jaki, Stanley L., *The Road of Science and the Ways to God,* Gifford Lectures. Chicago, University of Chicago Press, 1978.

Physics and cosmology require a theistic framework. Jaki is a learned and prolific Benedictine priest, physicist, and theologian. He tends to write intemperate and polemical apologetics disguised as history and philosophy of science.

Jaki, Stanley L., *Cosmos and Creation,* Edinburgh, Scottish Academic Press, 1980.
A more popular version of some of his technical work in theology and physics.

Jaki, Stanley L., "Teaching of Transcendence in Physics," *American Journal of Physics,* 55, 1987, pp. 884–888.

Jaki, Stanley L., *God and the Cosmologists,* Washington, DC, Regnery Gateway, 1989.
Develops a new version of the cosmological argument on the basis of the specificity, design, and contingency of the universe. Jaki has no use for process theology or for the metaphysics indulged in by many scientists because such perspectives undermine the classical view of God as omnipotent, omniscient, and future-determining. The book, though comprehensive and informed, is marred by Jaki's usual ad hominem attacks on Bohr, Einstein, Dirac, Hawking, et al.

Jantzen, Grace, *God's World, God's Body,* Philadelphia, Westminster Press, 1984.
A Canadian theologian who teaches in England argues that the cosmos is the embodiment of God.

Kitchener, Richard F., ed., *The World View of Contemporary Physics: Does It Need a New Metaphysics?* Albany, SUNY Press, 1988.
See Stapp's essay on Bell's theorem.

Layzer, David, *Cosmogenesis: The Growth of Order in the Universe,* New York, Oxford University Press, 1990.
A naturalistic theory of the emergence of order that connects cosmology and quantum mechanics with the second law of thermodynamics and the evolution of human mind and freedom. Layzer, the eminent Harvard astrophysicist, argues for the existence of genuine and unpredictable creativity in a world governed by physical laws.

Leslie, John, *Universes,* London, Routledge & Kegan Paul, 1989.
On God, cosmology, multiple worlds, anthropic explanations, and design arguments. Leslie is a philosopher at the University of Guelph, Canada, interested in the metaphysics of cosmology. He thinks it is a toss-up whether a creating and designing God or the many-world hypothesis best accounts for our fine-tuned universe.

Leslie, John, ed., *Physical Cosmology and Philosophy,* New York, Macmillan, 1989.
Includes an introduction and annotated bibliography by Leslie.

Liderbach, Daniel, *The Numinous Universe,* Mahwah, Paulist Press, 1989.
Signs of the transcendent presence of God in relativistic and quantum physics. The author did his doctorate in theology at St. Michael's at the University of Toronto.

Lightman, Alan, *Ancient Light: Our Changing View of the Universe,* Cambridge, Harvard University Press, 1991.
A lucid and comprehensive survey of recent cosmological theory, including such challenges to the Big Bang model as the proposed "great attractor" and the discovery of the "great wall" of galaxies.

Lightman, Alan, and Roberta Brawer, *Origins: The Lives and Worlds of Modern Cosmologists,* Cambridge, Harvard University Press, 1990.
Includes helpful essay, "An Introduction to Modern Cosmology," plus interviews with 27 scientists, including Hoyle, Sandage, De Vaucouleurs, Peebles, Rubin, Hawking, Page, Penrose, Weinberg, Guth, and Linde. Important for what some can (and cannot) affirm about God and purpose.

Linde, Andrei, *Inflation and Quantum Cosmology,* New York, Academic Press, 1990.
The Russian cosmologist, now at Stanford University, is the author of the "chaotic inflation" theory in which the universe—or multiverse—is eternal and infinitely branching.

McFague, Sallie, *Models of God: Theology for an Ecological, Nuclear Age,* Philadelphia, Fortress Press, 1987.
Theological reconstruction by one who sees both scientific and religious discourse as metaphoric.

McMullin, Ernan, ed., *Evolution and Creation,* Notre Dame, University of Notre Dame Press, 1985.
Essays by McMullin, Ayala, Leslie, Sloan, Lash, et al. On explanation in theology and science; cosmological and evolutionary theory in relation to concepts of creation and providence.

Mangum, John M., ed., *The New Faith-Science Debate: Probing Cosmology, Technology, and Theology,* Geneva and Minneapolis, WCC and Augsburg Fortress, 1989.
Essays by Peacocke, Peters, Russell, et al.

Mitchell, R. G., *Einstein and Christ,* Edinburgh, Scottish Academic Press, 1987.
Includes discussions of Schrödinger, Popper, and Eccles; theological anthropology.

Moltmann, Jürgen, *God in Creation: An Ecological Doctrine of Creation,* Gifford Lectures. Translated by Margaret Kohl. London, SCM Press, 1985.
A major essay in theological reconstruction.

Montefiore, Hugh, *The Probability of God,* London, SCM Press, 1985.
Cosmology, evolution, and natural theology. Montefiore is an Anglican bishop.

Murphy, Nancey, *Theology in the Age of Scientific Reasoning,* Ithaca, Cornell University Press, 1990.
Sees Lakatos (rather than Kuhn, Laudan, or Feyerabend) as the philosopher of science whose work is most helpful for relating theological and scientific methodologies.

Oliver, Harold H., "The Complementarity of Theology and Cosmology," in *Relatedness: Essays in Metaphysics and Theology,* Macon, Mercer University Press, 1984.

Overbye, Dennis, *Lonely Hearts of the Cosmos: The Scientific Quest for the Secret of the Universe,* New York, HarperCollins, 1991.
Inspired science journalism, sensitive to the personal motivations and meanings of the new cosmological theories.

Pagels, Heinz, *The Cosmic Code: Quantum Physics as the Language of Nature,* New York, Simon & Schuster, 1982.

Pagels, Heinz, *Perfect Symmetry: The Search for the Beginning of Time,* New York, Simon & Schuster, 1985.
Two books on cosmology and physics by the late theoretical physicist that remain open to the possibility of God.

Paul, Iain, *Science, Theology, and Einstein,* New York, Oxford University Press, 1982.
Metaphysical and epistemological implications of physics.

Peacocke, Arthur R., *Creation and the World of Science,* Oxford, Clarendon Press, 1979.
An important discussion of science and theology by the English physical biochemist, theologian, and Anglican priest.

Peacocke, Arthur R., ed., *The Sciences and Theology in the Twentieth Century,* Stocksfield, Oriel Press/Routledge, 1981.
Cosmology, quantum physics, creation, epistemology, ideology; sociology of science and religion. Essays by Peacocke, Pannenberg, McMullin, Hefner, Torrance, Bowker, Swinburne, Ravetz, Lash, Rudwick, Hess, et al.

Peacocke, Arthur R., *Intimations of Reality: Critical Realism in Science and Religion,* Notre Dame, University of Notre Dame Press, 1984.
Cosmology, epistemology, and divine activity in the world. A more popular presentation of ideas discussed in *Creation and the World of Science.*

Peacocke, Arthur R., *God and the New Biology,* London, J. M. Dent & Sons, 1986.

Continues Peacocke's interpretation of science and theology as compatible and convergent enterprises, and the reconstruction of the idea of creation. Includes discussion of thermodynamics, but emphasizes evolutionary biology, genetics, and sociobiology.

Peat, F. David, *Einstein's Moon: Bell's Theorem and the Curious Quest for Quantum Reality,* Chicago, Contemporary Books, 1990.

Peat is a Canadian physicist interested in philosophy and psychology. On the subject of the book, see also John S. Bell, *Speakable and Unspeakable in Quantum Mechanics,* New York, Cambridge University Press, 1987.

Peat, F. David, *Superstrings and the Search for the Theory of Everything,* Chicago, Contemporary Books, 1988.

The story and some implications of the theory that matter, forces, and space itself all consist of incredibly small 10-dimensional strings. This popular tour through postmodern physics includes chapters on Penrose's twistor theory, a mathematical theory connecting quantum mechanics and relativistic physics that helps explain the generation of fields (e.g., gravity) and of space itself.

Peat, F. David, "Mathematics and the Language of Nature," in *Mathematics and Science,* edited by Ronald E. Mickens, Teaneck, NJ, World Scientific, 1990, pp. 154-172.

Peat, F. David, *The Philosopher's Stone: Chaos, Synchronicity, and the Hidden Order of the World,* New York, Bantam Books, 1991.

An interpretation of the meaning of mathematics, matter, mind, and spirit by the coauthor (with David Bohm) of *Science, Order and Creativity,* 1987.

Penrose, Roger, *The Emperor's New Mind: On Computers, Minds, and the Laws of Physics,* Oxford University Press, 1989.

While not a religious thinker, the noted mathematician argues that classical physics, quantum mechanics, and natural selection are incapable of explaining the mind. Penrose believes mathematics makes "contact with Plato's world" of eternal forms. Provocative discussions of the Anthropic Principle, Big Bang cosmology, quantum physics, and entropy, and the limitations of Artificial Intelligence.

Peters, Ted, ed., *Cosmos as Creation: Theology and Science in Consonance,* Nashville, Abingdon Press, 1989.

A useful volume arising out of the work of the Center for Theology and the Natural Sciences at the Graduate Theological Union in Berkeley. Peacocke on theology and science; Peters on cosmos as creation; Barbour on creation and cosmology; Pannenberg on creation and science; Russell on cosmology and contingency.

Polkinghorne, John C., *The Particle Play: An Account of the Ultimate Constituents of Matter,* San Francisco, W. H. Freeman, 1979.

Formerly a mathematical physicist at Cambridge, Polkinghorne is also an Anglican priest who now concentrates on faith-and-science issues as president of Queen's College, Cambridge.

Polkinghorne, John C., *Creation and the Structure of the Physical World*, London, Christian Evidence Society, 1986.
A popular and more explicitly religious account of some of his earlier, technical work in quantum physics.

Polkinghorne, John C., *One World: The Interaction of Science and Theology*, Princeton, Princeton University Press, 1986.

Polkinghorne, John C., "Creation and the Structure of the Physical World," *Theology Today*, 44, April 1987, pp. 53–68.

Polkinghorne, John C., *Science and Creation: The Search for Understanding*, London, SPCK, 1988.
Relating scientific and theological world views; modern science and natural theology.

Polkinghorne, John C., *Science and Providence: God's Interaction with the World*, Boston, Shambhala, 1989.

Polkinghorne, John C., "God's Action in the World," *CTNS Bulletin*, 10, Spring 1990, pp. 1–12.
A symposium organized by the Center for Theology and the Natural Sciences, with responses by Wright, Murphy, Guagliardo, Russell, Barbour, and Peters, pp. 13–29.

Polkinghorne, John C., *Reason and Reality*, Philadelphia, Trinity Press International, 1991.
On the "cross-traffic" between science and theology. Includes careful analysis of the Anthropic Principle and other metaphysically laden issues arising in cosmology.

Pollard, William G., *Transcendence and Providence: Reflections of a Physicist and Priest*, Edinburgh, Scottish Academic Press, 1987.

Prigogine, Ilya, and Isabelle Stengers, *Order Out of Chaos*, New York, Bantam, 1984.
The emergence of order in nonequilibrium thermodynamics. Barbour and Peacocke are among those who have analyzed the theological implications of Prigogine's work.

Ravindra, Ravi, ed., *Science and Spirit*, New York, Paragon House, 1991.
A wide-ranging, scholarly survey of current issues in religion and science that includes Hindu perspectives, and a consideration of the cognitive power of mysticism as well as of physics. Ravindra teaches physics and religion at Dalhousie University in Halifax, Canada.

Robson, John M., ed., *Origin and Evolution of the Universe: Evidence for Design?* Kingston and Montreal, McGill-Queen's University Press, 1987.

North American and European scientists and philosophers reexamine design arguments in light of modern cosmology.

Rolston, Holmes, III, *Science and Religion: A Critical Survey,* New York, Random House, 1987.
A fine textbook by a philosopher best known for his work in environmental ethics.

Russell, Robert John, William R. Stoeger, and George V. Coyne, eds., *Physics, Philosophy and Theology,* Vatican City, Vatican Observatory, 1988. Subtitled "A common quest for understanding," this major collection brings together theologians, scientists, and philosophers on physics, cosmology, creation, natural theology, epistemology, etc. Papers by Barbour, McMullin, Buckley, Clarke, Hesse, Lash, Peters, Leslie, Tipler, Polkinghorne, Russell, et al.

Russell, Robert John, "The Physics of David Bohm and its Relevance to Philosophy and Theology," *Zygon: Journal of Religion and Science,* 20, June 1985, pp. 135–158.
Russell is Director of the Center for Theology and the Natural Sciences at Berkeley. His specialty is theology and cosmology; he has done research on Whitehead's theory of gravitation.

Schindler, David, ed., *Beyond Mechanism: The Universe in Recent Physics and Catholic Thought,* New York, University Press of America, 1986.

Seielstad, George, *At the Heart of the Web, The Inevitable Genesis of Intelligent Life,* New York, Harcourt Brace Jovanovich, 1989.
Uses Anthropic Principle to argue that observership "creates" the universe.

Sharpe, Kevin James, "Christian Theology and the Metaphysics, Physics and Mathematics of David Bohm," Ph.D. thesis, Boston University, 1987.

Sheldrake, Rupert, *The Rebirth of Nature: The Greening of Science and God,* London, Century, 1990.
A study of the new postmechanistic paradigm and the revival of animism. Sheldrake created the theory of "morphic resonance."

Stapp, Henry P., "Whiteheadian Approach to Quantum Theory and the Generalized Bell's Theorem," *Foundations of Physics,* vol. 9, nos. 1-2, 1979, pp. 1–25.
A physicist who uses process philosophy in his science. More recently, Stapp has done research in topological bootstrap theory and faster-than-light quantum "influences."

Stewart, Ian, *Does God Play Dice? The Mathematics of Chaos,* Oxford, Blackwell, 1989.
A good introduction to chaos theory. Despite the title, does not include theological discussion.

Stoeger, William R., "What Contemporary Cosmology and Theology Have to Say to One Another," *Center for Theology and the Natural Sciences Bulletin*, 9, Spring 1989, pp. 1–15.

A rich survey of the current dialogue by the Jesuit astrophysicist and cosmologist who works at the Vatican Observatory in Rome and who coedits the journal *Philosophy in Science.*

Swimme, Brian and Thomas Berry, *The Universe Story: From the Primordial Flaring Forth to the Ecozoic Era,* San Francisco, HarperCollins, 1992.

Talbot, Michael, *Beyond the Quantum,* New York, Macmillan, 1987.

A popular interpretation of the metaphysical implications of the new physics.

Templeton, John M., and Robert L. Herrmann, *The God Who Would Be Known: Revelations of the Divine in Contemporary Science,* New York, Harper & Row, 1989.

A wide-ranging survey by a supercapitalist who has published in, and has financially supported the faith-science dialogue, and by a biochemist with an informed evangelical outlook.

Tipler, Frank J., "The Omega Point Theory: A Model of an Evolving God," in *Physics, Philosophy, and Theology,* edited by Russell, Stoeger, and Coyne, Vatican City, Vatican Observatory, 1988, pp. 313–331.

The coauthor of *The Anthropic Cosmological Principle* writes, "It is the purpose of this paper to provide an argument for the existence of a Supreme Being who is also a Person. My analysis will be carried out entirely within physics itself." Cf. Barrow, 1988.

Torrance, Thomas F., *Christian Theology and Scientific Culture,* Theology and science at the frontiers of knowledge, edited by Thomas F. Torrance. Belfast, Christian Journals, 1980.

Torrance, of the Church of Scotland, is one of the major figures in the contemporary dialogue; he holds doctorates in theology, science, and literature. Most recently, he has been associated with the Center of Theological Inquiry at Princeton, one of the US centers for advanced research in science and religion.

Torrance, Thomas F., *Divine and Contingent Order,* Oxford, Oxford University Press, 1981.

Torrance, Thomas F., *Transformation and Convergence in the Frame of Knowledge: Explorations in the Interrelations of Scientific and Theological Enterprise,* Grand Rapids, Eerdmans, 1984.

Includes a discussion of the importance of Michael Polanyi's thought for understanding belief in science and religion.

Torrance, Thomas F., *The Christian Frame of Mind: Reason, Order, and Openness in Theology and Natural Science,* Colorado Springs, Helmers & Howard, 1989.

Continues his integrative work; science and theology are both concerned with the intelligibility of the universe, understood as a cosmos of divine and contingent order.

Toulmin, Stephen, *The Return to Cosmology: Postmodern Science and the Theology of Nature,* University of California Press, 1982.
See especially Part Three, "The Future of Cosmology: Postmodern Science and Natural Religion," in which Toulmin, a philosopher of science, suggests that the new physics and cosmology have opened up a path to the possible future reunion of natural science and natural theology.

Tracy, David, and Nicholas Lash, eds., *Cosmos and Theology,* 166, Concilium series, Edinburgh and New York, T. & T. Clark/ Seabury Press, 1983.
Brief but illuminating essays by theologians and cosmologists.

Van Till, Howard J., *The Fourth Day: What the Bible and the Heavens Are Telling Us About the Creation,* Grand Rapids, Eerdmans, 1986.
Van Till is a scholarly evangelical who is also an astrophysicist. This book and the one listed below are part of a large but unjustly neglected literature on science and religion produced by scientists from the evangelical wing of the Church. They are mostly theistic evolutionists; they are not "scientific creationists." They do object to the ideology of scientism.

Van Till, Howard J., Robert E. Snow, John H. Stek, and Davis A. Young, *Portraits of Creation: Biblical and Scientific Perspectives on the World's Formation,* Grand Rapids, Eerdmans, 1990.
Cosmology, geology, and theology of creation. Science and faith both necessary in interpreting the cosmos.

Viney, Donald, *Charles Hartshorne and the Existence of God,* Albany, SUNY Press, 1985.
Not the final word on its subject, but useful until more people begin reading and interpreting the thought of this most significant process theist.

Ward, Keith, *Rational Theology and the Creativity of God,* Oxford, Blackwell, 1982.
An example from the literature in theology and philosophy of religion on the question of divine creativity.

Wilber, Ken, ed., *Quantum Questions: Mystical Writings of the World's Great Physicists,* Boston, Shambhala, 1984.
Collects the religious opinions of Heisenberg, Schrödinger, Einstein, De Broglie, Jeans, Planck, Pauli, and Eddington. The editor insists that modern physics is completely unrelated to religious belief. It is interesting, however, that these twentieth-century scientists (and many more could have been included in such a volume) were profoundly religious, while not necessarily "orthodox" as Jews and Christians.

Wilkinson, D. A., "The Revival of Natural Theology in Contemporary Cosmology," *Science and Christian Belief,* October 1990, pp. 96–115.

A good introductory survey of the material. Wilkinson is an English astro-physicist and Methodist minister.

Wolf, Fred Alan, *Taking the Quantum Leap,* 2nd edition, New York, Harper & Row, 1989.

A physicist takes the reader on an informed, exhilarating, humorous, and well-illustrated romp through the weird world of quantum physics.

NOTES

◆

CHAPTER I

1. Kenneth Chilton, *Environmental Dialogue: Setting Priorities for Environmental Protection*, St. Louis, Washington University, Center for the Study of American Business, October 1991.
2. The memo, attributed to chief economist Lawrence Summers, was leaked by the Bank Information Center, a Washington watchdog group. It is reported in *New Scientist*, February 1, 1992, p. 13.
3. Anil Agarwal and Sunita Narain, *Global Warming in an Unequal World: A Case of Environmental Colonialism*, Centre for Science and the Environment, 807 Vishal Bhawan, 95 Nehru Place, New Delhi 110019, India.
4. Ramachandra Guha, "Radical American Environmentalism and Wilderness Preservation: A Third World Perspective," *Environmental Ethics*, Spring 1989, pp. 71–83.
5. "America's Ancient Forests: Cathedrals or Cornfields?" ABC Television, 1990.
6. Timothy Egan, "The Environmentalist as Bogeyman," *New York Times*, Jan. 4, 1992; also see Chip Berlet and William Burke, "Corporate Fronts: Inside the Anti-Environmental Movement," *Greenpeace*, Jan/Feb/Mar. 1991. Also see the *Nightline* report on anti-environmentalism, ABC-television, February 4, 1992.
7. George Reisman, *The Toxicity of Environmentalism*, Laguna Hills, CA, The Jefferson School of Philosophy, Economics, and Psychology, 1990.
8. For literature dealing with its Environmental Studies Program and other publications, write to the Competitive Enterprise Institute, 233 Pennsylvania Ave., SE, Suite 200, Washington, DC 20003.
9. A. Rosencranz and A. Scott, "Siberia's Threatened Forests," *Nature*, January 23, 1992.
10. Paul and Anne Ehrlich, "The Most Overpopulated Nation," *The Negative Population Growth Forum*, January 1991.

347

11. "Fifty *Difficult* Things You Can Do To Save The Earth," *Earth Island Journal*, Winter 1991, p. 12.

12. Kirkpatrick Sale, *Raise the Stakes: The Planet Drum Review*, San Francisco, Fall 1989, p. 3.

13. Jeremy Burgess, "Excuse Me for Being Alive," *New Scientist*, June 8, 1991, p. 52.

14. Abraham Maslow, *The Psychology of Science*, New York, Harper & Row, 1966, pp. 20–21.

15. Sigmund Freud, *Civilization and its Discontents*, translated by James Strachey, New York, W. W. Norton, 1962, pp. 13–14.

16. Galileo, "The Assayer" (1623) in *Discoveries and Opinions of Galileo*, translated by Stillman Drake, New York, Doubleday Anchor Books, 1957, p. 274.

CHAPTER 2

1. For the most accurate verbatim version of Chief Seattle's much misquoted message, see *The Washington Historical Quarterly*, 23:4, October 1931, pp. 243–276. The words I quote are not there. For this reason, I initially had some scholarly qualms about citing the chief—at least when it comes to the letter rather than the spirit of his surviving pronouncements. His famous speech addressed to "The Great Chief in Washington" (President Franklin Pierce) must be the most familiar of all Native American texts, primarily because of the eloquence with which it states the traditional vision of nature. But while the chief's message to the president was jotted down by a contemporary English-speaking witness in 1855, most of what is attributed to him today comes from a free "recreation" of that speech by the screenwriter Ted Perry written for a 1972 ABC television film titled *Home*. Perry heard Chief Seattle's words quoted at a rally on the first Earth Day in 1970. They inspired him to write a play about the pollution of the environment. He of course exercised some dramatic license with the chief's words. Most of what now goes out under Chief Seattle's name has come to be inextricably mixed with Perry's rewriting. In effect, what we have here is a piece of folklore in the making, a literary artifact mingling traditional culture with contemporary aspiration that has taken on a life of its own. The words have become precious to the environmental movement; but I have it on good authority from anthropologists I know that many (though not all) Native Americans honor the quotation as an accurate reflection of their people's understanding of the land. This is the passage that echoed in my mind on the

occasion I report. Whoever wrote or spoke these words, I quote them here for the nobility we have come to see in them.

2. Sigmund Freud, *A General Introduction to Psychoanalysis,* translated by Joan Riviere, New York, Washington Square Press, 1952, p. 296.

3. See Bruno Bettleheim, *Freud and Man's Soul,* London, Chatto & Windus, 1983, for a discussion of Freud's philosophical vocabulary.

4. Sigmund Freud, *Civilization and its Discontents,* translated by James Strachey, New York, W. W. Norton, 1962, p. 91.

5. R. D. Laing, *The Politics of Experience,* London, Penguin Books, 1967, pp. 61–62.

6. Activists For Alternatives is headquartered at 172 West 79th St., #2E, New York, New York 10024.

7. See Phil Brown, ed., *Radical Psychology,* New York, Harper Colophon Books, 1973, for a good basic selection of RT materials. Several local groups and publications continue the radical therapist's struggle. Among them: *Dendron News* (Eugene, Oregon), the National Association for Rights Protection and Advocacy (Minneapolis, Minnesota), Projects to Empower and Organize the Psychiatrically Labeled (Poughkeepsie, New York).

8. Sigmund Freud, *Beyond the Pleasure Principle,* translated by James Strachey, New York, Bantam Books, 1959, p. 70.

9. Sigmund Freud, *The Future of an Illusion,* translated by James Strachey, New York, W. W. Norton, 1961, p. 15.

10. Ernest Becker, *The Denial of Death,* New York, Free Press, 1973, pp. 282–283.

11. Quoted in Ernest Jones, *The Life and Work of Sigmund Freud,* New York, Basic Books, 1961, p. 407.

12. C. G. Jung, *Psychology and Alchemy,* Bollingen Series, 2nd edition, Princeton University Press, 1953, p. 218.

13. Jung quoted in Victor Mansfield, "The Opposites in Quantum Physics and Jungian Psychology," *Journal of Analytical Psychology,* February 1990, p. 1. Mansfield offers a basic survey of Jung's scientific speculation.

14. Barbara Hannah, *Jung, His Life and Work,* New York, Putnam, 1976, pp. 150–152.

15. C. G. Jung, *Modern Man in Search of a Soul,* New York, Harcourt Brace & Company, 1933, pp. 179–180, 187–188.

16. Sigmund Freud, *A General Introduction to Psychoanalysis,* New York, Washington Square Books, 1963, p. 280.

17. See, for example, Christopher Lasch, "Anti-Modern Mysticism: E. M. Cioran and C. G. Jung," *New Oxford Review,* March 1991, pp. 20–26.

18. Rollo May, "Contributions of Existential Psychotherapy," in Rollo May, et al., eds., *Existence: A New Dimension in Psychiatry and Psychology*, New York, Basic Books, 1958, pp. 61–64.

19. Ludwig Binswanger, "The Existential Analysis School of Thought," in Rollo May, et al., eds., *Existence: A New Dimension of Psychiatry and Psychology*, New York, Basic Books, 1958, p. 198.

20. Mary Midgeley, *Beast and Man*, Ithaca, New York, Cornell University Press, 1978, pp. 18–19.

21. Jay R. Greenberg and Stephen Mitchell, *Object Relations in Psychoanalytic Theory*, Cambridge, Harvard University Press, 1983, p. 248.

22. Abraham Maslow, *Toward a Psychology of Being*, New York, D. VanNostrand Co, 1968, Chapter 13.

23. U.S. Environmental Protection Agency Science Advisory Board, *Reducing Risk: Setting Priorities and Strategies for Environmental Protection*, Washington, DC, September 1990, pp. 9, 17.

24. Kenneth Chilton, *"Environmental Dialogue: Setting Priorities for Environmental Protection,"* St. Louis, Washington University, Center for the Study of American Business, October 1991, p. 16.

25. Viktor Frankl, *Man's Search for Meaning*, New York, Washington Square Press, 1959, pp. 178–179.

26. Sigmund Freud, *Civilization and its Discontents*, translated by James Strachey, New York, W. W. Norton, 1962, p. 91.

CHAPTER 3

1. I. M. Lewis, *Ecstatic Religion*, London, Routledge & Kegan Paul, 2nd edition, 1989, p. 178. Also see Iago Galdston, ed., *The Interface Between Psychiatry and Anthropology*, London, Butterworths, 1971, and Sudhir Kakar, *Shamans, Mystics, and Doctors*, New York, Knopf, 1982, chapter four.

2. Sigmund Freud, "On Psychotherapy," *Collected Papers*, New York, Basic Books, 1959, I:250.

3. Jane Murphy offers examples of psychosomatic healing in "Psychotherapeutic Aspects of Shamanism on St. Lawrence Island," in Ari Kiev, ed., *Magic, Faith, and Healing*, Glencoe, IL, Free Press, 1964.

4. E. Fuller Torrey, *Witchdoctors and Psychiatrists: The Common Roots of Psychotherapy and Its Future*, New York, Harper & Row Perennial Library, 1986.

5. John G. Niehardt, *Black Elk Speaks: The Life Story of a Holy Man of the Oglala Sioux*, New York, William Morrow, 1932. Also see Joseph Epes

Brown, ed., *The Sacred Pipe: Black Elk's Account of the Seven Rites of the Oglala Sioux,* University of Oklahoma Press, 1953.

6. Sigmund Freud, *Totem and Taboo,* translated by James Strachey, London, Routledge & Kegan Paul, 1961, p. 132.

7. Gene Weltfish, *The Lost Universe: The Way of Life of the Pawnee,* New York, Ballantine Books, 1965, pp. 403–406.

8. Gene Weltfish, *The Lost Universe: The Way of Life of the Pawnee,* New York, Ballantine Books, 1965, pp. 285–287.

9. Donald Sandner, *Navaho Symbols of Healing,* New York, Harvest Books, 1979, p. 131.

10. K. Rasmussen, *The Intellectual Culture of the Iglulik Eskimos,* Copenhagen, 1929, p. 56.

11. Jane Murphy, "Psychotherapeutic Aspects of Shamanism on St. Lawrence Island," in Ari Kiev, ed., *Magic, Faith, and Healing,* Glencoe, IL, Free Press, 1964, p. 64.

12. Paul Shepard, *Nature and Madness,* San Francisco, Sierra Club Books, 1982, pp. 7, 9, 128.

13. Robert Bly, *News of the Universe,* San Francisco, Sierra Club, 1980, p. 9.

CHAPTER 4

1. Bertrand Russell, "A Free Man's Worship," in Robert Egner, ed., *Basic Writings of Bertrand Russell,* New York, Touchstone Books, 1961, p. 72.

2. Richard Feynman, *QED,* Princeton University Press, 1985, p. 9.

3. Jacques Monod, *Chance and Necessity,* New York, Knopf, 1971, pp. 112–113.

4. Heinz Pagels, *The Cosmic Code,* New York, Bantam Books, 1983, p. 87.

5. Michael Murphy, *The Psychic Side of Sports,* Reading, MA, Addison-Wesley, 1978.

6. Stephen Hawking, *A Brief History of Time,* New York, Bantam Books, 1988, p. 60.

7. On Ponnamperuma, see *New Scientist,* May 19, 1990, p. 30. On Rebek, see *New Scientist,* April 28, 1990, p. 38.

8. E. Peter Volpe, *Understanding Evolution,* Dubuque, IA, Wm. C. Brown Company, 1972, p. 142.

9. Fred Hoyle and N. C. Wickramasinghe, *Lifecloud: The Origin of Life in the Universe,* London, J. M. Dent, 1978. For a critical response to Hoyle, see the article by H.N.V. Temperley in *New Scientist,* August 19, 1982, pp. 505–506, where it is objected that Darwinians do not believe the entire enzyme system was generated all at once, but that it evolved from "sim-

pler systems." The problem that arises from chopping one big improbability into an endless series of lesser improbabilities is to account for how each of the lesser improbabilities was selected for preservation and lasted long enough to compound into the whole evolutionary change.

10. F. B. Salisbury, "Natural Selection and the Complexity of the Gene," *Nature* (London) 1970, 224, issue 5217, p. 342. Hoimar Ditfurth has made a similar calculation for the chance evolution of a single enzyme, cytochrome C, one of the earliest complex proteins to emerge in the history of life on Earth. He asked what the probability is that the enzyme's protein sequence of 104 amino acids might have been randomly shuffled into place. He estimated the answer to be one chance in 10^{130}. At the rate of one random change per second, this would once again require more time than has passed since the Big Bang. See Hoimar Ditfurth, *The Origins of Life*, San Francisco, Harper & Row, 1982, p. 29.

11. Richard Dawkins, *The Blind Watchmaker*, New York, W. W. Norton, 1986, p. 47.

12. "Taming chance" through "cumulative selection by slow and gradual degrees" is the main thesis of Richard Dawkins, *The Blind Watchmaker*, New York, W. W. Norton, 1986. By such a process, Dawkins believes "we shall be able to derive anything from anything else."

13. John Polkinghorne, *Science and Creation*, Boston, New Science Library, 1989, pp. 47–48.

14. Jennifer Altman, "The Ghost in the Brain," *New Scientist*, May 12, 1990, p. 70.

15. Fang Lizhi, "Physics and Beauty," *Michigan Quarterly Review*, Summer 1991, p. 410.

16. John Gribbin and Martin Rees, *Cosmic Coincidences: Dark Matter, Mankind, and The Anthropic Principle*, New York, Bantam Books, 1989, pp. 15–18. For a convenient and accessible inventory of cosmic coincidences, see George Greenstein's list in the appendix to *The Symbiotic Universe*, New York, Morrow Quill, 1988.

17. Lawrence J. Henderson, *The Fitness of the Environment*, Boston, Beacon Hill, 1913; *The Order of Nature*, Cambridge, Harvard University Press, 1917. Also see the discussion of Henderson in Barrow and Tipler, *The Anthropic Cosmological Principle*, pp. 143–148.

18. Quoted in Alan Lightman and Roberta Brawer, *Origins: The Lives and Worlds of Modern Cosmologists*, Cambridge, Harvard University Press, 1991.

19. Brandon Carter in S. K. Biswas, et al., eds., *Cosmic Perspectives*, New York, Cambridge University Press, 1989.

20. John Wheeler, Foreword to John T. Barrow and Frank J. Tipler, *The Anthropic Cosmological Principle*, New York, Oxford University Press, 1986, p. v.

21. P. C. W. Davies, *The Accidental Universe*, New York, Cambridge University Press, 1982, pp. 110–111.

22. George Seielstad, *At the Heart of the Web, The Inevitable Genesis of Intelligent Life*, New York, Harcourt Brace Jovanovich, 1989, pp. 233, 271.

23. Fred Hoyle, from an unpublished article quoted in P. C. W. Davies, *The Accidental Universe*, New York, Cambridge University Press, 1982, p.118.

24. Hoyle quoted in John Barrow and Frank Tipler, *The Anthropic Cosmological Principle*, New York, Oxford University Press, 1986, p. 22.

25. Stephen Hawking, *A Brief History of Time*, New York, Bantam Books, 1988, p. 126.

26. John D. Barrow and Frank J. Tipler, *The Anthropic Cosmological Principle*, New York, Oxford University Press, 1986, pp. 677, 682.

27. Christian De Duve, "Prelude to a Cell," *The Sciences*, November/December 1990, p. 24. Along similar lines, in sources referred to previously, Brandon Carter, John Barrow, and Frank Tipler have devised probability distribution formulas that play off the number of crucial steps in human evolution that would have to take place in an ordered succession against the time available—which is the life span of main sequence stars like the sun. Such steps include the origination of the DNA code, aerobic respiration, glucose fermentation, the evolution of an eye precursor, etc. At various points different people are apt to say, "I can't believe so many unlikely events could happen in the right succession by accident." That would be their Credulity Index. Of course, hard-core randomists are always free to point out how unlikely *any* sequence of events is within some large enough framework of possibilities, and to settle for the fact that life did in fact evolve—and that's the way it is.

28. John Earman, "The SAP Also Rises: A Critical Examination of the Anthropic Principle," *American Philosophical Quarterly*, 24, 4, October 1987, p. 314.

29. Quoted in Alan Lightman and Roberta Brawer, *Origins: The Lives and Worlds of Modern Cosmologists*, Cambridge, Harvard University Press, 1991, p. 247.

30. Quoted in Alan Lightman and Roberta Brawer, *Origins: The Lives and Worlds of Modern Cosmologists*, Cambridge, Harvard University Press, 1991, p. 139.

31. See, for example, Gained Narlikar, "What If the Big Bang Didn't Happen?" *New Scientist*, March 2, 1991, pp. 48–51, and "The Extragalactic

Universe: An Alternative View," *Nature*, August 30, 1990, p. 807. For a quite quirky presentation of an opposing theory, see Eric J. Lerner's more than slightly paranoid *The Big Bang Never Happened: A Startling Refutation of the Dominant Theory of the Origin of the Universe*, New York, Times Books, 1991. For some dismissively critical views of the Anthropic Principle, see George Greenstein and Allen Kropf, "Cognizable Worlds: The Anthropic Principle and the Fundamental Constants of Nature," *American Journal of Physics*, August 1989, pp. 746–749, and N. Dowrick and N. McDougall, "Axions and the Anthropic Principle," *Physical Review*, December 15, 1988, pp. 3619–3624.

32. Errol Harris, *Cosmos and Anthropos*, New Jersey, Humanities Press International, 1991, p. 173.

CHAPTER 5

1. For a historical survey of the *anima mundi* in Western thought, see Conrad Bonifaci, *The Soul of the World*, Lanham, MD, University Press of America, 1978.

2. Lynn White, "The Religious Roots of Our Ecological Crisis," in *Machine Ex Deus: Essays in the Dynamism of Western Culture*, Cambridge, MIT Press, 1968.

3. D. P. Walker, *Spiritual and Demonic Magic from Ficino to Campanella*, South Bend, IN, University of Notre Dame Press, 1975. Also see Peter Finch, *John Dee: The World of an Elizabethan Magus*, London, Routledge & Kegan Paul, 1972.

4. For the social and psychological connection between the persecution of the witches and the rise of modern science, see Carolyn Merchant, *The Death of Nature*, New York, Harper & Row, 1980.

5. On Gilbert and other magician-scientists of the seventeenth century, see Brian Easlea, *Witch Hunting, Magic and The New Philosophy*, The Atlantic Press, 1980, chapter three.

6. James Lovelock, "Gaia: The World as Living Organism," *New Scientist*, December 18, 1986, p. 25.

7. John Postgate, "Gaia Gets Too Big For Her Boots," *New Scientist*, April 7, 1988, p. 60.

8. Steven Rose, *The Chemistry of Life*, New York, Penguin Books, 1966, pp. 78–9.

9. Roald Hoffmann and Shira Leibowitz, "Molecular Mimicry," *Michigan Quarterly Review*, Summer 1991, p. 386.

10. Richard Dawkins, *The Selfish Gene,* New York, Oxford University Press, 1976, p. 211.

11. Margie Patlak, "What Is Emotion For?" *San Francisco Examiner,* March 10, 1991, p. D16.95.

12. Quoted in Lawrence Henderson, *The Fitness of the Environment,* Boston, Beacon Press, 1913, p. 289.

13. Charles Darwin, *The Variation of Animals and Plants under Domestication,* London, Murray, 1875, pp. 7–8.

14. Charles Darwin, *The Origin of Species,* London, John Murray, 1859, chapter six, *passim.*

15. James Lovelock, *Gaia, A New Look at Life on Earth,* New York, Oxford University Press, 1979, pp. ix–x.

16. Lynn Margulis and Dorian Sagan, *Microcosmos: Four Billion Years of Microbial Evolution,* New York, Summit Books, 1986, pp. 115, 268.

17. Lynn Margulis and Dorian Sagan, *Microcosmos: Four Billion Years of Microbial Evolution,* New York, Summit Books, 1986, p. 117.

18. Lynn Margulis, "Big Trouble in Biology," in John Brockman, ed., *Doing Science,* New York, Prentice-Hall, 1991, p. 221.

19. In the debate over evolutionary imagery, the beat goes on. A study of dolphins published in 1991 includes the following observation in its preface by Lyall Watson. "Too much of our thinking is still based on views inherited from the nineteenth century and a model of nature that is red in tooth and claw. Naive observation of animal behavior in the days of Darwin led to a description of evolution as a ruthless struggle in which the winners take all. The truth is that there is no such war in nature. Cooperation, not competition, is the secret of survival." Exactly the position I take here. But one tougher-than-thou reviewer of the book characterized this viewpoint as "romantic New Age notions masquerading as science. Watson, like everybody else, is entitled to chat with the flowers or play flutes to the whales, but the danger is that some readers will accept his assertions as facts rather than wishful thinking." See *New Scientist,* April 13, 1991, p. 43. No doubt my remarks will elicit the same response; but I hope my intellectual sins will not be taken out on the dolphins or the whales.

20. James Lovelock, *The Ages of Gaia,* New York, Oxford University Press, 1988, p. 212.

21. Joshua Lederberg, "Medical Science, Infectious Disease, and the Unity of Humankind," *Journal of the American Medical Association,* August 5, 1988, p. 684.

CHAPTER 6

1. Ernest Haeckel, *The Riddle of the Universe*, New York, Harper & Brothers, 1900, pp. 225, 232.

2. Charles Darwin, *The Variation of Animals and Plants Under Domestication*, New York, Organe Judd, 1868, II, 204.

3. Errol Harris, *Cosmos and Anthropos*, New Jersey, Humanities Press International, 1991, p. 13.

4. Ludwig Von Bertalanffy, "System, Symbol, and the Image of Man," in Iago Galdston, ed., *The Interface Between Psychiatry and Anthropology*, London, Butterworths, 1971, p. 90. Also see his *Robots, Men and Mind: Psychology in the Modern World*, New York, Braziller, 1967.

5. M. J. Schleiden in 1842 quoted in Philip Ritterbush, *The Art of Organic Forms*, Washington, DC, Smithsonian Institution Press, 1968, p. 38.

6. Norbert Wiener, *Cybernetics*, 1948 and *The Human Use of Human Beings: Cybernetics and Society*, New York, Doubleday Anchor Books, 1954.

7. Norbert Wiener, *The Human Use of Human Beings*, New York, Doubleday Anchor Books, 1954, pp. 31, 40.

8. Tracy Kidder, *The Soul of a New Machine*, Boston, Little, Brown, 1981.

9. Bohr quoted in Sidney Fox, "In the Beginning Life Assembled Itself," *New Scientist*, February 27, 1969, p. 451.

10. Mario Bunge, "From Neuron to Mind," *News in Physiological Sciences*, October 1989, pp. 206–209. See Bunge's *A World of Systems*, Boston, Reidel, 1979.

11. Heinz Pagels, *The Dreams of Reason*, New York, Simon & Schuster, 1988, p. 222.

12. Richard Feynman quoted by P. C. W. Davies in *God and the New Physics*, London, Dent, 1983.

13. Sidney Fox, "In the Beginning, Life Assembled Itself," *New Scientist*, February 27, 1969, p. 450; "Spontaneous Order, Evolution, and Life," report on the second workshop on artificial life (Santa Fe, New Mexico, February 1990) *Science*, March 30, 1990, pp. 1543–1544.

14. Stephen Toulmin, *The Return to Cosmology: Postmodern Science and the Theology of Nature*, Berkeley, CA, University of California Press, 1982, pp. 230–234.

15. Errol E. Harris, *Cosmos and Anthropos*, New Jersey, Humanities Press International, 1991, p. 172.

16. Lancelot Law Whyte, "On the Frontiers of Science: This Hierarchical Universe," address delivered at the Harvard Club, New York, April 18, 1969. Also see Whyte's *Accent on Form*, New York, Harper & Brothers, 1954.

CHAPTER 7

1. Alexandre Koyré, *From the Closed World to the Infinite Universe*, New York, Harper Torchbooks, 1957.
2. Hubert Reeves, "Man in the Universe," in S. K. Biswas, et al., eds., *Cosmic Perspectives*, New York, Cambridge University Press, 1989, p. 73. Also see Reeves's remarks on the "essential role" played by chance in producing "the richness and diversity of forms in the realm of the living."
3. For example, see Steven Weinberg, *The First Three Minutes: A Modern View of the Origin of the Universe*, New York, Basic Books, 1977.
4. Charles Gillispie, *The Edge of Objectivity*, Princeton University Press, 1960, p. 402.
5. Harlow Shapley, *Flights From Chaos*, New York, Whittlesey House, 1930.
6. Norbert Wiener, *The Human Use of Human Beings*, New York, Doubleday Anchor Books, 1954, p. 11.
7. James Gleick, *Chaos: Making a New Science*, New York, Viking, 1987, pp. 308, 314.
8. Ilya Prigogine and I. Stengers, *Order Out of Chaos*, London, Heinemann, 1984.
9. Paul Davies and John Gribbin, *The Matter Myth: Toward 21st Century Science*, London, Viking, 1991, p. 266.
10. Erich Jantsch, *Design for Evolution*, New York, Braziller, 1975, p. 196.
11. Roger Lewin, "Look Who's Talking Now," *New Scientist*, April 27, 1991, p. 52.
12. Quoted in E. M. W. Tillyard, *The Elizabethan World Picture*, New York, Vintage Books, 1943, p. 39.
13. Wilkins quoted in Brian Easlea, *Witch Hunting, Magic and The New Philosophy*, The Atlantic Press, 1980, pp. 87–88.
14. Conrad Bonifaci, quoted in George Sessions, *Environmental Ethics*, Fall 1981, p. 277.
15. Pierre Teilhard de Chardin, *The Phenomenon of Man*, translated by Bernard Wall, New York, Harper Torchbooks, 1959, p. 251.
16. Warwick Fox, *Toward a Transpersonal Ecology: Developing New Foundations for Environmentalism*, Boston, Shambhala Books, 1990, pp. 20–21. Fox's book is the most thorough analysis so far of the many ecological schools of thought.
17. Pierre Teilhard de Chardin, *The Phenomenon of Man*, translated by Bernard Wall, New York, Harper Torchbooks, 1959, pp. 154–157
18. Robinson Jeffers, *The Double Axe*, New York, Liveright, 1977, p. xxi.

19. John Barrow and Frank Tipler, *The Anthropic Cosmological Principle*, New York, Oxford University Press, 1986, p. 290.
20. George Seielstad, *The Heart of the Web*, New York, Harcourt Brace Jovanovich, 1989, pp. 53–55.
21. John Gribbin and Martin Rees, *Cosmic Coincidences: Dark Matter, Mankind, and Anthropic Cosmology*, New York, Bantam Books, 1989, p. 93.
22. Paul Davies, *The Accidental Universe*, New York, Cambridge University Press, 1982, p. 29.
23. David Layzer, *Cosmogenesis*, New York, Oxford University Press, 1990, p. 37.

CHAPTER 8

1. Peter Bunyard, "Guardians of the Amazon," *New Scientist*, December 16, 1989.
2. See the television documentary "The Goddess and the Computer," produced by Andre Singer and Independent Communications Associates for WGBH, Boston, 1988.
3. Quoted in Fred Pearce, "Africa at a Watershed," *New Scientist*, March 23, 1981, pp. 34–40.
4. Joseph W. Bastien, *Mountain of the Condor*, Prospect Heights, IL, Waveland Press, 1985, p. 54. Originally published by the American Ethnological Society series as monograph 64. Also see Mac Chapin, "Losing the Way of the Great Father," *New Scientist*, August 10, 1991, pp. 40–44.
5. Paul Goodman, *The New Reformation: Notes of a Neolithic Conservative*, New York, Vintage Books, 1970, p. 191.
6. Peter Kropotkin, *Mutual Aid*, New York, Knopf, 1914, p. 9.
7. Goodman's basic contributions to Gestalt can be found in the volume he coauthored with Perls and Ralph Hefferline, *Gestalt Therapy*, New York, Delta Books, 1951. Walter Truett Anderson tells the bizarre story behind the writing of this odd but influential work in *The Upstart Spring*, Reading, MA, Addison-Wesley, 1983, pp. 94–96. Also see Taylor Stoehr, ed., *Nature Heals: The Psychological Essays of Paul Goodman*, New York, Dutton, 1977.
8. Gary Snyder, *Earth House Hold*, New York, New Directions, 1969, p. 112.
9. Marshall Sahlins, *Stone Age Economics*, New York, Aldine-Atherton, 1972, p. 37.
10. Arne Naess, "The Shallow and the Deep Ecology Movements," *Inquiry*, Oslo, Norway, 1973, vol. 16, pp. 95–100. For a fuller development of

Naess's ideas, see his *Ecology, Community, and Lifestyle*, New York, Cambridge University Press, 1989.

11. See Warwick Fox, *Toward a Transpersonal Ecology: Developing New Foundations for Environmentalism*, Boston, Shambhala, 1990, parts 2, 3, for a full critical survey of the varieties of Deep Ecology.

12. Murray Bookchin, later to become one of the severest critics of ecofeminism, speculatively but convincingly traces out the prehistoric "emergence of hierarchy" in man–woman relations in *The Ecology of Freedom*, Palo Alto, CA, Cheshire Books, 1981, chapter three. Also see the critical discussion of "Goddess Spirituality" in Charlene Spretnak, *States of Grace*, San Francisco, HarperCollins, 1991, pp. 127–133.

13. Merlin Stone's *When God Was a Woman*, New York, Dial Press, 1976, is one of the first feminist revisions of prehistory. Also see Riane Eisler, *The Chalice and the Blade*, San Francisco, Harper & Row, 1987; Susan Griffin, *Woman and Nature*, San Francisco, Harper & Row, 1978; Elinor Gadon, *The Once and Future Goddess*, San Francisco, Harper & Row, 1987; and above all Marija Gimbutas's landmark archaeological studies, *Goddesses and Gods of Old Europe*, University of California Press, 1982, *The Language of the Goddess*, San Francisco, Harper and Row, 1989, and *The Civilization of the Goddess*, San Francisco, HarperCollins, 1991.

14. Ynestra King, "The Ecology of Feminism and the Feminism of Ecology," in Judith Plant, ed., *Healing the Wounds: The Promise of Ecofeminism*, Philadelphia, New Society Publishers, 1989, p. 18.

15. Sharon Doubiago, "Mama Coyote Talks to the Boys," in Judith Plant, ed., *Healing the Wounds: The Promise of Ecofeminism*, Philadelphia, New Society Publishers, 1989, p. 40.

16. Betty Roszak, "The Spirit of the Goddess," *Resurgence*, London, January/February 1991, pp. 28–29.

17. Nancy J. Chodorow has studied the "strategies of accommodation" practiced by female analysts of the period 1930–60. See her *Feminism and Psychoanalytic Theory*, New Haven, Yale University Press, 1989, chapter ten. Some of the women worked from views about penis envy that were very much at odds with official Freudian doctrine, but they kept their reservations secret. For a survey of Freud's views of women, see Elizabeth Young-Bruehl, *Freud on Women: A Reader*, New York, W. W. Norton, 1990.

18. See the introduction to Charlene Spretnak, *Lost Goddesses of Early Greece: A Collection of Pre-Hellenic Myths*, Boston, Beacon Press, 1981.

19. Dorothy Dinnerstein, *The Mermaid and the Minotaur*, New York, Harper & Row, 1976, p. 94.

20. Marti Kheel, "Ecofeminism and Deep Ecology," in Irene Diamond, et al., *Reweaving the World: The Emergence of Ecofeminism,* San Francisco, Sierra Club Books, 1990, p. 129. For the most influential feminist extension of Object Relations, see Nancy J. Chodorow, *The Reproduction of Mothering: Psychoanalysis and the Sociology of Gender,* University of California Press, 1978, and *Feminism and Psychoanalytic Theory,* New Haven, Yale University Press, 1989.

21. Catherine Keller, "Toward a Postpatriarchal Postmodernity," in David Ray Griffin, ed., *Spirituality and Society,* Albany, SUNY Press, 1988, p. 72.

22. See Robert Bly, *Iron John,* Reading, MA, Addison-Wesley, 1991, and *A Little Book About the Human Shadow,* New York, Harper & Row, 1988, p. 53. On the contemporary men's movement, also see Sam Keen, *Fire in the Belly: On Being a Man,* New York, Bantam Books, 1991.

23. For a full how-to description of the Council of All Beings ritual, see John Seed, et al., *Thinking Like A Mountain,* Philadelphia, New Society Publishers, 1988. Also see Joanna Macy, *World as Lover, World as Self,* Berkeley, CA, Parallax Press, 1991, especially chapter 17, "The Greening of the Self."

CHAPTER 9

1. Lewis Mumford, *The Pentagon of Power,* New York, Harcourt Brace Jovanovich, 1970, p. 402.

2. Ernest Callenbach, *Ecotopia,* New York, Bantam Books, 1977.

3. Aldous Huxley, *Island,* New York, Bantam Books, 1962, p. 76.

4. Thomas Berry, *The Dream of the Earth,* San Francisco, Sierra Club Books, 1988. Also see Matthew Fox, *The Coming of the Cosmic Christ: The Healing of the Mother Earth,* San Francisco, Harper & Row, 1988, and Rosemary Ruether, *New Women/New Earth,* New York, Seabury Press, 1975.

CHAPTER 10

1. Sigmund Freud, *A General Introduction to Psychoanalysis,* translated by Joan Riviere, New York, Washington Square Press, 1952, pp. 423–425.

2. James F. Masterson, *The Search for the Real Self,* New York, Free Press, 1988. See chapter six.

3. Herbert Marcuse, *Eros and Civilization,* Boston, Beacon Press, 1955. See especially chapter eight.

4. Paul Goodman, Introduction to Ilse Ollendorff Reich, *Wilhelm Reich: A Personal Biography,* London, Elek, 1969, p. 3.

5. A survey of the antinarcissist literature of the seventies should include Daniel Bell, *The Cultural Contradictions of Capitalism*, New York, Basic Books, 1976; Peter Marin, "The New Narcissism," *Harpers*, October 1975; Christopher Lasch, *The Culture of Narcissism*, New York, W. W. Norton, 1978; Robert Nisbet, *The Twilight of Authority*, New York, Oxford University Press, 1975; Harvey Cox, *Turning East: The Promise and the Peril of the New Orientalism*, New York, Simon & Schuster, 1977; Edwin Schur, *The Awareness Trap: Self-absorption Instead of Social Change*, Chicago, Quadrangle Books, 1976. In a lighter but no less censorious vein, see Tom Wolfe, "The Me Decade and the Third Great Awakening," *New York*, August 23, 1976, R. D. Rosen, *Psychobabble*, New York, Atheneum, 1978.

6. Walter Truett Anderson, *The Upstart Spring*, Reading, MA, Addison-Wesley, 1983, is an excellent social history of Esalen Institute and Humanistic Psychology in general.

7. See especially Abraham Maslow, *Toward a Psychology of Being*, New York, D. Van Nostrand, 1968.

CHAPTER II

1. Sigmund Freud, *Inhibitions, Symptoms, and Anxiety*, translated by Alix Strachey, New York, W. W. Norton, 1959, p. 17.

2. Wilhelm Reich, *The Mass Psychology of Fascism*, translated by Vincent Carfagno, New York, Farrar, Straus & Giroux, 1970, p. xi.

3. Wilhelm Reich, *The Function of the Orgasm*, translated by Theodore Wolfe, New York, World Publishing Company, 1971, p. 89.

4. Georg Groddeck, *The Book of the It*, translated by the author, New York, Nervous and Mental Disease Publishing Company, 1928; *The World of Man as Reflected in Art, in Words, and in Disease*, London, C. W. Daniel, 1947.

5. D. W. Winnicott, "Mind and its Relation to the Psyche-soma," *Collected Papers*, New York, Basic Books, 1958, p. 246. On Winnicott's concept of environment, also see M. Gerard Fromm and Bruce L. Smith, eds., *The Facilitating Environment: Clinical Applications of Winnicott's Theory*, Madison WI, International Universities Press, 1989.

6. Dorothy Dinnerstein, *The Mermaid and the Minotaur*, New York, Harper Colophon, 1977, p. 94.

7. Madeline Davis and David Wallbridge, *Boundary and Space: An Introduction to the Work of D. W. Winnicott*, New York, Brunner/Mazel Publishers, 1981, p. 35.

8. Harold Searles, *The Nonhuman Environment In Normal Development and In Schizophrenia*, New York, International Universities Press, 1960.

9. Richard Byrne, "Brute Intellect," *The Sciences*, May/June 1991, pp. 42–47.

10. Nicholas Humphrey, *Consciousness Regained: Chapters in the Development of Mind*, New York, Oxford University Press, 1983, p. 27.

11. Jean Liedloff, *The Continuum Concept*, New York, Knopf, 1977.

12. Carl G. Jung, "Two Kinds of Thinking," *Symbols of Transformation, Collected Works*, vol 5, New York, Pantheon Books, Bollingen Series XX, 1956, p. 29.

13. Calvin Hall and Vernon Nordby, *A Primer of Jungian Psychology*, New York, Mentor Books, 1973, p. 40.

14. Sigmund Freud, *Totem and Taboo*, translated by James Strachey, London, Routledge & Kegan Paul, 1961, p. 158.

15. I am grateful to the Jungian therapist Meredith Sabini for drawing my attention to this direction in analytical theory. See Nathan Schwartz-Salant, ed., "The Body in Analysis," *Chiron: A Review of Jungian Analysis*, 1986.

16. William James, *The Varieties of Religious Experience*, New York, New American Library, 1958, p. 195.

CHAPTER 12

1. Erich Jantsch, *Design for Evolution*, New York, Braziller, 1975, p. 60.

2. Charlene Spretnak, "Ecofeminism: Our Roots and Flowering," in Irene Diamond, et al., *Reweaving the World: The Emergence of Ecofeminism*, San Francisco, Sierra Club Books, 1990, p. 13.

3. Nancy Chodorow, *Feminism and Psychoanalytic Theory*, New Haven, Yale University Press, 1989, pp. 159–162.

4. Anthony Weston, "Ethics Out of Place," *Environmental & Architectural Phenomenology Newsletter*, Winter 1992, p. 13.

BIBLIOGRAPHY

◆

Also see bibliographic appendix "God and Modern Cosmology." Several works used in this study appear listed there.

Anderson, Walter Truett, *The Upstart Spring*, Reading, MA, Addison-Wesley, 1983.

Barfield, Owen, *Saving the Appearances: A Study in Idolatry*, New York, Harcourt, Brace & World, 1976.

Bastien, Joseph W., *Mountain of the Condor*, Prospect Heights, IL, Waveland Press, 1985.

Berry, Thomas, *The Dream of the Earth*, San Francisco, Sierra Club, 1988.

Bertalanffy, Ludwig Von, *Robots, Men and Mind: Psychology in the Modern World*, New York, Braziller, 1967.

Biswas, S.K., et al., eds., *Cosmic Perspectives*, New York, Cambridge University Press, 1989.

Bly, Robert, *Iron John*, Reading, MA, Addison-Wesley, 1991.

Bly, Robert, *News of the Universe*, San Francisco, Sierra Club, 1980.

Bonifaci, Conrad, *The Soul of the World*, Lanham, MD, University Press of America, 1978.

Bookchin, Murray, *The Ecology of Freedom*, Palo Alto, CA, Cheshire Books, 1981.

Brockman, John, ed., *Doing Science*, New York, Prentice-Hall, 1991.

Brown, Joseph Epes, ed., *The Sacred Pipe: Black Elk's Account of the Seven Rites of the Oglala Sioux*, New York, Penguin Books, 1971.

Brown, Phil, ed., *Radical Psychology*, New York, Harper Colophon Books, 1973.

Bunge, Mario, *A World of Systems*, Boston, Reidel, 1979.

Callenbach, Ernest, *Ecotopia*, New York, Bantam Books, 1977.

Chodorow, Nancy J., *Feminism and Psychoanalytic Theory*, New Haven, Yale University Press, 1989.

Darwin, Charles, *The Origin of Species*, London, John Murray, 1859.

Darwin, Charles, *The Variation of Animals and Plants under Domestication*, London, John Murray, 1875.

Davis, Madeline, and David Wallbridge, *Boundary and Space: An Introduction to the Work of D. W. Winnicott,* New York, Brunner/Mazel Publishers, 1981.

Dawkins, Richard, *The Blind Watchmaker,* New York, W. W. Norton, 1986.

Dawkins, Richard, *The Selfish Gene,* New York, Oxford University Press, 1976.

Diamond, Irene, et al., *Reweaving the World: The Emergence of Ecofeminism,* San Francisco, Sierra Club Books, 1990.

Dinnerstein, Dorothy, *The Mermaid and the Minotaur,* New York, Harper & Row, 1976.

Ditfurth, Hoimar, *The Origins of Life,* San Francisco, Harper & Row, 1982.

Easlea, Brian, *Witch Hunting, Magic and The New Philosophy,* The Atlantic Press, 1980.

Eisler, Riane, *The Chalice and the Blade,* San Francisco, Harper & Row, 1987.

Feynman, Richard, *QED,* Princeton University Press, 1985.

Finch, Peter, *John Dee: The World of an Elizabethan Magus,* London, Routledge & Kegan Paul, 1972.

Fox, Matthew, *The Coming of the Cosmic Christ: The Healing of the Mother Earth,* San Francisco, Harper & Row, 1988.

Fox, Warwick, *Toward a Transpersonal Ecology: Developing New Foundations for Environmentalism,* Boston, Shambhala Books, 1990.

Frankl, Viktor, *Man's Search for Meaning,* New York, Washington Square Press, 1959.

Freud, Sigmund, *Beyond the Pleasure Principle,* translated by James Strachey, New York, Bantam Books, 1959.

Freud, Sigmund, *Civilization and its Discontents,* translated by James Strachey, New York, W. W. Norton, 1962.

Freud, Sigmund, *The Future of an Illusion,* translated by James Strachey, New York, W. W. Norton, 1961.

Freud, Sigmund, *A General Introduction to Psychoanalysis,* translated by Joan Riviere, New York, Washington Square Press, 1952.

Freud, Sigmund, *Inhibitions, Symptoms, and Anxiety,* translated by Alix Strachey, New York, W. W. Norton, 1959.

Freud, Sigmund, *Totem and Taboo,* translated by James Strachey, London, Routledge & Kegan Paul, 1961.

Fromm, M. Gerard, and Bruce L. Smith, eds., *The Facilitating Environment: Clinical Applications of Winnicott's Theory,* Madison WI, International Universities Press, 1989.

Gadon, Elinor, *The Once and Future Goddess,* San Francisco, Harper & Row, 1987.

Galdston, Iago, ed., *The Interface Between Psychiatry and Anthropology*, London, Butterworths, 1971.

Gillispie, Charles, *The Edge of Objectivity*, Princeton University Press, 1960.

Gimbutas, Marija, *Goddesses and Gods of Old Europe*, Los Angeles, University of California Press, 1982.

Gimbutas, Marija, *The Civilization of the Goddess*, San Francisco, HarperCollins, 1991.

Goodman, Paul, *The New Reformation: Notes of a Neolithic Conservative*, New York, Vintage Books, 1970.

Goodman, Paul, Frederick Perls, and Ralph Hefferline, *Gestalt Therapy*, New York, Delta Books, 1951.

Greenberg, Jay R., and Stephen Mitchell, *Object Relations in Psychoanalytic Theory*, Cambridge, Harvard University Press, 1983.

Griffin, David Ray, ed., *Spirituality and Society*, Albany, SUNY Press, 1988.

Griffin, Susan, *Woman and Nature*, San Francisco, Harper & Row, 1978.

Groddeck, Georg, *The Book of the It*, New York, Nervous & Mental Disease Publishing Company, 1928.

Groddeck, Georg, *The World of Man as Reflected in Art, in Words, and in Disease*, London, C. W. Daniel, 1947.

Haeckel, Ernest, *The Riddle of the Universe*, New York, Harper & Brothers, 1900.

Hall, Calvin, and Vernon Nordby, *A Primer of Jungian Psychology*, New York, Mentor Books, 1973.

Hawking, Stephen, *A Brief History of Time*, New York, Bantam Books, 1988.

Henderson, Lawrence J., *The Fitness of the Environment*, Boston, Beacon Hill, 1913.

Henderson, Lawrence J., *The Order of Nature*, Cambridge, Harvard University Press, 1917.

Hillman, James, *Revisioning Psychology*, New York, Harper & Row, 1975.

Hoyle, Fred, and N.C. Wickramasinghe, *Lifecloud: The Origin of Life in the Universe*, London, J. M. Dent, 1978.

Humphrey, Nicholas, *Consciousness Regained: Chapters in the Development of Mind*, New York, Oxford University Press, 1983.

Huxley, Aldous, *Island*, New York, Bantam Books, 1962.

James, William, *The Varieties of Religious Experience*, New York, New American Library, 1958.

Jantsch, Erich, *Design for Evolution*, New York, Braziller, 1975.

Jung, Carl G., *Modern Man in Search of a Soul*, New York, Harcourt, Brace & Company, 1933.

Jung, Carl G., *Psychology and Alchemy*, Bollingen Series, 2nd edition, Princeton University Press, 1953.

Jung, Carl G., "Two Kinds of Thinking," *Symbols of Transformation, Collected Works*, vol 5, New York, Pantheon Books, Bollingen Series XX, 1956.

Kakar, Sudhir, *Shamans, Mystics, and Doctors*, New York, Knopf, 1982.

Keen, Sam, *Fire in the Belly: On Being a Man*, New York, Bantam Books, 1991.

Kidder, Tracy, *The Soul of a New Machine*, Boston, Little, Brown, 1981.

Kiev, Ari, ed., *Magic, Faith, and Healing*, Glencoe, IL, Free Press, 1964.

Kropotkin, Peter, *Mutual Aid*, New York, Knopf, 1914.

Laing, R. D., *The Politics of Experience*, London, Penguin Books, 1967.

Lasch, Christopher, *The Culture of Narcissim*, New York, W. W. Norton, 1978.

Lasch, Christopher, "Anti-Modern Mysticism: E. M. Cioran and C. G. Jung," *New Oxford Review*, March 1991, pp. 20–26.

Lewis, I. M., *Ecstatic Religion*, London, Routledge & Kegan Paul, 2nd edition, 1989.

Liedloff, Jean, *The Continuum Concept*, New York, Knopf, 1977.

Lightman, Alan, and Roberta Brawer, *Origins: The Lives and Worlds of Modern Cosmologists*, Cambridge, Harvard University Press, 1991.

Lovelock, James, "Gaia: The World as Living Organism," *New Scientist*, December 18, 1986.

Lovelock, James, *The Ages of Gaia*, New York, W. W. Norton, 1988.

Lovelock, James, *Gaia, A New Look at Life on Earth*, New York, Oxford University Press, 1979.

Macy, Joanna, *World as Lover, World as Self*, Berkeley, CA, Parallax Press, 1991.

Mander, Jerry, *In the Absence of the Sacred: The Failure of Technology and the Survival of the Indian Nations*, San Francisco, Sierra Club Books, 1991.

Marcuse, Herbert, *Eros and Civilization*, Boston, Beacon Press, 1955.

Margulis, Lynn, and Dorion Sagan, *Microcosmos: Four Billion Years of Microbial Evolution*, New York, Summit Books, 1986.

Maslow, Abraham, *The Psychology of Science*, New York, Harper & Row, 1966.

Maslow, Abraham, *Toward a Psychology of Being*, New York, D. Van Nostrand, 1968.

Masterson, James F., *The Search for the Real Self*, New York, Free Press, 1988.

May, Rollo, et al., eds., *Existence: A New Dimension in Psychiatry and Psychology*, New York, Basic Books, 1958.

Merchant, Caroline, *The Death of Nature*, New York, Harper & Row, 1980.

Midgley, Mary, *Beast and Man: The Roots of Human Nature,* Ithaca, Cornell University Press, 1978.

Monod, Jacques, *Chance and Necessity,* New York, Knopf, 1971.

Mumford, Lewis, *The Pentagon of Power,* New York, Harcourt Brace Jovanovich, 1970.

Naess, Arne, "The Shallow and the Deep Ecology Movements," *Inquiry,* Oslo, Norway, 1973, vol 16, pp. 95–100.

Naess, Arne, *Ecology, Community, and Lifestyle,* New York, Cambridge University Press, 1989.

Niehardt, John G., *Black Elk Speaks: The Life Story of a Holy Man of the Oglala Sioux,* New York, William Morrow, 1932.

Pagels, Heinz, *The Cosmic Code,* New York, Bantam Books, 1983.

Pagels, Heinz, *The Dreams of Reason,* New York, Simon & Schuster, 1988.

Phillips, Adam, *Winnicott,* Cambridge, Harvard University Press, 1988.

Plant, Judith, ed., *Healing the Wounds: The Promise of Ecofeminism,* Philadelphia, New Society Publishers, 1989.

Rasmussen, K., *The Intellectual Culture of the Iglulik Eskimos,* Copenhagen, 1929.

Reich, Ilse Ollendorff, *Wilhelm Reich: A Personal Biography,* London, Elek, 1969.

Reich, Wilhelm, *The Function of the Orgasm,* translated by Theodore Wolfe, New York, World Publishing Company, 1971.

Reich, Wilhelm, *The Mass Psychology of Fascism,* translated by Vincent Carfagno, New York, Farrar, Straus & Giroux, 1970.

Ritterbush, Philip, *The Art of Organic Forms,* Washington, DC, Smithsonian Institution, 1968.

Roszak, Betty, "The Spirit of the Goddess," *Resurgence,* Jan-Feb 1991, pp. 28–29.

Roszak, Theodore, *Person/Planet,* New York, Doubleday, 1979.

Roszak, Theodore, *Unfinished Animal,* New York, Harper & Row, 1975.

Roszak, Theodore, *Where The Wasteland Ends,* Berkeley, CA, Celestial Arts, 1989.

Sahlins, Marshall, *Stone Age Economics,* New York, Aldine-Atherton, 1972.

Sandner, Donald, *Navaho Symbols of Healing,* New York, Harvest Books, 1979.

Searles, Harold, *The Nonhuman Environment In Normal Development and In Schizophrenia,* New York, International Universities Press, 1960.

Seed, John, Joanna Macy, Pat Fleming, Arne Naess, *Thinking Like a Mountain: Toward a Council of All Beings,* Philadelphia, New Society Publishers, 1988.

Shapley, Harlow, *Flights From Chaos,* New York, Whittlesey House, 1930.

Shepard, Paul, *Nature and Madness,* San Francisco, Sierra Club Books, 1982.

Snyder, Gary, *Earth House Hold,* New York, New Directions, 1969.

Spiegelman, J. Marvin, and Victor Mansfield: "Complex Numbers in the Psyche Matter," *Harvest* (England), 1990 and "The Opposites in Quantum Physics and Jungian Psychology," *Journal of Analytical Psychology,* February 1990.

Spretnak, Charlene, *Lost Goddesses of Early Greece: A Collection of Pre-Hellenic Myths,* Boston, Beacon Press, 1981.

Spretnak, Charlene, ed., *The Politics of Women's Spirituality,* New York, Doubleday Anchor Books, 1982.

Spretnak, Charlene, *States of Grace: Spiritual Grounding in the Postmodern Age,* San Francisco, HarperCollins Books, 1991.

Stoehr, Taylor, ed., *Nature Heals: The Psychological Essays of Paul Goodman,* New York, Dutton, 1977.

Stone, Merlin, *When God Was a Woman,* New York, Dial Press, 1976.

Teilhard de Chardin, Pierre, *The Phenomenon of Man,* translated by Bernard Wall, New York, Harper Torchbooks, 1959.

Torrey, E. Fuller, *Witchdoctors and Psychiatrists: The Common Roots of Psychotherapy and Its Future,* New York, Harper & Row Perennial Library, 1986.

Traherne, Thomas, *Poems, Centuries, and Three Thanksgivings,* New York, Oxford University Press, 1966.

Trefil, James, *The Dark Side of the Universe,* New York, Scribners, 1988.

Volpe, E. Peter, *Understanding Evolution,* Dubuque, IA, Wm. C. Brown Company, 1972.

Walker, D. P., *Spiritual and Demonic Magic from Ficino to Campanella,* University of Notre Dame Press, 1975.

Weinberg, Steven, *The First Three Minutes: A Modern View of the Origin of the Universe,* New York, Basic Books, 1977.

Wells, H. G., and Julian Huxley, *The Science of Life,* New York, Doubleday, Doran & Co., 1931.

Weltfish, Gene, *The Lost Universe: The Way of Life of the Pawnee,* New York, Ballantine Books, 1965.

Whitehead, Alfred North, *Science and the Modern World,* New York, Macmillan, 1924.

Whyte, Lancelot Law, *Accent on Form,* New York, Harper & Brothers, 1954.

Wiener, Norbert, *The Human Use of Human Beings,* New York, Doubleday Anchor Books, 1954.

Young-Bruehl, Elizabeth, *Freud on Women: A Reader,* New York, W. W. Norton, 1990.

INDEX

ABOUT THE AUTHOR

Theodore Roszak is Professor of History at California State University, Hayward. He is the author of several bestselling books, including *The Making of a Counterculture*, *Where the Wasteland Ends*, and a prize-winning novel, *The Memoirs of Elizabeth Frankenstein*. A Guggenheim Fellowship recipient, he has twice been nominated for the National Book Award and twice earned Goldman Environmental Foundation grants. A founder of ecopsychology, he lives in Berkeley, California, with his wife Betty.

ECOPSYCHOLOGY ON THE WEB

Further information and resources on ecopsychology can be found on the World Wide Web at:

www.cosmopolis.com/ecopsychology

An Alexandria Book

PHANES PRESS publishes quality books on
philosophy, mythology, ancient religions, the
humanities, cosmology, and culture.
To receive a copy of our catalogue, write:

Phanes Press
PO Box 6114
Grand Rapids, MI 49516
USA

www.phanes.com